Media Law and Policy in the Internet Age

Edited by
Doreen Weisenhaus and
Simon NM Young

OXFORD AND PORTLAND, OREGON
2017

Hart Publishing
An imprint of Bloomsbury Publishing Plc

Hart Publishing Ltd
Kemp House
Chawley Park
Cumnor Hill
Oxford OX2 9PH
UK

Bloomsbury Publishing Plc
50 Bedford Square
London
WC1B 3DP
UK

www.hartpub.co.uk
www.bloomsbury.com

Published in North America (US and Canada) by
Hart Publishing
c/o International Specialized Book Services
920 NE 58th Avenue, Suite 300
Portland, OR 97213-3786
USA

www.isbs.com

First published 2017

British Library Cataloguing-in-Publication Data
A catalogue record for this book is available from the British Library.

ISBN: HB: 978-1-78225-740-0
ePDF: 978-1-78225-738-7
ePub: 978-1-78225-739-4

Library of Congress Cataloging-in-Publication Data

Names: Weisenhaus, Doreen, editor. | Young, Simon NM, editor.

Title: Media law and policy in the internet age / edited by Doreen Weisenhaus and Simon NM Young.

Description: Oxford ; Portland, Oregon : Hart Publishing, an imprint of Bloomsbury Publishing Plc, 2017. | Includes bibliographical references and index.

Identifiers: LCCN 2016037922 (print) | LCCN 2016038128 (ebook) | ISBN 9781782257400 (hardback : alk. paper) | ISBN 9781782257394 (epub)

Subjects: LCSH: Mass media—Law and legislation. | Press law.

Classification: LCC K4240 .M4335 2017 (print) | LCC K4240 (ebook) | DDC 343.09/9—dc23

LC record available at https://lccn.loc.gov/2016037922

Typeset by Compuscript Ltd, Shannon
Printed and bound in Great Britain by CPI Group (UK) Ltd, Croydon CR0 4YY

MEDIA LAW AND POLICY IN THE INTERNET AGE

The Internet brings opportunity and peril for media freedom and freedom of expression. It enables new forms of publication and extends the reach of traditional publishers, but its power increases the potential damage of harmful speech and invites state regulation and censorship as well as manipulation by private and commercial interests.

In jurisdictions around the world, courts, lawmakers and regulators grapple with these contradictions and challenges in different ways with different goals in mind. The media law reforms they are adopting or considering contain crucial lessons for those forming their own responses or who seek to understand how technology is driving such rapid change in how information and opinion are distributed or restricted.

In this book, many of the world's leading authorities examine the emerging landscape of reform in nations with variable political and legal contexts. They analyse developments particularly through the prisms of defamation and media regulation, but also explore the impact of technology on privacy law and national security.

Whether as jurists, lawmakers, legal practitioners or scholars, they are at the front lines of a story of epic change in how and why the Internet is changing the nature and raising the stakes of 21st century communication and expression.

ACKNOWLEDGEMENTS

In 2013, the United Kingdom adopted historic reforms in defamation law in response to concerns its laws failed to take into account how technology, in the form of an increasingly crowded and sometimes rowdy Internet, was dramatically altering the way people distribute and consume information and opinion.

Lord Lester, a member of Parliament who played a major role in the development of the Defamation Act of 2013, saw the debates about the UK's reforms, which widened a public interest defence and raised the bar for probable harm, as a way to fuel a global dialogue on the new realities of the Internet age. He proposed a major conference of leading authorities on defamation, privacy and other issues, and suggested Hong Kong as a natural meeting ground. Hong Kong, like some other Asian jurisdictions, inherited the UK's common law system, though under Chinese sovereignty since 1 July 1997.

Lester's proposal eventually led to discussions in Hong Kong and to an alliance of three partners who conceived the strategic outline and determined the details of what became the international conference on 'Media Law and Policy in the Internet Age,' held at the University of Hong Kong on 18–19 October 2013. The partner-organisers were the Journalism and Media Studies Centre and the Centre for Comparative Law and Public Law at The University of Hong Kong, and Media Defence Southeast Asia, whose lawyers, journalists and advocates focus on media defence and freedom of expression challenges in the Southeast Asia region.

This book of 15 essays by a preeminent ensemble of media law and policy experts arises from that conference. As outlined in the introduction, their critical insights acutely reveal the complexities and contrasts in reform and provide an enduring framework for understanding the dynamics of technology-driven change. We gratefully acknowledge the expertise of our authors, including several who moderated or participated in conference panels. We also express our gratitude to our esteemed conference advisors, Robert Balin, Peter Noorlander, and Stewart Chisholm, and other distinguished speakers, including Pu Zhiqiang, Mark Stephens, Heather Rogers, Jennifer Robinson, Joseph Chan, Christiana Chelsia Chan, Dennis Kwok, Charles Mok, Bambang Harymurti, Marcelo Thompson, Chen Xinxin, Zheng Wenming, Zhu Wei, Malik Imtiaz Sarwar, M Ravi, and HR Dipendra. We were fortunate to have two outstanding keynote speakers, Lord Lester and Lord Dyson, and the assistance of moderators including Justice Michael Hartmann, Charles Glasser, Danny Gittings, Cliff Buddle, and Fu Hualing. We benefited greatly from the support of Professor Ying Chan of the JMSC and Professor Johannes Chan of the Faculty of Law. Finally, we extend our appreciation to the Open Society Foundations and Konrad Adenauer Stiftung, whose funding demonstrated their commitment to media freedom and freedom of expression, and helped us to compile what we proudly consider a timely book that also has lasting value.

Doreen Weisenhaus and Simon NM Young
October 2016, Hong Kong

CONTENTS

LIST OF CONTRIBUTORS

Peter Bartlett, Partner, Minter Ellison, Melbourne, Australia; practice focuses on media and communications law, including in regulatory compliance, breach of confidentiality, defamation, freedom of information, and data and personal privacy.

Ursula Cheer, Professor and Dean, School of Law, University of Canterbury, Christchurch, New Zealand; former legal adviser to the Prime Minister; author, *Media Law in New Zealand, Seventh Edition* (2015).

Lord Dyson, Master of the Rolls and Head of Civil Justice, England and Wales, 2012 to 2016.

Rick Glofcheski, Professor, Faculty of Law, The University of Hong Kong; Editor-in-Chief of the *Hong Kong Law Journal*; author of *Tort Law in Hong Kong*, 3rd edn (2012).

Lord Hunt of Wirral, Life Peer, House of Lords; Chairman, UK Press Complaints Commission, 2011 to 2014; Member of Parliament for Wirral, 1976 to 1997; member of the UK Government, 1979 to 1995, serving in the Cabinet as Secretary of State for Wales.

George Hwang, Director, George Hwang LLC, Singapore and founding member of Media Defence South East Asia Network; IP and media law specialist and counsel in cases defending bloggers and journalists.

Andrew T Kenyon, Professor, Melbourne Law School, Joint Director, Centre for Media and Communications Law, University of Melbourne; Editor of *Media & Arts Law Review*, 1999 to 2012; has published widely on comparative media law.

Adam Lazier, Associate, Levine Sullivan Koch & Schulz, LLP, New York.

Lord Lester of Herne Hill QC, Liberal Democrat Life Peer, House of Lords; Queen's Counsel, Blackstone Chambers, Temple, London; has argued many landmark cases on human rights and free expression, including in European Court of Human Rights; author of *Five Ideas to Fight For: How Our Freedom is Under Threat and Why it Matters* (2016).

T Mulya Lubis, Founder and Senior Partner, Lubis-Santosa & Maramis Law Firm, Jakarta, Indonesia; prominent commercial litigator as well as leading authority on media and human right issues, including as Chairman of Transparency International, in Indonesia.

Peter Noorlander, Director of Legal Programmes, Bertha Foundation, London, United Kingdom; CEO, Media Legal Defence Initiative, London, 2008 to 2016; expert on international human rights law and policy, particularly in digital rights and freedom of expression, in NGO sector.

Gillian Phillips, Director of Editorial Legal Services, Guardian News and Media Limited, London, United Kingdom; has advised *The Guardian* newspaper since 2009 on its content and coverage, including on the phone-hacking scandal, the Leveson Inquiry, Wikileaks and Edward Snowden.

H Harry L Roque, Jr, Former Director, UP Law Center Institute of International Legal Studies; founding Editor-in-Chief, *Asia-Pacific Yearbook of International Humanitarian Law.*

Paul Schabas, Partner, Blake, Cassels & Graydon LLP, Toronto; past President of the Canadian Media Lawyers Association; Adjunct Professor, University of Toronto; counsel in *Grant v Torstar* (2009), in which the Supreme Court adopted a new defence to libel, responsible communication in the public interest.

Rolf H Weber, Chair Professor, International Business Law, University of Zurich, Switzerland; member, Steering Committee of the Global Internet Governance Academic Network (GigaNet); member, panel of advisers of the Global Alliance for Information and Communication Technologies and Development.

Doreen Weisenhaus, Associate Professor and Director of the Media Law Project, Journalism and Media Studies Centre, The University of Hong Kong; author of *Hong Kong Media Law: A Guide for Journalists and Media Professionals*, 2nd edn (2014); former prosecutor and city editor, *The New York Times.*

Xu Xun, Professor and Executive Director of the Research Centre for Media Law and Policy, China University of Political Science and Law; former Director of Legal Services, China National Radio.

Simon NM Young, Professor and Associate Dean (Research), Faculty of Law, The University of Hong Kong; Barrister, Parkside Chambers; Co-Editor-in-Chief, *Asia-Pacific Journal on Human Rights and the Law.*

TABLE OF CASES

Africa

Australia

Brunei

Canada

European Court of Human Rights

European Court of Justice

Hong Kong

India

Inter-American Court of Human Rights

International Court of Justice

Ireland

Malaysia

New Zealand

The Philippines

Singapore

United Nations Human Rights Committee

United States

United Kingdom

TABLE OF LEGISLATION

Australia

Bill

Canada

China

Italy

Malaysia

Malta

New Zealand

The Philippines

Bill

United Kingdom

Bills

Statutory Instruments

Table of Codes, Guidelines and Professional Standards

Table of International Instruments

Introduction

DOREEN WEISENHAUS AND SIMON NM YOUNG

> *Freedom of opinion and freedom of expression are the foundation for every free and democratic society, a necessary condition to realise the principles of transparency and accountability we need to protect human rights (and) the basis for the full enjoyment of many other human rights … Though free speech was declared by the United Nations in 1948 to be a universal right, that is a hope, not reality.*[1]

A nation's media laws and policies are touchstones of its commitment to freedom of opinion and freedom of expression. A nation's openness to reform and willingness to balance competing interests in ways that enhance free speech are a product of its history, cultures, political contexts, and legal system.

In most jurisdictions, the process of reform in media law and policy has customarily moved slowly. Advocates on either side of a dispute sift generations of theory, custom, precedent, and practice to propose answers to new questions that arise in free speech. Reform considerations often grow out of major advances in media technology, from moveable type, for example, and on to the camera, radio, and television. In the early 1990s, the Internet arrived in a new user-friendly form known as the World Wide Web and changed communications forever. With its interactive global platforms, millions of websites, and billions of users, the Internet heavily taxes the capacity of all jurisdictions to devise legal and regulatory responses to questions that began coming into view at light speed.

Still, media law and policy reform has and is taking place, sometimes in a major and liberating way, such as with the UK's Defamation Act of 2013, but more often in patchwork and restrictive ways as courts, legislators and regulators wrestle with grand dilemmas presented by the Internet and for twenty-first century communications. Fundamental questions are being re-examined: who is a journalist, who is a publisher, and what is a publication? The questions are so large they seem philosophical, with no possible single answer, but the main purpose of media law and policy is to balance competing interests and uphold free speech.

In essays by some of the world's leading authorities on media law and policy in the Internet age, this book examines the opportunities and perils for media freedom and practice in an era of technology-driven change. The essays explore the complications and contradictions of change and the consequences now and in the future for 'traditional' publications and journalists, for new online publications, and for people who take to Internet platforms to distribute ideas and opinions, theirs or those of others, to anyone in the world with a computer, smartphone or technology not yet devised, and who sometimes unwittingly subject themselves, potentially, to legal sanctions.

[1] See Chapter 3 (Lester).

This book is not a catalogue of media law and policy reforms across the world, but instead is an examination of several key reforms to illuminate issues in current and historical, constitutional, and international contexts, with lessons and insights for those involved in different jurisdictions and stages of reform. Its authors also define the unique elements of the new media landscape and trace the 'very long process' of 'gradually protecting more speech' through both statute and case law in order to build a conceptual structure for considering the future.[2]

The book's authors include experts and leading thinkers at the frontlines of media law and policy reform: jurisprudence, legislation, litigation, and scholarship. Individually or with others, they are designing landmark legislation; litigating ground-breaking cases on multiple continents, and helping shape a universal Internet governance model that eschews sovereignty and commercial considerations in favour of principles of openness, neutrality, and inclusion.[3]

In the Internet age, international jurisprudence on balancing competing interests and justifying restrictions on media freedoms is of particular relevance, and so this book examines reform processes mainly through the prisms of defamation and the regulation of media to illustrate the challenges of law reform, but also explores how Internet technology impacts privacy law[4] and national security.[5]

> *Strict application of the publication rule … would be like trying to fit a square archaic peg into the hexagonal hole of modernity.*[6]

The Internet is a double-sided coin like no other in history: a global, two-way expressway for ideas and information as well as for publication on a scale previously unimaginable.[7] A dramatic example of the Internet's capacity for information dissemination came in early 2016 when members of a consortium of investigative journalists from 80 countries published stories, tailored for their respective audiences, that showed how politicians and others sheltered wealth in offshore tax havens; the so-called Panama Papers were gleaned from millions of encrypted documents originally leaked to a German newspaper.[8] Many courts, legislatures and regulators are struggling in many different ways to contend with this difficult duality, the inherent tendency of the Internet to greatly liberalise media freedoms but also to enable and greatly amplify harm, which can be stored in archives and remain hard to trace and remove.[9]

One of the book's major themes, however, is that while the Internet does require new legal approaches, it does not alter basic legal questions. For example, the core problem in defamation law reform in any era is finding the appropriate balance between free expression and reputational and privacy protection. The Internet yields new factual contexts to challenge the application and adaptation of existing law, but the fundamental issue is still the same. That idea, new Internet-produced factual contexts versus fundamental traditions,

[2] See Chapter 5 (Kenyon).

[3] See Chapter 11 (Weber).

[4] See particularly Chapters 13 (Cheer) and 14 (Bartlett).

[5] See Chapter 4 (Phillips).

[6] Justice Abella in *Wayne Crookes v Jon Newton* [2011] 3 SCR 269, [36], discussed in Chapter 6 (Schabas and Lazier).

[7] See Chapter 1 (Noorlander).

[8] See 'The Panama Papers', website of The International Consortium of Investigative Journalists, accessible at https://panamapapers.icij.org.

[9] See Chapters 1 (Noorlander), 7 (Glofcheski) and 11 (Weber).

was at the heart of a May 2016 ruling in the UK. A Supreme Court panel said that 'substantial Internet disclosure' outside the UK in a privacy case involving a celebrity and a sexual encounter with two other people did not justify the lifting of a court injunction preventing identification in the British press of the parties involved.[10] One media critic observed that the judges 'asserted the continuity of traditional legal values' despite a commercial media landscape 'utterly transformed by the Internet'.[11] Absent reform, according to UK media lawyer Mark Stephens, the case also illustrates how restrictive privacy and defamation laws encourage the powerful and the rich to seek to limit expression and information.[12]

The ruling in the so-called 'threesome case' mirrors a conundrum discussed in this book: courts are usually the first institutions to introduce change in media law and policy, but 'it may be asking too much of the courts to bear the full burden of law reform in the rapidly changing communications environment.'[13] It is also wrong to assume that courts are always inclined to liberalise the law in favour of media freedom.[14] The proper place for major, more far-reaching reform continues to be legislatures because as Lord Lester argues, 'judges are not lawmakers. They are constrained by past precedents.'[15] But, as with case law, legislative reform can also tilt the balance against media freedom.

Many issues in this book emerge from case law and media reform legislation developed in the cradle of the common law, in the UK; in only the past few years, in addition to the Defamation Act, new decisions have been rendered and legislative proposals debated that bear on free speech, freedom of information, privacy, and national security. These developments will have influence in jurisdictions that often cite UK authorities and statutes. Reform in the UK can be another double-sided coin. While in recent years the UK has abolished numerous speech crimes, including seditious libel and scandalising the court, a draft Investigatory Powers Bill, introduced in 2015, would grant sharply enhanced powers of Internet surveillance, a counter-intuitive step in a post-Snowden world.[16] It is seen as a particular threat to investigative journalism because unnamed sources can no longer be assured of confidentiality if they communicate with a journalist via a computer or smartphone.[17] Chinese authorities have already cited the bill to rationalise China's ever-expanding web of Internet censorship practices.[18]

In the end, the Internet can be seen as a 'tool'.[19] It can be put to different uses, depending on the purposes of who wields it. It can liberalise media freedoms by opening expression-and-opinion doors to a vast new interactive community, but the technology of it can also be manipulated to shut the same doors. In the hands of judges who believe, as Lord Dyson writes, that 'the public has a right to understand what (judges) are doing', it enables

[10] *PJS v News Group Newspapers* [2016] UKSC 26, [28].

[11] Owen Bowcott, 'Ruling on "threesome" injunction establishes significant precedent', *The Guardian*, 19 May 2016.

[12] Jane Martinson, 'Are privacy injunctions on the brink of a comeback?', *The Guardian*, 23 April 2016, quoting UK media lawyer Mark Stephens.

[13] See Chapter 7 (Glofcheski).

[14] Read the cases from the Philippines and Singapore criticised in Chapters 9 (Roque) and 10 (Hwang).

[15] See Chapter 3 (Lester).

[16] Investigatory Powers Bill, read first and second times in the House of Commons on 19 May 2016, http://services.parliament.uk/bills/2015-16/investigatorypowers/documents.html.

[17] Gavin Millar, 'This surveillance bill threatens investigative journalism', *The Guardian*, 6 November, 2015. See also the discussion of the issue in Chapter 4 (Phillips) and in Singapore in Chapter 10 (Hwang).

[18] Simon Denyer, 'China's scary lesson to the world: Censoring the Internet works', *The Washington Post*, 23 May 2016.

[19] See Chapter 1 (Noorlander).

live-streaming and tweeting of courtroom proceedings.[20] But it also facilitates surveillance on levels never seen before. The benefit and the danger have the same binary origin.

> *Virtually unchanged for centuries, defamation law is now adapting in different ways to a very different world.*[21]

The UK, the nation that introduced defamation law to the common law world, enacted a historic and sweeping package of reforms with the Defamation Act of 2013. The reforms, the outgrowth of the failure to achieve reliable reform through case law, addressed major fault lines that had appeared in traditional English libel law and fuelled an on-going global dialogue on how to balance free speech and reputation and privacy in the Internet age.

As law, the Defamation Act was evolutionary. It made it more difficult for plaintiffs to sue and strengthened available defences in ways intended to end the UK's reputation for 'libel tourism.'[22] Plaintiffs now have to show serious harm to reputation, whereas, before, they had to show none, and companies are barred from bringing an action unless they can prove substantial financial harm. The Defamation Act also broadened a public interest defence while simplifying and codifying other defences.[23]

The Defamation Act took into account a revolution in technology, which was 'changing the ways in which people, including journalists, communicate, disseminate and seek out information and opinions.'[24] The Act, for instance, replaced a multiple publication rule that made Internet publishers particularly vulnerable because it started the clock each time an item was downloaded, with a single publication rule with a one-year limitation.

The Defamation Act is strong evidence of the notion that reform that protects and enhances media freedom best occurs through legislation, but 49 years earlier, in a ruling that reverberated across the common law world, the US Supreme Court posited a powerful reform in libel law in cases involving public-official plaintiffs: they had to prove the words of defendants were false and that defendants had acted with actual malice (knowledge that the words were false or with reckless disregard for the truth). The case arose in the context of social and political turmoil surrounding civil rights campaigns in the American south. The ruling in *New York Times v Sullivan* was based on the premise that 'good-faith participation in public debate without fear of liability is fundamental to democratic discourse.'[25]

Over the next three decades, the influence of *Sullivan* on defamation law reform varied significantly across jurisdictions. Its influence 'lay particularly in one of its rationales—the chilling effect imposed by traditional public defamation law on public speech' and that idea 'gradually gained traction outside the US.'[26] It was first embedded in UK law in 1993, in *Derbyshire County Council v Times Newspapers*,[27] in a decision that foreclosed the ability of local governments to file defamation claims because of 'public interests considerations.'[28]

[20] See Chapter 2 (Dyson).
[21] See Chapter 6 (Schabas and Lazier).
[22] Doreen Weisenhaus, *Hong Kong Media Law*, 2nd edn (Hong Kong, Hong Kong University Press, 2014).
[23] See Chapter 3 (Lester).
[24] See Chapter 7 (Glofcheski).
[25] See *New York Times v Sullivan*, 376 US 254 (1964), discussed in Chapters 5 (Kenyon), 6 (Schabas and Lazier) and 9 (Roque).
[26] See Chapter 5 (Kenyon).
[27] *Derbyshire County Council v Times Newspapers* [1993] AC 534 (HL), discussed in Chapter 5 (Kenyon).
[28] See Chapter 5 (Kenyon).

The decision pushed UK courts further down a path that led in 1999 to *Reynolds v Times*,[29] which 'gave much greater weight' to the 'value of informed public debate of significant public issues.'[30] As with *Sullivan*, *Reynolds* grew out of social and political debates—the UK's adoption a year earlier of its Human Rights Act. It incorporated into domestic law rights contained in the European Convention on Human Rights of 1950, including the freedom of expression.

Reynolds broke ground by applying qualified privilege to the mass media as long as publication was in the public interest and the product of responsible journalism. The second part of the test immediately introduced a major issue, how to define 'responsible journalism.' *Reynolds* provided a 10-part guide, which lower courts interpreted in different ways, but the 'focus on responsible publication meant actions would be focused on the conduct of defendants before publication rather than, for example, the truth or falsity of the publication at issue.'[31] While *Reynolds* was a 'liberalisation of defamation law,' it 'remained subject to the sorts of criticism that were raised against the traditional law decades ago, about complexity, cost, predictability and public debate.'[32]

Courts attempted to resolve *Reynolds* issues in further rulings,[33] but continuing criticism and the growing impact of the Internet during the first decade of the twenty-first century only heightened *Reynolds*' shortcomings. Momentum for the idea that major statutory reform was needed began to build in public and legislative forums, and in 2013, the Defamation Act was enacted. It eliminated the *Reynolds* defence and provided broader protection not only for traditional journalists but also for a new generation of online contributors: a public interest defence now turned on whether the defendant was reasonable in believing the statement was in the public interest, not on the complicated and often elusive standard of 'responsible journalism.'

The Defamation Act can be seen as a second UK reaction to *Sullivan*, and one likely to influence other common law jurisdictions with deep experience in the process of civil defamation law reform over the last half century. In some parts of the world, however, weak development of civil defamation law[34] or stronger competing interests have given way to punitive criminal defamation laws. In more than 140 countries, including China, Russia and Vietnam, but also countries with liberal democratic values, such as France, Germany and Spain, speech remains subject to criminal prosecution. A report by the Vienna-based International Press Institute, published in January 2015, found that over half of European Union member states had convicted journalists of criminal defamation in the previous five years.[35]

Criminal defamation, particularly in authoritarian nations, has an inherently more chilling effect on freedom of expression. Some states apply the laws against students and

[29] *Reynolds v Times Newspapers Ltd* [2001] 2 AC 127.

[30] See Chapter 5 (Kenyon).

[31] Andrew Kenyon, *Defamation: Comparative Law and Practice* (Abingdon, UCL Press, 2006) 226–29.

[32] See Chapter 5 (Kenyon).

[33] See, eg, *Jameel (Mohammed) v Wall Street Journal Europe* [2007] 1 AC 349 (HL); *Joseph v Spiller* [2011] 1 AC 852 (UKSC).

[34] See Chapter 8 (Xu).

[35] International Press Institute, 'IPI special investigation: The application of criminal defamation laws in Europe', 15 September 2015, accessible at http://legaldb.freemedia.at/2015/09/15/ipi-special-investigation-the-application-of-criminal-defamation-laws-in-europe/.

dissenters as well as journalists. It is common in such countries for individuals critical of the government or commercial interests to be charged in multiple defamation cases, or given suspended prison sentences that enable them to remain free, but silent, for fear of another conviction and immediate imprisonment.

A chilling trend in media law development remains in the passage and use of coercive speech crimes to punish or imprison journalists for criticising prosecutors, reporting allegations against government officials, and scandalising courts. Equally alarming is the use of anti-terrorism, national security, and public order laws to restrict or hinder the work of journalists, for traditional as well as new media, as they pursue stories about matters of public interest. The consequences of the use and abuse of law are reflected in two major developments: first, in 2014, the largest decline in more than a decade in an index that measures media freedom around the world in terms of democracy, human rights, and press freedom;[36] second, more than half of imprisoned journalists today were prosecuted under libel and national security laws.[37]

Many laws invite abuse because they lack clearly defined terms or judicial safeguards. Some egregious intrusions on freedom of expression and opinion occur in emerging or young democracies, such as Indonesia, where a Twitter user was imprisoned after being convicted of defaming a politician under a new Electronic Information and Transaction Law enacted to protect personal data.[38] But even in countries with long traditions of building safeguards into law, cybercrime, anti-terrorism, national security, and surveillance laws are being used to investigate whistle-blowers and individuals through widespread surveillance of Internet traffic.

Despite statutory and other legal reforms in freedom of information, defamation, and privacy in the UK cited earlier in this introduction, coercive laws still pose threats to media freedom there and intrude upon journalistic practice. A media lawyer in the UK needs to have 'more than a passing knowledge' of the Official Secrets Act, the Computer Misuse Act 1990, the Protection from Harassment Act 1997, the Malicious Communications Act 1998, the Fraud Act 2006, the Serious Crimes Act 2007, and the Bribery Act 2010—all in addition to data protection and injunctions.[39]

> *History has taught us that the instinct of those in power to 'control' the press is a strong one … [T]he struggle to 'free' the media took hundreds of years, and is an achievement that should not be taken lightly.*[40]

Media freedom matters. Where media is free, truth emerges from unfettered exchange of information and expression. But throughout history, the first instinct of official power, when confronted with information or opinion contrary to its interests, is to control media.

[36] Freedom House, 'Freedom of the Press 2014', 1 May 2014, accessible at https://freedomhouse.org/report/freedom-press/freedom-press-2014.

[37] Committee to Protect Journalists, '2014 prison census: 221 journalists jailed', 1 December 2014, accessible at https://cpj.org/imprisoned/2014.php. Increasingly, foreign journalists are being prosecuted, such as *Washington Post* correspondent Jason Rezaian, who was convicted in Iran in 2015 on charges of espionage, 'collaborating with hostile governments,' 'propaganda against the establishment,' and allegations that he gathered information about internal and foreign policy. Rezaian was released in 2016 after the intervention of US President Barack Obama.

[38] See Chapter 15 (Lubis).

[39] See Chapter 4 (Phillips).

[40] ibid.

The Internet raises the heat of this tension. With its capacity to shine wider spotlights on official misconduct and abuse of power with content and ideas that unsettle existing authority, the Internet increases the temptation of authority to restrict access to truth.

Today, the temptation to restrict is not limited to traditional media operating (online and offline) within the laws and regulations of particular jurisdictions, but also to an entirely new interactive universe of producers and information recipients who use Internet technology to drive content and ideas across borders and into archives not easily emptied of information deemed harmful or threatening to individual or national interests.

The technology also enables new levels of purely social interaction and commercial partnerships. The onset of multiple globalised forms of communications forces reconsideration of sovereign borders and the importance of 'legal rules and systems' based on the 'principle of territoriality' and the need to redefine the 'competence of states to regulate cross-border activities.'[41] In international forums, the reconsideration and redefining have led to two main ideas for Internet governance. One is built on an open and neutral system for distributing power to Internet users with no traditional role in sovereign power, such as non-governmental organisations. The other rests on a 'cyber-sovereignty' concept under which governments regulate Internet activities accessible to domestic audiences. The US and other western nations came to favor the first; China, Russia, and others came to embrace the second, and have used filtering and other technology to block and censor content.

What China has constructed—a system for managing what nearly 700 million people, or almost 1 in 4 of the world's online users, can read, see, and hear—does not bode well for people who live in authoritarian countries. China is promoting its vision of cyber-sovereignty as 'a model for the world' and was expected in 2016 to approve legislation that 'would codify, organise, and strengthen its control of the Internet.'[42] Other nations are already well down China's path.[43]

At the same time, however, in western nations, the 'open and neutral' picture is clouded for a different reason. As wielded by commercial and private interests, technology itself can become a de-facto regulator, replacing traditionally open processes of rulemaking. It can happen, for example, in the use of so-called digital rights management systems that limit access to content through 'code', a binary way of aligning the law, markets, and social norms by using the 'architecture' of Internet hardware and software to 'code' content into systems that automatically execute. Code is not law, nor transparent, and so the 'question of who is in control of and responsible for code is of utmost social importance.'[44]

The use of Internet technology to regulate content in different ways alarms Internet activists and scholars. The Internet has become such a part of everyday life that, in the absence of common rules across jurisdictions, a new 'universal media governance framework' with regulations having their own 'special characteristics and particularities is needed to create legal certainty.'[45] Akin to international private law, the focus must be on 'on societal

[41] See Chapter 11 (Weber).

[42] Simon Denyer, 'China's scary lesson to the world: Censoring the Internet works', *The Washington Post*, 23 May 2016.

[43] In an annual survey of 88% of the world's Internet users, 34.3% of the world's nations had Internets that were rated 'not free', 22.7% 'partly free', 31% 'free', and 12% not rated, see *Freedom on the Net*, 2015, accessible at www.freedomhouse.org.

[44] See Chapter 11 (Weber).

[45] ibid.

interests' that include the removal of 'democratic deficits' accruing from media ownership, filtering, and censorship.[46]

In March 2014, Sir Tim Berners-Lee, the British computer scientist and inventor of the World Wide Web, which connects the computer networks comprising the Internet, called for a similar universal governance structure because the Internet had come under increasing government and corporate attack. He said an online Magna Carta was needed to protect an 'open, neutral' Internet.[47]

Magna Carta was granted in 1215 by the King of England to enshrine two main principles, government accountability and protection of individual rights, but it had birthing problems similar to those in media self-regulation in the UK.[48] Self-regulation for print media in the UK began in 1953 with the creation of the Press Council, but in the 1980s it came to be seen as an ineffective regulator of unethical press conduct.[49] Rather than seek to impose statutory controls, the government commissioned a report, which led to a Code of Practice and a new self-regulatory agency, the Press Complaints Commission.

History began repeating itself in 2011, in the wake of a phone-hacking scandal involving illegal acts by journalists from the *News of the World* newspaper. The scandal led to another government-commissioned report into the practices and ethics of the British press. The Leveson Report resulted in the scrapping of the Press Complaints Commission because it 'became apparent that the public and politicians had lost confidence in the existing system.'[50] It also led, in 2014, to the creation of another self-regulatory body, the Independent Press Standards Organisation (IPSO).

The IPSO was designed to ensure self-regulation was independent through a series of safeguards against government or political interference that included audits and standards established by the media, but overseen by an independent panel. The system introduced standards far beyond those of the existing Code of Practice. But it can be difficult for IPSO to determine to whom its standards apply. Who is 'entitled to source protection rights' and does it 'matter whether an individual' is a journalist? 'Should the focus be on 'output' and apply to any publication 'that is in the public interest, irrespective of the status of the writer?'[51]

Other common law nations struggle with regulatory dilemmas in similar, but also unique ways. In New Zealand, its Law Commission recommended a 'grand regulator' in the form of a News Media Standards Authority for all media, but the government rejected the proposal. In the place of a grand regulator, New Zealand has a patchwork of laws and regulatory conventions.[52] For example, its Press Council, a volunteer self-regulatory body for print media, began offering membership to digital media. Meanwhile, the nation's Broadcast Standards Authority, a statutory agency that co-regulates content with its members (by

[46] ibid.

[47] Jemina Kiss, 'An online Magna Carta: Berners-Lee calls for bill of rights for web', *The Guardian*, 12 March 2014.

[48] See JC Holt, *Magna Carta*, 2nd edn (Cambridge, Cambridge University Press, 1992).

[49] See Chapter 12 (Hunt).

[50] ibid.

[51] See Chapter 4 (Phillips). While IPSO has been joined by a majority of the UK press—with the notable exceptions of *The Guardian*, *Independent* and the *Financial Times*—another organisation (IMPRESS) has emerged as a possible alternative regulator, appealing to smaller, non-traditional publications. Mark Sweney, 'Press regulator Impress unveils first members and makes charter submission', *The Guardian*, 20 January 2016.

[52] See Chapter 13 (Cheer).

reviewing cases of complainants dissatisfied with a broadcaster's response), began working with its members to establish a new set of standards. Separately, the broadcasters set up a new Online Media Standards Authority, an industry-led group, to regulate online content.[53] Sorting out the regulatory quandaries presented by the Internet in jurisdictions large and small are very much works in progress.

Newsgathering in the 21st century is a risky business.[54]

That axiom is certainly true for traditional and online media in today's world, in both authoritarian and developed countries. A theme of this book centres on the idea that the Internet liberalises and restricts media freedom; the Internet and its technology are now so woven into daily routines that most would have a hard time navigating life without access to the URLs they turn to for interaction of one sort or another every day. The imposition of restrictions is so potentially harmful and the threat of them so alarming.

From their positions at the frontlines of media law and policy, the contributors to this book have assembled a body of knowledge with lessons and insights for media law and policy reform across the world. They have examined the significance of setbacks and obstacles, but also demonstrated that the scale and pace of change have led to many positive reforms. As they have shown here and in their work and scholarship, the processes of reform occur in different ways, through statutory reform, new regulations and evolving case law, often sharpened by strategic litigation. The authors also have shown how reform can occur through new national and international networks of civil society partners and media freedom advocates, and how sometimes it is prompted by a confluence of events—scandal, public support, the emergence of a visionary 'political champion' who supports 'both the process and most outcomes' and brings people together.[55]

A political threat can also lead to reform, as was the case in Australia in 2006, when the attorney generals in each of six states agreed to a set of defamation reforms to obviate a Commonwealth threat to impose laws enforceable only within the scope of traditional Commonwealth power. As one commentator said then: 'from the perspective of the media, [the Commonwealth's] original proposal was so appallingly bad that it changed the politics of defamation reform.'[56]

Even political paralysis can lead to positive change; in countries where legislative reform is frozen due to political conflict, civil society groups with no stakes in local power struggles can have impact, particularly if they seek redress in regional courts. For example, the Media Legal Defense Initiative, which pursues media law and policy reform through strategic intervention in cases across the world, has reported a 70 percent success rate over the last five years and won standard-setting judgments on issues such as defamation and the protection of sources at the European Court of Human Rights, African Court of Human and Peoples' Rights, and other courts and tribunals.[57]

[53] ibid.

[54] See Chapter 4 (Phillips).

[55] Michael Kirby, 'Reforming Law Reform: Concluding Reflections,' in Michael Tilbury, Simon NM Young and Ludwig Ng (eds), *Reforming Law Reform* (Hong Kong, Hong Kong University Press, 2014) 264.

[56] Andrew Kenyon 'Six Years of Australian Uniform Defamation Law: Damages, Opinion and Defence Meanings' (2012) 35 *University of New South Wales Law Journal* 31. See also Chapter 14 (Bartlett).

[57] See Chapter 1 (Noorlander). See, eg, *Lohé Issa Konaté v Burkina Faso*, African Court of Human and People's Rights, Application No 004/2013, judgment of 5 December 2014 (condemning the practice of imprisonment for defamation).

On the other hand, as this book cautions, judicial insistence on applying traditional principles in cases with new twenty-first century realities can delay in some jurisdictions the development of a set of reforms to define the boundaries of media landscapes forever altered by technology. By nature, as noted at the outset of this introduction and as demonstrated by defamation law history, reform processes move slowly and sometimes ineffectively. But technology moves fast and is being used effectively to restrict or threaten free speech, censor content and manipulate data for commercial interests in non-transparent ways. Media law and policy reformers face great challenges in the Internet age. As Lord Lester warns, 'This is no time for apathy'.[58]

[58] See Chapter 3 (Lester). See also Anthony Lester, *Five Ideas to Fight For: How Our Freedom is Under Threat and Why it Matters* (London, Oneworld Publications, 2016).

Part A

Conceptual Perspectives of Media Law and Policy

1

Defending Media Freedom in the Internet Age

PETER NOORLANDER

Introduction

This chapter provides an overview of media law cases and issues encountered by media across Asia, Africa and Europe, as seen from the vantage point of the Media Legal Defence Initiative—a London-based organisation that provides legal aid to journalists and independent media in these regions.[1] Most of the cases concern what used to be known as 'countries in transition'—relatively new democracies. This chapter focuses on the challenges to defending media freedom in what will be loosely referred to as 'the Internet age', but also takes stock of opportunities brought by online publishing.

There can be no doubt that the Internet has brought unique publishing opportunities. It is much easier for new entrants to establish themselves online, and in countries with restrictive print laws or media markets dominated by political interests, online media have been able to gain significant audiences with a thirst for news from an independent point of view. For example, Malaysia's media scene would be very poor without Malaysiakini, a website whose readership exceeds that of the country's traditional politically-aligned media. The Internet has also transformed investigative journalism—revolutionising data-gathering and analysis—and with increasing numbers of people on smart phones or other Internet-enabled devices, anyone can be a 'citizen journalist'.

Furthermore, the Internet has brought opportunities for cross-border publishing that simply did not exist 15 years ago. A well-known example is that of the UK newspaper, the *Guardian*, which since 2010 has run a series of stories based on leaked information that could not have been published in the UK and which instead have been reported together with US newspapers, under the protection of the First Amendment of the US Constitution. It is a publishing model also practised by exiled media such as Sahara Reporters—who publish on Nigerian corruption issues from New Jersey—under the protection, again, of the First Amendment.

[1] Since 2009, when it was established, the Media Legal Defence Initiative has provided legal assistance to over 1,000 journalists in 40 countries, and won standard-setting judgments on issues such as defamation and the protection of sources at the European Court of Human Rights, African Court of Human and Peoples' Rights, and other courts and tribunals. See www.mediadefence.org/our-impact (accessed July 2016) for an overview of its work.

To a large extent, however, all these media operate under very similar legal obstacles as traditional media. In particular, the threat of libel proceedings looms large, even over exiled media. Generally speaking, while the advent of the Internet and online publishing has brought new publishing opportunities and has allowed international media with swift feet the opportunity to shield some of their publishing activities in jurisdictions with strong pro-speech laws, the main obstacles to media freedom in many countries are very similar to those that existed 20 years ago. In many 'new' as well as 'old' democracies, a lingering but fundamental resistance among the rich and powerful to have their actions scrutinised, coupled with a legal framework that is often weighted against free speech, feeds an on-going barrage of legal actions against the media. Globally, national security laws—in various guises—along with criminal libel and broadly defined public order offences account for the majority of journalists in prison.[2] These are traditional, 'old media' and 'old law' challenges to media freedom that remain current in the Internet age. New challenges have cropped up in the form of liability for user-generated content, enhanced penalties for defamatory statements made online, the risk of cross-border liability and being sued in jurisdictions other than one's own, and various forms of filtering and blocking of content.

Challenges to Media Freedom in the Internet Age

The main challenges to media freedom can be grouped together under two headings: 1. Laws designed to protection privacy and reputational interests; and 2. Laws designed to protect national security and public order interests.[3] There is also a growing body of laws designed to regulate or restrict online media which do not themselves impose content-specific restrictions but rather aim to regulate issues of liability or to require registration of website owners and editors.

Laws that Protect Reputation and Privacy

Like everyone else in society, the media and journalists, including bloggers and citizen journalists, are subject to the 'regular' laws and regulations that exist in every country. This includes laws on content—such as libel laws—as well as corporate and tax laws. While the former arguably affect the media more than others in society, nevertheless they are laws of general application that apply to all. Prime among these is the law on libel. A recent case from Rwanda, which was litigated all the way up to the country's Supreme Court and is currently pending before the African Commission on Human and Peoples' Rights, provides a perfect example of how these laws can be abused to silence journalism.

In 2010, the Rwandan newspaper, *Umurabyo*, a publication with a small circulation in Kigali, reported allegations that President Kagame was shielding an army general suspected

[2] 132 out of a total of 221 journalists jailed at the end of December 2014. See '2014 prison census: 221 journalists jailed worldwide' (Committee to Protect Journalists, 1 December 2014) www.cpj.org/imprisoned/2014.php accessed July 2016.

[3] Following the structure of Art 19(3) of the International Covenant on Civil and Political Rights.

of corruption.[4] A criminal defamation case was taken out against the paper's editor, Agnes Uwimana, on the grounds that the allegation was 'insulting' to the President's honour. Following a quick trial in which the judge required her to prove the absolute truth of the allegations, she was sentenced to a year in prison. Her defence arguments that she was merely reporting on a debate in society and that there were strong indications (if not absolute proof) that the President was shielding corrupt individuals was not accepted.[5]

The case is by no means unusual or an isolated example: criminal libel laws are in active use in the majority of countries around the world, and many of these laws provide for imprisonment as a sanction. Globally, a dozen journalists every year are reported to be imprisoned for defamation.[6] The African Court of Human and Peoples' Rights condemned this practice in a December 2014 judgment brought by the Media Legal Defence Initiative on behalf of a journalist from Burkina Faso who served a one-year prison sentence for having 'insulted' a local prosecutor.[7] This has led to a change of the law in Burkina Faso and similar petitions being brought before other courts in Africa. For example, the East African Court of Justice has begun hearing a case challenging the criminal defamation laws of Uganda.[8]

Even when libel laws do not result in imprisonment, they can still have a serious chilling effect. Damages are a particular issue: in many countries, courts routinely award high damages against media outlets as well as individual journalists. Large libel judgments issued over the past few years include a US$1.5 million award to Tommy Suharto, son of Indonesia's former President, for an article that branded him a 'convicted murderer'. In 2002, Suharto had been convicted of ordering the killing of a supreme court judge, but the South Jakarta District Court held that he had 'served his sentence and since the completion of the term he has fully regained his rights as a citizen and [the right] for his past to not be mentioned'.[9] In another example, Southeast Asian supermarket chain Tesco Lotus pursued a three-year case against three Thai journalists for a total of US$36 million in damages. Two of the journalists were forced to apologise; only one of them managed to win his case.[10] In Sierra Leone, newspaper publisher Rodney Sieh served time in prison for his refusal to pay a US$1.5 million libel award obtained against his newspaper by a government minister. He was eventually released on compassionate grounds, following a sustained campaign by his lawyers bolstered by pressure from the international community.[11]

Libel laws are used not only to suppress domestic dissent. From time to time attempts are made to suppress criticism abroad as well: in 2011, for example, the Bahrain government

[4] 'A Review of the Crimes Committed in 16 Years', *Umurabyo* No 23 (Rwanda, 17-31 May 2010).

[5] *Le Ministère Public v Uwimana Nkusi and Mukakibibi* Case No RPA 0061/11/CS (SC 4 April 2012) paras 74–75 (Rwanda).

[6] According to the 'prison census' published annually by the Committee to Protect Journalists.

[7] *Lohé Issa Konaté v Burkina Faso,* African Court of Human and People's Rights, Application No 004/2013, judgment of 5 December 2014.

[8] *Ronald Walusimbi v The Attorney General of the Republic of Uganda*, East African Court of Justice, Reference No 16 of 2014.

[9] 'Court Awards Tommy $1.5 Million Damages for "Convict" Article', *Jakarta Globe* (Jakarta, 24 May 2011) www.thejakartaglobe.com/indonesia/court-awards-tommy-15-million-damages-for-convict-article/442917 accessed July 2016.

[10] 'The lotus position' (Media Legal Defence Initiative, 16 June 2010) www.archive.today/saMtg accessed July 2016.

[11] 'Rodney Sieh released from prison permanently', *Heritage News Liberia* (Monrovia, 9 November 2013) www.allafrica.com/stories/201311121014.html accessed July 2016.

instructed a London law firm to sue the daily newspaper *The Independent* for its very critical coverage of the killing of protesters.[12] While foreign media outlets can usually weather relatively 'small' libel cases such as this, fighting larger cases is more difficult and can be a significant drain on their resources. The *Far East Economic Review* (FEER), for example, fought a lengthy battle with Singapore's Minister Mentor Lee Kuan Yew over an article in which FEER alleged that Lee Kuan Yew used the country's libel laws to suppress any criticism of them. Lee Kuan Yew sued and won.[13] Since then, foreign media have been noticeably more careful in their reporting of the actions of Lee Kuan Yew and his son, Prime Minister Lee Hsien Loong (Lee Kuan Yew passed away in March 2015).

Privacy laws—whether civil or criminal—are a close corollary to libel laws. Where the latter purport to protect reputational interests, privacy laws can be used to restrict any reporting that concerns a person's private or family life. Courts around the world have defined 'private and family life' very loosely to include extramarital affairs involving top officials and politicians.[14] They are similarly easily abused to restrict public criticism.

Over the last decade or so, media freedom advocates have put significant effort into reforming libel and insult laws so as to ensure a better balance with the right to freedom of expression. Some notable successes have been achieved as regards decriminalisation of defamation[15] and on bringing down the size of libel awards. In a series of judgments beginning with the landmark case of *Tolstoy Miloslavsky v the United Kingdom* (1995) 20 EHRR 442, the European Court of Human Rights has held that awarding a disproportionate sum of money in a libel case violates the right to freedom of expression, even if a defendant journalist cannot prove the truth of a defamatory allegation. In deciding what constitutes a 'disproportionate' award, courts have to bear in mind not only the size of the overall award but also the impact it has on the defendant journalist or media outlet, and whether the award would have a wider 'chilling effect' on other media outlets.[16] In the case of *MGN v United Kingdom* (2011) ECHR 18, the European Court of Human Rights held that a situation whereby a newspaper had to pay more than £1 million in legal costs as a result of losing a privacy case violated the newspaper's right to freedom of expression.[17] It will take time for these high-level international human rights judgments to trickle down and be adopted by national courts, but this trend provides hope to media outlets around the world.

[12] As reported by the Bahrain News Agency on 14 June: 'IAA to Start Legal Procedures against The Independent' *Bahrain News Agency* (Manama, 14 June 2011) www.bna.bh/portal/en/news/460799 accessed July 2016.

[13] *Review Publishing Co Ltd and Another v Lee Hsien Loong and Another Appeal* [2009] SGCA 46.

[14] Eg, Rwandan journalist Bosco Gasasira was convicted for invasion of privacy for a story reporting an extramarital affair involving one of the country's top prosecutors, who had used his office to threaten other journalists not to report the story. See 'The minister, the journo and the ladies', Kanyarwanda (Rwanda, 11 April 2010) republished on the Rwanda Democracy Watch blog www.rwandarwabanyarwanda.over-blog.com/article-rwanda-the-minister-the-journo-and-the-ladies-sex-and-power-in-rwanda-48440287.html accessed July 2016.

[15] In recent years, defamation has been 'decriminalised' in Armenia, Ghana, Ireland, the Maldives, Mexico, Papua New Guinea, Timor Leste and the UK; and Indian government ministers have indicated that moves are underway to decriminalise defamation. 'We'll consider defamation law change', *Times of India* (New Delhi, 19 February 2011) http://articles.timesofindia.indiatimes.com/2011-02-19/india/28625531_1_criminal-defamation-law-minister-journalists accessed July 2016.

[16] See *Tolstoy Miloslavsky v the United Kingdom* (1995) 20 EHRR 442, no 18139/91, 13 July 1995; *Steel and Morris v the United Kingdom* [2005] EMLR 314, no 68416/01, 15 May 2005; *Koprivica v Montenegro* no 41158/09, 22 November 2011; *Filipovic v Serbia* no 27935/05, 20 November 2007; *Krone Verlag GmbH v Austria* no 27306/07, 19 June 2012.

[17] *MGN Limited v the United Kingdom* no 39401/04, 12 June 2012.

National Security, Anti-terror and Public Order Laws

There is no doubt that countries may restrict the publication of reports that genuinely endanger national security. For example, in times of war the publication of details on troop movements can be restricted. However, national security laws are easily abused by governments to restrict publications and even imprison journalists for political ends. Even in relatively developed democracies, judges have a strong tendency to defer to the authorities when national security interests are asserted,[18] while in some 'new' democracies there is hardly any judicial inquiry when national security-related charges are brought. It is telling that of the 221 journalists imprisoned at the end of 2014, more than half were jailed on national security charges.[19]

The case of the same Rwandan journalists that I used to illustrate the abuse of criminal libel laws also illustrates the abuse of national security laws. In addition to the report that alleged that the President shielded corrupt officials, the journalists also published a report that was critical of President Kagame's security policies. One article pointed out that since Kagame had come into power:

> killings have increased in intensity instead of arrests [and] insecurity has spread beyond the borders ... Rwanda has become an enemy of its neighbours, ethnic discrimination has separated Rwandans, the economy continues to malfunction, education has lost value, orphans and widows live in poor conditions, and there are indications that the RPF government dares to kill people and blame their murder on genocide survivors.[20]

Another article complained that farmers were forced to grow cash crops, and a final article criticised the system of so-called Gacaca courts through which genocidaires had been prosecuted.[21] The Rwandan courts found that these reports endangered state security and the two journalists responsible were sentenced to three years imprisonment each.[22] The Supreme Court reasoned, with regard to the article that criticised the Gacaca courts, that:

> The report argues that the purpose of creating the gacaca courts was vengeance, opposing people against one another and causing conflicts between parents and children ... These words ... may be the source of disorder within the population. [These were] rumours that had the purpose of inciting people to rise up against those in power.[23]

The Rwandan courts did not examine in any detail whether there was any real likelihood that national security would be undermined as a result of the articles, or whether the articles even had a tendency to undermine national security—the courts merely asserted, without reasoning, that national security was endangered. The journalists' case is now pending before the African Commission of Human and Peoples' Rights.

[18] For an overview of US judicial practice, see Robert M. Chesney, 'National Security Fact Deference' (2009) 95 *Va. L. Rev.* 1361, 1366-1435.

[19] '2014 prison census: 221 journalists jailed' (*Committee to Protect Journalists*, 1 December 2014) www.cpj.org/imprisoned/2014.php accessed July 2016.

[20] 'King Kigeli is heading to Gasabo', *Umurabyo* No. 29 (Rwanda, 5–19 July 2010).

[21] 'Kagame in difficult times', *Umurabyo* No 21 (Rwanda, 1-15 May 2010).

[22] *Le Ministère Public v Uwimana Nkusi and Mukakibibi*, above n 5.

[23] ibid [35]–[36].

As well as cases such as this in relatively young democracies, there is a worrying trend over the last decade of increasing use of national security laws against the media in 'old' democracies. A high-profile example is the on-going case in the UK of David Miranda, the partner of journalist Glen Greenwald, who was stopped at Heathrow Airport under the UK Terrorism Act 2000. Greenwald was one of the journalists who published materials that had been leaked by NSA whistleblower, Edward Snowden. Miranda was en route from Berlin to Rio de Janeiro, where he and Greenwald lived, and was carrying a hard disk with some of the materials that had been deemed too sensitive to email. UK anti-terror officials knew that he would be passing through Heathrow, to change planes, and had a strong desire to interrogate him. The Terrorism Act 2000 provided the perfect legal power to stop him: Schedule 7 of the Act allows border officials to stop anyone for the purpose of determining whether they are involved in terrorism, *regardless of whether they have any suspicion*.[24] Coupled with a vague definition of what entails 'terrorism', this gives extremely broad discretion to police officers to stop almost anyone.[25] Miranda was held for hours, and his belongings—including an encrypted hard drive believed to contain classified materials—were taken from him.[26] Even in the US, with its strong constitutional protection for freedom of speech, anti-terror laws have been used to force journalists to reveal their confidential sources and to justify raids on newspaper offices. New York Times reporter, James Risen, faced prison because of his refusal to disclose the sources for a book he wrote revealing the extent of CIA wrongdoing under the Bush administration;[27] and in May 2013, Associated Press (AP) had two months' of its phone records seized by the US Justice Department.[28]

Undoubtedly one of the biggest threats to media freedom is the use of surveillance technology, in the name of national security and the 'war on terror'. Following the Snowden revelations, it is now clear that western security agencies have used loopholes in surveillance laws to engage in vast and widespread surveillance of Internet traffic. The ostensible aim of this is to 'fight terrorism', but it is clear that numerous journalists have been caught in the crossfire.[29]

A November 2008 report commissioned by the Council of Europe, 'Speaking of Terror', surveyed the use of national security laws against the media in 47 countries across Europe

[24] Terrorism Act 2000, Sch 7, Port and Border Controls, [2].

[25] The UK Supreme Court found that this legislation was compatible with human rights law in the case of *Beghal v DPP*, [2015] UKSC 49. This case has now been brought to the European Court of Human Rights (no application number has been allocated as yet). The case of Miranda is pending before the UK Court of Appeal and will be heard in December 2015. No decision is expected until 2016.

[26] As reported in the High Court: *Miranda v Secretary of State for the Home Department & Ors* [2014] EWHC 255 (Admin), 19 February 2014.

[27] The book described, amongst things, how the CIA sought to have a former Russian scientist provide flawed nuclear weapons blueprints to Iran, as part of a scheme intended to disrupt that country's nuclear program. The US Supreme Court declined to hear the case on 2 June 2014 (13-1009, *James Risen v US et al*, certiorari denied) and the threat of imprisonment was lifted only in January 2015, when the US Department of Justice confirmed he would not be compelled to testify: 'Times Reporter Will Not Be Called to Testify in Leak Case', *New York Times* (New York, 12 January 2015) www.nytimes.com/2015/01/13/us/times-reporter-james-risen-will-not-be-called-to-testify-in-leak-case-lawyers-say.html accessed July 2016.

[28] As reported by AP, see Mark Sherman, 'Gov't obtains wide AP phone records in probe', *AP* (Washington, 13 May 2013) www.ap.org/Content/AP-In-The-News/2013/Govt-obtains-wide-AP-phone-records-in-probe accessed July 2016.

[29] See Ewen Macaskill and Gabriel Dance, 'NSA Files: Decoded', *Guardian* (Washington, 1 November 2013) www.theguardian.com/world/the-nsa-files accessed July 2016.

on issues ranging from access to information to the use of wiretaps and the protection of journalistic sources. The report finds a worrying trend in the introduction of new laws:

> which have serious effects on the abilities of journalists to gather and disseminate information. Terrorism is often used as a talisman to justify stifling dissenting voices in the way that calling someone a communist or capitalist were used during the Cold War …

The report also criticises the courts in established democracies for not exercising sufficient scrutiny, and the European Court of Human Rights—the last bulwark for claimants in legal cases—for being 'inconsistent', and for allowing cases to go on for years without offering much by way of a remedy even if they do find in the claimant's favour.

Cases such as this in the US and Europe are troubling in and of themselves, but also provide cover for authoritarian governments to abuse national security laws to silence their critics and opponents. One of the primary problems in defending journalists accused of national security offences, particularly, anti-terror related offences, is the vague standards set by these laws. The legal definition of terrorism is very vague. This is open to abuse but in countries where there is a strong tradition of the rule of law and constitutional protection of human rights, the abuse is limited. But when these laws are used in a country where there is little respect for the rule of law and human rights, those constitutional protections fall away. A clear case of that is Ethiopia, where anti-terror laws that have been drafted with input from US and UK experts are now being abused to imprison hundreds of journalists and human rights activists.[30]

Laws Designed to Regulate or Restrict Online Media

Certain laws are specifically aimed at regulating the media. Many countries still have specific laws to regulate the print media, and virtually all countries in the world have laws to regulate the broadcast media. In an attempt to control the wild west of libel and unruly comment that some governments perceive the Internet to be, efforts are made to bring online media within the ambit of these laws. A controversial recent example is Russia, where new legislation was enacted in 2014 requiring bloggers who attract more than 3,000 visitors per month to register.[31]

But Russia is neither alone nor the leader in this type of legislation. Both Belarus and Kazakhstan, for example (neither of them known for their love or understanding of media freedom) have restrictive print media laws that allow only 'approved' businesses to publish newspapers, and both have legislated to extend these laws to Internet media. In the case of Belarus, this has meant that all online publications have to be pre-approved by the

[30] See especially, the Human Rights Watch report 'Ethiopia: Terrorism Law Used to Crush Free Speech' (Human Rights Watch, 27 June 2012) www.hrw.org/news/2012/06/27/ethiopia-terrorism-law-used-crush-free-speech accessed July 2016. In July 2015, a small number of them were released in advance of a visit from US President Barack Obama, but dozens of others are still imprisoned: 'Ethiopia releases journalists and bloggers ahead of Obama visit', *Guardian* (London, 9 July 2015) www.theguardian.com/world/2015/jul/09/ethiopia-releases-journalists-bloggers-obama-zone-9 accessed July 2016.

[31] Federal Law On Amendments to the Federal Law on Information, Information Technologies and Protecting Information and Certain Legislative Acts of the Russian Federation on Regulating Information Exchange Via Information and Telecommunications Networks, 5 May 2014.

government; while in the case of Kazakhstan, all social media were brought under the scope of the country's print media act, rendering them vulnerable to action by a special agency set up to control Internet content.[32]

The trend to apply 'traditional' media laws to Internet-based outlets is visible not only in authoritarian countries: courts in Italy have sanctioned blogs for not registering as required under Italy's Press Law,[33] and the UK's Independent Press Standards Organisation has taken jurisdiction over websites run by traditional media.[34] While to some extent, it is unavoidable—and perhaps even desirable—to have a degree of regulation for websites (it makes little sense that a member of the public could complain about an article published in a newspaper, but has no recourse if that same article is published online), any regulation for online media should be no more than is strictly necessary and must take into account the specific nature of the Internet.[35]

A particular legal frontline has emerged in recent years over the question of whether online media are liable for comments left on their site by their readers. Online media value user comments for the different insights and viewpoints that readers may have on issues that they report, and some treat them as an integral part of their journalism. This leads to legal problems, however, particularly as regards whether media should be liable for these comments. It is impossible for media to check the thousands of comments before they go online, and even if they could it would be impossible to check the veracity of comments or whether they might be defamatory or otherwise illegal in the various jurisdictions in which they publish. Broadly speaking, countries fall into three categories: (1) online media are held fully liable for user comments; (2) online media are liable only for comments if they have been notified that a comment is defamatory or otherwise illegal and they still keep it up; (3) media are exempted from liability.[36] The US would be an example of the latter regime; while most European countries and Hong Kong fall in the second category. China and other authoritarian countries fall in the first category, holding media fully liable for any comments that appear on their sites. This has resulted in the imposition of a suspended prison sentence for a Thai news website editor, for allowing comments to be published that were defamatory of the monarchy;[37] and a libel action by the Malaysian Prime Minister,

[32] 'In bad company: Kazakhstan takes page from Belarus' (Committee to Protect Journalists, 22 March 2010) https://cpj.org/blog/2010/03/osce-leader-kazakhstan-takes-page-from-belarus.php accessed July 2016.

[33] 'Freedom on the Net 2011: Italy' (Freedom House, March 2011) www.freedomhouse.org/sites/default/files/inline_images/Italy_FOTN2011.pdf accessed July 2016.

[34] See www.ipso.co.uk/IPSO/regulatedpublications.html (accessed July 2016) for the full list of 1100 online media over which IPSO has jurisdiction.

[35] A Declaration issued by the special mandates for the protection of freedom of expression at the United Nations, Organisation of American States, African Union and the Organisation for Security and Cooperation in Europe in June 2011 states that, '[a]pproaches to regulation developed for other means of communication—such as telephony or broadcasting—cannot simply be transferred to the Internet but, rather, need to be specifically designed for it.'—'Joint Declaration on Freedom of Expression and the Internet' (Article 19, June 2011) www.article19.org/pdfs/press/international-mechanisms-for-promoting-freedom-of-expression.pdf accessed July 2016.

[36] See Cynthia Wong and James X Dempsey, 'The Media and Liability for Content on the Internet', *Mapping Digital Media Reference Series*, No 12 (Open Society Foundations, May 2011) www.opensocietyfoundations.org/sites/default/files/mapping-digital-media-liability-content-internet-20110926.pdf accessed July 2016.

[37] Pravit Rojanaphruk, 'Lèse majesté cases creating climate of fear, critics say', *The Nation* (Thailand, 10 May 2011) www.nationmultimedia.com/2011/05/10/national/Lese-majeste-cases-creating-climate-of-fear-critic-30154978.html accessed July 2016.

Mohd Najib Tun Razak, against the news website Malaysiakini for a series of comments left by users under its 'Your Say' page.[38]

Media Law in the Internet Age: Opportunities

Even in the face of the legal obstacles described above, the 'age of the Internet' has allowed online media to thrive and offers the public a choice of media outlets it never had before. Malaysian website, Malaysiakini is perhaps the best example of this: launched in 1999 by journalists who were disenchanted with the heavily (self) censored newspaper scene in the country, it started with a staff of five and a budget of US$100,000. Within months, its fiercely independent journalism gained it a readership of 100,000 visitors a day, and by 2014 it had a readership of more than 2,000,000 and was acknowledged as the main news website in the country. It achieved this status despite an on-going barrage of defamation suits against it, many of them defended by lawyers acting pro bono, including—at the time of writing—a libel suit taken out by the Prime Minister.

One of the reasons for the success of Malaysiakini and other news websites in the country is the Malaysian government's on-going 'Multimedia Super Corridor' policy. This is a programme of laws and regulations designed to promote online commerce, and which includes a 'Bill of Guarantees' that effectively acts as a constitution for all online activity. Article 7 of this Bill promises 'no censorship of the Internet'.[39] MSC Malaysia continues to provide publishing opportunities, sometimes intended—as through the Malaysian 'no censorship' promise—but sometimes unintentional.

While MSC Malaysia is a program of laws specifically designed to promote e-commerce, other laws and legislative advances that have had the effect of furthering the enjoyment of the right to freedom of expression in recent years are unconnected to the advent of the Internet or other technological advances. The following paragraphs will examine two of the most important opportunities: (1) cross-border publishing opportunities that allow media to take advantage of more speech-friendly legal regimes, and (2) the emergence of freedom of information laws.

Publishing in the Age of the Internet: Taking Advantage of Strong Pro-speech Laws

The editor of UK-based newspaper and website, the *Guardian*, Alan Rusbridger, recalls how in 2010, he said to the editor of the *New York Times*: 'We have the thumb drive, you have the first amendment.'[40] The thumb drive that Rusbridger referred to contained the 'US

[38] As reported by many, including Mong Palatino, 'A First for Malaysia: Prime Minister Sues Website for Libel', *The Diplomat* (Malaysia, 12 June 2014) http://thediplomat.com/2014/06/a-first-for-malaysia-prime-minister-sues-website-for-libel/ accessed July 2016.

[39] MSC Malaysia Bill of Guarantees, Guarantee No 7: To ensure no censorship of the Internet www.mscmalaysia.my/bogs#bog7 accessed July 2016.

[40] Alan Rusbridger, 'David Miranda, schedule 7 and the danger that all reporters now face', *Guardian* (London, 19 August 2013) www.theguardian.com/commentisfree/2013/aug/19/david-miranda-schedule7-danger-reporters

Embassy Cables' tranche of Wikileaks documents that *Guardian* journalists took possession of in 2010. It would have been impossible for the *Guardian* to publish these in the United Kingdom, and so Rusbridger struck up a deal with Bill Keller, editor of the *New York Times*. The Wikileaks materials would be edited and published out of the US, under the protection of the First Amendment. This deal continued when the Edward Snowden materials came into the possession of *Guardian* journalists—and Brazil, the home base of *Guardian* journalist Glen Greenwald, was added to the list of locations from which journalistic work was done. In a globalised publishing world, this construction allowed cutting-edge journalism on issues of the highest public interest to be produced under the protective umbrella of robust free speech protections, and be published online as well as in the print editions of the *Guardian* in the UK and other news media across the world.

It is not only the large globalised media outlets that take advantage of these publishing constructions. A particular class of media that thrives on this model is the exiled media. Two examples are Sahara Reporters, which is based in the US and reports on corruption and human rights issues in Nigeria, and the Zambian Watchdog, which reports on news and governance issues from Zambia but is published from the UK. Both are edited by journalists in self-imposed exile and cannot return to their countries for fear of legal action and almost certain imprisonment. Both Zambia and Nigeria have highly restrictive laws on libel and national security—of the variety described above—that would surely end their publishing activities.[41] By going into exile, the editors of both websites can make use of a network of anonymous reporters—sometimes in high positions in government ministries—who provide information on issues such as corruption and instances of mismanagement of public finances, which is then edited and published to an audience of hundreds of thousands in the countries concerned. Both sites have broken major stories and report on issues that cannot be reported on by media who are based inside the countries. Both face legal threats: Sahara Reporters has, with the help of NGOs and pro bono lawyers, fended off libel suits in the US that would have otherwise cost it hundreds of thousands to defend; and the Zambian Watchdog faces constant threats to its local reporters as well as denial of service attacks. But both are able to weather these threats and carry on reporting, filling an important void in the media markets in their home countries.

Laws that Promote Media Freedom

A small number of countries have in recent years legislated to specifically protect the right to freedom of expression—and the Icelandic Modern Media Initiative (IMMI) is probably

accessed July 2016. In the same article, Rusbridger also tells of the pointless destruction of a MacBook Pro in the basement of the *Guardian* offices by British intelligence officers who sought to satisfy themselves that no confidential materials should fall into the hands of any passing Chinese intelligence officers. See also, Joe Coscarelli, 'Guardian to Borrow New York Times' First Amendment Rights for NSA Leaks', *New York Magazine* (New York, 23 August 2013) http://nymag.com/daily/intelligencer/2013/08/guardian-ny-times-team-up-snowden-leaks.html accessed July 2016.

[41] According to the International Press Institute, the editor of the Zambian Watchdog faces charges of contempt of court and defaming the president that date back to 2010: Naomi Hunt, 'REPORT: Zambia press freedom performance gets mixed reviews from local journalists' *International Press Institute* (Vienna, 10 October 2012) http://ipi.freemedia.at/newssview/article/report-zambia-press-freedom-performance-gets-mixed-reviews-from-local-journalists.html accessed July 2016.

the best example. IMMI is a parliamentary initiative spearheaded by Icelandic 'poetician' Birgitta Jónsdóttir,[42] tasking the Icelandic Government to introduce legislation to render Iceland a 'safe haven' for freedom of expression.[43] It seeks legislative reform on a number of fronts:

1. A Freedom of Information Act;
2. Strong protection for whistleblowers as well as for journalistic sources;
3. Limiting prior restraint;
4. Strong protection of communication data flows;
5. Strong protection for intermediaries such as Internet service providers;
6. Protection from 'libel tourism';
7. Enacting a realistic statute of limitations for Internet publications, making it clear that not every 'click' constitutes a new publication;
8. Ensuring that legal processes are not abused to restrict free speech;
9. Allowing the creation of virtual limited liability companies.

It is clear that IMMI is a project for the digital age: much of it is concerned with ensuring that regulators do not use technology or technology-based arguments to undermine media freedom. The process to draft and pass the various laws that will be needed to finalise is likely to take several years. According to the latest progress report, a new access to information law was passed in 2013; source protection has been significantly strengthened; a bill to protect whistleblowers was laid before parliament in 2015; blasphemy was de-criminalised in July 2015; and work on the other headings remains 'in progress'.

The other relatively recent law that has been enacted with the explicit aim of enabling media freedom is Georgia's[44] 2004 Law on Freedom of Speech.[45] This is technology neutral (some might say, old-fashioned) by comparison. It does not mention intermediaries or protecting transborder data flows, but is instead concerned with ensuring a proper balance between free speech, privacy and reputation, the protection of political speech, ensuring that any regulation of the media is content neutral, and ensuring strong protection of journalistic sources of information. The law has unquestionably created a very liberal environment for the media as far as content-regulation is concerned. Since the introduction of the Law, few legal cases against Georgian media have been reported internationally.[46] It should be noted, however, that there has been a rising trend in incidences of violence against the media whilst political interference in the work of the broadcast regulator also impacted on media freedom.[47] In other words, the existence of liberal content laws alone does not suffice to guarantee a free media.

Besides media freedom laws and initiatives such as Iceland's IMMI, Malaysia's MSC and Georgia's Law on Freedom of Speech, one of the biggest opportunities offered by legal

[42] See 'Board of Directors', *International Modern Media Institute* https://en.immi.is/about-immi/board-of-directors/ accessed July 2016.

[43] See 'About IMMI', *International Modern Media Institute* https://en.immi.is/about-immi/ accessed July 2016.

[44] The country in the Caucasus, not the US State.

[45] See Law of Georgia on the Freedom of Speech and Expression www.idfi.ge/uploadedFiles/files/Law_of_Georgia_on_the_Freedom_of_Speech_and_Expression.pdf accessed July 2016.

[46] The International Freedom of Expression Exchange, www.ifex.org, carries very few alerts of legal matters from Georgia.

[47] As reported by Freedom House, Freedom of the Press Report 2014 (Washington DC, 2014) https://freedomhouse.org/report/freedom-press/2014/georgia accessed July 2016.

developments is the emergence around the world of freedom of information laws, along with an acceptance by international human rights courts as well as national courts that access to information is a human right. So-called 'freedom of information' (FOI) laws allow the media—along with everyone else—to obtain access to information held by public bodies, and hold them to scrutiny. While the libel, national security and other laws reviewed in the preceding sections restrict media freedom, FOI laws aim to empower the media. Along with constitutional provisions recognising the right to freedom of expression, they are among the very few laws to do so.

The last decade has seen an expansive growth in the number of FOI laws around the world. As of 2013, 95 countries around the world had specific freedom of information laws, the vast majority of them enacted in the last 15 years.[48] The European Court of Human Rights, along with the Inter-American Court of Human Rights and the UN Human Rights Committee, have accepted that access to information is part and parcel of the right to freedom of expression, particularly when used by journalists to gather information on issues of public interest.[49]

The spirit of FOI laws is to provide transparency of government. As such, they serve society as a whole and not just the media. However, good use by the media of FOI laws can result in strong stories and issues of high public interest coming to light. Recent examples of stories published through the use of FOI laws by journalists range from the mundane to the extraordinary, including a scandal in the UK on how MPs were abusing their expenses allowances that resulted in resignations and the imprisonment of some of them,[50] and how the FBI maintained a watchlist of anti-war and environmental campaigners.[51]

Unfortunately, many of the 85 FOI laws that were enacted recently have been very poorly implemented. In some cases, government agencies have apparently remained blissfully unaware that they are under any legal obligation to disclose any information at all, and in others civil society organisations have had to push governments to implement the legislation. For example, a recent study has found that Indonesia's Freedom of Information Law, passed in 2008 and entered into law in May 2010, has not been implemented;[52] Maltese journalists criticised their government for taking four years to implement their Freedom of Information Act 2008;[53] while media and civil society in Uganda struggle to gain access

[48] According to the right2info website, which catalogues freedom of information law and practice: *Access to Information Laws: Overview and Statutory Goals* (*Right2Info*, September 2013) www.right2info.org/access-to-information-laws/access-to-information-laws accessed July 2016.

[49] For ECHR jurisprudence, see especially, *Roşiianu v Romania*, No 27329/06, 24 June 2014; *Társaság a Szabadságjogokért v Hungary*, No 37374/05, 14 April 2009; *Youth Initiative for Human Rights v Serbia*, No 48135/06, 25 June 2013; *Kenedi v Hungary* No 31475/05, 26 May 2009. For the Inter-American Court see *Claude Reyes and ors v Chile, Merits, reparations and costs*, IACHR Series C no 151, 19 September 2006. For UN Human Rights Committee, see *Toktakunov v Kyrgyzstan*, Communication No 1470/2006, 28 March 2011.

[50] 'Expenses: How MP's expenses became a hot topic', *Daily Telegraph* (London, May 8, 2009) www.telegraph.co.uk/news/newstopics/mps-expenses/5294350/Expenses-How-MPs-expenses-became-a-hot-topic.html accessed July 2016.

[51] '40 noteworthy headlines made possible by FOIA, 2004-2006', *National Security Archive* http://nsarchive.gwu.edu/nsa/foia/stories.htm accessed July 2016.

[52] Yayasan Tifa, 'Fulfilling the Right to Information: Baseline Assessment on Access to Information in East Nusa Tenggara Timur-Indonesia' (Article 19, November 2010) www.article19.org/pdfs/publications/fulfilling-the-right-to-information.pdf accessed July 2016.

[53] Kevin Aquinila, 'Information freedom at last', *Times of Malta* (Malta, 22 August 2012) www.timesofmalta.com/articles/view/20120822/opinion/Information-freedom-at-last.433866 accessed July 2016.

to more than the most mundane information under legislation enacted in 2005.[54] Even in developed democracies, journalists are frustrated that the stock response to many FOI requests appears to be 'no'. A British reporters' group guide to FOI includes the tips, 'Appeal, appeal, appeal, because they're counting on you not to', as well as the observation that 'FoI is a negotiation, not a right.'[55] It seems that concerted civil society action and pressure from domestic media will be necessary to fulfill the promise that FOI laws unquestionably harbour.

Concluding Observations

Defending media freedom in the 'Internet age' means to take advantage of the opportunities that are there whilst being realistic about the challenges that remain. The Internet is a tool, not a panacea, and technology can be used to promote freedom of expression as well as to clamp down on it. One of the biggest threats to media freedom online—and freedom online in general—is posed by surveillance technology and its use in the name of national security. But even in the face of this surveillance, and while its full extent remains unclear, the Internet has offered publishing opportunities and promoted freedom in ways that were unthinkable 20 years ago. Independent media have flourished online and can use cross-border publishing strategies to allow them to publish in speech-friendly legal regimes.

It is striking, however, that many of the challenges faced by media in the Internet age are the same as those that were challenged by media 20 years ago. The abuse of libel and national security laws accounts for more than half of all journalists and bloggers in prison. This alone is a chilling statistic. In too many countries, the legal regime lacks safeguards to prevent abuse of the law to silence critical journalism. Western countries use the rhetoric of the 'war on terror' to introduce—and use—anti-terror laws that are easily abused against journalists, and new democracies follow their lead.

But good lawyering and civil society campaigning can have an impact. The Media Legal Defence Initiative sees an overall success rate of 70 per cent in the cases that it works on, and broad-based civil society campaigns to reform libel laws have been successful in the UK and elsewhere. In Malaysia, Gambia and in Sri Lanka, all countries with weak traditions of democracy, journalists have defeated criminal trials against them on the back of civil society efforts, and the explosive growth in FOI laws is in no small part due to sustained campaigning on the issue by a number of NGOs.

With new NGOs dedicated to defending individual cases and bringing strategic law suits to help media defend their rights, and existing ones strongly campaigning for better recognition in law of the right to freedom of expression, international civil society is arguably well positioned to take action. However, the scale of the challenge facing them should not be underestimated and it is necessary for these organisations to up their efforts and work together if they are to score more results.

[54] 'Freedom of Information Laws struggle to take hold in Africa' (*Committee to Protect Journalists*, 5 February 2010) www.cpj.org/blog/2010/02/freedom-of-information-laws-struggle-to-take-hold.php accessed July 2016.

[55] 'How to get the most out of FOI requests', Fleet Street Blues, 5 January 2010.

2

Advances in Open Justice in England and Wales

LORD DYSON MR*

Introduction

Open justice is a principle that has long been a central feature of our justice system. When civil trials were conducted before a jury drawn from the local community, justice was done under the eyes of ordinary citizens. They performed a central role in the process. Ordinary citizens also had free access to the courts if they wished to see what was going on inside them.

As a general rule, the days of the civil jury trial are now long gone. When the Defamation Act 2013 came into force, the presumption became that civil jury trials will be confined to proceedings for civil fraud, malicious prosecution and false imprisonment.[1]

The days when the general public would attend civil trials in large numbers are long gone. Television may secure high ratings for legal and courtroom dramas, but an interest in compelling fiction does not translate into increased attendance to witness real proceedings. This may have something to do with a general impatience and unwillingness these days to sit through long and often rather dull hearings with no guarantee of excitement. The falling attendances at county cricket matches in England and Wales may be another example of this.

The decline in public attendance at court, as well as the decline in media reporting of civil proceedings in general, poses a problem. This is a problem identified by the great nineteenth century philosopher and advocate of law reform, Jeremy Bentham. Professor Neil Andrews, of Cambridge University, succinctly described the problem nearly twenty years ago. He put it this way:

> Justice administered behind closed doors will soon reek to high heaven. This is the procedure of a despotic legal system, not an open and liberal one. Bentham supplied the theory. He insisted that justice should take place publicly in order that the judges be kept up to scratch: [He said this] 'Publicity is the very soul of justice. It is the keenest spur to exertion, and the surest of all guards against improbity. It keeps the judge himself, while trying, under trial.'[2]

* I wish to thank John Sorabji for all his help in preparing this lecture.

[1] See Senior Courts Act, s 69; Defamation Act 2013, s 11.

[2] Neil Andrews, *Principles of Civil Procedure*, 1st edn (Sweet & Maxwell 1994) 23–24.

Professor Andrew's solution to the problem was to suggest that 'The principle of publicity [ought to] be emblazoned on a banner and displayed aloft the Royal Courts of Justice.'[3]

Such a banner would have the virtue of making it plain to everyone passing by the courts that they know the courts are there and that they are open to the public. That was 20 years ago. It was a suggestion from an era when the Internet was in its infancy; mobile phones were a long way from being smart; and social media platforms like Twitter were unknown.

Today I want to discuss the steps we have taken and are considering taking, in the light of 20 years of advances in communication technology, to raise a metaphorical banner over our courts; a banner which will give practical reality in the twenty-first century to what Lord Brown has described as that highest of constitutional principles: open justice.[4] I shall focus on the following specific issues: televising courts; the use of social media; and the Judicial Communications Office and the Judicial Media Panel.

Televising Courts

It is nearly one hundred years now since photography in courts was banned by section 41 of the Criminal Justice Act 1925. The first UK television broadcast was not made until 1929. With the advent of national television, the ban was extended to cover filming as well as photography. The reason why photography was banned was that there was a growing concern that newspaper coverage of trials, specifically criminal trials, was becoming increasingly sensationalist. The issue had first come to a head in 1912 following the murder trial of Frederick Seddon. After he had been convicted, photographs were taken of him in court whilst he was being sentenced to death. The question arose whether the photographs were taken with permission of the relevant authorities. It seemed that no permission had been sought or granted. Questions were then raised in Parliament and the Prime Minister was asked to consider whether legislation should be brought in to render the publication of such photographs unlawful.[5] The issue was, we would say now, kicked into the long grass until 1925.

The rationale behind the ban was to stop sensationalism in reporting. Photographs of defendants being sentenced to death did little to inform the public of what occurred in the court that could not be communicated fairly and accurately in writing. They did however, excite a degree of prurience, perhaps resembling a little that exhibited by those who in earlier times used to go to Tyburn to witness hangings. At all events, the ban stood in England and Wales from 1925 until the creation of the UK Supreme Court. The ban did not apply to that Court, since it is not by definition a court of England and Wales.

The Supreme Court was, therefore, able to come to an arrangement with Sky Television to provide live coverage on its News Channel of appeal hearings and the delivery of judgments.[6] It is now possible for the public and aspiring barristers to watch some of the best advocates in the country argue before its highest court from the comfort of their homes, their smart phones or their laptops. Apparently approximately 22,000 people do so each

[3] ibid.

[4] *Al-Rawi v Security Services* [2012] 1 AC 531, [84] (Lord Brown).

[5] HC Deb 21 March 1912, vol 35, col 2067.

[6] Supreme Court Live http://news.sky.com/supreme-court-live accessed July 2016.

month.[7] As someone who sat in that court for more than two years, I can honestly say that I did not find the TV cameras (which were very unobtrusive) at all disconcerting. In fact, I rarely even thought about their presence. And my indifference to them was not always brought about because I was dazzled by the brilliance of the legal argument that I was hearing. Nor did I ever have any sense that the behaviour of any of my colleagues or the advocates was in any way influenced by an awareness that they were being televised. I believe that the President of the Supreme Court, Lord Neuberger, commented that he had been told off by his wife and daughter for slouching on camera and having an evidently smug smile.[8] I cannot of course comment on that other than to say that, if he was guilty as charged, it is good proof the presence of the camera is not causing any change in behaviour on the part of the judges.

Following the introduction of live televised broadcasts of proceedings in the Supreme Court, it was understandable that the question would be asked: why limit them to the Supreme Court? The ensuing discussions led to a government consultation paper in May 2012, which proposed introducing filming of both civil and criminal appeals in the Court of Appeal, and at some future date sentencing remarks in the Crown Court. Filming would not extend to the High Court. The government said that it was 'aware of concerns that televising our courts may open the judicial process to sensationalism and trivialise serious processes to a level of media entertainment.'[9] Those concerns were, of course, as applicable to the Crown Court as the High Court, and the consultation paper noted the danger of criminal trials becoming show trials if they were to be televised.[10] Subsequent to the consultation, televising the courts was made lawful by section 32 of the Crime and Courts Act 2013. This provision gives the Lord Chancellor the power, with the concurrence of the Lord Chief Justice, to make an order disapplying section 41 of the 1925 Act.

We are proceeding cautiously. A pilot scheme has been introduced in the Court of Appeal. The government, in its consultation, took the view that opening up the courts to television cameras, so that the public can understand how courts work, and how in particular the sentencing process works, was 'critical to confidence in the system and to its effectiveness in ensuring that justice was done.'[11] Greater accessibility should help to blow away the mystery that surrounds the process. Public ignorance as to what goes on in courts is not surprising in view of the fact that so few individuals have the time or inclination to visit a court during the working day. The reform will certainly help to promote open justice.

There are those who fear that televising court proceedings will undermine the due administration of justice and that it will encourage the very kind of prurience that saw Parliament ban photography almost a century ago. In these days when anyone can see almost anything on the website, it seems to me that it is absurd to worry about prurience. But we do need to make sure that televising court proceedings does not harm justice itself.

[7] Ministry of Justice, 'Proposals to allow the broadcasting, filming, and recording of selected court proceedings', London, May 2012, 10. www.gov.uk/government/uploads/system/uploads/attachment_data/file/217307/broadcasting-filming-recording-courts.pdf accessed July 2016.

[8] Joshua Rozenberg, 'Judicial review is increasingly essential, judges warn government', *The Guardian*, 13 February 2008 www.theguardian.com/law/2013/feb/13/judicial-review-judges-supreme-court accessed July 2016.

[9] Ministry of Justice, above n 7, 8.

[10] ibid 21.

[11] ibid 23.

I can see no objection to filming appeals at any level of our system. Why limit television to appeals to the Supreme Court? The experience of that court has shown that the televising of appeals has been an unqualified success. Different considerations arise in those few appeals in the lower courts where evidence is given during the course of the appeal. The general consensus in England and Wales, so far as one can tell, is that the camera should be excluded from trials at which witnesses give evidence and from all jury trials. Some may say that this is rather pusillanimous. My personal view is that, as a general rule, we should not exclude the camera even from witness trials, but that the judge should have the power to direct that certain cases are not televised if he or she considers this to be necessary in the interests of justice. For example, it is difficult to conceive circumstances in which it would be in the interests of justice to televise proceedings involving children. But having expressed my personal view, I think it is wise that we are proceeding on a step by step basis and that each step of the way is the subject of a pilot study. There are many who do not share that view. There is also a range of practices in different countries. We need to examine their experiences.

The reforms provide an important means of bringing court proceedings to a far wider public audience than in the past. It is true that reforms often carry certain risks and we should be cautious in how we proceed. But legal proceedings have evolved over time in response to changes in society and they will undoubtedly continue to do so. We live in an age of television and technology. Opening up courts to the cameras is a necessary reform of this age. It is one that we must make work in the public interest. Television has been with us for a long time. I need to turn to some of the other technological changes which are relevant to my theme. With that in mind I propose to consider the changes that social media has brought about.

Social Media

Not so long ago, if court reporters wanted to report what was going on in particular proceedings, or to report the outcome of a trial or a judgment, they had to wait in court and then, when they had the information they needed, they would make a dash for the public phones within the court building. With the advent of the mobile phone there was no need to dash; the reporter could just walk out of the courtroom and make a call to the news desk. The dash to the public phone now seems to be a rather quaint piece of history; and even the use of the mobile is receding into the past. This is because of the arrival of smart phones and social media. As most of us know, it is now possible to report in 140 characters or less and to give a running commentary of whatever you want in real time through Twitter. Equally it is possible through the use of mobile email to file a report with the news desk from within the courtroom itself or to put a report onto a live blog.

But the opportunity for court reporting by means of the Internet and the use of smart phones was frustrated by the prohibition on the use of mobile phones within the court. The ban was explained in the Lord Chief Justice's 2011 Consultation on the use of mobile technology in courts, because of the potential they have:

> to interfere with the proceedings, and the fact they may be used with ease to make illegal sound or video recordings, or to take photographs. [In addition the] blanket prohibition against the use of

> mobile telephones in court is also easier for court staff and security officers to enforce than if there were some permitted uses and some prohibited uses.[12]

The blanket ban meant that whatever benefits might arise via smart phones and the Internet could not be realised.

In December 2010 the Lord Chief Justice issued Interim Guidance to the courts that provided an initial framework for the use by the media of mobile phones in court, so that live text-based reporting could be carried out in court.[13] This was followed by a formal consultation on whether and if so how such reporting should be permitted.[14] In December 2011 formal Practice Guidance was issued.[15] It covered the use of mobile email, social media and Internet-enabled laptops in and from courts in England and Wales to provide livetext-based communications. It emphasised that the court has the overriding responsibility to ensure that proceedings are conducted consistently with the proper administration of justice, and that open justice is a fundamental aspect of that. It noted however that there are exceptions to open justice; that photography from court and making sound recordings of proceedings was prohibited.

It went on to say:

> (8) The normal, indeed almost invariable, rule has been that mobile phones must be turned off in court. There is however no statutory prohibition on the use of live text-based communications in open court.
>
> (9) Where a member of the public, who is in court, wishes to use live text-based communications during court proceedings an application for permission to activate and use, in silent mode, a mobile phone, small laptop or similar piece of equipment, solely in order to make live, text-based communications of the proceedings will need to be made. The application may be made formally or informally (for instance by communicating a request to the judge through court staff).
>
> (10) It is presumed that a representative of the media or a legal commentator using live, text-based communications from court does not pose a danger of interference with the proper administration of justice in the individual case. This is because the most obvious purpose of permitting the use of live, text-based communications would be to enable the media to produce fair and accurate reports of the proceedings. As such, a representative of the media or a legal commentator who wishes to use live, text-based communications from court may do so without making an application to the court.
>
> (11) When considering, either generally on its own motion, or following a formal application or informal request by a member of the public, whether to permit live, text-based communications, and if so by whom, the paramount question for the judge will be whether the application may interfere with the proper administration of justice.

The Guidance noted that the issue of improper interference with the administration of justice was likely to be most acute in relation to criminal proceedings. Witnesses outside court would be able to read evidence given in court via Twitter or live blogs. Inadmissible

[12] Judicial Communications Office, 'A Consultation on the Use of Live, Text-Based Forms of Communications from Court for the Purposes of Fair and Accurate Reporting', London, February 2011, 9 (JCO *Consultation*).

[13] Judicial Communications Office, 'Interim Guidance: The Use of Live Text-based Forms of Communication (including Twitter) from Court for the Purposes of Fair and Accurate Reporting' www.judiciary.gov.uk/wp-content/uploads/2011/12/ltbc-guidance-dec-2011.pdf accessed July 2016. (JCO Interim Guidance).

[14] JCO *Consultation*, above n 12.

[15] JCO Interim Guidance, above n 13.

evidence posted on Twitter might influence the jury. Live reporting in any proceedings might serve to create pressure on witnesses or litigants more generally, distracting them or worrying them so as weaken the quality of their evidence.

It is perhaps not surprising that, following the publication of the Guidance, there were some teething problems. For example, shortly after it came into force, the criminal trial for tax evasion of Harry Redknapp, a famous football manager, was interrupted because a journalist had tweeted the name of a juror and some of the evidence given by a witness in the absence of the jury. A fresh jury had to be sworn in, the matter was referred to the Attorney-General and tweeting was barred for the rest of the proceedings.[16] But since then, as far as I am aware, court-based tweeting and blogging has taken place without any significant hitches. The recent High Court action concerning David Miranda, the partner of the US journalist Glenn Greenwald, was for instance live tweeted by *The Guardian* newspaper with no apparent difficulty.[17]

It is difficult for the judiciary to know to what extent live tweeting and blogging from court is finding an audience. No doubt the means exist to discover how many people follow such tweets and blogs, but I am not aware of any research yet which has collated such data as exists. It would, I think, be useful if someone were to undertake the research. In the absence of such evidence, and on the assumption that there is an audience for such court reporting whether through journalistic tweets tied to a newspaper or TV channel or by members of the public or legal bloggers, I think it can be said that the use of technology is enabling important advances to be made in opening up the courts to the public. As long as technology can continue to be used in a way that does not impede the proper administration of justice, its use should continue to be permitted.

The Judicial Communication Office and Media Panel

I now want to say a few a words about the Judicial Communication Office (JCO) and the Judicial Media Panel. The traditional attitude of the judiciary to the media was one of deep suspicion. Generally speaking, reporters were not to be trusted. The judges behaved like Trappist monks. They spoke only through their judgments and, occasionally, through lectures. The media knew that this was the convention. Therefore, if they wanted a judicial view on an issue, they tended to seek out retired judges. There were one or two of these, usually people who had had fairly undistinguished judicial careers. They enjoyed the publicity which they had not previously enjoyed. The silence of the serving judges was imposed on them by the Kilmuir Rules.[18] So from 1955, when they were framed, until 1987 when Lord Mackay set them aside, they effectively barred public comment by members of the judiciary.[19] In this there was no conflict with the principle of open justice. The intention

[16] See Friederike Heine, 'Judge bans court tweeting from Harry Redknapp trial', *Legal Week*, 24 January 2012.

[17] See, David Miranda, 'David Miranda lawyers seek high court injunction—live tweets' *The Guardian*, 22 August 2013 www.theguardian.com/world/2013/aug/22/david-miranda-high-court-tweets accessed July 2016.

[18] Letter from Lord Kilmuir LC (12 December 1955) reprinted in 'Barnett, Judges and the media—the Kilmuir Rules' [1986] *Public Law* 383, 384–385.

[19] See Lord Mackay LC, *The Administration of Justice* (Stevens & Co, 1993) 25–26.

behind the prohibition was to help secure public confidence in the judiciary by preventing them from being drawn into political and other controversies.

The relaxation of the Kilmuir Rules in 1987 did not lead to a rush of judges jostling to give interviews with the press nor did it lead to pressure from the media for comment from the judiciary. Where such comment was called for in respect of the judiciary or judicial decisions, the Lord Chancellor would make it under his historic duty to defend the independence of the judiciary. Occasionally, the Lord Chief Justice would speak. But his public utterances were comparatively rare and not always an unqualified success. Lord Taylor's one and only appearance on the TV show 'Question Time' alongside politicians was generally regarded as unsuccessful.

In 2005, however, our constitutional arrangements were changed by the Constitutional Reform Act. The effect of this legislation was that the Lord Chancellor lost his tripartite role of being a member of the executive and legislative branches of our constitution as well as Head of the Judiciary; and the Lord Chief Justice become the Head of the Judiciary of England and Wales instead.

The 2005 Act imposed a duty on the Lord Chancellor to uphold the independence of the judiciary, thereby maintaining his historic duty to defend the judiciary from adverse public or media comment of the kind that is likely to reduce public confidence in the judicial system. But the wider role of representing the judiciary to the media and the public passed to the Lord Chief Justice and with it, as the House of Lords' Constitution Committee noted the duty to 'increase public understanding of the judges and the justice system, … [as well as to] help the judiciary to place constructive pressure on the executive over areas where there is disagreement or unease'.[20] Informing and educating both the public and the executive about what goes on in the courts is clearly an important aspect of open justice administered in an open society. Increasing an understanding of what is done and, most importantly, why it is done is an essential element of securing public confidence in an independent judiciary and thereby the rule of law.

To help the Lord Chief Justice to carry out this duty effectively the JCO and the Judicial Media Panel were created. The JCO is the judiciary's press office and carries out the role that the Lord Chancellor's press office used to play prior to the 2005 reforms. It was created with the explicit aim of increasing 'the public's confidence in judges … as part of an overall requirement to enhance public confidence in the justice system.'[21] It operates in a number of ways. It maintains the judicial website, which contains a wealth of information about the judiciary, its role and function, about judicial independence and accountability. It published important judgments as well as summaries of judgments which outline the key factual and legal issues and the reasons for the decision (something the JCO shares with the UK Supreme Court, which routinely publishes such summaries at the same time as it hands down judgments).[22] It also published judicial lectures and speeches, judicial responses to government consultation papers, as well as reports and Practice Directions and Guidance.[23]

[20] See House of Lords' Select Committee, *Constitution*, (HL 2006-2007, 6th Report) at [156] www.publications.parliament.uk/pa/ld200607/ldselect/ldconst/151/15106.htm accessed July 2016. (HL *Constitution Report*).

[21] ibid (Lord Woolf LCJ).

[22] UK Supreme Court website www.supremecourt.gov.uk/news/latest-judgments.html accessed October 2013.

[23] UK Judiciary website www.judiciary.gov.uk accessed July 2016.

The JCO does not simply ensure that the judiciary has a web presence, as important as that might be today. It also ensures that, wherever possible, a member of its press team is available to talk to the press on issues of interest that arise, in particular contentious issues that arise from judgments. The Office cannot explain or interpret judgments or a judge's sentencing remarks. What the judge says in his or her judgment or sentencing remarks must speak for itself. But the Office can help to place the judgment or sentencing remarks in their proper context by, for instance, ensuring that the press is aware of the full picture. If an enquiry relates to the length of a sentence handed down for a certain criminal offence, it can for instance ensure that the enquirer is aware of the relevant sentencing guidelines. What might at first blush have appeared to be a very lenient sentence can then be seen in its proper context. The aim of the Office is to ensure that the sentence, or judgment, is reported fairly and accurately. In this way, if the sentence or judgment still appears to be unsatisfactory once the context has been fully explained and understood, the issue may be seen as one for political debate concerning whether the law itself should be changed rather than an occasion for criticising the judge.

One interesting issue that was raised by the respected legal journalist Joshua Rozenberg shortly after the JCO was created was whether it should 'act as the public spokesman for the judges'.[24] By this he meant: should it employ a trained lawyer, or perhaps as others suggested a panel of senior or retired judges, who could comment on judgments so as to 'correct inaccuracies, highlight significant sections in judgments or sentencing remarks, and possibly even explain complex points of law to facilitate more informed media coverage?'[25] It seems to me that the idea that a senior judge could play such a role is a non-starter. First, the judge would not be able to sit on an appeal from such a decision. But more importantly, it would risk undermining judicial comity and judicial independence. It is one thing for a judge's decision to be overturned on appeal. The risk of that happening is an incident of judicial life which every judge accepts. But I would regard as unacceptable the risk of being exposed to adverse criticism by another judge without the benefit of adversarial argument.

There is perhaps something to be said for a legally trained spokesman or a retired judge explaining complex points of law or the background to sentencing remarks so as to facilitate accurate reporting. This is an idea that we might perhaps consider in the future, although given the existence of the judge's media panel it is perhaps an unnecessary development or one that carries with it too great a danger of the spokesman drifting into the realm of defending judgments or explaining that when the judge said X he or she really meant to say Y.

Let me turn then to the media panel. It too was created following the 2005 reforms. It is the responsibility of the Judges' Council's communications sub-committee. I can best describe its role by setting out how my predecessor as Master of the Rolls, Lord Clarke, explained its role to Parliament in 2009. In evidence to the Culture, Media and Sport Select Committee he said this:

> The media panel was set up as a means by which the judiciary could clear up media confusion which can simply and easily be rectified and thereby improve public understanding and confidence

[24] HL *Constitution Report*, above n 20, [166].

[25] ibid.

in the justice system. It does not exist to enter into a debate with the media or to respond to adverse comment by the media …

The panel is selective in respect of the interviews it gives. Panel judges are not available 'on tap' on any and every topic. There are occasions when we feel that an objective opinion voiced by a judge will be helpful eg, where confusion has arisen about bail decisions, sentencing and housing repossession processes. There are also matters on which panel judges cannot comment. They never comment, for example, on individual judgments, sentencing or other judicial decisions. Equally, there are areas on which panel judges decline and will continue to decline giving interviews ie, on matters that are overtly political, raise social policy issues or concern party political argument. Media attention on bail is a good example of where an issue developed and become too political for it to be appropriate for judges to give interviews about it. Once it became political and an announcement was made to review the law on bail it was decided that any interview would draw the judge into a conversation about what changes should be made.[26]

How does the panel work? A small group of judges of wide experience is given media training. If the media seek judicial comment on a particular subject, they can approach the JCO. It checks with the Lord Chief Justice and the relevant Head of Division, say the President of the Queen's Bench Division, whether comment would be appropriate. If it would be appropriate, the JCO arranges for a panel judge with relevant experience to speak to the media. Panel judges do not comment on individual cases. They deal with issues that are raised by cases, but only in a generalised way.

At the time when this evidence to the Select Committee was given, the media panel was 'still in its infancy'.[27] Few requests for interview had been granted. In fact, only 12 interviews had been given. Since then, the panel has not been called upon to speak as often as might have been expected. This may reflect the care that has been taken to ensure that the members of the panel are not available to comment on issues which are perceived to be too controversial. But the creation of the JCO and the Panel shows that since 2005 there has been an acceptance that the voice of the judiciary should not only be heard through their judgments.

Like Parliament and the Executive, the judicial arm of the state needs to engage with the public and to explain its role. Engagement—a form of openness—as a means of furthering public legal education is essential if public confidence is to be maintained in the justice system. We are feeling our way and proceeding with care. I think this is the right thing to do. A careful balance has to be struck. On the one hand, people think that the majesty of the law should be preserved. One aspect of this is that judges should keep their distance. If judges become too familiar, there is a danger that respect for the law will be undermined. On the other hand, what judges do is of enormous importance to the maintenance of the stability and well-being of our society. Judges should act in the public interest. Ultimately, they are public servants. That is why the public has a right to understand what they are doing. I can well imagine that what has been done since the 2005 Act came into force to inform the public about the work of the judiciary is only a start and that both the JCO and the media panel will develop their respective roles further in the years to come.

[26] Lord Clarke, Written Submission to the House of Commons' Select Committee on Culture, Media and Sport, *Press Standards, Privacy and Libel* (HC 2009–2010 2nd Report), Ev201–202. www.publications.parliament.uk/pa/cm200910/cmselect/cmcumeds/362/362ii.pdf accessed July 2016.

[27] ibid.

Conclusion

But to return to my main theme, it is perhaps fitting that I should conclude my presentation by noting something that was said by another of my predecessors as Master of the Rolls: Lord Donaldson. He famously noted that:

> The judges administer justice in the Queen's name on behalf of the whole community. No one is more entitled than a member of the general public to see for himself that justice is done.[28]

It is true, as he went on to acknowledge in another case, that there are circumstances which justify limits being placed on public access to the courts[29]—where, for instance, such limits are strictly necessary to ensure that justice is done. But apart from these situations, all steps should be taken to secure public scrutiny of the courts. This is essential to maintain public confidence in the justice system, and by that means the rule of law itself.

In the past, the public could exercise their right to see justice done by going to court. They could also read press reports. But necessarily these could only be read hours, if not days, after the event; and a journalist's summary of court proceedings is highly selective and hardly a satisfactory substitute for witnessing the real thing. Anyway, the days when a journalist sat in court all day have gone. In the nineteenth century we reformed our courts and their procedures to make them fit for an industrial age. A system that had evolved to serve the needs of an agrarian society was no longer regarded as sufficient to deliver justice. We now live in a technological age. We have the means to enhance public access to the courts. If we want justice to be truly public, for the courts to be properly open, we will have to continue to build upon recent advances and utilise that technology as far as we can, as far as is consistent with our commitment to making sure that justice is done.

[28] *R v Chief Registrar of Friendly Societies, ex parte New Cross Building Society* [1984] QB 227, 235.

[29] *A-G v Leveller Magazine Ltd* [1979] AC 440, 450; *Scott v Scott* [1913] AC 417, 437.

3

Free Speech, Reputation and Media Intrusion: Law Reform Now

LORD LESTER OF HERNE HILL QC*

The Defamation Act 2013 received Royal Assent on 25 April 2013 and came into force in England and Wales on 1 January 2014. The Act is designed to remove the notorious chilling effects on free expression of the common law of libel. It reflects the public interest in freedom of expression while protecting the right to a good reputation and respect for personal privacy against unwarranted media intrusion. Parliament also abolished outdated common law and statutory speech offences.

Much attention has been concentrated on the future of independent press regulation. For many months, the British press faced the danger of a punitive regime with statutory backing being imposed upon them by politicians. That would have chilled the freedom of speech of the print media and its readers. Instead the new Independent Press Standards Organisation (IPSO) was established in September 2014 to replace the Press Complaints Commission. In this chapter, I review recent developments and reforms in the law of civil defamation, speech crimes, and press regulation in the UK.

The Defamation Act 2013

Before the Defamation Act, English libel law did not strike a fair balance between free speech and reputation. It had these characteristics:

1. The claimant was presumed to have and to enjoy an unblemished reputation. Once the claimant had proved publication and that the words are defamatory, the law presumed in the claimant's favour that the words are false. As falsity and damage were presumed, the burden was then on the defendant to establish a defence.
2. Anyone who took part in the process of publication could be liable for defamatory statements made in that publication. Liability did not depend on the intention of the publisher but the fact that the defamatory material had been published. It did not

* The author would like to thank Zoe McCallum, his Parliamentary Legal Officer, for her assistance in preparing this article. Parts of this chapter were originally published in 'Free Speech, Reputation and Media Intrusion: British Law Reform and its Implications for Hong Kong and Beyond' (2012) 42 *Hong Kong Law Journal* 731.

depend on how the words were actually understood. Instead, it proceeded on the basis that a publication had a 'single meaning', worked out by reference to what the ordinary person would, reasonably, have understood the publication to mean.

3. The principle that each communication was a separate publication meant that for limited purposes, time started to run again whenever the defamatory matter was communicated afresh. That gave rise to special difficulties for defendants who publish material on the Internet.
4. There was uncertainty about the effects of electronic communication on liability for defamatory publication. There was a failure to reformulate the relevant principles or to recognise technology-specific exception.
5. The media had not traditionally been regarded as having any special duty to inform the public so as to create a separate head of common law qualified privilege. The so-called '*Reynolds* privilege', developed by the House of Lords and Supreme Court was difficult to apply in practice and led to a number of costly appeals; it lacked legal certainty.
6. There was uncertainty about the scope of the defence of fair comment. That had a chilling effect on freedom of speech, including academic and scientific discussion and debate. Despite the valuable contribution made by the Hong Kong Court of Final Appeal in *Cheng v Tse Wai Chun*,[1] the case law developed a defence beset by onerous and unnecessary technicalities, including the relationship between fact and comment.
7. The statutory defences of qualified privilege for reports of various proceedings and matters were out-of-date and far too restrictive.
8. The chilling effect was increased by the ability of claimants to bring cases even where a publication had caused no significant harm and by the reluctance of claimants and their lawyers to settle cases expeditiously and at low cost.
9. There were too few incentives to avoid litigation, for example by alternative dispute resolution or mediation.

The aims of sensible civil defamation reform should be to:

1. strike a fair balance between private reputation and public information as protected by the common law constitutional right to freedom of expression;
2. simplify and clarify the law so as to assist the claimant whose reputation has been significantly and unjustifiably damaged in having effective access to justice;
3. require claimants to demonstrate that they have suffered or were likely to suffer real harm as a result of the defamatory publication of which they complain;
4. modernise the defences to defamation proceedings in accordance with the overriding requirements of the public interest, so that freedom of expression is not chilled by self-censorship and coercive litigation;
5. discourage so-called 'libel tourism';
6. encourage the speedy resolution of disputes, including the use of mediation and alternative dispute resolution and wise, firm and early case-management by the courts;
7. make the normal mode of trial, trial by judge alone rather than by judge and jury;
8. modernise statutory privilege; and
9. operate a costs regime that ensures a level playing field between the strong and the weak.

[1] *Cheng v Tse Wai Chun* (2000) 3 HKCFAR 339.

Prior to the Defamation Act 2013, the unsatisfactory state of English defamation law was notorious both in the UK and abroad. In 2008, the UN Human Rights Committee had expressed concern that

> The practical application of the [English] law of libel has served to discourage critical media reporting on matters of serious public interest, adversely affecting the ability of scholars and journalists to publish their work, including through the phenomenon known as 'libel tourism'. The advent of the internet and the international distribution of foreign media also creates the danger that [an]... unduly restrictive libel law will affect freedom of expression worldwide on matters of valid public interest.[2]

In 2009, a number of controversial and high-profile media law cases prompted the House of Commons Culture, Media and Sport Select Committee to enquire into the balance of the freedom of the press against the rights of citizens to privacy. They included the exposé of Formula One President Max Mosley's unusual private activities with prostitutes and the repeated allegations that the parents of Madeleine McCann, a young child who went missing on holiday in Portugal, were responsible for her death. The Committee published its report, *Press Standards, Privacy and Libel* in February 2010.[3]

In the same year, three free speech NGOs—*English PEN*, *Index on Censorship* and *Sense About Science*–published a joint report on the impact of English libel law on freedom of expression, entitled *Free Speech is not for Sale*.[4] It concluded that English libel law had a negative impact on freedom of expression, both in the UK and around the world. It made recommendations for a new libel bill to simplify the law, restore the balance between free speech and reputation and reflect the impact of the internet on the circulation of ideas and information.

With expert help,[5] I prepared a private member's bill to implement those recommendations. It was given a second reading on 9 July 2010, and the coalition government undertook, by way of response, to introduce its own bill.[6]

There was pre-legislative scrutiny by a Joint Parliamentary Committee,[7] and public consultation.[8] The actual Bill was scrutinised in the House of Commons.[9] Following the Second Reading debate in the House of Lords,[10] the Bill was then scrutinised in Grand Committee in December 2013.

[2] UN Doc CCPR/C/GBR/CO/6, [25].

[3] HC 362-I Second Report of Session 2009-10. Their report made various recommendations with respect to libel, including that the defences should be strengthened and clarified; that the burden of proof in libel should remain on the defendant; and that additional hurdles should be put in place to prevent libel tourism. With respect to privacy and press regulation, they concluded that privacy legislation was unnecessary, but that the Press Complaints Commission should do more to uphold standards and to protect people from press intrusion; and that there should be an incentive for newspapers to comply with self-regulation, perhaps through reductions in the costs burden in defamation cases.

[4] See The Libel Reform Campaign website at www.libelreform.org/our-report/download-the-report accessed July 2016.

[5] From Sir Brian Neill and Heather Rogers QC.

[6] HL Hansard 9 July 2010, Vol 720, Col 477.

[7] Report of the Joint Committee on the Draft Defamation Bill, Session 2012-2012: HL 203 HC 930-I.

[8] Draft Defamation Bill Consultation CP3/11, Mar 2011.

[9] Second Reading Debate: HC Hansard 12 June 2012, Col 177. Committee Debate: HC Hansard 19, 21 and 26 June 2012. Report and Third Reading Debate: HC Hansard 12 Sept 2012, Col 309.

[10] HL Hansard 9 Oct 2012, Col 932.

The key changes the Defamation Act makes are well reviewed in an article in the Media Law Center Bulletin.[11] I gratefully adopt their summary, as follows:

- Claimants must satisfy a threshold requirement of showing serious harm—a requirement likely to prevent trivial libel claims and which will underpin all defences to libel complaints.
- Companies can only sue if they prove serious financial loss—a hurdle they will find difficult to surmount.
- A defence of public interest applies where the statement concerns a matter of public interest and the defendant reasonably believed that the statement was in the public interest. This is wider than the former *Reynolds* common law defence. In deciding whether the defendant's belief was reasonable, the court is likely to consider whether the journalism was responsibly conducted.
- The defences of truth and honest opinion replace the defences of justification and fair comment. They are codified and simplified, but the burden of proof remains upon the defendant and the rule against repetition of a libel remains.
- There is a new defence for operators of websites under section 5 of the Act where the operator can show that he did not publish the statement on the website. The Defamation (Operators of Websites) Regulations 2013 were made by Statutory Instrument to define the steps the complainant and operator must take where the poster of the libel cannot be identified.
- Qualified privilege is extended to peer-reviewed statements in scientific or academic journals which should prevent cases such as that brought by the *British Chiropractic Association v Simon Singh.*[12]
- Various categories of statutory privilege are extended worldwide rather than being limited to EU bodies or courts or international courts or organisations to which the UK belongs.
- A single publication rule is introduced providing for a proper one-year limitation period provided the subsequent publication is not materially different from the original.[13]
- Libel tourism is much less likely. Cases may only be brought against a non-EU or Lugano Convention country citizen if it can be shown that England and Wales is clearly the most appropriate jurisdiction for the libel action to be heard.[14]
- Trial by jury for libel actions is effectively abolished, except in rare cases. This shortens and reduces the cost of libel actions.
- The court has power to order a summary of its judgment in a defamation claim to be published
- Where the defamatory statement is published online and judgment has been given for a claimant, the court can order the operator of a website to take it down.

[11] David Hooper, Brid Jordan and Oliver Murphy, 'The New Defamation Act 2013: What Difference Will It Really Make?' (August 2013) Issue No 1, *Media Law Center Bulletin*, 3-16.

[12] *British Chiropractic Association v Simon Singh* [2010] EWCA Civ 350.

[13] S 8 Defamation Act 2013.

[14] Even before the Defamation Act came into force, a court used its existing discretion to discourage libel tourism by striking out a claim by a Russian against a British-based fund manager on the basis that the applicant's connection to Britain was exiguous. See *Karpov v Browder* [2013] EWHC 3071 (QB).

The civil procedure rules were reviewed in 2014 to ensure that the courts encourage the early resolution of key issues.[15] The Ministry of Justice also carried out a consultation in September 2013 on procedural measures aimed at capping costs and better case management. It promised to implement reform by April 2014 but to date, it has not delivered. These reforms are vital to ensure access to justice and equality of arms between the strong and the weak.

Another difficult problem has arisen since the enactment of the Defamation Act. Under our system of devolved government, the Westminster Parliament may legislate in this area for England and Wales, but not for Scotland and Northern Ireland to whose governments and legislatures public powers has been devolved. Defamation law is a devolved subject.

Historically, the law of defamation has been the same in England and Wales and Northern Ireland. Scotland's government has adopted some very limited aspects of the legislation.[16] Northern Ireland's coalition government of opposing parties[17] indicated initially that it had no plans to review the law of defamation.[18]

It was ironical that the Democratic Unionist Party, committed to keeping Northern Ireland within the UK should decide to sever Northern Ireland from England and Wales in this area of law. During a debate in the House of Lords in June 2013,[19] reference was made to the view of a senior Belfast lawyer[20] who wrote this:

> The refusal of the Northern Ireland Executive to extend to Northern Ireland the remit of the Defamation Act, and the legal clarity and free speech protection it brings, is quite simply unjustifiable. Why should the citizens and journalists of Northern Ireland not be afforded the same protection as those in the rest of the United Kingdom, whether they are expressing opinions online or holding government to account? Why, as the rest of the United Kingdom embraces the digital revolution, should Northern Ireland be confined by archaic and unfocused freedom of expression laws, some of which were conceived when computing was in its infancy?
>
> The development of a dual defamation system may also have consequences extending across the Irish Sea. Publishers and broadcasters may be forced to sanitise their once uniform national output lest they fall foul of the antiquated laws still operating in Belfast. Investigations in the public interest which concern well-funded organizations will effectively be subject to censorship by the back door, as regional publications will be unable to report on matters for fear of court action in this libel-friendly, free speech limiting UK outpost.

[15] Rule 26.11 was changed to reflect the removal by Act of Parliament of trial by jury in defamation cases. However, the Master of the Rolls concluded that the court's existing case management powers were sufficient to ensure early resolution of defamation cases and 'are fully aware if the importance of using these powers'. Source: The Rt Hon Lord Dyson, Master of the Rolls and Head of Civil Justice, Statement Regarding Defamation Cases, 2 January 2014.

[16] Sections 6 and 7(9) conferring qualified privilege on academic and scientific peer reviewed journals and conferences. The Legislative Consent Memorandum (Motion S4M-04380) through which these provisions were adopted concluded: 'In light of the fact that there has been no requirement identified for reform of the law of defamation in Scotland and that the wider body of Scots law on defamation appears robust enough for present purposes, it is not proposed that the Legislative Consent Motion should seek to extend any further changes to Scotland other than the limited scientific and academic related provisions.'

[17] The Democratic Unionist Party and Sinn Féin.

[18] The Finance and Personnel Committee of the Northern Ireland Assembly took evidence on the Defamation Act. See Finance and Personnel Committee, *Minutes of Evidence*, Northern Ireland Assembly www.niassembly.gov.uk/officialreport/minutesofevidence.aspx accessed July 2016.

[19] HL Debate 27 June 2013, vol 746, col GC 330–46.

[20] Paul McDonnell, a partner in the law firm, McKinty and Wright.

This impasse undermined the very essence of the new statutory scheme, fashioned with such care and democratic scrutiny. Without reform in Northern Ireland, any media that publishes across the UK will have to comply with the antiquated common law and its chilling effects in Northern Ireland. Publishers cannot choose to publish only in England and Wales.

On 13 September 2013, 31 leading authors and others from Northern Ireland and the Irish Republic wrote to Northern Ireland's First Minister, Peter Robinson, and his deputy, Martin McGuinness warning that 'Northern Ireland may become a new forum for libel bullies.' The letter said:

> As writers, we are particularly concerned about the impact of the unreformed libel laws on the freedom to write: biographers, historians, journalists and even novelists will remain vulnerable to libel actions on trivial and vexatious grounds. The mere threat of a libel action is enough to discourage publishers from touching controversial subjects.

On 19 September 2013, Mike Nesbitt, the leader of the Ulster Unionist Party, launched a Private Members' Bill to extend the legislation to Northern Ireland. Simon Hamilton, the new Finance Minister, soon after commissioned an official report by the Northern Ireland Law Commission on whether the legislation should be extended to Northern Ireland. In February 2014, pro-reform peers in Westminster attempted to put pressure on the Northern Ireland executive to speed up the process, by introducing an amendment in the House of Lords to extend the Defamation Act 2013 to Northern Ireland.[21] However, it was opposed by the government, who argued that:

> [T]his is a devolved issue and it is important that we respect that devolution ... it is for the Assembly and not the Government to hold the Executive to account, and it is for the Assembly to seek an explanation ... We recognise the concerns involved, but we cannot abandon the principle of devolution just because we deplore the decisions of the devolved Administration concerned ...[22]

The Northern Ireland Law Commission completed its public consultation in February 2015. However, the Department of Justice decided that it could no longer afford a Law Commission. The Commission was abolished a month later and responsibility for the report passed to the Department of Finance and Personnel.[23] Though the strong weight of the responses favoured reform equivalent to the 2013 Act,[24] the Department of Finance and Personnel is unable or unwilling to approve new expenditure to take it forward. Meanwhile Mike Nesbitt's Bill will not proceed further. It remains to be seen, therefore, whether the problem will be resolved—either politically or by the courts. There is a similar problem about applying the Defamation Act to Scotland but libel claims are less common there and damages are modest.

[21] Amendment 3 to the Northern Ireland (Miscellaneous Provisions) Bill, debated at report stage on 25 February 2014.

[22] Hansard HL Deb 25 Feb 2014 Col 880-884.

[23] A final report by Dr Andrew Scott of the London School of Economics was submitted to the Finance Minister in June 2016 with two recommended draft bills. One would be equivalent to the UK Defamation Act; the other recommended revisions to the honest comment defence.

[24] Hansard NI Assembly Committee for Finance and Personnel, Reform of Defamation Law in Northern Ireland: Northern Ireland Law Commission, 4 March 2015.

Speech Crimes

Section 5 of the Hong Kong Defamation Ordinance makes it an offence to publish a libel known to be false, with liability to imprisonment for two years and an unlimited fine.[25] In Britain, we have abolished the common law speech offences of criminal libel, seditious libel, blasphemous libel and obscene libel,[26] with their origins in the medieval ecclesiastical courts and the Court of Star Chamber. The government explained that they were 'arcane offences which have largely fallen into disuse' and that they 'stem from a bygone age when freedom of expression was not seen as the right that it is today'.[27] The Minister expressed the hope that the abolition would help the UK to take the lead in challenging similar laws in other countries when they are used to suppress free speech.[28] These reforms to our criminal law accord with the General Comments by the UN Human Rights Committee on Article 19 of the International Covenant on Civil and Political Rights.[29]

The Contempt of Court Act 1981 codified much of the law on contempt of court. The Law Reform Commission of Hong Kong recommended in 1986 that there should be a comprehensive Contempt of Court Ordinance containing clear guidelines, including[30] a public interest defence on the lines of section 5 of the UK Act where a publication is made as part of a discussion in good faith of public affairs or other matters of public interest, and the risk of impediment or prejudice to particular legal proceedings is merely incidental to the discussion.

The report does not appear to have been implemented a quarter century later. The original British statute did not repeal the archaic crime of scandalising the court. In 2012, however, the government accepted my amendment to the Crime and Courts Bill. It gave effect to the Law Commission's recommendation that this sweepingly broad offence be abolished,[31] which Parliament did in 2013.[32] The Law Commission has recently published two further reports to reform the law of contempt so as to reduce vagueness and uncertainty.[33] Some of those changes, including making it a criminal offence for jurors to conduct their own research, were enacted in the Criminal Justice and Courts Act 2015.

It was on the basis of that outmoded common law crime of scandalising the court that the Court of Appeal in Singapore upheld the conviction of Alan Shadrake, the veteran journalist, for having insulted Singapore's judiciary in his book *Once a Jolly Hangman: Singapore*

[25] Defamation Ordinance (Cap. 21), s 5 provides that 'Any person who maliciously publishes any defamatory libel, knowing the same to be false, shall be liable to imprisonment for 2 years, and, in addition, to pay such fine as the court may award'.

[26] Criminal Justice and Immigration Act 2008, s 79, and Coroners and Justice Act 2009, s 73.

[27] Speech by Lord Bach, Under-Secretary of State, Ministry of Justice, Coroners and Justice Bill, Report Stage HL Deb, 28 October 2009, vol 713, col 1173.

[28] ibid.

[29] General Comment No 34 CCPR/C/GC/34.

[30] Law Reform Commission of Hong Kong, *Report on Contempt of Court* (Hong Kong 1986) [5.38].

[31] HL Debate 10 Dec 2012, vol 741, col 871–76. See also Law Commission Consultation Paper 207 *Contempt of Court: Scandalising the Court* (2012).

[32] See s 33 of the Crime and Courts Act 2013.

[33] See *Contempt of Court 1: Juror Misconduct and Internet Publications* (Law Commission Report No 340), 9 December 2013; *Contempt of Court 2: Court Reporting* (Law Comm 344, 25 March 2014).

Justice in the Dock. He received a sentence of six weeks' imprisonment, a fine and an order to pay costs to the Attorney General.[34]

If the British approach were adopted in Hong Kong, the common law could be repealed. Alternatively, it could be replaced by a narrowly drawn statutory offence to accommodate the extreme facts that resulted in the Court of Appeal's decision in *Wong Yeung Ng v Secretary for Justice*.[35] In that case, a media company was fined HK$5 million and one of its editors was sentenced to four months in prison for contempt of court. They had published articles sharply critical of two judges and conducted a paparazzi-style campaign against one of the judges.

Blasphemous libel is still unlawful in Hong Kong, as a common law speech crime. It is listed together with 'offences against religion' and 'publishing blasphemous, seditious or defamatory libels' in the Magistrates Ordinance.[36] Offences protecting against 'insult' are used in many parts of the world to suppress or punish political criticism or dissent. I wrote in 2012 about 'the right to offend'.[37] Our Parliament successfully resisted calls by British Muslim leaders to extend blasphemous libel to protect Islam and ensured that the statutory offence of inciting religious hatred is narrowly defined to protect freedom of speech.

Section 5 of the Public Order Act 1986 makes it an offence to use 'threatening, abusive or insulting words or behaviour'. It was amended in 2013,[38] removing 'insulting' from the definition of the offence, as was done in relation to religious hate speech[39] and homophobic hate speech.[40] Section 5 had been used to arrest or prosecute religious campaigners against homosexuality, a British National Party member who displayed anti-Islamic posters in his window, and people who swore at the police.

In much of the world, speech crimes for blasphemy and insult have very harsh consequences. In particular, the phenomenon of imprisoning bloggers on charges of insulting religion is becoming widespread in Muslim countries. Maikel Nabil Sanad, an Egyptian political activist, published a blog entitled 'Yes, I'm a blasphemer. Get over it.'[41] He was threatened with prosecution for 'insulting Islam', though charges were ultimately dropped. In 2011, he was sentenced to three years in prison for insulting the military.[42] Egypt has some 20 speech crimes, including criticising the president, parliament, the military or the judiciary, and criticising a foreign president, such as Mahmoud Ahmadinejad or Bashar Al-Assad. A Shiite, Mohammed Asfour, was also sentenced to three years' imprisonment in July 2011 for speaking against the crimes committed by followers of the Prophet Mohammed.

I doubt whether Hong Kong courts would uphold the constitutionality of blasphemous libel if a prosecution were brought. It is an archaic and potentially divisive offence and is incompatible with the fundamental right to freedom of expression.

[34] *Shadrake Alan v Attorney-General* [2011] SGCA 26.

[35] *Wong Yeung Ng v Secretary for Justice* [1999] 2 HKLRD 293 (CA).

[36] Magistrates Ordinance (Cap. 227), Sch 2, Pt III.

[37] In Sir Nicolas Bratza's *liber amicorum* 'Freedom of Expression' (Wolf Legal Publishers, Oct 2012).

[38] Crime and Courts Act 2013, s 57.

[39] Racial and Religious Hatred Act 2006. Debate on the Bill: HL Debate 25 October 2005, vol 674, col 1070.

[40] Criminal Justice and Immigration Act 2008, s 74.

[41] See Maikel Nabil Sanad, 'Yes, I'm a blasphemer. Get over it.', *Foreign Policy*, 19 October 2012 http://transitions.foreignpolicy.com/posts/2012/10/19/yes_i_m_a_blasphemer_get_over_it accessed July 2016.

[42] He was released after serving 10 months.

Independent Press Regulation and the Leveson Report

In the UK, we have also been wrestling with how to improve our system of press regulation. The print media used to regulate itself ineffectively through the Press Complaints Commission (PCC), a voluntary body funded and controlled by the press themselves. It was widely criticised for lacking independence from newspaper proprietors and editors, and for failing to provide effective remedies for victims of press malpractice. In 2009, a disgraceful example of press abuse emerged. *The News of the World* had illegally hacked phones on a huge scale to retrieve private information for news stories. The scandal resulted in prosecutions and one national title being closed down.

Our existing criminal law is adequate to prosecute and convict those involved in such conduct. However, the scale of the scandal—which led to more than 100 arrests, including at least 40 current or former journalists, and more than a dozen convictions—exposed the shortcomings of self-regulation by the toothless PCC. Public outrage at the scale of the disgraceful and unlawful activities of newspaper staff in pursuit of salacious stories about celebrities; the targeting of the families of victims of terrible tragedies; and the apparent complicity or willful blindness by the police and politicians led some to call for a statutory system of regulation of the print media, similar to the OFCOM system of regulation of the broadcast media.[43] The Prime Minister ordered a public inquiry chaired by a Court of Appeal judge, Lord Justice Leveson.

The previous scheme operated by the Press Complaints Commission did not command public confidence. On the other hand, a system of state regulation of the print media would rightly be rejected as incompatible with freedom of speech and freedom of the press. The last chairman of the Press Complaints Commission, Lord Hunt of Wirral, gave extensive evidence to the Leveson Inquiry recognising the need for a new regulator. His proposals had the support of most editors of national newspapers, who strongly oppose statutory regulation.[44]

Lord Justice Leveson's report into the culture, practices and ethics of the press was published in November 2012.[45] It fully diagnosed the problems of abuse by the media. However, his recommendations for a new regulatory system were more controversial. They were a classic example of overkill: burning the house to roast the pig. It opened the way to political pressure for intrusive and punitive statutory regulation. Instead of encouraging effective self- regulation, it united press opposition against much needed reform, and polarised the mutual hostility of bruised politicians and newspaper bruisers.

Lord Justice Leveson recommended:

- financial penalties to be inflicted on publishers, large and small, for failure to join the new system of regulation;
- a narrowing of the exemptions from data protection law for investigative journalism;

[43] OFCOM is the communications regulator, established by the Communications Act 2003, with responsibility for regulating television and radio, telecoms and postal services, see www.ofcom.org.uk.

[44] See, eg, 'A Free Society Needs a Free Press', *The Sunday Times* editorial, 21 October 2012.

[45] Lord Justice Leveson, *An inquiry into the culture, practices and ethics of the press: report* (The Stationery Office, 2012).

- Strong powers of interference by the new regulator, including a power to direct the nature, extent and placement of apologies, and to impose financial sanctions of up to one per cent of turnover, with a maximum of £1 million on any subscriber found to be responsible for serious and systemic breaches of the standards code or governance requirements of the regulator;
- an arbitral process in relation to civil legal claims against subscribers which would be fair, quick and inexpensive, inquisitorial and free for complainants to use. The arbitrator would have the power to dispense with hearings;
- exemplary damages (renamed punitive damages) to be available against non-members of the scheme, for actions for breach of privacy, breach of confidence and similar media torts, as well as for libel and slander.

The three political parties had protracted talks and agreed to create a Royal Charter to give legal recognition to an independent regulator fulfilling Leveson's criteria. The Royal Charter model is a convoluted way of avoiding direct statutory underpinning. It is backed by statutory provisions providing for a punitive regime of costs and damages for newspapers unwilling to comply with the scheme.[46] Punitive damages offend the right to free expression and their use has been criticised across the free world.[47] It is also backed by statute that would enable a future Parliament to amend the Charter by a two-thirds majority in both Houses, giving rise to fears of further political interference in future.[48]

The Charter scheme, however, cannot become operative unless some or all of the Press agree to put forward a regulator for recognition. Instead of doing so, the newspaper industry boycotted the scheme by pushing ahead with its own plans for a new and independent regulator, the Independent Press Standards Organisation (IPSO). The standoff between politicians and the press over the two rival schemes led to the government allocating £250,000 in February 2014 to recruit an appointment panel for the charter scheme—at the same time as IPSO advertised for a Chairman of its Board. Yet whilst not a single UK news publisher agreed to seek recognition under the terms of the Charter, over 90 per cent of UK publishers have signed up to IPSO—some 75 publishers with over 1,400 publications and 1,000 websites.[49] The Secretary of State for Culture, Media and Sport finally conceded in April 2014 that it was 'a decision for the Press' whether to be governed by IPSO or by

[46] Crime and Courts Act 2013, ss 34–42 provide for a punitive regime of costs and damages for newspapers unwilling to comply with the scheme.

[47] 'Editorial' *New York Times* (New York, 20 March 2013); Ben Webster, David Brown, Anne Barrowclough, 'World media condemns attack on press freedom' *The Times* (London, 22 March 2013).

[48] Enterprise and Regulatory Reform Act 2013, s 96, provides that any future attempt to amend the Royal Charter must have parliamentary approval.

[49] There are three national newspapers who have not yet joined IPSO: *The Guardian* (and its sister paper, the *Observer), The Independent* and the *Financial Times*, see Mark Sweney, 'Press regulation: new government must decide on independent watchdog', *The Guardian* 23 March 2015 www.theguardian.com/media/2015/mar/23/press-regulation-independent-watchdog-ipso. accessed July 2016. These newspapers opted instead for their own internal mechanisms to handle complaints: www.independent.co.uk/service/code-of-conduct-and-complaints-6280644.html, www.theguardian.com/info/2014/sep/12/-sp-how-to-make-a-complaint-about-guardian-or-observer-content, and <http://aboutus.ft.com/2014/09/05/update-on-independent-system-for-editorial-complaints/#axzz4GBH2Xv6d, accessed July 2016.

Royal Charter.[50] The new Chair of IPSO, Sir Alan Moses, former Lord Justice of Appeal, was appointed and IPSO was launched on 8 September 2014.[51]

One radical journalist observed that the Leveson inquiry into the phone-hacking scandal of the late *News of the World* became:

> a pretext for a mission to purge the entire 'popular' press, using high-profile victims as human shields, high-ranking celebrities as voice-over artists, and high-minded talk of "ethics" as a code for advancing an elitist political and cultural agenda ... Far from needing more regulation and regimentation, what the press needs is greater freedom and openness.[52]

I do not go so far but am closer to his views than to those who support coercive measures to regulate the print media. The UK needs independent self-regulation to provide effective remedies and promote professional standards, with the courts intervening only where the press has abused its powers. There are early signs that IPSO will deliver this far better than the discredited PCC—and without resorting to the chilling threat of coercive penalties for failure to join the scheme. Already its daily complaints service has seen that newspapers are dealing with complaints faster than before and for the first time, where appropriate, providing corrections in a place and on terms dictated by the regulator.[53] It has also launched a consultation process with the aim of providing an arbitration scheme for civil legal disputes with the press, on issues such as defamation and privacy.[54] IPSO under its robust chair Sir Alan Moses has shown its effectiveness but parliamentarians continue to press the government to implement coercive measures that threaten freedom of the press.

Conclusion

Freedom of opinion and freedom of expression are the foundation for every free and democratic society, a necessary condition to realise the principles of transparency and accountability we need to protect human rights. It is the basis for the full enjoyment of many other human rights, including freedom of assembly and association and the right to vote.

Though free speech was declared by the United Nations in 1948 to be a universal right, that is a hope, not reality. In Hong Kong, as with many countries all over the world, vague and dangerously broad offences threaten free speech and the expression of political opposition—including criminal defamation, contempt of court and blasphemous libel.

As the Law Reform Commission of Hong Kong has recognised, the project of modifying the law and striking a fair balance between free speech, reputation and the rights of others

[50] Rachel Sylvester and others, 'Press Will Choose Way Ahead Over Regulation, says Javid', *The Times* (London, 26 April 2014).

[51] Alex Spence and Frances Gibb, 'Soham murders Judge will head press regulator', *The Times* (London, 30 April 2014).

[52] Mick Hume, *There is No Such Thing as a Free Press* (Imprint Academic, 2012).

[53] See Sir Alan Moses, 'Whither IPSO: IPSO and the Future of Independent Press Regulation', address at the invitation of the LSE Media Law Policy Project, 12 March 2015, 13.

[54] 'IPSO Launches Consultation Process on Arbitration Scheme', IPSO Press Release, 15 June 2015.

must not be left to the courts. Judges are not lawmakers. They are constrained by past precedents. If they clarify and modernise the law, it is through cases that happen at random. Their task is to do justice in particular circumstances, not consult experts and the public and consider the general application of the law. Wider reforms require the intervention of the legislature. With the advent of the internet, the case for modernising the law has become yet more pressing.

Of course, no law can save our right to free speech without the support of a strong, popular culture of liberty. As Justice Brandies observed long ago 'the greatest menace to freedom is an inert people'.[55] Across the world, one of the greatest threats to free speech comes from the dogmatic intolerance of those who seek to impose their 'fighting faiths'[56] (whether political, religious or secular) on others. There is a right (but not a duty) to offend. We need to defend free expression against them as well as against censorship by the arms of the State: 'freedom for the thought that we hate'.[57] There is no time for apathy.

[55] *Whitney v California* 274 US 357 (1927), p376.

[56] The memorable phrase used by Holmes J. in his celebrated dissenting judgment in *Abrams v United States* 250 US 616 (1919), 626. 'Persecution for the expression of opinions seems to me perfectly logical. If you have no doubt of your premises or your power and want a certain result with all your heart you naturally express your wishes in law and sweep away all opposition ... But when men have realized that time has upset many fighting faiths, they may come to believe even more than they believe the very foundations of their own conduct that the ultimate good desired is better reached by free trade in ideas ... The best test of truth is the power of the thought to get itself accepted in the competition of the market, and that truth is the only ground upon which their wishes safely can be carried out.'

[57] The title of Anthony Lewis's biography of the First Amendment (2007) borrowing the phrase of Justice Holmes Jr.

4

Independence of the Press as a Constitutional Necessity

GILLIAN PHILLIPS

A free press stands for the kind of liberties and tolerances that are vital and precious to all of us. As John Stuart Mill and John Milton both recognised, we need to believe and have faith that in a free and equal encounter with falsehood, truth will emerge, that differences of opinion encourage debate and help truth emerge, and that by this process we have a better chance of getting the whole picture and not a partial one fed to us by those in positions of power or influence. As the then Lord Chief Justice, Lord Justice Judge put it so eloquently in his keynote speech to the Justice Human Rights Law Conference in London in November 2011, 'In a country governed by the rule of law, the independence of the press is a constitutional necessity.'[1]

The press, no more than any other institution, are not perfect, make mistakes and get things wrong. But that is the price that you have to pay if you believe in free speech.

Carl Bernstein, the legendary co-author of Watergate, used the phrase 'the best obtainable version of truth' to describe what journalists, at their best, seek to achieve.[2] Alan Rusbridger, the Editor of the *Guardian* likes to remind people of the description of a newspaper given by the late sage of the Washington press corps, David Broder:

> a partial, hasty, incomplete, inevitably somewhat flawed and inaccurate rendering of some of the things we have heard about in the past 24 hours—distorted, despite our best efforts to eliminate gross bias, by the very process of compression that makes it possible for you to lift it from the doorstep and read it in about an hour. If we labelled the product accurately, then we could immediately add: But it's the best we could do under the circumstances, and we will be back tomorrow, with a corrected and updated version.[3]

In the nineteenth and twentieth centuries, the press, traditionally the print media but joined more recently by broadcasters, have taken upon themselves the protection of some of the liberties and rights referred to by Milton and Mill, in particular the free speech rights now encapsulated in Article 19 of the Universal Declaration of Human Rights and recognised

[1] Lord Justice Judge, 'Keynote Address' (Justice Human Rights Law Conference, London, 19 October 2011) www.theguardian.com/media/2011/oct/19/lord-chief-justice-press-regulation accessed July 2016.

[2] Carl Bernstein, 'The Idiot Culture', *The New Republic*, 8 June 1992, 24.

[3] David Border, Pulitzer Prize acceptance speech, 1973, reprinted in David S Broder, *Behind the Front Page* (New York: Simon and Schuster, 1987) 14–15 and cited in Alan Rusbridger, 'The importance of a free press', *Guardian* (London, 6 October 2011).

in the International Covenant on Civil and Political Rights and Article 10 of the European Convention on Human Rights and the First Amendment in the US (even though these are rights which belong to the individual citizen and are not the exclusive preserve of 'organised' or commercial media) but also rights such as those contained in Article 6 of the European Convention, namely that justice should be done in open court.

That the press should take these responsibilities on, is not new, nor is the conflict that this role can create with the state, even a democratically elected one. Within 10 years of William Caxton setting up the first printing press in London, in 1476, Henry VII was complaining about 'forged tydings and tales'.[4] Throughout history, ever since the arrival of printing, there have been attempts by the state to regulate the press. In 1542, the Privy Council took action against individuals for 'seditious' 'unfitting' or 'unseemly wordes' and 'evil opinions.'[5]

In 1638, following an order of the Star Chamber in 1637, John Lilburne was dragged through the streets and put in the pillory for distributing copies of an unlicensed pamphlet criticising Charles I.[6] Although the Star Chamber was abolished in 1641, a Licensing Order was introduced in 1643 which re-introduced most of the stringent controls of the 1637 decree.[7] Indeed it was this that prompted John Milton to publish *Areopagitica: A Speech for the Liberty of Unlicensed Printing* in 1644.[8]

Under the Licensing of the Press Act of 1662 (long title 'An Act for preventing the frequent Abuses in printing seditious treasonable and unlicensed Bookes and Pamphlets and for regulating of Printing and Printing Presses.') printing presses could not be set up without notice to the Stationers' Company[9] and the importation of books, the appointment of licensers, and the number of printers and founders were controlled by the state.[10] A king's messenger had power by warrant of the King to enter and search for unlicensed presses and printing. Severe penalties by fine and imprisonment were available.

In 1663, Sir Roger L'Estrange, the 'Surveyor of the Press', who had overall responsibility for licensing printers, published 'Considerations and Proposals in Order to the Regulation of the Press.' Within months of this being published, the premises of John Twyn of Cloth Fair were raided and he was found guilty of unlicensed printing. He was hung, disemboweled and quartered.[11]

While attempts to impose state licensing may have ultimately languished, they were replaced by various stamp acts, which were aimed at taxing the press. The 1712 Stamp Act, for example, taxed the press initially at a penny a paper, rising over the years to four pence a paper.[12] With the new tax taking a large slice out of newspapers profits, journalists reportedly resorted to taking bribes in order to make a living—so the ruling Tories

[4] Louis Edward Ingelhart, *Press and Speech Freedoms in the World, From Antiquity until 1998: A Chronology* (Westport, Conn., Greenwood Press, 1998) 16-17.

[5] ibid 21.

[6] ibid 49–50.

[7] ibid 55.

[8] ibid 57.

[9] The Stationers' Company was formed as a Guild in 1403; it received a Royal Charter in 1557. It held a monopoly over the publishing industry and was officially responsible for setting and enforcing regulations until the enactment of the Statute of Anne in 1709.

[10] Ingelhart, above n 4, 67–68.

[11] ibid 68–69.

[12] ibid 87.

paid secret subsidies to pro-government newspapers using public funds—even Sir Robert Walpole bribed Daniel Defoe to write pieces that ostensibly opposed him. When George III came to the throne in 1760 he appointed as his Prime Minster, the Earl of Bute. Bute used public money to bribe Tobias Smollett to produce a weekly newspaper—the Briton—to pour abuse on his predecessor—William Pitt. It was this that prompted John Wilkes to launch his satirical attack on Bute and the monarchy—culminating in Wilkes' published accusation that the King had lied when he gave the traditional Monarch's speech opening parliament. Wilkes (and everyone connected with his publication) were hounded and arrested and accused of treason.[13]

The irony of stamp duty was that it only applied to papers of a certain size and content, so while the quality press struggled, there was an increase in smaller, unstamped newspapers, and only the well to do could afford to buy the more mainstream papers that were published.

Foreshadowed by Gladstone's free trade budget of 1853, stamp duty on newspapers was eventually removed in 1855.[14] The so-called 'freeing' of the press that resulted, ultimately created an environment which allowed the mass media of the time 'to act as an independent critic and formulator of public opinion' and led to the vibrant press environment that the UK still possesses today.[15]

History has taught us that the instinct of those in power to 'control' the press, is a strong one, that regulation—whether by taxes or by laws distorts and restricts people's access to the truth, and that the struggle to 'free' the media took hundreds of years, and is an achievement that should not be lightly discarded to satisfy short term demands.

In the post-Leveson, post-Snowden landscape, these lessons should not be forgotten. The UK media already operate under a claimant-friendly libel regime. Even with the Defamation Act 2013, which came into force in January 2014 and is generally regarded as a liberalising measure that was 'good news for free speech', the burden of proof still lies on a defendant.[16]

More and more, ordinary people are part of the newsgathering process, whether as whistleblowers, bloggers, witnesses, or experts. Journalism is no longer a prerogative of the elite few. Everyone can be a publisher. The age of the citizen journalist is already here. Social media forum are newsgathering and news breaking. Subterfuge and secret recording is open to everyone with a smartphone. Yet the risks multiply. Newsgathering in the twenty-first century is a risky business. According to the Committee to Protect Journalists, in 2014, more than 60 journalists were killed because they were journalists—ie this was the deliberate motive for their death.[17]

In the United Kingdom, there are a multiplicity of civil and criminal statutes that are inimical to free speech, pose real risks to journalists and investigative journalism and give serious cause for concern as to how sources can be protected. When I started practising in

[13] ibid 109–110.

[14] ibid 146.

[15] Michael Bromley and Hugh Stephenson, *Sex, Lies and Democracy: The Press and the Public* (London, Longman, 1998) 4.

[16] 'Defamation Act 2013 aims to improve libel laws', *BBC News* (London, 31 December 2013) www.bbc.co.uk/news/uk-25551640 accessed July 2016.

[17] See Committee to Protect Journalists website https://cpj.org/killed/2014/ accessed July 2016.

the media field, as an in-house lawyer at the BBC, in 1987, the average in-house lawyer might have considered as their stock in trade, a need to know about the law of libel, copyright, contempt, trespass, and breach of confidence; in addition, a passing knowledge of obtaining a pecuniary advantage by deception and, the Official Secrets Act was useful. Today, in addition to these areas, a UK media lawyer needs to have more than a passing knowledge of the Official Secrets Act, and needs to know about data protection, privacy, injunctions, the Computer Misuse Act 1990, the Protection from Harassment Act 1997, the Malicious Communications Act 1998, Regulation of Investigatory Powers Act, the Communications Act 2003, the Fraud Act 2006, the Serious Crimes Act 2007, the Bribery Act 2010, plus a wide range of offences under various Terrorism Acts.

Even in the UK, we live in times where a 50-year-old journalist working on a local paper can be arrested and have her home and office searched and her papers seized.[18] On 8 May 2007, eight detectives entered the home of Sally Murrer, a journalist working for the Milton Keynes Citizen, and seized her address book, her mobile phone, her laptops and bank statements, they tapped her phones, and secretly recorded conversations that took place between her source in the source's car. They searched the offices of the newspaper where she worked, kept her in custody isolated from her two teenage daughters and autistic son for 24 hours, and strip-searched her. She was charged with aiding and abetting misconduct in a public office, along with her source, Mark Kearney, a police sergeant, who was charged under the common law offence of misconduct in a public office. Eventually, a judge ruled that evidence gathered by police from bugging her conversations should be excluded under laws that protected the rights of journalists and their sources. The ruling resulted in the prosecution case collapsing before the trial began.

It has long been accepted that an independent press is one of the fundamentals of a democracy. As a result, journalists, their sources and materials have received protection under both the English common law and under the European Convention on Human Rights.[19] Article 10 gives strong protection to journalists when acting as the public's watchdog over the activities of government—and when publishing responsibly in the public interest. In this situation a compelling case has to be made out *on the facts* that the protection of the public interest in national security and the like justifies a restraint on press freedom as necessary in a democratic society.

In August 2013, David Miranda, a Brazilian citizen, was detained at Heathrow airport, and material he was carrying, as well as his phone and computer, was seized, using legislation designed to stop terrorists, Schedule 7 of the 2000 Terrorism Act. Miranda, a Brazilian national, was stopped in transit between Berlin and Rio de Janeiro after meeting the documentary film-maker Laura Poitras. Poitras was one of three journalists, along with Glenn Greenwald and Ewan McAskill from the *Guardian*, who initially met up with the former NSA contractor, Edward Snowden, in Hong Kong in June 2013. Miranda had been carrying encrypted files, including an external hard drive containing 58,000 highly classified UK intelligence documents, 'in order to assist the journalistic activity of Greenwald', his partner, who had published a number of reports about US and UK government surveillance programmes, based on the disclosures by Edward Snowden.[20]

[18] Nick Cohen, 'Meet Sally. Her case should scare us all', *Guardian* (London, 21 September 2008).

[19] *Financial Times Ltd v United Kingdom* [2009] ECHR 821/03.

[20] *David Miranda v The Secretary of State for the Home Department* [2014] EWHC 255, [8] (Admin).

For many journalists, especially investigative journalists, travel is an essential and indispensible aspect of their job. Indeed, many journalists have to travel to dangerous or sensitive locations including locations in which terrorism or related civil disorder are rife. Journalists are therefore particularly vulnerable to the use (and misuse) of Schedule 7 of the 2000 Act. A decision to detain and search a journalist or person carrying confidential journalistic material carries with it the potential to gravely interfere with the freedom of the press and, specifically, the right to free journalistic expression. This is particularly so where a broad power is conferred upon public officials to detain and search a journalist and seize material in his or her possession.

In February 2014, three high court judges—Lord Justice Laws, Mr Justice Ouseley and Mr Justice Openshaw—concluded that Miranda's detention at Heathrow under Schedule 7 was legal, proportionate and did not breach European human rights protection of freedom of expression. In their judgment dismissing Miranda's judicial review challenge[21] into the legality of his detention,[22] the Court made clear it did not think journalists should be doing anything connected with national security (contrast that with the US National Security Agency's own lawyer, who said that it was for governments to keep their secrets and the press to publish in the public interest if governments fail in their endeavours of secrecy). Despite the judgment paying lip service to the recognition that a modern, democratic society requires a free media, it appears to leave no room for investigative journalism. The judges declined to accept that the seized files were primarily 'journalistic material', describing them as stolen 'raw data'.[23]

The judgment worryingly downplays the role that journalists have to play in a democratic society. While Lord Justice Laws accepted that there was an indirect interference with journalistic rights, he found that the interference was justified.[24] While he acknowledged that 'the protection of journalistic expression is an important sub-class of the law's more general care for free speech', he went on to disagree with some of the leading judicial pronouncements on free speech protection, suggesting that free speech was not in fact an ally of democratic government and that suggestions to that effect were, in his view, false.[25] He debunked three propositions that many might think were the bedrock of the role of journalists in a democratic society, namely that:

1) 'journalists, like judges, have a role in a democratic State to scrutinise actions by government',[26] 2) 'the function of the free press is inhibited by an insistence that anything (in the security field) which the journalist seeks to publish must be stifled because it may be part of the "jigsaw" from which a knowing terrorist may draw harmful inferences.'[27] 3) 'there is a balance to be struck, again in the security field, between the responsibility of government and the responsibility of journalists'.[28]

[21] ibid, [90].

[22] Miranda was given permission to appeal the decision: Owen Bowcott, 'David Miranda allowed to appeal against ruling on Heathrow detention', *Guardian* (London, 15 May 2014) www.theguardian.com/world/2014/may/15/david-miranda-appeal-high-court-ruling-detention-heathrow accessed July 2016.

[23] *Miranda* (HC), above n 20, [64].

[24] ibid [72].

[25] ibid [42]–[43].

[26] ibid [70].

[27] ibid [58].

[28] ibid [70].

Lord Justice Laws said that 'Taken at their height these propositions would confer on the journalists' profession a constitutional status which it does not possess.'[29] Statements such as this contribute to a serious undermining of the constitutional necessity of an independent press, not just in the UK, but globally.

Fortunately, in early 2016, the Court of Appeal went some way towards ameliorating the damage potentially caused by the remarks of Lord Justice Laws. Ruling on David Miranda's appeal from the High Court's judgment, the Court held that the police officers had lawfully detained David Miranda, relying on their powers under Schedule 7 of the Terrorism Act.[30] The court also upheld the lower court's finding that the use of those stop powers against Miranda was a justified and proportionate interference with his right to freedom of expression as a journalist, on the basis that the Government's national security concerns outweighed his Article 10 rights. However, the Court went on to rule that, where journalists were concerned, the Schedule 7 stop powers lack sufficient legal safeguards and as such were not prescribed by law and so were incompatible with Article 10 of the European Convention. They made a declaration of incompatibility.[31]

In some powerful passages, delivered by the Master of the Rolls, relying in particular on the Grand Chamber decision of *Sanoma Uitgevers v the Netherlands*, the Court emphasised that the protection of journalistic sources (whether confidential or not) must be accomplished by legal procedural safeguards commensurate with the importance of the Article 10 principle at stake.[32] First and foremost among those safeguards was the guarantee of review by a judge or other independent and impartial decision-making body of any requirement that a journalist hand over material concerning a confidential source. The Court could find 'no reason in principle for drawing a distinction between disclosure of journalistic material *simpliciter* and disclosure of journalistic material which may identify a confidential source.'[33]

In a strong passage, the Court noted, 'If journalists and their sources can have no expectation of confidentiality, they may decide against providing information on sensitive matters of public interest. That is why the confidentiality of such information is so important.'[34]

While David Miranda lost the substantive part of his appeal, these passages represent an encouraging reassertion of judicial recognition of the importance of journalism. No one is suggesting that journalists can act with impunity and have no responsibilities. As journalists in the UK know to their cost, they are not above the law.[35] But journalism plays a special role in a democracy and while that brings with it responsibilities, it also necessitates appropriate protections and safeguards.

From an ethical perspective, for the print media (there is a separate system of regulation for broadcasters), there is a voluntary system of independent self-regulation. The Independent Press Standards Organisation (IPSO), the successor organisation to the much maligned Press Complaints Commission, was launched in September 2014 and currently

[29] ibid [71].
[30] *R (David Miranda) v Secretary of State for the Home Department* [2016] EWCA Civ 6.
[31] ibid [119].
[32] ibid [100], citing *Sanoma Uitgevers v The Netherlands* [2011] EMLR 4, [88] (ECtHR).
[33] *Miranda* (CA), above n 30, [107].
[34] ibid [113].
[35] www.pressgazette.co.uk/subject/Phone-hacking accessed July 2016.

acts as the main regulator for most of the newspaper and magazine industry in the UK.[36] It seeks to 'uphold the highest standards of journalism by monitoring and maintaining the standards' set out in a Code of Practice, which was framed by a Committee of Editors. Not all national UK newspapers have joined IPSO,[37] and there are alternative regulators waiting in the wings (for example IMPRESS).[38] The aim of the regulator is to impose standards beyond simply what the law deems necessary. What is becoming much harder, is to determine who to apply what standards to. Who is entitled, for example, to source protection rights? Does it matter whether an individual is a 'journalist'? Should the focus rather be on output—ie apply protections to any publication that is in the public interest, irrespective of the status of the writer?

As we celebrated the twenty-fifth anniversary in 2014 of the creation of the World Wide Web, it remains important that there is an open and secure Internet, in word and deed, so as to ensure that individuals and businesses can have faith, confidence and trust in the online world. The twenty-first century digital model needs to be open and transparent, as well as safe and private. The United States National Security Agency (NSA) and its British partner, the Government Communications Headquarters (GCHQ)—in conjunction both wittingly and unwittingly with the Internet and telecommunications giants—have used their technical skills to 'master the Internet'. Thanks to Edward Snowden, we have come to realise and appreciate the dangers that arise from the widespread use of state surveillance of communications, not only on citizens' ability to enjoy a private life, freely express themselves and enjoy their other fundamental human rights but also on journalists' ability to carry out their duties and responsibilities freely, uninhibited by the state.

> Modern communications technology provides a powerful tool for democracy, by vastly increasing individuals' access to information and facilitating their active participation in society. However, it has also contributed to a blurring of lines between the public and private sphere, and made possible unprecedented levels of interference with the right to privacy. Concerns have been raised recently over the broad scope of security surveillance regimes and the potential for intrusions which have been facilitated by modern technologies used in this context.[39]

According to the annual index of media freedom, published by the US-based Freedom House, an NGO established in 1941 that has been ranking countries worldwide since 1980 in relation to democracy, human rights and press freedom, global press freedom in 2014 fell to its lowest level in over a decade.[40]

> The year's declines were driven by the desire of governments—particularly in authoritarian states or polarized political environments—to control news content, whether through the physical harassment of journalists covering protest movements or other sensitive news stories; restrictions on foreign reporters; or tightened constraints on online news outlets and social media. In addition,

[36] www.ipso.co.uk/IPSO/index.html accessed July 2016.

[37] See www.theguardian.com/media/greenslade/2014/sep/04/press-regulation-ipso accessed July 2016.

[38] See http://impressproject.org and www.theguardian.com/media/2015/may/20/ipso-rival-impress-to-seek-recognition-under-royal-charter accessed July 2016.

[39] Navi Pillay, UN High Commissioner for Human Rights;—opening remarks at discussion on 'How to safeguard the right to privacy in the digital age' (24th session of the UN Human Rights Council, Geneva, September 2013). www.ohchr.org/EN/NewsEvents/Pages/DisplayNews.aspx?NewsID=13758&LangID=E accessed July 2016.

[40] 'Freedom of the Press 2015: Harsh Laws and Violence Drive Global Decline https://freedomhouse.org/sites/default/files/FreedomofthePress_2015_FINAL.pdf accessed July 2016.

press freedom in a number of countries was threatened by private owners—especially those with close connections to governments or ruling parties—who altered editorial lines or dismissed key staff after acquiring previously independent outlets.[41]

As the 2015 Freedom House report noted:

The steepest declines worldwide relate to two factors: the passage and use of restrictive laws against the press—often on national security grounds—and the ability of local and foreign journalists to physically access and report freely from a given country, including protest sites and conflict areas. Paradoxically, in a time of seemingly unlimited access to information and new methods of content delivery, more and more areas of the world are becoming virtually inaccessible to journalists.[42]

Britain dropped five places from 31st place in 2013 to 36th in 2014, ranking it alongside Malta and Slovakia and dropped even further in 2015, to 38th place.[43]

According to the 2013 report:

The United Kingdom registered both positive and negative trends in 2013, leading to a net decline from 21 to 23 points. A long-awaited reform of the libel laws raised the threshold for initiating cases and has the potential to curb 'libel tourism.' However, a number of negative developments stemmed from the government's response to the revelations of surveillance by the NSA and its British counterpart, Government Communications Headquarters (GCHQ). Authorities used the Terrorism Act to detain the partner of investigative journalist Glenn Greenwald, who broke the story; raided the offices of the Guardian newspaper and destroyed hard drives containing potentially sensitive source materials; and subsequently threatened the Guardian with further action. In the wake of the 2011 News of the World phone-hacking scandal and the Leveson inquiry that followed, the establishment of a new regulatory body to oversee print media also raised concerns among some observers.[44]

Most recently, two reports in 2015, by the UK's Independent Reviewer of Terrorism Legislation, David Anderson QC[45] and the Royal United Services Institute[46] into the interception and collection of information and communications by public authorities in the UK, have expressed serious concerns about the absence of sufficient robust and independent judicial safeguards in the exercise of state surveillance in the UK. Of most concern, were reports that state authorities in the UK, including the police, had been using the Regulation of Investigatory Powers Act 2000 (RIPA) to bypass journalistic safeguards built into other legislation[47] in order, effectively, to seize journalists' data and obtain information as to their sources,

[41] Karin Deutsch Karlekar and Jennifer Dunham, 'Press Freedom in 2013: Media Freedom Hits Decade Low', Freedom of the Press 2014, Freedom House, 1 https://freedomhouse.org/sites/default/files/FOTP2014_Overview_Essay.pdf accessed July 2016.

[42] 2015 Report, page 1.

[43] http://freedomhouse.org/report/freedom-press/freedom-press-2015 accessed July 2016.

[44] Karlekar and Dunham, 'Press Freedom in 2013' ibid 12.

[45] 'A Question of Trust: Report of the Investigatory Powers Review' by David Anderson QC, https://terrorismlegislationreviewer.independent.gov.uk/wp-content/uploads/2015/06/IPR-Report-Print-Version.pdf accessed July 2016.

[46] 'A Democratic Licence to Operate: Report of the Independent Surveillance Review' available at www.rusi.org/downloads/assets/ISR-Report-press.pdf accessed July 2016.

[47] For example Police and Criminal Evidence Act 1984, Schedule 1.

via their private telephone calls and text messages.[48] Under RIPA, warrants permitting the gathering of communications data are not subject to judicial approval, rather they are approved internally by members of the relevant authority.

Conclusion

It is not appropriate to encapsulate what is happening in the UK at the moment as a 'little bit of local difficulty'; if UK journalism is being strangled and submerged by a complex mass of civil and criminal law and regulation, without sufficient judicial empathy and awareness of the vital role that the media plays in a democracy, this sets the tone for other jurisdictions. It becomes the justification for repression and suppression across the world.

[48] See www.thetimes.co.uk/tto/news/medianews/article4503608.ece; www.telegraph.co.uk/news/uknews/law-and-order/11752529/Anti-terror-laws-used-to-spy-on-Plebgate-journalists.html and www.dailymail.co.uk/news/article-3170190/Met-used-terror-law-spy-reporters-phones-Plebgate-scandal-Three-journalists-launch-legal-action-claims-human-rights-violated.html accessed July 2016.

Part B

Media Law Reform and Defamation

5

Rethinking *Reynolds*: Defending Public Interest Speech

ANDREW T KENYON*

Defamation law has long been criticised. Close to 70 years ago, witnesses to the Porter committee commented on defamation law and practice in terms such as: 'unnecessarily complicated'; 'unduly costly'; 'difficult to forecast the result of an action both as to liability and ... damages'; and 'liable to stifle discussion upon matters of public interest and concern'.[1] Many years later in the 1970s, the Faulks committee observed 'much force' in similar criticisms.[2] The concerns are seen in a host of reform reports on the law in England and Wales and comparable jurisdictions.[3]

Such long-standing concerns about complexity, cost, predictability and public debate are worth noting when considering the 2013 reforms to English defamation law.[4] In the decades since the Porter committee report, reform through case law and legislation has increased the protection for defamatory speech, but during the same period the environment for public speech has changed markedly, and public understanding of what speech warrants protection has also expanded substantially. Thus the changes in law have not countered criticisms about defamation stifling public interest speech, even less have they countered the other areas of complaint. The 'target' of protecting public interest speech has shifted as much as, or more than, the law has changed.

While the literature includes calls for more extensive alteration of defamation law, the changes that have been suggested through law reform reports have generally been

* This paper has benefitted from research funding from the Australian Research Council, 'Defamation and Privacy: Law, Media and Public Speech' (DP0985337). Thanks to Sophie Walker for research assistance.

[1] Porter Committee, *Report of the Committee of the Law of Defamation* (Cmd 7536, 1948) [6] (Porter Committee).

[2] Faulks Committee, *Report of the Committee on Defamation* (Cmd 5909, 1975) [20].

[3] See, eg, Supreme Court Procedure Committee, *Report on Practice and Procedure in Defamation* (1991) (Neill Committee); Australian Law Reform Commission, *Unfair Publication: Defamation and Privacy* (Report 11, 1979) ('ALRC'); New South Wales Law Reform Commission, *Defamation* (Report 75, 1995) (NSWLRC).

[4] Defamation Act 2013. Litigation under earlier law in England and Wales will continue for several years as the 2013 Act applies to causes of action accruing after it comes into force: s 16. A brief commentary is provided by Alastair Mullis and Andrew Scott, 'Tilting at Windmills: the Defamation Act 2013' (2014) 77 *Modern Law Review* 87; longer analyses are in James Price and Felicity McMahon (eds), *Blackstone's Guide to the Defamation Act 2013* (Oxford University Press 2013); Matthew Collins, *Collins on Defamation* (Oxford University Press 2014). The Act has not been applied in Northern Ireland, but the question has been referred to the Law Commission; see Northern Ireland Law Commission, *Consultation Paper: Defamation Law in Northern Ireland*, NILC 19 (2014). Provisions of the 2013 Act that protect scientific and academic refereed publications apply to Scotland: s 17 and Scottish Government, *Legislative Consent Memorandum—Defamation Bill*, LCM (S4) 13.1 (2012).

incremental.[5] Evolutionary change—wide-ranging but not radical overall[6]—may also be a good description for the United Kingdom's Defamation Act 2013, although there is scope for more substantial interpretation through case law.[7] And although the reforms are wide-ranging, important matters left requiring attention after the Act was passed included the perennial challenges of litigation practice and costs.[8]

Reynolds to Section 4

One aspect of the statutory reforms is examined here: the public interest defence in section 4 of the Defamation Act 2013 that has replaced the *Reynolds* defence.[9] The public interest defence was repeatedly referred to as 'the heart of the Bill' in parliamentary debates,[10] and was a significant element of the concerns raised by reformers.[11] The public character, strength and duration of the reform movement preceding the 2013 Act were all especially strong. The situation could hardly have been further from the reforms introduced by the Defamation Act 1952, which were described at that time as matters of 'lawyer's law' arousing little public interest.[12] The importance of wide public debate and the effects of defamation law on such debate are understood very differently today. While a number of changes in the 2013 Act are notable,[13] the public interest defence was an emblematic aspect of the reforms. This chapter explores aspects of 'the heart of the Bill' and how it might operate.

Traditionally, privilege has been one of the main ways in which defamation law considers free speech.[14] Privilege defences provide 'limited enclave[s] of partially or wholly

[5] A notable exception being NSWLRC, above, n 3.

[6] Collins, above, n 4 ix.

[7] See Gavin Phillipson, 'The "Global Pariah", the Defamation Bill and the Human Rights Act' (2012) 63 *Northern Ireland Legal Quarterly* 149. On possible effects from Art 8 of the ECHR see eg Alastair Mullis and Andrew Scott, 'The Swing of the Pendulum: Reputation, Expression and the Re-Centring of English Libel Law' (2012) 63 *Northern Ireland Legal Quarterly* 27; Tanya Aplin and Jason Bosland, 'The Uncertain Landscape of Article 8 of the ECHR: The Protection of Reputation as a Fundamental Human Right?' in Andrew T Kenyon, *Comparative Defamation and Privacy Law* (Cambridge University Press).

[8] See Alexander Horne, 'Defamation Bill [Bill no 5 of 2012-13]—Commons Library Research Paper' (2012) RP 12/30, which also summarises events preceding the 2013 Act; Price and McMahon, above, n 4, 1-11 outlines major steps in the reform process. See also HL Deb 23 April 2013, vol 744, col 1379. During parliamentary debates, Lord McNally provided 'assurances that we will make sure that the cost issue is clearly dealt with before this Bill comes into force'. While the statutory reforms have largely left costs unchanged, judge alone trial becoming the default position under s 11 could be expected to reduce costs in England.

[9] Named after *Reynolds v Times Newspapers* [2001] 2 AC 127 (*Reynolds*).

[10] HL Deb 5 February 2013, vol 743, cols 194-95 (Lord McNally); HL Deb 9 October 2012, vol 739, col 939 (Lord Browne), cols 953-54 (Lord Lester).

[11] See eg Jo Glanville and Jonathan Heawood, *Free Speech is Not for Sale: The Impact of English Libel Law on Freedom of Expression* (report by English PEN and Index on Censorship, 2009) 9.

[12] William A Leitch, 'Recent UK Legislation' (1953) 2 *International and Comparative Law Quarterly* 120, 127.

[13] Eg Defamation Act 2013, s 1 which provides 'A statement is not defamatory unless its publication has caused or is likely to cause serious harm to the reputation of the claimant' (cf first instance decision in *Thornton v Telegraph Media Group* [2009] EWHC 2863 (QB)); s 6 which provides a privilege defence for 'peer-reviewed statements in scientific or academic journals'; s 8 which sets out a single publication rule; s 10 which limits actions against persons who are not the author, editor or publisher of the statement in question.

[14] Eg Eric Barendt, *Freedom of Speech*, 2nd edn (Oxford, OUP 2005) 203-204. Another is through the defence for fair comment or honest opinion; it warrants separate consideration.

free speech'.[15] To a similar end, the 2013 Act provides a defence for publication on a matter of public interest where a defendant reasonably believed publication was in the public interest. The new defence is another step in a very long process of gradually protecting more speech within defamation law. Historically, this has happened on two fronts.[16] First, fair report privileges were expanded by statute to address concerns that public interest speech lacked sufficient protection. More recently, English case law developed a generally available qualified defence in *Reynolds* for publications made 'responsibly', with similar developments preceding or following that in many comparable jurisdictions (see, for example, Australia, Brunei, Canada, Hong Kong, India, Ireland, Malaysia, New Zealand and South Africa).[17] A prominent alternative to that general form of defence is seen in US law which increases the burden placed on most plaintiffs under the *Sullivan* rules.[18] In requiring more form most plaintiffs, the approach established through *New York Times v Sullivan* (and subsequent cases) is not a defence like the developed forms of qualified privilege, but it responds to similar concerns about traditional defamation law's effects on speech. Compared with the traditional law, the US approach offers clarity and strong protection for speech. In order to make out their case, public plaintiffs must establish that a false defamatory fact was published about them with 'actual malice'—the speaker knew the matter was false or entertained serious doubts about its falsity—and this has to be established to a 'clear and convincing' standard, which is a higher standard of proof than usual in civil matters.[19]

Since *Reynolds*, English law protected more speech, but not in the predictable or accessible fashion that would substantially reduce the uncertainties that face publishers.[20] It does not seem unfair to suggest that *Reynolds* was primarily available to some well-resourced publishers—largely mainstream 'serious' news media—rather than being a generally accessible defence for speech of public value. *Reynolds* could be used to dissuade claimants from pursuing litigation because actions would be even less predictable and more expensive than under the traditional law. In addition, the focus on responsible publication meant actions would be focused on the conduct of defendants before publication rather than, for example, the truth or falsity of the publication at issue.[21] While these differences from traditional law could also pose challenges for defendants, the challenges may have been

[15] Michael Chesterman, *Freedom of Speech in Australian Law: A Delicate Plant* (Ashgate 2000) 81.

[16] See Andrew T Kenyon, 'Protecting Speech in Defamation Law: Beyond Reynolds-Style Defences' (2014) 6 *Journal of Media Law* 21.

[17] *Reynolds*, above, n 9; see eg in Australia: *Theophanous v Herald & Weekly Times* (1994) 182 CLR 104 and *Lange v Australian Broadcasting Corporation* (1997) 189 CLR 520; Brunei: *Rifli bin Asli v New Straits Times Press (Malaysia) Berhad* [2001] Brunei LR 251 and [2002] Brunei LR 300; Canada: *Grant v Torstar* [2009] 3 SCR 640; Hong Kong: *Abdul Razzak Yaqoob v Asia Times Online* [2008] 3 HKC 589; India: *Rajagopal v State of Tamil Nadu* [1995] All India Reporter 264; Ireland: *Hunter v Gerald Duckworth & Co* [2003] IEHC 81, *Irish Times Law Report* (8 December 2003) 18 (now see Defamation Act 2009 s 26); Malaysia: *Anwar Bin Ibrahim v Mahathir Bin Mohamad* [2001] 2 MLJ 65 and *Irene Fernandez v Utusan Melayu* [2008] 2 CLJ 814; New Zealand: *Lange v Atkinson* [2000] 3 NZLR 385; South Africa: *National Media v Bogoshi* [1999] 1 Butterworth's Constitutional LR 1.

[18] Named after *New York Times v Sullivan*, 376 US 254 (1964) (*Sullivan*). On the US position see eg Rodney A Smolla, *Law of Defamation*, 2nd edn (Clark Boardman Callaghan 1999–2014). Overviews are provided by Raymond E Brown, *Defamation Law: A Primer*, 2nd edn (Carswell 2013) 385–486; Collins, above, n 4, 653–62.

[19] See *Sullivan*, ibid, 270, 279–80; *Curtis Publishing v Butts*, 388 US 130 (1967); *St Amant v Thompson*, 390 US 727, 731 (1968).

[20] Eric Barendt, '*Reynolds* Privilege and Reports of Police Investigations' (2012) 4 *Journal of Media Law* 1, 10.

[21] Eg Andrew T Kenyon, *Defamation: Comparative Law and Practice* (UCL Press 2006) 226–29.

easier for well-resourced defendants to face, especially in relation to classic investigative publications.[22] However, if attempts to dissuade claimants from suing failed and litigation proceeded, *Reynolds* might only offer a defence where publishers were prepared, and had sufficient resources, to appeal all the way to the Supreme Court. None of this suggests that *Reynolds* has been an easy defence for many publishers. It can be seen as a liberalisation of defamation law, but one that remained subject to the sorts of criticism that were raised against the traditional law decades ago, about complexity, cost, predictability and public debate. In that, the position under *Reynolds* appears to have been markedly different from the *Sullivan* rules in the US, especially after the 1986 US decision in *Anderson v Liberty Lobby*. It required public plaintiffs to prove actual malice with convincing clarity before trial rather than merely at trial,[23] which made it far easier for defendants to dispose of most cases quickly and cheaply.[24]

There are real questions whether the public interest defence in section 4 of the 2013 Act will operate expansively—a stronger defence than *Reynolds*, as it generally operated, appears to have been intended by the reforms—or whether section 4 will substantially repeat problematic aspects of the *Reynolds* defence. I have considered elsewhere the possibilities that could be offered by 'discursive' privilege defences in comparison with defences in the style of *Reynolds*. Discursive models provide a defence, but only where some form of statement by way of response has also been published where requested by a potential claimant, as seen in many fair report privileges.[25] This form of defence may allow speech and reputation to reach a better accommodation than has generally been achieved in defamation law. A related point is that the 2013 reforms have done comparatively little with regard to remedies. John Fleming long ago observed that courts, when recognising a need to protect speech in the public interest, have tended to enlarge defences rather than address remedies (for example, by reducing the quantum and availability of damages, or providing for a right of reply).[26] Indeed, in *Sullivan* one of the alternative arguments offered by the media's counsel, but not adopted by the judges, was for the law to require public officials to prove economic loss.[27] Paying attention to matters other than remedies has also been the approach in many statutory reforms to defamation law. Calls for different remedies, seen for decades within the English language literature,[28] remain unfulfilled even though remedial changes might deal better with the interests at stake in at least some instances of defamation. Of course, one factor that could be considered under the *Reynolds* defence was

[22] The difficulties of Conditional Fee Agreements complicated the picture substantially for defendants; but they can be seen as a distinct issue from litigating a *Reynolds* defence.

[23] *Anderson v Liberty Lobby*, 477 US 242 (1986). There have also been changes to pleading requirements in federal courts, making it harder for plaintiffs to resist motions to dismiss: see Robert D Sack, '*New York Times Co v Sullivan*—50-Year Afterwords' (2014) 66 *Alabama Law Review* 273, 289; *Bell Atlantic Corp v Twombly*, 550 US 554 (2007); *Ashcroft v Iqbal*, 556 US 662.

[24] See, eg, David A Anderson, 'An American Perspective' in Simon Deakin, Angus Johnston and Basil Markesinis, *Markesinis and Deakin's Tort Law*, 5th edn (Clarendon Press 2003) 725; David A Anderson, 'Freedom of the Press' (2002) 80 *Texas Law Review* 429, 484 and its footnote 298.

[25] Kenyon, 'Beyond Reynolds', above, n 16.

[26] John G Fleming, 'Retraction and Reply: Alternative Remedies for Defamation' (1978) 12 *University of British Columbia Law Review* 15, 16.

[27] See David A Anderson, 'Weschler's Triumph' (2014) 66 *Alabama Law Review* 229, 240.

[28] See, eg, Kenyon, 'Beyond Reynolds', above, n 16, 31–33 for one review noting more than 10 calls for reforms that would have involved remedial change.

the degree to which the defamatory publication included the claimant's version of events,[29] and notable litigation explored whether a comment would always need to be sought before publication.[30] But that aspect of *Reynolds* is a lesser step than, for example, the terms of a defence that itself supports publication of a response after a defamatory publication has been made.[31] That is something many fair report privileges attempt to do and have done so for more than a century. In any event, a list of factors as set out in *Reynolds* was expressly excluded from section 4 due to concerns that any list would lead to overly restrictive interpretations—repeating weaknesses that were seen to have existed under *Reynolds*.[32] So the public interest defence is general in its express terms.

The Terms of Section 4

The Defamation Act 2013 abolishes the *Reynolds* defence,[33] replacing it with a statutory public interest defence. Section 4(1), headed 'Publication on a matter of public interest', provides a defence where the defendant shows:

(a) the statement complained of was, or formed part of, a statement on a matter of public interest; and
(b) the defendant reasonably believed that publishing the statement complained of was in the public interest.[34]

The court 'must have regard to all the circumstances of the case' in applying section 4(1),[35] subject to two specific provisions related to reportage and editorial judgment. Where the defendant publishes an 'accurate and impartial account of a dispute' involving the claimant, the court must disregard any omission by the defendant to take steps to verify the statement at issue.[36] In determining whether the defendant reasonably believed publishing was in the public interest, 'the court must make such allowance for editorial judgment as it considers appropriate'.[37]

In its literal terms, the defence differs from *Reynolds*, which protected publication on matters of *public interest* made *responsibly*. Section 4 protects publication on matters of *public interest* where *publication was reasonably believed to be in the public interest. Reynolds*

[29] *Reynolds*, above, n 9, 205 (Lord Nicholls) with the 10 listed factors including whether 'comment was sought' from the claimant, although that would 'not always be necessary' and whether 'the article contained the gist' of the claimant's 'side of the story'.

[30] See, eg, *Jameel (Mohammed) v Wall Street Journal Europe* [2007] 1 AC 359 (*Jameel*).

[31] See Kenyon, 'Beyond Reynolds', above, n 16.

[32] See, below, n 48 to n 52 and accompanying text.

[33] Defamation Act 2013, s 4(6).

[34] ibid s 4(1).

[35] ibid s 4(2).

[36] ibid s 4(3). On reportage under the 2013 Act see Price and McMahon, above, n 4 [5.62] to [5.66]; Collins, above, n 4 [12.86] to [12.104]. On reportage prior to the Act see, eg, *Al-Fagih v H H Saudi Research and Marketing (UK)* [2002] EMLR 13; Jason Bosland, 'Republication of Defamation under the Doctrine of Reportage—The Evolution of Common Law Qualified Privilege in England and Wales' (2011) 31 *Oxford Journal of Legal Studies* 89; Eric Barendt, 'Balancing Freedom of Expression and the Right to Reputation: Reflections on Reynolds and Reportage' (2012) 63 *Northern Ireland Legal Quarterly* 59.

[37] ibid s 4(4). The defence also explicitly applies to opinion as well as fact: s 4(5).

incorporated a list of ten illustrative factors about 'responsible publication' which courts could consider if relevant to the circumstances of publication.[38] The factors concerned matters such as the publication's public importance, urgency and tone, and the steps taken by the publisher in verification. Most commentary has suggested that lower courts applied the factors restrictively—in effect as distinct hurdles, requiring each one to be cleared[39]—even though the House of Lords and Supreme Court called for a flexible and less restrictive approach to be taken.[40] The restrictive approach to *Reynolds* by lower courts means that its main effects may well have been *outside* the case law. In short, *Reynolds* helped some well-resourced media to reduce the legal risk in publishing particular allegations by conducting pre-publication investigations that had been shaped to reflect the requirements of the defence.[41] In this, the defence fitted with traditional and serious news reporting and investigation. Other speakers did not necessarily benefit in the same manner from the *Reynolds* defence, whether NGOs, satirical entertainment-style news publications, or individual online critics.

The *Reynolds* defence contained elements about *public interest* in relation to both the overall story and the allegation at issue, and about *responsible* conduct in relation to the act of publication. For the first element concerning public interest, *Jameel* illustrates the approach under the former law.[42] This asked if the publication as a whole was on a subject of public interest and then allowed room for editorial judgment about the inclusion of particular details. As Lord Hoffmann stated in *Jameel*, 'the question of whether the defamatory statement should have been included is often a matter of how the story should have been presented. And on that question, allowance must be made for editorial judgment.'[43] On paper, section 4 differs slightly from this as it refers to editorial judgment expressly in relation to *reasonable belief*, but not in relation to *public interest*.

Under the new defence, it is sufficient that the 'statement complained of was, or formed part of, a statement on a matter of public interest'.[44] There may be a limit on what allegations are recognised as 'forming part of' a statement on a matter of public interest, but it is worth noting that no intention appears in the parliamentary debates to limit any judicial recourse in that regard to the concept of editorial discretion. As explored below, express reference was made in parliamentary debates to the new defence being no more limited than the case of *Flood*.[45] That decision confirmed the importance of editorial judgment in general. This could suggest that editorial judgment in relation to the allegation at issue may be considered broadly under both elements of the statutory defence, concerning *public interest*

[38] *Reynolds*, above, n 9, 205 (Lord Nicholls).

[39] Eg Barendt, 'Balancing', above, n 36, 61 (approach of courts 'dashed' hopes that *Reynolds* would greatly expand media freedom); Eric Descheemaeker, '"A man must take care not to defame his neighbour": The Origins and Significance of the *Reynolds* Defence', unpublished, copy on file ('not … controversial to say that the potential (or intended) impact of Reynolds is greater than the actual impact it has had so far').

[40] See *Jameel*, above, n 30; *Flood v Times Newspapers* [2012] 2 AC 273 (*Flood*).

[41] Russell Weaver, Andrew T Kenyon, David F Partlett and Clive P Walker, *The Right to Speak Ill: Defamation, Reputation and Free Speech* (Carolina Academic Press, 2006) 240–42.

[42] *Jameel*, above, n 30.

[43] ibid [51]

[44] Defamation Act 2013, s 4(1)(a)

[45] *Flood*, above, n 40.

and *reasonable belief* that publication was in the public interest. In *Flood*, Lord Brown JSC stated:

> The courts ... give weight to the judgment of journalists and editors not merely as to the *nature and degree of the steps to be taken* before publishing material, but also as to the *content of the material to be published in the public interest*. The courts must have the last word in setting the boundaries of what can properly be regarded as acceptable journalism, but within those boundaries the judgment of responsible journalists and editors merits respect.[46]

Similarly, Lord Dyson JSC stated:

> although the question of whether the story as a whole was a matter of public interest must be determined by the court, the question of whether defamatory details should have been included is often a matter of how the story should have been presented. On that issue, allowance must be made for editorial judgment.[47]

Parliamentary Debates

Section 4 changed during the parliamentary process. When introduced, it provided a statutory form of *Reynolds* defence where 'the defendant acted responsibly in publishing the statement complained of' and included a non-exhaustive list of factors adapted from *Reynolds*.[48] The proposed defence received strong criticism in both parliamentary chambers and it was replaced in the House of Lords. A prominent matter of debate was whether a list of factors should be included at all. In the House of Lords, any statutory list was thought to be detrimental to the central aim of considering all the circumstances of each case.[49] In criticising *Reynolds*, Viscount Colville reported the list of factors was 'being used as a stick with which to beat journalists in an attempt to prevent publication' and that costs for publishers were beyond what could be justified,[50] while Lord Marks voiced concerns about 'oppressive' costs being incurred before action because of the way the list of factors was being used.[51] Overall, the *Reynolds* list was seen as either unworkable, or as not working well enough to warrant the retention of any list.[52]

Wording close to the final form of the defence had been suggested in earlier debates in the House of Commons. It read: 'having regard to all the circumstances of the case, the defendant could properly have considered that the publication of the statement complained of

[46] ibid [137] (emphasis added), see also [180].

[47] ibid [194].

[48] Defamation Bill 2012, s 4.

[49] The central aim is reinforced by the explicit requirement that 'the court must have regard to all the circumstances of the case': Defamation Act 2013, s 4(2).

[50] HL Deb 9 October 2012, vol 739, col 944 (Viscount Colville).

[51] ibid col 967 (Lord Marks).

[52] Eg Lord Mawhinney, who chaired the Joint Committee: HL Deb 9 October 2012, vol 739, col 946, col 939 (Lord Browne), cols 953–54 (Lord Lester); HL Deb 19 December 2012, vol 741, cols GC 542–43 (Lord May), col GC 546 (Lord Bew), col GC 547 (Lord Triesman); HL Deb 5 February 2013, vol 743, cols 194–95 (Lord McNally).

was in the public interest'.[53] An even closer proposal was made in the House of Lords by Lord Lester, quoting Sir Brian Neill, someone with very long experience in defamation law:

> it is a defence ... (a) for the defendant to show that the statement complained of was on, or formed part of a publication on, a matter of public interest, and (b) if the defendant honestly and reasonably believed at the time of publication that the making of the statement was in the public interest.[54]

This defence would also have involved allowing wide editorial discretion. Notably, the proposed defence would also have been subject to a correction being published if requested by the claimant. However, the idea of a correction was not pursued in the debates.[55]

From these suggestions came the wording of section 4, which has been called a 'rather neat formulation'[56] but also a formulation that 'is at best ambiguous' and misleading for the law.[57] The requirement for a reasonable belief that publication was in the public interest can be traced to *Flood* where Lord Brown JSC described the *Reynolds* defence as amounting to one overall question:

> the judge, on true analysis, is deciding but a single question: could whoever published the defamation, given whatever they knew (and did not know) and whatever they had done (and had not done) to guard so far as possible against the publication of untrue defamatory material, properly have considered the publication in question to be in the public interest?[58]

Lord Clarke JSC expressly agreed.[59] Both judgments noted that 'a host of different considerations are in play' in answering the question.[60] While one would expect this approach to involve reference to the publisher's conduct, the 'emphasis is on the public interest aspect of the publication'[61] and the judgment of the defendant 'as to the nature and content' of the publication 'merits respect'.[62]

A related point of focus during parliamentary debates was whether the statutory defence, in its initial or reformed wording, would protect speech as much as the decision in *Flood* which had confirmed the importance of editorial judgment. In part, the debate linked to concerns that the need to demonstrate a reasonable belief would entail too much attention being placed on the speaker's motives. This led to a *Pepper v Hart* statement being made in the House of Lords,[63] which referred explicitly to *Flood*:

> The courts have made it clear in cases such as *Flood* that considerations about motive are usually irrelevant, so it is highly unlikely that they would entertain them if any such arguments were to arise. We are satisfied that our wording accurately captures the essence of the *Flood* judgment.

[53] HC Deb 19 July 2012, col 73 (Paul Farelly) quoting from 'an eminent QC' who from later debates would appear to have been Sir Brian Neill.

[54] HL Deb 9 October 2012, above, n 52 (Lord Lester).

[55] See further Kenyon, 'Beyond Reynolds', n 16, 30–31.

[56] HL Deb 19 December 2012, n 52 (Lord Bew).

[57] Eric Descheemaeker, 'Three Errors in the Defamation Act 2013' [2015] 6 *Journal of European Tort Law* 24.

[58] *Flood*, above, n 40 [113].

[59] ibid [184].

[60] ibid [113] and [184].

[61] Barendt, 'Police Investigations', above, n 20, 5.

[62] *Flood*, above, n 40 [180] (Lord Brown JSC).

[63] *Pepper (Inspector of Taxes) v Hart* [1993] AC 593 (HL); see, eg, Aileen Kavanagh, '*Pepper v Hart* and Matters of Constitutional Principle' (2005) 121 *Law Quarterly Review* 98.

> In addition, the emphasis that the Government have placed—in debates, and which I reiterate today—on our intention to reflect *Flood* will leave the courts in no doubt that that is the case.[64]

While expressly linked here to the question of a publisher's motives, the wider references to *Flood* in parliamentary debates (and indeed in related documents such as the Joint Committee of Human Rights report on the Defamation Bill),[65] suggest broader aims to capture the strength of that decision. As the contributors to *Blackstone's Guide to the Defamation Act 2013* have noted, it seems that the words of Lord Brown from *Flood* quoted above must be taken as 'the best indication of legislative intention'.[66] Those words 'succinctly' express the new defence.[67]

Stronger than *Reynolds*?

What might be the effect of the new defence? Even after the decision in *Flood*, Eric Barendt commented:

> A major criticism of *Reynolds* privilege, as it has been developed by the courts, is that it has done much too little to reduce the 'chilling effect' of libel laws. Editors and journalists are uncertain, for example, whether judges will uphold an argument that publication was in the public interest and how much room will be allowed for editorial judgment in this respect.[68]

Equally, much ordinary public debate lay outside the defence: 'Passionate participants in public controversies say harsh things, often in haste'[69] and much of what they say may be about matters of public interest. Such speech would have been difficult, at the very least, to bring within *Reynolds*. The *Reynolds* defence was crafted before widespread use of social media and the list of factors did not necessarily lend themselves to contemporary public speech or the potential for easy publication using networked digital communications.[70] It is not yet clear how the new law will differ from that defence, and it is possible that section 4 will emerge through case law as being effectively the same as *Reynolds* at least as the *Reynolds* defence was interpreted by the House of Lords and Supreme Court. But the overall sense of the movement preceding the 2013 Act, the parliamentary debates and the statutory wording itself suggests something more.

Uncertainty will exist in relation to the new defence, initially at least.[71] Ironically, this may happen particularly in relation to *Reynolds*' greatest strength; namely, the way the checklist

[64] HC Deb 16 December 2013, col 271 (Simon Hughes).

[65] Joint Committee on Human Rights, *Legislative Scrutiny: Defamation Bill* (Seventh Report of Session 2012–13) HL Paper 84 HC 810 (4 December 2012).

[66] Price and McMahon, above, n 4 [5.12]. Collins, above, n 4 [158] to [1.61] provides a concise outline of the limited role that legislative intention takes in statutory interpretation in England and Wales.

[67] Mullis and Scott, 'Windmills', above, n 4, 91.

[68] Barendt, 'Police Investigations', above, n 20,10.

[69] Justice Peter Applegarth, 'Distorting the Law of Defamation' (2011) 30 *University of Queensland Law Journal* 99, 109.

[70] See, eg, Jabob Rowbottom, 'In the Shadow of the Big Media: Freedom of Expression, Participation and the Production of Knowledge Online' [2014] *Public Law* 491, 498–99. See also the chapter by Rick Glofcheski in this collection.

[71] Eg William McCormick, 'Defamation Defences: Reynolds Privilege and Publication on Matter of Public Interest' in *Insight* (Westlaw UK) (accessed August 2015).

of factors allowed investigations to be shaped so that publications could come within the defence. 'Without guidance from the courts on which circumstances might be relevant and what their relevant weight might be, advising pre-publication is likely to become less certain again, at least in the early years of the defence.'[72] However, there is potential for case law to interpret section 4 to provide stronger protection than the former law. If a speaker reasonably believes that it is the public interest to publish, the defence, on its face, should apply. The reasonable belief test may be easier than *Reynolds* for lower courts to apply flexibly to different speakers and their individual circumstances. Section 4 offers the possibility of better differentiating between speakers—such as individual social media users and mass media publishers—about what is required for a reasonable belief that publication is in the public interest.[73] There could well be more room for the section 4 defence to operate, for it to apply to more varied styles of publication, and for it to be a more generally available defence for speech of public value. As observed in the House of Lords, the defence 'is a genuine attempt to strengthen freedom of speech and should be seen as such'.[74]

There may be, however, a tension between that attempt to strengthen freedom of speech and the references to capturing the essence of *Flood*. Even though *Flood* can be seen as strengthening the defence in light of at least some prior decisions on *Reynolds*, there may be ambiguity for courts as to whether the statutory defence is, in essence, *Flood* or is stronger than the common law of which *Flood* was a part.[75] Courts may still refer to some of the factors considered under *Reynolds*, but that should only be done where relevant to the new statutory test. The Reynolds list has lost its 'status' within the defence.[76] Clearly, an important matter will be how 'reasonable' is interpreted. The word 'is notoriously slippery and undetermined'.[77] It is the sort of 'broad and general' term, 'inherently open and flexible in meaning' which is all the more open to reinterpretation by courts under the Human Rights Act.[78] Courts have interpreted 'reasonable' in varied ways historically in defamation, only sometimes in a restrictive manner; they have moved, in part at least, with 'the temper of the times'.[79]

[72] Price and McMahon, above, n 4, [5.59].

[73] Eg Rowbottom, above, n 70. In addition, Andrew Scott and Alastair Mullis suggested that less might be expected of an individual blogger than a well-resourced journalist under the defence, when approving the defence in its Lord Lester and Sir Brian Neill wording: Andrew Scott and Alastair Mullis, 'A New Style Public Interest Defence in Libel Law?' *Inforrm* (8 November 2012) http://inforrm.wordpress.com accessed July 2016. Notably, that wording included the requirement to publish a reasonable response if requested, which appears to have been a significant aspect in the authors' support for the defence. See also Collins, above, n 4 [12.77] with regard to s 4 and bloggers.

[74] HL Deb 19 December 2013, col GC 558 (Lord McNally).

[75] Price and McMahon, above, n 4 [5.45] to [5.47] note the apparent disjunction between parliamentary statements about the aim to strengthen the protection of free speech over the prior law and 'to embrace and reflect *Flood*' in the prior law (the quoted words are from Lord McNally); cf eg Descheemaeker, 'Three Errors', above, n 57, who suggests that s 4, in the end, should be substantially equivalent to the law after *Flood*, while David Hooper, Kim Waite and Oliver Murphy, 'Defamation Act 2013—What difference will it really make?' (2013) 24(6) *Entertainment Law Review* 199 see s 4 as wider and more flexible than the prior law, as part of reforms that will 'significantly assist' defences (206), but also as something that may well follow the approach in *Flood*: 201.

[76] McCormick, above, n 71.

[77] Descheemaeker, 'Neighbour', above, n 39.

[78] The quoted words are from Phillipson, above, n 7, 165 who makes the point about the reforms more generally.

[79] Applegarth, above, n 69, 114.

A Second Generation of Reform?

In any event, the new defence continues one element of *Reynolds*. It offers a complete defence without requiring, for example, publication of a form of response from the subject of the defamation where that might be appropriate in the context of the original publication and contemporary communication technology. Some forms of fair report privilege require an explanation to be published, but this defence does not. Perhaps more surprisingly, this is so despite Sir Brian Neill's wording initially requiring the publication of a reply if requested. Instead, courts are left with wording in section 4, which offers the potential at least for a broader defence. If I was to offer a prediction, it would be that the defence will be interpreted initially to similar effect as *Flood*. In that, the new defence will be stronger than some of the broadly similar defences in other jurisdictions (notably the Australian *Lange* and statutory defences).[80] Over time, however, that sort of interpretation of section 4 will be seen as insufficiently protecting public debate because of its distance from being a defence for public interest speech in general. Calls will then emerge for further statutory reform, or case law will make more of the flexibility in section 4 and give greater weight to the margin of appreciation for the speaker that can be seen to lie 'at the very core of the defence'.[81] Indeed, the flexibility within section 4, through its comparative brevity and lack of a list of factors, may come to be seen as a benefit more than a weakness. If section 4 does develop into a genuine public interest defence through case law, which may be more likely over time, there could well be pressures for further reform to *Reynolds*-style defences in other jurisdictions. And there may also then be pressures for remedial developments, in the UK and elsewhere, so that a better accommodation is made for all relevant interests at stake in defamation claims.

If it does receive a stronger interpretation in case law, the public interest defence may become the start of a 'second generation' of reform in common law defamation jurisdictions outside the US. A first generation of reform occurred in many places during the last two decades.[82] The reforms had important similarities to, but also significant differences from, *Sullivan*.[83] In some places, the reforms have been seen as responding insufficiently to the challenge posed by *Sullivan*. The influence of *Sullivan* on the reforms lay particularly in one of its rationales—the chilling effect imposed by traditional defamation law on public speech. To a notable degree, that idea has gradually gained traction in law outside the US. At first, cases and law reform reports said simply that *Sullivan* did not apply outside the US constitutional context and that it was not wanted in any event.[84] Even after such rejections, *Sullivan* remained at play in reform debates and case law with its clear and strong enunciation of a chilling effect. That rationale began to 'catch' and affect Commonwealth law.

[80] See, eg, Kenyon, *Defamation*, above, n 21, 233–36; also P D T Applegarth SC, 'When Reasonableness is Unreasonable', *Gazette of Law and Journalism* (8 June 2005).

[81] McCormick, above, n 71.

[82] See above, n 17.

[83] See further Andrew T Kenyon and Megan Richardson, 'Reverberations of *Sullivan*? Considering Defamation and Privacy Law Reform' in Kenyon, *Comparative*, above, n 7, 309.

[84] Eg Faulks Committee (n 2); *Hill v Church of Scientology* [1995] 2 SCR 1130, 1187 (Cory J) ('I simply cannot see that the [traditional] law of defamation is unduly restrictive or inhibiting').

Perhaps the most important example is the unanimous 1993 decision of the House of Lords in *Derbyshire County Council v Times Newspapers*.[85] The decision ended the ability of local government bodies to bring actions in defamation. Lord Keith held that the requirement for defendants to prove truth imposed too great a chill, at least for public speech about local authorities. While *Sullivan* and other US decisions 'related most directly to the provisions of the American Constitution concerned with securing freedom of speech, the public interest considerations which underlaid them are no less valid in this country. What has been described as "the chilling effect" induced by the threat of civil actions for libel is very important.'[86]

With such judicial recognition, the need for larger developments in defamation law became accepted and change followed in a host of countries. In England that happened through *Reynolds*, and with the 2013 Act English law has made a further attempt at reform—in some sense, a second response to *Sullivan*'s recognition of a chilling effect. The change made by *Reynolds* came to be seen as too weak in protecting public speech, so a new form of defence has been enacted. Of course, 'reasonableness' as required under section 4 does not look at all like the First Amendment rules, but the English defence has the potential of amounting to a relative simple test that is available widely on matters of public interest. In that, it could come to provide a faint echo of *Sullivan*. And it may offer a partial response to longstanding concerns with defamation law's complexity, high cost of litigating, unpredictability and the limitations it imposes on public debate. If some of that does emerge in English law, the efficacy of the recently developed defences in other jurisdictions such as Australia, Canada and New Zealand are likely to be further questioned with pressure for further reform. Section 4 and a broad interpretation of it in cases may offer one guide.

Conclusion

The 'heart' of the Defamation Bill has become a defence that exhibits aspects of the former law while attempting to transcend some of its weaknesses. The statutory public interest defence may offer a more flexible approach to protecting public speech of varied forms, emanating from diverse speakers, and published in differing circumstances. But the reform has not on its face gone as far as the recommendation of one long-term analyst of comparative defamation law. In the same year as the Defamation Act 2013 was passed, Raymond Brown concluded his overview of defamation law with a simple recommendation in relation to a public interest defence: there should be a traditional style qualified privilege defence available for widespread publications of general public interest.[87] The English reforms, though different in form, have something of that aim. The degree to which a workable public interest defence is achieved in practice may depend on how skilfully the courts draw from *Reynolds* case law when considering all the circumstances of the

[85] [1993] AC 534.

[86] *Derbyshire County Council v Times Newspapers* [1993] AC 534, 547.

[87] Brown, above, n 18, 494.

case at hand under section 4. Those earlier decisions, although made under a defence that has been explicitly abolished, are likely to receive continued consideration for the ways in which they illustrate particular circumstances of publication and the manner in which English law can defend public interest speech.[88] But they should not limit the statutory aim to create a stronger defence for a wide variety of speakers.

[88] Eg Collins, above, n 4, [12.35] to [12.77] discusses earlier decisions on *Reynolds* factors at length in relation to s 4; Price and McMahon, above, n 4, [1.39] notes the 'particular resonance' of the question of how earlier case law will be used in relation to s 4.

6

Defamation Law in Canada and England: Emerging Differences

PAUL SCHABAS AND ADAM LAZIER*

Historically, Canadian defamation law has closely followed English law.[1] But in recent years the laws of the two countries have diverged. In England, courts and now Parliament have adopted new principles, while in Canada libel law has gone through its own process of modernisation. Since 2008, the Supreme Court of Canada and provincial appellate courts have decided a series of landmark cases, reconsidering long-standing common law rules. As a result, and especially following the enactment of the English Defamation Act 2013, significant differences have developed between Canadian and English law. While England has chosen to codify new principles, Canadian law continues to develop more slowly, one case at a time. This chapter reviews these developments and contrasts Canadian law with approaches now taken in England.

The Long Road to the Responsible Communication Defence

Libel Law before the Canadian Charter of Rights and Freedoms

Prior to 1982, there was no constitutional protection for freedom of expression in Canada. Although Canada had a written constitution,[2] it was concerned primarily with the structure of public institutions and the division of powers between the federal government and the provinces. It contained no protection for individual rights. Nonetheless, courts sometimes found ways to protect individual rights, including freedom of expression. In 1938, for instance, the Supreme Court of Canada used principles of federalism to strike down an Alberta law requiring newspapers to publish government responses to criticisms of its policies.[3] Relying on the fact that Canada had 'a Constitution similar in principle to that of

* Mr Schabas was counsel in *Grant v Torstar Corp* and *Breeden v Black*, two cases discussed below.

[1] See *Hill v Church of Scientology* [1995] 2 SCR 1130, [116] (*Hill*) ('The character of the law relating to libel and slander in the 20th century is essentially the product of its historical development up to the 17th century, subject to a few refinements such as the introduction and recognition of the defences of privilege and fair comment'.)

[2] Constitution Act 1867 (UK).

[3] *Re Alberta Statutes* [1938] SCR 100.

the United Kingdom',[4] Chief Justice Duff wrote that 'it is axiomatic that the practice of this right of free public discussion of public affairs, notwithstanding its incidental mischiefs, is the breath of life for parliamentary institutions.'[5] In 1957, in striking down a Québec law that prohibited the profligation of communism or bolshevism 'by any means whatsoever', Justice Rand wrote that '[a]part from sedition, obscene writings and criminal libels, the public law leaves the literary, discursive and polemic use of language, in the broadest sense, free'.[6]

Despite the rhetoric, this approach had obvious limitations. The use of federalism principles did not impose any limitations on the power of the federal government to regulate speech, only the provinces. It also did not apply to the common law, which meant that defamation law was immune to the Supreme Court's early attempts to protect freedom of expression. Canadian libel law therefore remained fiercely loyal to its roots in old English law. If the words were defamatory and the defendant was unable to prove them true, he or she was limited to a very narrow range of defences. As a strict liability tort, a defendant could be required to pay damages without proof of any negligence, fault, or even damage to the plaintiff.

Even opportunities to expand the common law defences were rejected. The Supreme Court refused to expand the traditional qualified privilege defence to protect media reports on matters of public interest four times in the 1950s and 1960s.[7] Beginning with its 1951 decision in *Douglas v Tucker*, the Court relied on old English cases to hold that no privilege attaches to publications made 'to the world'. In *Boland v Globe and Mail*, decided in 1960, Justice Cartwright did not seem troubled by the implications this had for freedom of speech, writing that recognising a privilege for honestly-held statements of fact dealing with public interest issues would be 'harmful to the common convenience and welfare of society' and that the fair comment defence was all the protection the media and the public interest required.[8] It was even held that where a statement—such as a political candidate's speech to voters—would ordinarily be protected by qualified privilege, that privilege was nullified if the candidate knew the media would cover the speech.[9]

The Early Charter Years

The *Canadian Charter of Rights and Freedoms* was enacted in 1982, as part of a series of constitutional reforms.[10] The *Charter* provided constitutional protection for individual rights, including freedom of expression in section 2(b). Courts have the power to declare laws that are inconsistent with the *Charter* of no force and effect. *Charter* rights are not absolute,

[4] Constitution Act 1867, above n 2, Preamble.

[5] *Re Alberta Statutes*, above n 3, 133.

[6] *Switzman v Elbling* [1957] SCR 285, 305.

[7] *Douglas v Tucker* (1951) [1952] 1 SCR 275 (*Douglas*); *Globe and Mail v Boland* [1960] SCR 203 (*Boland*); *Banks v Globe and Mail* [1961] SCR 474; *Jones v Bennett*, [1969] SCR 277 (*Jones*).

[8] *Boland*, ibid 208–09.

[9] *Douglas*, above n 7, 287; *Jones*, above n 7, 284.

[10] The Canada Act 1982 (UK) c 11, passed in Westminster at the request of the Canadian government, finally completed the patriation of Canada's constitution, ending the necessity of having amendments approved by the UK Parliament.

however, as section 1 allows for 'reasonable limits prescribed by law as can be demonstrably justified in a free and democratic society'.[11]

When the *Charter* was enacted, some suggested that the new constitutional right to freedom of expression would mark a long-awaited turning point for libel law.[12] To the south, the American First Amendment right to free speech formed the basis for the US Supreme Court's landmark 1964 decision in *New York Times v Sullivan*, which held that the common law of libel did not adequately protect expression. The Court in *Sullivan* modified the common law so that a defendant could not be held liable for defaming a public figure unless the plaintiff proved that the words were false, and that the defendant acted with 'actual malice'—ie, knowledge that the words were false, or with reckless disregard for the truth.[13] The contrast between *Sullivan*, which turned libel law on its head, and the rigid 1960s jurisprudence of the Supreme Court of Canada is striking.[14]

The Supreme Court's early *Charter* jurisprudence suggested that it might reconsider libel law's balance, which so strongly favoured protecting reputation over freedom of expression. In 1989, in recognising the critical role of the press in covering courts and obtaining information about public institutions, the Court wrote that 'it is difficult to imagine a guaranteed right more important to a democratic society than freedom of expression'.[15] Three years later, in *R v Zundel*, it struck down a criminal law prohibiting the deliberate dissemination of false news. The majority rejected an argument that false speech—even deliberately false speech—did not deserve constitutional protection:

> Exaggeration—even clear falsification—may arguably serve useful social purposes linked to the values underlying freedom of expression. A person fighting cruelty against animals may knowingly cite false statistics in pursuit of his or her beliefs and with the purpose of communicating a more fundamental message, eg, 'cruelty to animals is increasing and must be stopped'. A doctor, in order to persuade people to be inoculated against a burgeoning epidemic, may exaggerate the number or geographical location of persons potentially infected with the virus. An artist, for artistic purposes, may make a statement that a particular society considers both an assertion of fact and a manifestly deliberate lie; consider the case of Salman Rushdie's *Satanic Verses*, viewed by many Muslim societies as perpetrating deliberate lies against the Prophet.
>
> All of this expression arguably has intrinsic value in fostering political participation and individual self-fulfilment. To accept the proposition that deliberate lies can never fall under s. 2(*b*) would be to exclude statements such as the examples above from the possibility of constitutional protection. I cannot accept that such was the intention of the framers of the Constitution.[16]

[11] Section 1 creates a proportionality test: *R v Oakes* [1986] 1 SCR 103. In the free expression context, it has been invoked to uphold hate speech laws (see *Saskatchewan (Human Rights Commission) v Whatcott* (2013) SCC 11) and restrictions on commercial speech (see *Irwin Toy v Québec (SG)*, [1989] 1 SCR 927), among other things.

[12] See Darlene Madott, 'Libel Law, Fiction, and the Charter' (1983) 21 *Osgoode Hall LJ* 741, 785–86.

[13] *New York Times v Sullivan*, 376 US 254 (1964).

[14] *New York Times v Sullivan* and its progeny, such as *Gertz v Robert Welch, Inc* 418 US 323 (1974) (*Gertz*), have led to a dramatic decline in successful defamation suits against the media in the US. According to one American commentator, 'a reasonable publisher should worry about having to pay substantial libel damages as much as she worries about being struck by lightning'. See David A. Logan, 'Libel Law in the Trenches: Reflections on Current Data on Libel Litigation' (2001) 87 *Va L Rev* 502, 508, 510, 520, 529.

[15] *Edmonton Journal v Alberta (AG)* [1989] 2 SCR 1326, 1336 (Cory J).

[16] *R v Zundel* [1992] 2 SCR 731, 754-55 (McLachlin J).

Initial hopes for change were dashed in 1995, when the Court got its first chance to consider whether the common law of libel infringed the *Charter* in *Hill v Church of Scientology*.[17] The case had unusual facts. A lawyer representing the Church of Scientology stood in his barrister's gown on the steps of the Toronto courthouse and alleged before the assembled media that a Crown prosecutor had misled a judge and breached sealing orders. The media organisations settled before trial, so only the Church and its lawyer were left as defendants. On the other side, the plaintiff was a respected Crown counsel. At trial there was significant evidence that the Church had acted maliciously and a jury awarded Hill $1.6 million (CAD), at the time the highest libel damages award in Canadian history. They were bad facts indeed.

Those who expected the Supreme Court to follow *Sullivan* were sorely disappointed. The Court did recognise that the common law had to evolve in accordance with '*Charter* values', including freedom of expression.[18] As a consequence, it made a minor change in the law of qualified privilege, extending it to cover the publication of court pleadings.[19] But the Court rejected arguments that the *Charter* right to freedom of expression required that Canadian law adopt the 'actual malice' standard from *Sullivan*. It effectively stood by what it had written in *Globe and Mail v Boland*[20] some 35 years earlier: that the meagre defences available at common law were all the protection freedom of expression required.

Sullivan was based on the premise that even false speech on matters of public interest has value, so long as it is presented without knowledge that it is untrue, or recklessness to its truth. Good-faith participation in public debate without fear of liability is fundamental to democratic discourse. The Canadian Supreme Court had recognised similar values in *Zundel*. In *Hill*, however, the Court emphatically rejected the value of defamatory statements. Justice Cory, the same judge who found it 'difficult to imagine a guaranteed right more important to a democratic society than freedom of expression', wrote that 'defamatory statements are very tenuously related to the core values which underlie s 2(b)' and are 'harmful to the interests of a free and democratic society'.[21] Indeed, Justice Cory went further, concluding that 'I simply cannot see that the law of defamation is unduly restrictive or inhibiting. Surely it is not requiring too much of individuals that they ascertain the truth of the allegations they publish.'[22] At the same time that he denigrated the value of defamatory speech, Justice Cory discussed the importance of reputation—which is not mentioned in the *Charter*—in reverent terms: 'A defamatory statement can seep into the crevasses of the subconscious and lurk there ever ready to spring forth and spread its cancerous evil. The unfortunate impression left by a libel may last a lifetime.'[23] Perhaps the most disappointing thing about *Hill* was that the Supreme Court went so far in defending the constitutionality

[17] *Hill*, above n 1.

[18] ibid [91]–[98].

[19] ibid [153]–[54].

[20] *Boland*, above n 7.

[21] *Hill*, above n 1, [106].

[22] ibid [137].

[23] ibid [166]. Cory J was particularly taken with the importance of reputation for lawyers, commenting, 'In the present case, consideration must be particular significance reputation has for a lawyer. The reputation of a lawyer is of paramount importance to client, to other members of the profession and to the judiciary'. See also *Botiuk v Toronto Free Press Publications* [1995] 3 SCR 3, [92]. The irony, of course, is that the public generally holds lawyers in low regard.

of the common law of defamation when it was unnecessary to consider the issues at all, given the finding of malice and the absence of media defendants.

Hill indicated that the Supreme Court still considered the protection of reputation to be more important than freedom of expression, a view confirmed three years later. In *R v Lucas*,[24] the Court upheld the constitutional validity of the rarely-used criminal offence of defamatory libel.[25] The majority judgment, again written by Justice Cory, reiterated the low value placed on defamatory speech, and emphasised the importance of reputation in even stronger terms than *Hill*, stating that 'defamatory libel is far from and indeed inimical to the core values of freedom of expression', and that freedom of expression does not override reputation, characterised as 'the attribute which is most highly sought after, prized and cherished by most individuals'.[26]

Grant v Torstar: Recognising Responsible Communication

The Court in *Hill* did not consider adopting a responsible journalism defence, even though a similar concept was put forward by at least one intervener in the case.[27] There had been shifts in the direction of a public interest defence in Australia, in *Theophanus v Herald & Weekly Times*,[28] and since the 1970s American courts had applied a negligence standard to plaintiffs who are not public figures in cases involving defamatory speech on matters of public concern.[29]

In light of the important role that English libel law continued to play in Canada, the responsible journalism defence could not be ignored after the House of Lords first recognised it in *Reynolds v Times Newspapers*[30] and confirmed it in *Jameel v Wall Street Journal Europe*.[31] In the years following *Reynolds*, a number of Canadian provincial courts cited *Reynolds* and held that—notwithstanding the Supreme Court's previous jurisprudence—the defence of qualified privilege could protect statements made by the media to the public, where, for example, the media was reporting allegations on matters of public interest.[32] In some cases, they did this explicitly on freedom of expression grounds.[33] In another example of the gradual effect of the *Charter* on Canadian libel law, courts adopted the

[24] *R v Lucas* [1998] 1 SCR 439 (*Lucas*).

[25] Criminal Code RSC 1985, c C-46, s 300: 'Everyone who publishes a defamatory libel that he knows is false is guilty of an indictable offence and liable to imprisonment for a term not exceeding five years.'

[26] *Lucas*, above n 24, [93]–[94].

[27] Counsel for the Canadian Civil Liberties Association, led by Professor Robert Sharpe (later Sharpe JA of the Ontario Court of Appeal), argued that 'where a public official sues [for defamation] there should be no liability if the defendant can establish reasonable grounds for a genuine belief in the truth of the facts which form the basis of the alleged libel.'

[28] *Theophanus v Herald & Weekly Times* (1994) 124 ALR 1 (HCA). The Court in *Hill* discussed the *Theophanus* case, but mentioned only that '[a]lthough a plurality of the seven judges sitting on the High Court held that the existing law of defamation curtailed the constitutionally protected right to political discussion, it rejected the adoption of the "actual malice" standard', and distinguished *Theophanus* on the basis that the case before it did not involve the media or political commentary. See *Hill*, above n 1, [135], [139].

[29] *Gertz*, above n 14; *Dun & Bradstreet v Greenmoss Builders* 472 US 749 (1985), 766, 770 (White J).

[30] *Reynolds v Times Newspapers* [2001] 2 AC 127 (*Reynolds*).

[31] *Jameel v Wall Street Journal Europe* [2006] UKHL 44 (*Jameel*).

[32] This law was summarised by the Ontario Court of Appeal in *Cusson v Quan* 2007 ONCA 771, [63]–[71].

[33] See *Young v Toronto Star Newspapers Limited* (2003) 66 OR (3d) 170, [176] (Ont SCJ); affirmed (2005) 77 OR (3d) 680 (CA).

Polly Peck rule[34] permitting defendants to plead their own meanings because 'it strikes a more appropriate balance between protection of reputation and freedom of expression and freedom of the press'.[35]

In 2007 and 2008, the Ontario Court of Appeal went further. In two cases, that court held that the common law of libel was inconsistent with the *Charter* and explicitly recognised the *Reynolds* responsible journalism defence as something 'fundamentally different in nature from traditional qualified privilege.'[36] In the first case, *Cusson v Quan*, the Court (Sharpe JA) wrote:

> [The defence] represents a natural extension of the law as it has been developing in recent years, an incremental change necessary to keep the common law in step with the dynamic and evolving fabric of society ... The public interest responsible journalism defence recognizes that in relation to matters of public interest, the traditional common law unduly chills freedom of expression but, at the same time, rejects the notion that media defendants should be afforded a licence to defame unless the innocent plaintiffs can prove deliberate or reckless falsehood. It rights the common law imbalance in favour of protection of reputation and creates a proper balance between that value and freedom of expression.[37]

In the second case, *Grant v Torstar Corp*,[38] the Court applied the new defence for the first time.

Both *Grant* and *Cusson* went to the Supreme Court of Canada, giving the Court an opportunity to revisit the standard for liability for defamatory statements of fact. This time the Court held that the common law struck the wrong balance, and it established a new defence, which it named 'public interest responsible communication'.

Grant was the main decision. The case arose from a lengthy investigative article by an experienced reporter published in the *Toronto Star*, Canada's largest newspaper, about the plaintiff's proposed personal golf course development on land he wished to purchase from the Crown by a lake in northern Ontario. The article reported on the concerns of neighbouring cottagers, environmental and regulatory issues, the plaintiff's economic power in the area (his lumber company was one of the largest employers in the region), his financial support of the governing party in the province, and his friendship with the Premier of Ontario. The plaintiff, Peter Grant, had refused to talk to the newspaper. When the reporter persisted in seeking his side of the story, he threatened to sue if the *Star* published an article. He followed through on his threat, asserting the *Star* suggested he had improperly used his influence and economic power to obtain favours from the government. The trial judge rejected the responsible communication defence (which in early 2007 had not yet been recognised by any Canadian court), holding that even if the defence existed it would not apply because the article was primarily of local importance and carried a 'negative tone'. Despite the absence of any evidence of harm, but after a charge to the jury that mis-stated the fair comment defence, a jury in Grant's small home town awarded him and his company $1.475 million (CAD) in damages.

[34] See *Polly Peck (Holdings) v Trelford* [1986] QB 1000 (CA).

[35] *Pizza Pizza v Toronto Star Newspapers Limited* (1998) 42 OR (3d) 36, [21] (Div Ct) (Sharpe J as he then was).

[36] *Cusson v Quan* 2007 ONCA 771, [148]; see also [137] (*Cusson*).

[37] ibid [139], internal quotation omitted.

[38] *Grant v Torstar Corp* 2008 ONCA 796. In *Cusson*, the defence had not been advanced at trial. While the Court of Appeal took the opportunity to recognise the existence of the defence in that case, it refused to apply it to the facts. See *Cusson*, above n 36, [149]–[50].

The Ontario Court of Appeal (in a decision written by Feldman JA) directed a new trial, finding the trial judge had not properly considered the responsible communication defence (by then recognised in *Cusson*) because he had conflated it with traditional qualified privilege, and because the portion of the trial judge's charge to the jury respecting the fair comment defence was seriously flawed. Grant appealed to the Supreme Court, and the *Star* cross-appealed arguing that the Court of Appeal should simply have found that the defence applied and dismissed the action.

The Supreme Court's decision, written by Chief Justice McLachlin, turned away from the approach taken in *Hill* and *Lucas*. It began by recognising that the common law had a problematic 'chilling effect' on freedom of expression:

> The existing common law rules mean, in effect, that the publisher must be certain before publication that it can prove the statement to be true in a court of law, should a suit be filed ... Information that is reliable and in the public's interest to know may never see the light of day.[39]

While the *Hill* decision classified defamatory speech as having no more value than hate speech, in *Grant* the Court held that two of the core reasons for the protection of freedom of expression apply to false defamatory speech on matters of public interest: it strengthens the proper functioning of democratic governance, and it enhances the search for truth.[40] In *Hill* the Court suggested that it was not too much to expect someone to ascertain the truth of what he or she said, but it recognised in *Grant* that 'to insist on court-established certainty in reporting on matters of public interest may have the effect of preventing communication of facts which a reasonable person would accept as reliable and which are relevant and important to public debate.'[41] The contrast between *Hill* and *Grant* is striking.

The 'responsible communication' defence, as Chief Justice McLachlin named it, follows the structure of the House of Lords's analysis in *Jameel v Wall Street Journal Europe*.[42] The Supreme Court adopted a two-part test: the defendant must prove first that the publication complained of related to a matter of public interest; and, second, that 'publication was responsible, in that he or she was diligent in trying to verify the allegation(s), having regard to all the relevant circumstances'.[43]

Since the Court based the responsible communication defence on the English common law *Reynolds* defence, it is not surprising that the Canadian defence is more similar to the *Reynolds* defence than its statutory successor. There are, however, a number of significant differences between the Canadian public interest responsible communication defence and the *Reynolds* defence. First, the Supreme Court of Canada listed a set of factors for establishing whether publication was responsible, but it did not simply adopt the ten *Reynolds* factors. It instead recognised seven non-exhaustive factors including:

(a) the seriousness of the allegation;
(b) the public importance of the matter;
(c) the urgency of the matter;

[39] *Grant v Torstar Corp* 2009 SCC 61, [53] (*Grant* SCC). The Supreme Court reversed the Court of Appeal's decision in *Cusson* on the basis that the Court of Appeal erred by not applying the new defence: *Quan v Cusson* 2009 SCC 62.

[40] *Grant* SCC, above n 39, [47]–[57], [64].

[41] ibid [53].

[42] *Jameel*, above n 31.

[43] *Grant* SCC, above n 39, [98].

(d) the status and reliability of the source;
(e) whether the plaintiff's side of the story was sought and accurately reported;
(f) whether the inclusion of the defamatory statement was justifiable; and
(g) whether the defamatory statement's public interest lay in the fact that it was made rather than its truth ('reportage').[44]

As in *Jameel*, the Court emphasised that these factors should not be treated as 'hurdles' which must all be surmounted for the defence to apply.[45] Chief Justice McLachlin's decision also made clear that the defence applies not only to professional journalists, but to 'anyone who publishes material in the public interest'—which is reflected in the name of the defence.[46] This holding is another welcome development—one which reflects the rise of bloggers and citizen journalists. It remains to be seen whether courts will hold citizen journalists and others to the same standards as professionals in determining whether they acted responsibly.

Another significant difference between *Grant* and the *Reynolds* factors is the Supreme Court's rejection of the importance of an article's tone. As the Court correctly noted, placing too much emphasis on tone risks holding writers to a 'standard of stylistic blandness … The best investigative reporting often takes a trenchant or adversarial tone.'[47] This demonstrates a welcome appreciation of what really constitutes fairness. A reporter who concludes after a responsible investigation that the subject has done something wrong should be free to express that conclusion.[48] Tone can form an integral part of a writer's expression, and ought not to be a bar to the defence—as the trial judge had viewed it in *Grant*.

The English and Canadian approaches may also differ with respect to malice. *Grant*'s discussion of malice is brief and cryptic:

> [T]he defence of responsible communication obviates the need for a separate inquiry into malice. (Malice may still be relevant where other defences are raised.) A defendant who has acted with malice in publishing defamatory allegations has by definition not acted responsibly.[49]

The breadth of this statement is troubling. If the malice relates to publishing for an improper or ulterior motive, as the concept is understood in the context of qualified privilege, the statement may be understandable. But what if the malice emerges, as it sometimes does, through evidence of spite or ill-will? An early email by a journalist may disclose a distaste for the subject of the investigation, or a desire to expose someone suspected of misdeeds—to 'get someone'.[50] However, if the journalist then acts responsibly in investigating and reporting the story, his or her original motivation should not matter. In this context, the English approach, set out by Lord Hoffmann in *Jameel*, is preferable. Lord Hoffmann wrote that the malice inquiry in such circumstances is unnecessary because '[t]here is no question of the privilege [i.e. the defence] being defeated by proof of malice because the propriety

[44] ibid [126].
[45] ibid [73].
[46] ibid [96], quoting *Jameel*, n 31, [54].
[47] ibid [123].
[48] See ibid. ('Neither should the law encourage the fiction that fairness and responsibility lie in disavowing or concealing one's point of view').
[49] ibid [125].
[50] This type of malice was found in *Leenen v Canadian Broadcasting Corp* (2000) 48 OR (3d) 656 (SCJ), affirmed (2001) 54 OR (3d) 626 (CA).

of the conduct of the defendant is built into the conditions under which the material is privileged.'[51] If a defendant behaves responsibly in publishing an article relating to a matter of public interest his or her motivation should be irrelevant to whether the publication is protected.

Just as it seemed Canadian law had caught up with developments in England, the goal posts have moved again with the enactment of the Defamation Act 2013, which abolishes the '*Reynolds* defence' and creates a new 'public interest' defence.[52] The effect of the statutory defence remains to be seen: subsection 4(1) resembles the two-step *Jameel/Grant* approach, but the test is different, asking on the second branch simply whether 'the defendant reasonably believed that publishing the statement complained of was in the public interest.' Does this do away with the due diligence requirement of publishing 'responsibly'? Perhaps in some cases it does. Subsection 4(2) directs courts, vaguely and generally, to 'have regard to all the circumstances of the case', and subsection 4(4) codifies making 'allowances for editorial judgment'. Only time will tell whether the new 'public interest' defence in subsection (4) of the Defamation Act 2013 will mark a further liberalising of libel law or whether it may mark the end of the common law developments favouring free speech seen in *Reynolds*, *Jameel*, *Flood v Times Newspapers*,[53] and even *Derbyshire County Council v Times Newspapers*.[54] However, as long as provincial legislatures in Canada do not follow the UK Parliament's lead—and there is no indication they will—the new defences in Canada and England may well develop more differences than similarities.

Another significant difference relates to the role of the jury. Under the English approach set out in *Reynolds* and *Jameel*, the jury is responsible for fact-finding, but the decision on whether the defence applies on the proven facts is left to the judge.[55] Now, with the passage of the Defamation Act 2013, English libel cases will presumptively be tried by judge alone.[56] In Canada, however, Chief Justice McLachlin pronounced that 'the jury's participation ... is firmly entrenched in the psyche of defamation law'.[57] In *Grant*, the majority held that while the judge must decide the preliminary question of whether the publication is on a matter of public interest, it is the jury that must assess whether the publication was responsible having regard to all the relevant factors.[58] The Court, otherwise unanimous, divided 8–1 on this issue. The lone dissenter, Justice Abella, would have left the whole task of applying the defence to the judge. As she pointed out, there is 'very little conceptual difference between deciding whether a communication is in the public interest and whether it is responsibly made', and applying the defence is 'is a highly complex legal determination with constitutional dimensions' in the form of balancing competing *Charter* values.[59]

[51] *Jameel*, above n 31, [46].

[52] Subsection 4(1) states: 'It is a defence to an action for defamation for the defendant to show that—(a) the statement complained of was, or formed part of, a statement on a matter of public interest; and (b) the defendant reasonably believed that publishing the statement complained of was in the public interest.'

[53] *Flood v Times Newspapers* [2012] UKSC 11.

[54] *Derbyshire County Council v Times Newspapers* [1993] 2 WLR 449 (HL).

[55] *Reynolds*, above n 30, 205.

[56] Defamation Act 2013, c 26, s 11 (UK) (Defamation Act 2013)

[57] *Grant* SCC, above n 39, [144] (Abella J). In some provinces, defamation actions are presumptively tried by juries: see, eg, the Alberta Jury Act, RSA 2000, c. J-3, s 17(1); however, in other provinces, including Ontario, a jury trial only takes place if a party requests it, and many defamation cases are tried by judge alone.

[58] *Grant* SCC, ibid, [132]–[35].

[59] ibid [142]–[45].

It remains too early to assess whether the lower courts are applying the responsible communication test in a manner that protects freedom of expression in the way the Supreme Court intended. Results have been mixed in the few cases that have applied the defence thus far.[60] There are, however, hopeful signs that it has begun to thaw libel chill in Canadian newsrooms and encourage investigative reporting on controversial issues.[61]

Modernising the Fair Comment Defence

The responsible communication defence in Canada applies only to defamatory statements of fact.[62] It is therefore narrower than England's new statutory public interest defence, which in another change to the common law now applies to both statements of fact and opinion.[63] However, Canada's fair comment defence is now broader than the analogous honest opinion defence in England. In *WIC Radio v Simpson*,[64] a case decided a year before *Grant,* the Supreme Court of Canada constitutionalised the fair comment defence, broadening its scope and departing from an unfortunate 1970s decision, *Cherneskey v Armadale Publishers*.[65]

In *Cherneskey*, a newspaper in Saskatoon, Saskatchewan had published a letter to the editor accusing a local alderman of racism. The alderman sued the newspaper. Relying once again on old English law, the majority held that the newspaper was not entitled to rely on fair comment, because that defence required proof that the comment in question was honestly held. The newspaper admitted that it did not believe the alderman to be a racist, and there was no evidence whether the writers themselves honestly held the opinion expressed in their letter.[66] In a strong dissent, Justice Dickson—later Chief Justice– advocated an objective test requiring a defendant to prove only that anyone could honestly have expressed the opinion based on proven facts.[67]

The majority decision in *Cherneskey* made no reference to the importance of freedom of expression (it was a pre-*Charter* case), and reaction was harsh. Provinces promptly amended their defamation legislation to protect newspapers that publish opinions with which they disagree.[68] But it was not until *WIC*, almost 30 years later, that the Court addressed the

[60] For examples of cases where the defence was successful, see *Shavluk v Green Party of Canada* 2010 BCSC 804; affirmed 2011 BCCA 286; *Vellacott v Saskatoon StarPhoenix Group* 2012 SKQB 359; *Jiang v Sing Tao Daily* 2014 ONSC 287. For examples of cases where the defence was unsuccessful, see *Hansen v Harder* 2010 BCCA 482; *James v Black Press Group* 2012 BCSC 1969; *Vigna v Levant* 2010 ONSC 6308; *Warman v Veck* 2015 ONSC 486.

[61] One example of this is the *Toronto Star*'s decision to report in May 2013 on the existence of a video showing Toronto mayor Rob Ford smoking crack cocaine and making racist and homophobic statements—a story subsequently reported around the world—even though the newspaper did not have possession of the video. For an interesting discussion of the role played by the law in the coverage of Ford, see Ivor Tossell, 'The Story Behind the Rob Ford Story', *The Walrus*, 11(2) (March 2014).

[62] *Grant* SCC, above n 39, [140].

[63] Defamation Act 2013, above n 56, s 4(5).

[64] *WIC Radio v Simpson* 2008 SCC 40 (*WIC*).

[65] *Cherneskey v Armadale Publishers* [1979] 1 SCR 1067.

[66] ibid 1088.

[67] ibid 1100–01.

[68] See Libel and Slander Act RSO 1990 (Ontario), c L12, s 24 ('Where the defendant published defamatory matter that is an opinion expressed by another person, a defence of fair comment by the defendant shall not fail

common law defence again, and this time it was prepared to consider the implications for freedom of expression.

The plaintiff in *WIC* was Kari Simpson, a well-known homophobic opponent of teaching about the 'gay lifestyle' in schools. The case related to comments that Rafe Mair—a prominent radio host—made on his show, describing Simpson's speech at a parents' meeting:

> It could have been blacks last Thursday just as easily as gays. Now I'm not suggesting that Kari was proposing or supporting any kind of holocaust or violence but neither really—in the speeches, when you think about it and look back—neither did Hitler or Governor Wallace or [Orval Faubus] or Ross Barnett. They were simply declaring their hostility to a minority. Let the mob do as they wished.

Simpson sued Mair and the radio station. Although Mair specifically said that he was not suggesting Simpson supported violence—only that he believed Simpson to be an intolerant bigot—the trial judge nonetheless agreed with Simpson that Mair's comments implied that Simpson 'would condone violence toward gay people'. The problem was that even though Mair did not intend to convey this meaning and Mair did not honestly believe that Simpson would condone violence, according to *Cherneskey* he could not rely on the fair comment defence. But was it fair to deny him the protection of fair comment for not believing something that he did not believe he had said and never meant to say?

The Supreme Court held that this result would not be consistent with the requirement that the common law comply with *Charter* values, including freedom of expression. In language that presaged *Grant* and marked the Court's first significant departure from *Hill*, Justice Binnie wrote on behalf of the majority that:

> [o]f course 'chilling' false and defamatory speech is not a bad thing in itself, but chilling debate on matters of legitimate public interest raises issues of inappropriate censorship and self-censorship. Public controversy can be a rough trade, and the law needs to accommodate its requirements.[69]

He noted the importance of protecting cartoonists or satirists who 'exercise a democratic right to poke fun at those who huff and puff in the public arena.'[70] The Court reversed *Cherneskey* and adopted the test for fair comment advocated in Justice Dickson's dissent:

> (a) the comment must be on a matter of public interest; (b) the comment must be based on fact; (c) the comment, though it can include inferences of fact, must be recognisable as comment; (d) the comment must satisfy the following objective test: could any [person] honestly express that opinion on the proved facts?; (e) even though the comment satisfied the objective test the defence can be defeated if the plaintiff proves that the defendant was [subjectively] actuated by express malice.[71]

The Canadian fair comment defence therefore now differs from the English law of honest opinion. Section 3 of the Defamation Act 2013 reflects Canadian law as it existed before *WIC* by denying the defence if the defendant did not honestly hold the opinion—except where the defendant is re-publishing a statement made by someone else.[72] The Canadian

for the reason only that the defendant or the person who expressed the opinion, or both, did not hold the opinion, if a person could honestly hold the opinion') (Ontario LSA).

[69] *WIC*, above n 64, [15].

[70] ibid [48].

[71] ibid [28]. Emphasis in original removed.

[72] Defamation Act 2013, n 56, ss 3(4)-(6).

fair comment defence may therefore be broader than the English defence. On the other hand, the English have attempted to liberalise the defence by protecting opinions based on facts whether or not those facts were known at the time. Canadian and English law also apply different definitions of malice in the context of fair comment. Although section 3 of the Defamation Act 2013 no longer refers to malice at all, the rule that 'the defence is defeated if the claimant shows that the defendant did not hold the opinion' appears to fill the role of malice. In *WIC*, on the other hand, the Supreme Court of Canada defined malice in this context as 'an indirect or improper motive not connected with the purpose for which the defence exists'.[73]

While *WIC* marked an important extension of the fair comment defence, the defence still has troubling limitations. Justice Binnie required that the factual foundation of the opinion must be 'properly disclosed or sufficiently indicated', unless the facts are 'so notorious as to already be understood by the audience.'[74] Since the *WIC* decision, the British Columbia Court of Appeal applied this requirement in a strict way and held that a press release and website criticising the protection of the salmon fishery were not protected by fair comment because they did not describe some of the detailed scientific evidence upon which the opinions were based.[75] Even hyperlinking to that evidence, the Court held, would not be enough unless the link was accompanied by a notice that it contained facts upon which the opinion was based and information about where to find those facts in the hyperlinked document.[76]

This approach is problematic. Expecting a commenter—a newspaper editorialist, a cartoonist, or even a Twitter user—to accompany his or her comment with a laundry list of all facts relied on is unrealistic and contrary to the reality that people choose to express themselves in different ways. It is also unnecessary in the Internet age, where an interested reader may easily do the background research necessary to assess the validity of the opinion independently.[77]

Is the approach different in England? The answer is unclear. In *Spiller v Joseph*, the UK Supreme Court rejected the notion that a comment must identify the facts relied upon with specific particularity to allow a reader to judge whether it is well-founded. But a comment must still 'identify at least in general terms what it is that has led the commentator to make the comment, so that the reader can understand what the comment is about and the commentator can, if challenged, explain by giving particulars of the subject matter of his comment why he expressed the views that he did.'[78] The Defamation Act 2013 appears to retain that standard for the new statutory 'honest opinion' defence, requiring that 'the statement complained of indicated, whether in general or specific terms, the basis of the opinion.'[79]

[73] *WIC*, above n 64, [1]. In *Tse Wai Chun Paul v Albert Cheng* (2000) 3 HKCFAR 339, 360-1, Lord Nicholls defined malice in the context of fair comment in terms similar to the Defamation Act—'proof that the defendant did not honestly hold the belief he expressed'.

[74] *WIC*, ibid [25].

[75] *Mainstream Canada v Staniford* 2013 BCCA 341, leave to appeal denied [2013] SCCA No 332.

[76] ibid [45]–[46].

[77] Brian MacLeod Rogers, 'The Supreme Court of Canada and Free Expression 2008-13: Tidal Wave or Tidal Wash?' (2013) 1 *MLRC Bulletin* 25, 29.

[78] *Spiller v Joseph* [2010] UKSC 53, [104].

[79] Defamation Act 2013, above n 56, s 3(3).

Defamation Law and the Internet

Protection for Hyperlinking and Intermediaries

In a case dealing with hyperlinking, the Supreme Court of Canada showed an appreciation for the challenges the Internet raises for defamation law. In *Crookes v Newton*,[80] the defendant published an article online about the plaintiff. None of the article's text was defamatory, but it included links to other websites that contained material defaming the plaintiff. Because a plaintiff must demonstrate that the defendant has 'published' the words complained of by communicating them to a third party, the issue was whether the plaintiff had republished that defamatory material by including hyperlinks to it.

The Supreme Court unanimously found for the defendant, in three separate opinions. Although the majority acknowledged that applying traditional publication principles likely would have captured hyperlinks to defamatory material,[81] concern about protecting expression on the Internet led it to modify its approach. According to the majority, hyperlinking to defamatory content will not lead to liability unless the defendant actually repeats the defamatory material.[82] As put by Justice Abella, who wrote for the majority:

> The Internet cannot, in short, provide access to information without hyperlinks. Limiting their usefulness by subjecting them to the traditional publication rule would have the effect of seriously restricting the flow of information and, as a result, freedom of expression. The potential 'chill' in how the Internet functions could be devastating, since primary article authors would unlikely want to risk liability for linking to another article over whose changeable content they have no control. Given the core significance of the role of hyperlinking to the Internet, we risk impairing its whole functioning. *Strict application of the publication rule in these circumstances would be like trying to fit a square archaic peg into the hexagonal hole of modernity*.[83]

The majority's recognition that technological change requires it to do more than apply old rules to new situations is refreshing, and may have implications for other areas where the Internet engages defamation law.

Just as important is Justice Abella's decision to adopt a clear and predictable rule, rather than the contextual analysis proposed by the two concurring opinions.[84] Uncertainty in any area of defamation law may chill expression, but these concerns are particularly relevant in the case of hyperlinking, as the content of links may change. Hyperlinking affects a broad cross-section of society: essentially anyone who posts content to the Internet. Expecting ordinary people to evaluate their exposure to liability based on complex contextual standards and on an ongoing basis is unrealistic and unfair.[85]

[80] *Crookes v Newton* 2011 SCC 47 (*Crookes*).

[81] ibid [16]–[18]; see also *Hill*, above n 1, [176] (accepting that expressing approval of a defamatory statement constituted publication).

[82] *Crookes*, above n 80, [24], [42].

[83] ibid [36], [emphasis added].

[84] McLachlin CJ and Fish J proposed that a defendant be liable where the text surrounding the hyperlink indicates 'adoption or endorsement' of the link's content: see ibid [48]. In the other concurrence, Justice Deschamps suggested that a defendant should be liable where the link makes the material 'readily available': see ibid [59].

[85] Iris Fischer and Adam Lazier, '*Crookes v Newton*: the Supreme Court Brings Libel Law into the Internet Age' (2012) 50 *Alta LR* 205, 214–15.

The *Crookes* decision is also significant for its recognition that 'some acts are so passive that they should not be held to be publication'. It accepts English jurisprudence holding that online intermediaries—such as message boards, search engines, or Internet service providers—are 'mere conduits' that are not publishers of defamatory material they unknowingly transmit.[86] Intermediaries form the backbone of the Internet, and imposing liability on them for the content they transmit risks forcing intermediaries either to pass these costs on to their users—raising the cost of using the Internet and limiting its accessibility—or to refuse to transmit content that does not come from a 'trusted' source. Limiting intermediary liability is therefore an important part of protecting the democratic nature of the Internet.[87]

The Canadian approach in *Crookes* appears to also be consistent with the direction taken in the Defamation Act 2013, which appears to limit liability for Internet hosts, service providers and even operators of websites where they comply with requirements that may lead to removing defamatory material.[88]

The Single Publication Rule

The Court in *Crookes* was right to celebrate the Internet's power to enhance free expression, but the Internet also poses new risks. Libel actions in Canada are generally subject to strict notice requirements and limitation periods. In Ontario, for example, the general limitation period is two years, but a plaintiff suing for libel in a newspaper or broadcast must give notice of an intention to sue within six weeks of finding out about the publication and actually commence the action within three months.[89] The purpose of these rules is closely connected to freedom of expression. They ensure that the threat of potential libel suits against media organisations does not linger, and that defendants are able to prepare a full defence while the facts remain fresh, or publish a correction in a timely way to limit liability.[90] The traditional common law rule, which dates back to the nineteenth century, holds that each publication of a defamatory statement constitutes a new cause of action.[91] Because an article can remain available on the Internet indefinitely, this rule—the multiple publication rule—means that the clock restarts for notice and limitation purposes every time someone sees it for the first time online, or it is republished online even if that happens years after the article was first published. As one American court has recognised, this creates the:

> potential for endless retriggering of the statute of limitation, multiplicity of suits and harassment of defendants …
>
> …

[86] *Crookes*, above n 80, [21], citing *Bunt v Tilley* [2006] EWHC 407 (QB), *Metropolitan International Schools v Designtechnica Corp* [2009] EWHC 1765 (QB). See also *Crookes*, ibid [87] (Deschamps J).

[87] Fischer and Lazier, above n 85, 211.

[88] Defamation Act 2013, above n 56, ss 5, 10. See also The Defamation (Operators of Websites) Regulations SI 2013 No 3028 (UK).

[89] Ontario LSA, above n 68, ss 5(1), 6 (limitation period and notice requirement for actions for libel in newspaper or broadcast); Ontario Limitations Act 2002, SO 2002, c 24, s 4 (general limitation period).

[90] *Butler v Southam* 2001 NSCA 121 [129], [135].

[91] See *Duke of Brunswick v Harmer* (1849) 117 Eng Rep 75.

> Inevitably, there would be a serious inhibitory effect on the open, persuasive dissemination of information and ideas over the Internet, which is, of course, its greatest beneficial promise.[92]

In light of these concerns, American courts have adopted the single publication rule, meaning that the clock starts to run for the purposes of limitation laws when the defamatory statement is first published.[93] Although English courts persisted with the multiple publication rule,[94] the single publication rule has now been adopted in section 8 of the Defamation Act 2013. This reform has made no real headway in Canada yet. The issue has yet to reach the Supreme Court, but the single publication rule has been rejected by appellate courts in British Columbia and Ontario.[95] Both cases cited traditional English jurisprudence.[96] It remains to be seen whether future courts faced with this issue will take the new English rule into account.

The Law of Jurisdiction: The Next Capital of Libel Tourism?

Another change brought by the Internet has been the growth in libel tourism as potential plaintiffs shop for the forum with laws most favourable to them. If the defendant's website is accessible around the world, the plaintiff may have a case for jurisdiction anywhere. Due to plaintiff-friendly laws, London has become a centre for libel tourism. But the Defamation Act 2013 may now change that. Along with making English libel law arguably less plaintiff-friendly, the Act provides that English courts do not have jurisdiction to hear libel cases against people who do not reside in Europe unless England 'is clearly the most appropriate place in which to bring an action'.[97]

In Canada, on the other hand, the Supreme Court has rolled out the welcome mat for libel tourists. In two cases in 2012, the Court endorsed a very liberal view of jurisdiction. The first case, *Breeden v Black*,[98] involved a lawsuit by Conrad Black, the disgraced British peer, former publisher of *The Daily Telegraph*, and former Chairman of US media company Hollinger International, against members of a special committee of directors and its advisor, Richard Breeden, that issued Hollinger press releases and a report to the Ud S Securities and Exchange Commission regarding Black's conduct. In the second, *Éditions Écosociété v Banro Corp*,[99] an Ontario-based mining company sued a publisher based in Québec over an allegedly defamatory book. Out of nearly 5,000 copies of the book, 108 were available for purchase or loan in Ontario. The book was also available for sale from the publisher's website. While in both cases the plaintiff had ties to Ontario and may not have been a

[92] *Firth v State of New York* 775 NE 2d 463, 456–66 (NY Ct App 2002) (*Firth*).

[93] See *Canatella v Van de Kamp*, 486 F.3d 1128, 1134–35 (9th Cir.2007).

[94] See *Godfrey v Demon Internet* [1999] EWHC QB 244, [33].

[95] *Carter v BC Federation of Foster Parents Association* 2005 BCCA 398, [14]–[20]; *Shtaif v Toronto Life Publishing Co* 2013 ONCA 405, [27]–[40] (*Shtaif*).

[96] The Court in *Shtaif*, ibid [32], noted that the rule 'does not fit comfortably' with the fact that limitation periods under Ontario law begin to run when the plaintiff became aware of the alleged libel, rather than the date of publication.

[97] Defamation Act 2013, above n 56, s 9(2).

[98] *Breeden v Black* 2012 SCC 19 (*Breeden*).

[99] *Éditions Écosociété v Banro Corp* 2012 SCC 18 (*Banro*).

'tourist' (although for some time Black was in an American prison and inadmissible to Canada), the Court held that Ontario courts had jurisdiction in a way that opens the door to libel tourism.

In *Breeden*, the Court held that '[i]t is well established in Canadian law that the tort of defamation occurs upon publication of a defamatory statement to a third party'.[100] This means that when a defamatory news article is downloaded from a foreign website by someone in Canada even a single time, or where a single copy of a foreign print publication makes its way into Canada, the tort of defamation has been committed in Canada. The court of the province in which that occurred will have presumptive jurisdiction over any non-resident defendant.[101]

The Supreme Court in *Breeden* explicitly rejected a jurisdictional test based on either the place of substantial publication, or on the subject matter and conduct giving rise to the defamatory statement. It did this—and purported to apply established law—without any discussion of the implications these rules had for freedom of expression in the context of the Internet.

The Court did express some concern about libel tourism in *Banro*, the companion case, and left open the possibility that the usual rule for tort claims in Canada—that the applicable law is that of where the tort occurred (the principle known as *lex loci delicti*)—might not apply in defamation cases. It suggested that the law of the place of the most substantial harm to reputation, as has been adopted in some Australian states by statute, may be a more appropriate choice of law rule in defamation matters.[102]

This does not mean that Canadian courts will welcome all libel tourists. A *forum non conveniens* argument may still prevail where a party has little connection to the jurisdiction, but this is a vague, discretionary test that may be applied unevenly and may have no regard for protecting freedom of expression.[103]

The Serious Harm Test

Many libel suits are brought not because a plaintiff has suffered significant reputational harm, but simply to muzzle criticism. Corporations often sue for libel when they have suffered no special—or actual financial—damages. Yet defendants are put to the expense of lengthy litigation, or capitulation, by deep-pocketed plaintiffs. In England, section 1 of the Defamation Act 2013 may provide a way to avoid such chilling actions. In an extraordinary departure from the long-standing common law presumption of harm from defamatory statements, subsection 1(1) provides that '[a] statement is not defamatory unless its publication caused or is likely to cause *serious* harm to the reputation of the claimant' [emphasis added]. And for corporations (other than non-profits), the 'serious harm' test is only met if the statement 'has caused or is likely to cause the body serious financial loss'.[104]

100 *Breeden*, above n 98, [20].

101 ibid.

102 *Banro*, above n 99, [56]–[62].

103 See, eg, *Goldhar v Haaretz.com et al.* 2016 ONCA 515. The Ontario Court of Appeal split 2-1 on the application of the forum non conveniens test, allowing an action to proceed where jurisdiction existed solely because a small number of people had read an Israeli newspaper story on the internet in Canada.

104 Defamation Act 2013, above n 56, s 1(2).

These provisions may be the most significant changes introduced by the Defamation Act 2013. They provide a high threshold for plaintiffs to meet to pursue an action, and give defendants a basis to seek early dismissal. At a practical level, the 'serious harm' test may create a powerful new defence.

No such defence exists in Canada, yet. The presumption of harm from publication continues to be the law,[105] and while the rule is that damages to corporations are to be modest in the absence of specific loss, businesses can still sue where there is no provable loss or harm.[106] However, a related development in Canada is the introduction of laws intended to curb strategic lawsuits against public participation (SLAPP). Like the 'serious harm' requirement in the Defamation Act 2013, anti-SLAPP legislation is intended to give courts the power to summarily dismiss frivolous claims that could undermine freedom of expression. It can be expensive to defend even groundless claims, and the threat of having to incur defence costs can itself chill expression.

Anti-SLAPP legislation was first enacted in the US. The civil-law province of Quebec enacted an anti-SLAPP law in 2009.[107] Following recommendations from the Uniform Law Commission of Canada, which adopted a model anti-SLAPP law in 2010,[108] Ontario, Canada's most populous province, enacted the Protection of Public Participation Act 2015.[109] Under this Act, a lawsuit that relates to expression on a matter of public interest will be dismissed unless the plaintiff can demonstrate that (a) there are grounds to believe the action has 'substantial merit' and the defendant has no valid defence, and (b) that the harm suffered by the plaintiff as a result of the expression is sufficiently serious that the public interest in allowing the case to continue outweighs the public interest in dismissing the case.[110] Under this test, it may be difficult for a defamation case to proceed that relates to a matter of public interest in the absence of serious harm to the plaintiff.

Related Causes of Action

Breach of Privacy

Privacy litigation is much less common in Canada than it is in England. This may be because the Canadian *Charter*, unlike the European Convention for Human Rights, contains

[105] *Grant SCC*, above n 39, [28].

[106] *Walker v CFTO* (1987) 59 OR (2d) 184, [24]–[31] (CA).

[107] An Act to amend the Code of Civil Procedure to prevent improper use of the courts and promote freedom of expression and citizen participation in public debate, SQ 2009, c 12. British Columbia also enacted a SLAPP law in 2001, but the law was repealed only a few months later following a change of government: see Michaelin Scott and Chris Tollefson, 'Strategic Lawsuits Against Public Participation: The British Columbia Experience' (2010) 19 *Rev of Eur Comp & Int Env Law* 45.

[108] Model Prevention of Abuse of Process Act, accessible at www.ulcc.ca/en/uniform-acts-new-order/current-uniform-acts/641-abuse-of-process-prevention/1403-uniform-prevention-of-abuse-of-process-act accessed July 2016.

[109] Protection of Public Participation Act 2015, 2015, S.O. 2015 C. 23.

[110] ibid s 2. The Act also allows a defendant who succeeds on such a motion to recover all reasonable costs they have incurred in defending the action, as well as damages from the plaintiff if the court finds that the plaintiff brought the action in bad faith or for an improper purpose: see ss 2(7), 2(9).

no explicit right to privacy.[111] In the absence of an express constitutional privacy right, Canadian law has developed a patchwork of remedies for privacy violations. For instance, the Québec Charter of Human Rights and Freedoms, which applies only in that province, contains a privacy right.[112] In *Aubry v Éditions Vice-Versa*, the Supreme Court relied on this right to hold that someone could sue a magazine for publishing a picture taken of her (and only her) in a public place without her consent.[113] The plaintiff in that case was not a public figure, was 17 years old when the picture was taken, and was not in a place where she would have expected to be included in a photograph.

Four other provinces have used legislation to create a tort of invasion of privacy, but it is asserted infrequently.[114] In Ontario, after years of uncertainty, in 2012 the Court of Appeal held in *Jones v Tsige* that there is also a narrow common law tort of 'intrusion upon seclusion'.[115] In order to be liable, the defendant must have intentionally or recklessly invaded the plaintiff's private affairs or concerns without lawful justification in a way that a reasonable person would consider 'highly offensive causing distress, humiliation or anguish'. The plaintiff need not prove economic harm.[116]

Jones did not involve the media—the case concerned a bank employee who had surreptitiously and repeatedly looked at bank records belonging to her boyfriend's ex-wife. Significantly, Justice Sharpe (who wrote the decision) observed that the tort might apply differently where it threatened freedom of expression:

> Finally, claims for the protection of privacy may give rise to competing claims. Foremost are claims for the protection of freedom of expression and freedom of the press. As we are not confronted with such a competing claim here, I need not consider the issue in detail. Suffice it to say, no right to privacy can be absolute and many claims for the protection of privacy will have to be reconciled with, and even yield to, such competing claims. A useful analogy may be found in the Supreme Court of Canada's elaboration of the common law of defamation in *Grant v Torstar* where the court held, at para. 65, that '[w]hen proper weight is given to the constitutional value of free expression on matters of public interest, the balance tips in favour of broadening the defences available to those who communicate facts it is in the public's interest to know.'[117]

Damages for breach of privacy in Canadian law are also quite low. The plaintiff in *Aubry* was awarded only $2,000 (CAD). In *Jones*, the Court stated that in the absence of pecuniary loss damages for common law intrusion upon seclusion should not exceed $20,000 (CAD).[118] This is consistent with the damage awards under provincial privacy legislation.[119] Although aggravated and punitive damages are available both at common law and under privacy statutes, such awards are generally reserved for 'truly exceptional circumstances.'[120]

[111] In *Hill*, above n 1, [121], the Court recognised privacy as a *Charter* value that should play a role in the development of the common law.

[112] RSQ, c C-12, s 5.

[113] *Aubry v Éditions Vice-Versa* [1998] 1 SCR 591.

[114] See British Columbia Privacy Act, RSBC 1996, c 373; Manitoba Privacy Act, RSM 1987, c P125; Saskatchewan Privacy Act, RSS 1978, c P-24; Newfoundland and Labrador Privacy Act, RSN 1990, c P-22.

[115] *Jones v Tsige* 2012 ONSC 32.

[116] ibid [71].

[117] ibid [73]. In *Trout Point Lodge Ltd. v Handshoe* 2012 NSSC 245 the Court refused to apply the tort where freedom of expression was engaged.

[118] ibid [87].

[119] ibid app B.

[120] ibid [88].

Negligence

As in England,[121] Canadian courts have allowed plaintiffs to sue in negligence over statements that cause harm. In *Young v Bella*—a case where two university professors falsely reported to colleagues and the police that a student had sexually abused children—the Supreme Court of Canada cited the House of Lords' decision in *Spring v Guardian plc* and wrote that:

> '[t]here is no reason in principle why negligence actions should not be allowed to proceed where (a) proximity and foreseeability have been established, and (b) the damages cover more than just harm to the plaintiff's reputation (i.e. where there are further damages arising from the defendant's negligence)'.[122]

In a negligence action, of course, the defendant has no access to the defences available to a defamation claim. Someone could conceivably be held liable in negligence for a statement that is true, constitutes fair comment, or is subject to privilege. This would not fit with the Supreme Court's holding in *WIC* and *Grant* that the defamation defences are essential to ensuring adequate protection for freedom of expression. However, a decision from the Ontario Court of Appeal has provided reassurance for the media. In *Shtaif v Toronto Life Publishing Co*, the Court held that there is no duty of care in negligence between a magazine and the subject of its reports. Justice Laskin, who wrote the decision, suggested that the process of investigating and reporting a story would not give rise to a duty of care unless there is a pre-existing relationship between the parties. In *Shtaif*, reporters for the magazine had contacted one of the plaintiffs twice before publication, to interview him and verify the accuracy of some of his statements:

> But to say, as the plaintiffs have, that these contacts by themselves gave rise to a duty of care would mean that in virtually every case a plaintiff could proceed with a negligence claim as well as a defamation claim. The principle in *Young v Bella* does not go that far.
>
> …
>
> The case before us is quite different [from *Young v Bella*]. Two telephone calls, part of journalists' ordinary diligence in writing a story, do not establish a pre-existing relationship that give[s] rise to a duty of care. The plaintiffs' action is an action for defamation and nothing more. Even the claims for income and business losses are essentially consequential financial losses, compensable under the law of defamation.[123]

Conclusion

It took more than 25 years for Canada's *Charter of Rights and Freedoms* to have a meaningful effect on defamation law. But in recent years the process of constitutionalising libel law has

[121] See *Spring v Guardian Assurance plc* [1995] 2 AC 296 (HL).
[122] *Young v Bella* 2006 SCC 3, [56].
[123] *Shtaif*, above n 95, [82], [85] (Laskin JA).

moved quickly. The Supreme Court now clearly recognises that the law of defamation must evolve to comply with the constitutional protection of freedom of expression and the needs of a modern and democratic society. As there is no indication that Canadian provincial legislatures are considering significant statutory change, however, there will likely be more divergence between Canadian and English law. The public interest/responsible communication and fair comment/honest opinion defences now have significant differences. Juries are presumptively displaced in England but are alive and well in Canada, where they may even assess responsible communication. The Defamation Act 2013 creates a 'serious harm' threshold[124] which may see many cases struck out at an early stage in England—a process lacking in Canada. As all of these changes, in both countries, are very recent, it will take time to assess their impact. Virtually unchanged for centuries, defamation law is now adapting in different ways to a very different world.

[124] Defamation Act 2013, above n 56, s 1.

7

The Internet and Politics in the Development of Hong Kong Defamation Law

RICK GLOFCHESKI

As elsewhere, defamation law in Hong Kong is in a state of flux. This is so largely because modern information technology is changing the ways in which people, including journalists, communicate, disseminate and seek out information and opinions. Although the impact of the new technology should not be over-stated and the pre-Internet era law is adaptable and capable of application in most cases, there can be no doubt that problems created by the new technology and new habits of communication are requiring a high degree of creativity from the courts to the point where statutory intervention may be unavoidable.

Hong Kong defamation law is under pressure for another reason. The rules of defamation law seek to strike a balance between free speech and the protection of reputation, but these interests and the value attached to them change over time. In recent years there is evidence of increased expectations on the part of civil society for greater political freedoms, including freedom of expression. The one country, two systems model has worked well enough since the 1997 handover, but Hong Kong is facing new issues in its political evolution. In the absence of an accountable government, but in the expectation of one, a free and active press has a vital role to play in the transition to the next stage of political development.

In Hong Kong, defamation law is governed largely by the common law.[1] The Defamation Ordinance, dating to the nineteenth century and modelled on English legislation, is the principal piece of defamation legislation, but does little more than provide minor modifications of some of the rougher aspects of the common law, in particular the defences, many of which are relevant to the press. There have been no significant amendments to the Defamation Ordinance for decades, the few that did take place being cosmetic in nature. It is probably fair to say that the Ordinance has a 'passed its use-by date' feel about it. Indeed, a good portion of the Ordinance is concerned with criminal libel and procedure, provisions that are certainly outdated, not to say controversial, and not surprisingly have not been applied by the courts for decades. Leaving aside the need for substantive reform of defamation law brought about by changes in communications technology and changing

[1] For the continuation of the common law in Hong Kong after the transfer of sovereignty to China in 1997, see Basic Law of the Hong Kong Special Administrative Region, Art 8. For a critical discussion of the effect of this article, see P Y Lo, *The Hong Kong Basic Law* (LexisNexis/Butterworths 2011) 46–54.

social expectations, the Ordinance is in need of an overhaul, if only to give it a modern look and to make it more relevant.

In the United Kingdom (UK), the jurisdiction with laws closest to Hong Kong's, a package of defamation law reforms was enacted in 2013[2] to address some of the problems triggered by the new technology. There was also a concern about so-called 'libel tourism', a phenomenon derived from a perception that, because of its favourable jurisdictional[3] and procedural rules and the low threshold for qualifying for substantial damages, the English courts had become the forum of choice of international litigants looking for a plaintiff-friendly venue to file their defamation claims.[4] The 2013 reforms attempt to address that issue as well, while codifying and smoothing over some of the common law principles that were considered to be in need of tweaking.[5]

In Hong Kong there is as yet no talk of statutory reform, despite defamation laws broadly similar to those of the UK.[6] Indeed, law reform is a rare event in Hong Kong in any area of the law.[7] This generalised legal inertia is sometimes explained by reference to the laissez-faire, non-interventionist governance philosophy that has been practiced by a succession of Hong Kong governments both pre- and post-handover.[8] More recently, and perhaps more accurately, it can be explained by a governance paralysis brought about by a fear of backlash from a public increasingly suspicious of any change initiated by a non-representative

[2] Defamation Act 2013, c 26. The Act came into force on 1 January 2014.

[3] The libel tourism problem is exacerbated by the Internet and its capacity to facilitate widespread publication, giving rise to a right to bring an action wherever the Internet exists and material can be downloaded.

[4] Commentators have differed over the extent of the 'problem', as to whether it is more perception than reality. See for instance Centre for Democracy and Technology, *Defamation in the Internet Age: Protecting Reputation without Infringing Free Expression* www.cdt.org/files/pdfs/Defamation-Internet-Age.pdf accessed July 2016. Nonetheless, the situation was viewed with such concern by US law-makers that Congress passed a law in 2010 with the express purpose of preventing British defamation judgments from being recognised and enforced in the US—see the Speech Act www.gpo.gov/fdsys/pkg/PLAW-111publ223/html/PLAW-111publ223.htm accessed July 2016. Despite its similarly plaintiff-friendly libel laws, there is no indication that Hong Kong has become favoured by international libel litigants—at least not yet.

[5] The Act introduces additional protection for secondary publishers such as booksellers and for website operators in relation to material posted by users of sites which they host (s 5), supplementing the provisions introduced by the Defamation Act 1996. A defence is available if it can be shown that the website operator was not the one who posted the statement on the website. Subsection 5(3) provides for the defence to be defeated if the claimant can show that it was not possible for him or her to identify the person who posted the statement; that they gave the operator a notice of complaint in relation to the statement; and that the operator failed to respond to that notice in accordance with provision contained in the regulations. The Act reforms the multiple publication rule that, as applied to online archives and other Internet publications, can keep libels actionable long after the expiry of limitation periods (s 8). The new law abolishes the presumption in favour of a jury trial in defamation cases (s 11), thereby significantly decreasing the cost and time to resolve claims. In order to discourage trivial claims it introduces a requirement for a claimant to demonstrate that the published material has caused serious harm (s 1). It restricts the jurisdiction of English courts to hear cases involving foreign defendants (s 9). It replaces the common law defences of justification and fair comment with statutory versions (ss 2 and 3) that are easier to understand and apply, and that to some degree reflect developments in the case law, and it puts the *Reynolds* public interest defence on a statutory footing (s 4).

[6] Before the extensive reforms of the Defamation Act 2013 there were only minor differences: the Hong Kong limitation periods is six years, compared to one year in England; in Hong Kong there is no equivalent of s 1 of Defamation Act 1996 detailing responsibility for publication and the Electronic Commerce (EC Directive) Regulations 2002 extending protection to secondary publishers including website operators.

[7] See generally M Tilbury, SNM Young and L Ng (eds), *Reforming Law Reform: Perspectives from Hong Kong and Beyond* (Hong Kong, Hong Kong University Press, 2014) ch 1.

[8] For a description of this governance ethos in a labour law context, see Rick Glofcheski, 'Job Security Issues in a Laissez-Faire Economy' in Blanpain et al (eds), *The Modernization of Labour Law and Industrial Relations in a Comparative Perspective* (The Netherlands, Kluwer, 2009) 425–26.

government that has for the most part lost the public trust. In this environment, it falls to the judiciary to initiate change in areas of the law thought to be in need of reform. Thus, defamation law reform in Hong Kong is by necessity a slow, cautious and to some degree random process, dependent on cases coming to the courts, but also constrained by the common law process itself, which does not permit of wholesale breaks with existing precedents.

From a review of the post-handover defamation case law it can be seen that the Hong Kong courts, in particular the Court of Final Appeal, are prepared to take the lead and introduce change where it is needed.[9] However, it may be asking too much of the courts to bear the full burden of law reform in the rapidly changing communications environment. Certainly, judge-made common law has advantages over legislation in that as computer software and other information technology continue to develop and become more sophisticated, the common law may prove a more adaptable process than legislation, which runs the risk of being overtaken by new technology. On the other hand, it is hard to imagine how the courts can achieve reforms of the nature of some of those introduced in the UK's Defamation Act 2013, for instance, the repeal of the statutory presumption in favour of jury trials,[10] or of greater urgency, the abolition of the much-criticised multiple publication rule, which treats each new publication of a libelous statement as a fresh defamation, thereby restarting the limitation period and perpetuating its actionability. This is surely a major issue in defamation law given the Internet's capacity to multiply defamatory material over time. In this environment, statutory reform cannot be deferred for much longer.

The New Media

It is now a cliché but it must be said, the Internet has brought about a communications revolution that has changed the ways in which ideas and opinions are communicated and disseminated for almost everyone, the media included. This communications revolution is impacting on defamation law in significant ways.[11] The temptation to publicly share one's thoughts is greater than ever, in part because of the so-called 'liberating effect' that the Internet has had on its users, each of whom now has a convenient and cheap tool for communicating with potentially limitless numbers of people. There is now a considerable industry cashing in on this tendency, through the construction of social media platforms, blogging services, discussion forums and other online services that encourage participation and the expression of ideas, often on an anonymous basis. The news media has also adapted to this environment, providing embedded discussion threads through which its readers can

[9] In particular see *Cheng v Tse Wai Chun* (2000) 3 HKCFAR 339 in which the court revised the common law defence of fair comment to strengthen the protection of freedom of speech.

[10] High Court Ordinance (Cap 4), s 33A(1).

[11] Among the many legal problems triggered by the new technology, Collins identifies six major features that have implications for libel law: the Internet's unlimited geographical reach; the emergence of a new layer of participants in the publication process, in particular, Internet intermediaries; the Internet's capacity for re-publication; website hyper-links; new and multiple forms of communication (text, audio, video, etc); and indefinitely accessible communications. See Matthew Collins, *The Law of Defamation and the Internet*, 3rd edn (Oxford, OUP, 2010) 36–42.

express their opinions, engage in discussion with one another, and even hurl insults, in real time and on an anonymous basis.

All of this is forcing a re-think of basic defamation concepts, for instance, what constitutes publication for the purposes of defamation law, who can be considered a publisher of a given piece of writing, how much liability should be imposed given the Internet's capacity for infinite storage and hence its unlimited reach geographically and over time, whether the court should even hear the case given that the protagonists may have little connection with Hong Kong other than that the material was downloaded there, and indeed whether the sorts of spontaneous and anonymous online utterances that comprise much of this new communication should even be taken seriously, as defamatory, given the context of the technology and changing social practices and perceptions.[12] Some of these problems have already reached the Hong Kong courts, while for others it is just a matter of time.

Website Hosts and Discussion Sites

Of the many issues triggered by the new technology, the liability of Internet intermediaries has proven to be one of the most contentious. Intermediaries play an important role in facilitating the free flow of ideas and opinions through the provision of discussion forums, blogging sites and the like. On the other hand, it is in the nature of these discussion sites that users will be tempted to engage in impulsive and often ill-advised communications, some of which inevitably are defamatory in nature. It is not surprising that victims of such communications will look to the Internet intermediary, instead of or in addition to the creator of the post, for a remedy either in the form of a damages award or a court order to take down the offending material, or both. How such cases are decided will be critical in the free speech debate. To find intermediaries jointly liable with the maker of the statement may very well cause the intermediaries to cease or scale back their operations, denying Internet users a convenient and powerful means of expression and access to larger audiences.[13] While the empowering capacity of the Internet for the free expression of ideas cannot be overstated,[14] its potential to wreak harm is also great; therein lies the central dilemma for the modern law of defamation.

We now know that the determination of intermediary liability for libelous material uploaded by a user will to some degree depend on the actual role played by the intermediary in the production and dissemination of the material. For instance, was it providing content, or was it providing a place for content to be uploaded? The former will most certainly attract liability under established principles, the latter might.

[12] In the context of the social media platform Twitter, see Paul Bernal, 'A Defence of Responsible Tweeting' [2014] *Comms L* 12, commenting on the fallout from the decision in *Lord McAlpine of West Green v Bercow* [2013] EWHC 1342 (QB).

[13] A phenomenon often referred to as the 'chilling effect' of defamation law.

[14] The European Court of Human Rights in its landmark decision in *Yildirim v Turkey* (3111/10) November 18, 2012 at [56], stated: 'the Internet has now become one of the principal means by which individuals exercise their right to freedom of expression and information, providing as it does essential tools for participation in activities and discussions concerning political issues and issues of general interest.'

The poor fit between established common law principles and the new communications environment was to some degree exposed in the first such case to reach the Court of Final Appeal, *Oriental Press Group Ltd v Fevaworks Solutions Ltd*.[15] The defendant was a company that provided and managed a website that hosted a popular Internet discussion forum, which boasted up to 5,000 postings an hour and 30,000 users at any given time. The plaintiff newspaper group was defamed in three anonymous postings made in 2007 and 2008. After identifying and settling with the users who posted the libelous statements,[16] the plaintiff proceeded to sue the website host itself for its role in the production and publication of the defamatory statements. The case raises the central question—who is a publisher of online text? No doubt the maker of the statements was a publisher, but what of the defendant website host?

Given the complete absence of legislation regulating online postings,[17] the reasoning of the court was based on the ordinary common law of defamation as developed in the era of print media. The decision runs to 134 paragraphs, provides a background and history of defamation law and makes some fine legal distinctions, most of which are not necessary for the purposes of the present discussion.

As summarised by the court, at common law:

> a person is liable for publishing a libel if by an act of any description, he could be said to have intentionally assisted in the process of conveying the words bearing the defamatory meaning to a third party, regardless of whether he knew that the article in question contained those words.[18]

However, that law makes a distinction between primary and subordinate publishers. Primary publishers are those who are involved in the creation of the material, while subordinate publishers play a role in its distribution. Classic examples of subordinate publishers are booksellers, news agents and libraries, though the list is potentially much longer. Subordinate publishers may be eligible to rely upon a special defence under common law.

The plaintiff argued that the defendant was a primary publisher, having participated in the production and distribution of the statement in its role as discussion forum operator. That would have left the defendant with no arguable defence.

Perhaps not surprisingly, the court preferred to characterise the defendant as a subordinate publisher. Under a long-established common law principle, such a publisher can avoid liability if three conditions are satisfied:

> (1) that he was innocent of any knowledge of the libel contained in the work disseminated by him, (2) that there was nothing in the work or the circumstances under which it came to him or was disseminated by him which ought to have led him to suppose that it contained a libel, and (3) that, when the work was disseminated by him, it was not by any negligence on his part that he did not know that it contained the libel.[19]

Of the three defamatory postings under consideration, the defendant had removed two of them from the website within hours of learning of their existence, and so was entitled to the

[15] *Oriental Press Group Ltd v Fevaworks Solutions Ltd* (2013) 16 HKCFAR 366 (*Fevaworks*).

[16] They were identified through *Norwich Pharamacal* orders, see ibid [14].

[17] There is nothing in Hong Kong comparable to the Electronic Commerce (EC Directive) Regulations 2002, which identify the conditions under which Internet hosts will be liable for material they carry but did not create.

[18] *Fevaworks*, above n 16, [19].

[19] *Vizetelly v Mudie's Select Library Limited* [1900] 2 QB 170, 180, cited with approval, *ibid* [27].

innocent dissemination defence. As for the third, which remained on the website for eight months after it was made known to the defendant, the defendant was found liable. A more prompt response was required.

There are at least two important observations that can be made about this conclusion and the reasoning that supported it. On the face of it, the plaintiff's argument that the defendant was a primary publisher was not without force. After all, the defendant participated in the publication of those postings from the beginning. It set up the mechanism for uploading postings, and was in the very business of disseminating those postings. The situation was analogous less to well-established categories of subordinate publishers such as a bookseller or news agent than it was to a print newspaper that publishes the opinions of readers on the letters page, or the opinions of syndicated columnists on the op-ed page. The only difference is in the volume of material, and thus the practicality of moderating the content. Booksellers and newsagents become involved only after the text is produced and published. A discussion forum host such as the defendant's, like the print newspaper, involved from the beginning, has the power to prevent or delete postings, however resource-intensive and inconvenient that might prove to be. The finding that the defendant was not a primary publisher avoids the so-called chilling effect that such a decision would have on freedom of Internet speech, but the poor fit with the conventional subordinate publisher/innocent dissemination defence demonstrates the contortions that are required in achieving defamation reform in a legal environment devoid of the benefits of fit-for-purpose statutory regulation. These kinds of contortions make a strong case for statutory intervention.

The second observation concerns the application of the three conditions of the innocent dissemination defence. The defence applies if it was not by any negligence on the defendant's part that he did not know that the publication contained the libel. The standard required will vary with the circumstances. This implies that a monitoring mechanism may be required in appropriate circumstances. For print media this may require putting in place a system whereby some pre-distribution monitoring is at least possible.[20] According to Ribeiro PJ, this would be an impractical and unrealistic standard to apply to a heavy-traffic discussion forum such as the defendant's. However, an obvious concern with this reasoning is that it implies that monitoring may not be impractical or unrealistic for a low-traffic discussion forum. This triggers the question: is it fair to penalise those commercially less successful website hosts in this way? Can there really be a rational basis for discriminating in this way?

The decision leaves unaddressed a host of other questions about the liability of online service providers. For instance, if busy websites have no duty to moderate, where is the line to be drawn as to when the duty to moderate and screen arises?[21] How will the court's reasoning apply, for instance, to the popular phenomenon of reader discussion threads embedded in an online newspaper? These discussion forums have proved immensely popular in Hong Kong and elsewhere. Will the news website be characterised differently, as a

[20] *Chau Hoi Shuen Solina Holly v SEEC Media Group Ltd* [2016] 2 HKC 80 (CFA).

[21] There are other aspects of the court's reasoning that also expose the difficulty of applying libel principles developed in the print media era to the modern context. One of these concerns an analogy with club notice boards, and another with contemporaneous television broadcasts, but these will not be taken up here. See generally Anne SY Cheung, 'Liability of Internet Host Providers in Defamation Actions: From Gatekeepers to Identifiers' in András Koltay (ed), *Media Freedom and Regulation in the New Media World* (Hungary, Wolters Kluwer Ltd, 2014).

primary publisher, since the thread is embedded in the news story itself?[22] And how will the court respond in those cases where the Internet host has voluntarily taken more of a hands-on role in discussion forum moderation? What about the liability of search engines for search results that prove to be libelous?[23] What about hyper-links in a website—will the creator of the article containing the hyper-link be liable for any libelous material that the hyper-link leads to?[24] Or in performing only an editing function?

That all such questions were not answered is to some degree inevitable as it is not open to the court to go beyond the specific liability issues raised by the facts of the case. This again demonstrates the limitations of judge-made as opposed to statutory law.

Automated Internet Search Suggestions

The decision in *Fevaworks* did lay the foundation for the more recent interlocutory decision in *Albert Yeung v Google Inc*,[25] a factually more interesting and potentially ground-breaking decision that sits at the very cutting edge of libel law and the new technology. This case was not concerned with Internet posts or website text, but search engine suggestions that, according to counsel for Google, were not even written by humans but produced algorithmically by the Autocomplete search suggestions in the Google drop-down menu. The plaintiff, a prominent entertainment mogul in Hong Kong, complained that when the first few characters of his name are typed into the search field, Googlebot (Google's web crawling bot or 'spider') automatically produces libelous search suggestions such as 'Albert Yeung triad'. The plaintiff commenced an action for defamation and obtained an order permitting service of the writ on Google in the US. The defendant brought an application under Order 12 rule 8 of the Rules of the High Court (RHC) seeking an order to set aside service on the basis that the Hong Kong court did not have jurisdiction to hear the case, and on the basis that the case did not satisfy Order 11 rule 1(1)(f) of the RHC requiring that 'the claim is founded on a tort and the damage was sustained, or resulted from an act committed, within the jurisdiction'. In essence, the defendant argued that as the Autocomplete was produced without human intervention, the defendant could not be a publisher of the material. The expert evidence accepted by the court showed that Autocomplete suggestions for a given search term were based on algorithms tabulating a number of factors, including users' preferences. The more frequently a search term was entered into the Google search field, the

[22] The outcome may depend on the degree of control exercised by the news provider over the embedded comment section, as in *Delfi AS v Estonia* App no 64569/09 (ECtHR, 10 October 2013) http://hudoc.echr.coe.int/sites/fra/pages/search.aspx?i=001-126635 accessed July 2016 (the decision was upheld by the Grand Chamber on June 16, 2015 http://hudoc.echr.coe.int/eng?i=001-155105#{"itemid":["001-155105"]} accessed July 2016. Note that Delfi had also determined which comments were to be published and which were not, and only it could remove or change them. To similar effect, the English High Court held in *Kaschke v Gray* [2010] EWHC 690 (QB) that an ISP of a web blog lost the protection of the EC Directive Regulations because it corrected the spelling and grammar of entries posted by bloggers. It was found to have been actively engaged with the content, such that the extent of its control had gone beyond the mere storage function, an essential criterion of a host in order to qualify for protection under Regulation 19 of the EC Directive Regulations. Such rulings give rise to the irony that by taking a less careful, less detailed approach in the management of the discussion thread, liability might be avoided. If so, this cannot be a public policy position a court would want to endorse.

[23] As in *Metropolitan International Schools Ltd v Designtechnicia Corporation* [2011] 1 WLR 1743.

[24] *Crookes v Newton* [2011] 3 SCR 269.

[25] *Dr Yeung, Sau Shing Albert v Google Inc* [2015] 1 HKLRD 26 (CFI).

more likely the search term would pop up as a search suggestion for a subsequent user. This, according to Google, was outside its control.

On one view this is a remarkable argument, akin to a scientist creating a robot programmed to randomly commit acts of destruction, and then claiming no responsibility because the robot is programmed to act on its own prompting. As the plaintiff argued, the programme was functioning precisely as Google intended[26] in producing pop-up search suggestions. On the other hand, it is not an entirely unreasonable argument from Google's perspective, given the implications of a finding that Google was a publisher. Such a ruling might very well have the effect of shutting down the Google search suggestions tool.

The threshold for establishing an arguable question of law in what is in effect a striking-out application is not very high. The court was satisfied that, Google having set up the programme that was now functioning in the way that Google intended, and given that Google did have the capacity to edit out search suggestions, however impractical it might be given the volume of searches undertaken and the unpredictable nature of the algorithm system, there was an arguable case that Google was a publisher of the offending material. Thus, the case was sent for trial, at which time the issue can be fully explored and finally decided.[27]

Like *Fevaworks*, this case challenges the traditional principles of libel law. On a conventional analysis, Google could conceivably be found to be a primary publisher, given its role in producing the software programme that generates the libelous material, involved from the beginning and having liability from the moment of the production of the offending search results. That would be a disastrous result for Google, effectively requiring it to withdraw the Autocomplete function from its search engine. On the other hand, on the reasoning in *Fevaworks*, Google could be found to be a subordinate publisher, liable on a notice and take-down basis only. This would be more acceptable, but not entirely convenient for Google, requiring as it would, prompt action when Autocomplete libels are reported. It is unlikely that Google would be required to implement a monitoring mechanism, something that would be very difficult to administer in view of the apparently unpredictable nature of the Autocomplete function. Exempting Google from a monitoring function would be consistent with *Fevaworks*, where the court found monitoring not required for hosts with large-volume postings.

Public Interest

This public interest defence goes by different names. It is often referred to as *Reynolds* privilege, taking its name from the English House of Lords decision in which it was introduced in 2001.[28] The decision was a major breakthrough for mainstream journalism. In *Reynolds*

[26] The same argument succeeded in Australia against Google regarding text and image search engine results—see *Trkulja v Google* (No 5) [2012] VSC 533. Note that the correctness of the decision in *Trkulja* was doubted by McCallum J in the interlocutory injunction in *Bleyer v Google Inc* [2014] NSWSC 897.

[27] In the Tribunale Ordinario di Milano, a case with similar facts was decided by Judge Padova Marie Luisa against Google—see case 10847 of 2011 decided March 31, 2011 (plaintiff's name suppressed by the court). Case BGH, VI ZR 269/12, in the Federal Court of Justice in Karlsruhe Germany, was also decided against Google May 14 2013.

[28] *Reynolds v Times Newspapers Ltd* [2001] 2 AC 127.

the English courts recognised for the first time a form of qualified privilege for the news media when reporting on matters of public interest. Lord Nicholls identified ten non-exhaustive factors that should be taken into account for a news publisher to avoid liability for a libelous report. Among the factors to be taken into consideration before publishing an article, the seriousness of the allegation, the nature and reliability of its source, the urgency attaching to the subject matter and the opportunity given to the defamed person were paramount. Despite the apparent breakthrough, Lord Nicholls' formulation produced a body of lower court case law that rigidly applied those ten factors, thereby diluting the effect of reforms intended by the decision.[29] Subsequently, in *Jameel v Wall Street Journal Europe,*[30] Lord Hoffmann clarified that Lord Nicholls' ten factors were relevant but should not be strictly applied or treated as hurdles or conditions. What was crucial was for the defendant to demonstrate that it satisfied the standards of responsible journalism in the circumstances. Verification of sources and an opportunity for the defamed person to respond to the allegations were paramount. In *Seaga v Harper* the Privy Council took the development further, holding that such journalistic privilege could apply to 'publications made by any person who published material of public interest in any medium'.[31] Most recently, in *Flood v Times Newspapers Ltd,*[32] the Supreme Court confirmed the importance of the public interest requirement of responsible journalism:

> the judge … is deciding but a single question: could whoever published the defamation, given whatever they knew (and did not know) and whatever they had done (and had not done) to guard so far as possible against the publication of untrue defamatory material, properly have considered the publication in question to be in the public interest?[33]

On the face of it, the extension of the defence in *Seaga* to include non-professional journalists and publishers was an important development for bloggers and other non-professional journalists. Nonetheless, one may well question how the *Reynolds* defence as currently fashioned is suitable to online non-professional journalism. The *Reynolds* defence was introduced in the context of traditional journalism and news reporting. Many of the factors enumerated by Lord Nicholls may not be appropriate to online journalism when practiced by bloggers and other non-professionals. *Reynolds'* criteria require some legal expertise, and resources to do follow up and pose questions carefully to sources and the subjects of the postings, who are often prominent figures such as politicians. Small, low-volume publishers and bloggers will not have access to such resources or any realistic way to get the attention of politicians to give the other side of the story before blogging. If requirements are imposed that cannot be met, the defence will be of no value to anyone lacking the resources and standing of large-scale commercial publishers.[34] It remains to be seen whether the extension of the *Reynolds* privilege will offer any protection to the online community.[35]

[29] In Hong Kong, the decision in *Yaqoob v Asia Times Online Ltd* [2008] 4 HKLRD 911(discussed below) is such an example.

[30] *Jameel v Wall Street Journal Europe* [2007] 1 AC 359.

[31] *Seaga v Harper* [2009] 1 AC 1, 11.

[32] *Flood v Times Newspaper Ltd* [2012] 2 AC 273.

[33] Ibid 308, per Lord Brown. Lord Clarke agreed.

[34] See Jacob Rowbottom, 'In the Shadow of the Big Media: freedom of expression, participation and the production of knowledge online' [2014] *Public Law* 491.

[35] It will be particularly difficult, for instance, in the case of Twitter, where 140 characters and its spontaneous character would hardly allow for verification and inclusion of the other side of the story: see Bernal, above n 12.

In this regard the simplicity of section 4 of the Defamation Act 2013 is to be noted. The codified version of the *Reynolds* defence does not contain a list of conditions or criteria for responsible journalism or even mention responsible journalism, but only requires that the statement complained of be on a matter of public interest, and that the publisher had a reasonable belief that publication was in the public interest.[36]

The *Reynolds* public interest defence[37] has met with mixed success in the Hong Kong courts. In *Yaqoob v Asia Times Online Ltd*,[38] the defendant online news service based in Hong Kong published an article attributing a range of criminal conduct (money laundering, terrorist financing and drug trafficking) to the Dubai-based plaintiff businessman and two companies he was associated with. The article was removed from the defendant's website the day following its publication. The plaintiffs sued the defendant in defamation, and the defendant pleaded the public interest defence. Reyes J applied Lord Nicholls' ten factors and concluded that, far from having satisfied the requirements of responsible journalism, the failure to verify sources, and to properly give the plaintiff the opportunity to respond to the allegations and to publish his side of the story, and the absence of any urgency to the article, were all fatal to the defence. Substantial damages were awarded in favour of all three plaintiffs.

Blakeney-Williams v Cathay Pacific Airways[39] concerned a labour dispute in which a group of dismissed airline pilots sued their former employer alleging wrongful termination based on their participation in trade union activities. In a press release following the terminations, the defendant asserted that the terminated pilots could not be relied upon to act in the best interests of the company. This was defamatory. In the Court of Appeal, the defendant's attempt to rely on the public interest defence was accepted as proper, by reference to *Seaga*. However, the defence failed because the defendant could not satisfy its requirements—there was insufficient material on which to base the allegation and because the statement failed to include the pilots' version or their response to the defendant's statement. As noted by the court,

> [t]he present case is different from one in which an independent journalist or writer engages in investigative journalism and publishes his result. Cathay and the Union were using the public arena to conduct a public communication campaign. But once Cathay decided to make public the underlying reason for dismissal, it had to act fairly and responsibly. The principle of responsible public dissemination of information demanded a degree of fairness: either the other side's story was also to be told or the fact was that the other side was not prepared to give its story.

Finally, *Pui Kwan Kay v Ming Pao Holdings Ltd*, decided at trial by a judge and jury, concerned an editorial written by a senior editor of the defendant newspaper about possible match-fixing in the Hong Kong Football Association.[40] The editorial referred to the plaintiff, the Vice-Chairman of the Hong Kong Football Association and a former club director, by name, as having provided inconsistent answers in a post-press conference question

[36] Defamation Act 2013, s 4(1).

[37] In Hong Kong the defence is referred to variously as 'responsible public dissemination'—see *Blakeney-Williams v Cathay Pacific Airways* [2011] 1 HKLRD 901 (CA), and 'responsible journalism'—see *Law Chi Ching v Apple Daily Ltd* (unreported, HCA 2155/2009, 21 August 2015, CFI).

[38] *Yaqoob v Asia Times Online Ltd* [2008] 4 HKLRD 911 (CFI).

[39] *Blakeney-Williams*, above n 37.

[40] *Pui Kwan Kay v Ming Pao Holdings Limited* (unreported, CACV 201/2013, 17 November 2015); [2015] HKEC 2421.

session regarding the funding sources of one of the teams under suspicion for match-fixing, a team that the plaintiff had once been associated with. The editorial, based on an article written by the defendant's reporter who attended the post-press conference question session, was found by the jury to be defamatory in raising suspicions about the plaintiff himself being connected with possible match-fixing. The court found the factual basis for the suspicion—the plaintiff's equivocation in answering the questions about the team's source of funding—could not be made out, and that the reporter committed factual errors in his note-taking of the question session. The court rejected the public interest defence because the senior editor who wrote the editorial had drawn insufficient attention in the editorial to the plaintiff's reply to the defendant newspaper's follow-up inquiries and had not sought verification of the events beyond the report provided by the defendant's own reporter. In the court's view, in order to meet the standards of responsible journalism, the defendant should have read the other newspapers that reported on the press conference (seven in number), and included the substance of those reports in the editorial.

Lam V-P, giving the judgment of the Court of Appeal, agreed with Lord Phillips in *Flood v Times Newspapers Ltd*[41] that the determination of the public interest defence by a judge at first instance was not an exercise of discretion, and 'whether an appellate court should interfere in a particular case must depend on the context'. He found that the errors made by the trial judge—in particular, applying the defence by reference to a meaning not attributable to the jury (that there were reasonable grounds to suggest that the plaintiff was involved in match-fixing and that the ICAC should investigate the plaintiff)—made this such a case. Moreover, the trial judge had applied too strict a standard, requiring too much of the defendant in satisfying the standards of responsible journalism. It was not necessary for a newspaper to consult the reports in other newspapers. At any rate, how could the accuracy of those reports be verified? In the absence of anything that might prompt the need for further verification, there was no reason why the defendant could not rely on the report prepared by its own reporter, who after all was present at the press conference and question session when the plaintiff gave the allegedly equivocal responses. Also, on the undisputed facts, the defendant's reporter had made telephone contact with the plaintiff, who replied that his equivocation was caused by a mere memory-lapse. Moreover, the summary of that conversation was included in an article published by the defendant in the same issue as the impugned editorial, and was cross-referenced in the editorial. In the court's view this was sufficient to satisfy the requirements of the public interest defence.

The decision itself aside, the Court of Appeal judgment in this case puts the public interest defence on a more solid footing. The tone of the judgment and its adoption of some strong statements by Lords Phillips and Mance about the importance of the public interest defence for a free press, the need to 'look at the position in the round and [that] some latitude should be given to the content and presentation of news items',[42] and how in the application of the defence, 'the courts must give due weight to the editorial judgments of journalists given their role in the overall equation of public interest'[43] bode well for the press in Hong Kong and certainly move the defence beyond the literal application of Lord

[41] Above n 32.

[42] *Flood v Times Newspapers Ltd,* above n 32, [131] and [132], per Lord Mance.

[43] *Pui Kwan Kay v Ming Pao Holdings Limited,* above n 40, [40].

Nicholls' 10 factors that had obstructed the defence in the early days. However, it is only the second successful application of the defence in Hong Kong, and much remains to be seen. The defence will surely be tested again soon.

Reportage

It is a well-established principle that to repeat a defamatory statement attracts liability in the same way as if made as an original statement. This is known as the repetition rule.[44] However, sometimes what is of public interest is the fact that a particular statement was made by someone on a particular occasion, regardless of its truth. It is important that some flexibility be introduced to soften the strictness of the repetition rule to allow for such reporting. The UK Supreme Court case of *Flood v Times Newspapers Ltd*[45] was concerned with the publication of an article in the defendant's newspaper reporting that allegations of wrongful disclosure of information and corruption were made against a police officer. The court identified a distinction to be made between the standard of verification required in cases of 'reportage', where the gist of the publication is that allegations have been made by others, and cases of original allegation:

> Reportage is a special, and relatively rare, form of *Reynolds* privilege. It arises where it is not the content of a reported allegation that is of public interest, but the fact that the allegation has been made. It protects the publisher if he has taken proper steps to verify the making of the allegation and provided that he does not adopt it.

This is a less exacting verification standard than is required for original allegations, for which the 'privilege will normally only be earned where the publisher has taken reasonable steps to satisfy himself that the allegation is true before he publishes it'. It is important that the defendant not adopt the statement as his own. The development of the defence is in its early stages. It is not yet clear whether the defence is available only when reporting a public dispute, or at least some sort of dispute, and whether both sides of the dispute must be reported, or whether a dispute is required at all.[46]

In *Oriental Daily Publisher Ltd v Ming Pao Holdings Ltd*,[47] the defendants, a newspaper and its proprietors, published stories about a person (X) who called himself 'Hong Kong Bin Laden'. X was known to have made threats of violence against the Chief Executive and senior government officials. In 2002, X was convicted of offences related to his having poisoned different food products in supermarkets and was imprisoned. In 2007 X was convicted of criminal intimidation of the plaintiffs involving letters he had sent to them. In 2008 the defendant newspaper published an article which referred to X's claim that the criminal intimidation case against him was a setup and that he was wrongly convicted. Just above the article the defendants included a photograph of X outside the High Court

[44] *Lewis v Daily Telegraph Ltd* [1964] AC 234. The rule is that 'if A makes a defamatory statement about B and C repeats it, C cannot succeed in the defence of justification by showing that A made the statement: C must prove the charge against B is true': *Roberts v Gable* [2008] QB 502.

[45] *Flood*, above n 32.

[46] *Gatley on Libel and Slander*, 12th edn (London, Sweet & Maxwell, 2013) 664–66.

[47] *Oriental Daily Publisher Ltd v Ming Pao Holdings Ltd* [2011] 3 HKLRD 393 (CA).

displaying a banner in which X accused the plaintiffs of forgery and false claims against him. The next day, the defendants reported the plaintiffs' denials of X's allegations, and the defendants later published a statement that X's allegations were his alone and untrue. Nonetheless, the plaintiffs complained that in publishing the article and the photograph of X carrying the defamatory banner, the defendants had thereby repeated the defamation and so sued the defendants in defamation. The defendant argued that no reasonable person would have believed the accusations of X and maintained that it had not adopted the truth of X's allegations nor sought to justify them. The court held that adoption of the truth of the allegation was not essential to liability under the repetition rule. However much it was likely that most people might not believe the allegations, looking at the article as a whole and the context, the article was not so incredible that no reasonable reader could believe it, according to the court. The defendants were liable in defamation.

With respect, the decision is overly restrictive. The harm done to the plaintiff by the defamation in question was minor but the consequences of the decision for free speech and the public's right to know serious. In Hong Kong where universal suffrage is absent, public demonstrations and protests take place frequently. For many, they are important vehicles of political expression. Complete and accurate media coverage of such events is hardly possible without photographs, which are bound to contain images of protestors waving banners highly critical and at times defamatory of politicians and other public figures. This decision runs the very real risk of forcing the media into a form of self-censorship, brushing out images of protestors' signage thereby depriving the Hong Kong public of full and accurate coverage of these events. It seems to place insufficient weight on freedom of expression and the public's right to know.[48] The decision was hampered by the defendant's abandonment at trial of the public interest defence.[49] Full argument on the defence may have provided the opportunity for a full airing of the issues. Whether the defendant would have qualified for the defence of the reportage version of *Reynolds* privilege remains an open question. Certainly there should have been a closer consideration of the consequences for the news media in its reporting of political and other public demonstrations and protests that take place on an almost weekly basis in Hong Kong. The case was decided before the decision in *Flood v Times Newspapers Ltd*.[50] One can reasonably speculate that the defence may not have been abandoned and a full hearing on the issue would have taken place if counsel had the benefit of the Supreme Court ruling in *Flood*.

In the meantime the defence of reportage has been accepted in Hong Kong in the CFI decision in *Jigme Tsewang Athoup v Brightec Ltd*.[51] The defendant magazine published an article submitted by an author, apparently under a pseudonym. The article contained a number of statements libelous of the plaintiff, a person of some prominence in a particular sect of Tibetan Buddhism. The defendant had previously and in the same issue of the magazine published articles written by those who supported the plaintiff regarding the issues under contention. The defendant argued that it was providing a neutral forum for the publication of these differing views, and therefore came within the reportage defence.

[48] Unfortunately, this issue was not the subject of comment by the Court of Final Appeal, where damages assessment, but not liability, was under review (see *Oriental Daily Publisher Ltd v Ming Pao Holdings Ltd* (2012) 15 HKCFAR 299).

[49] Referred to in the Court of Appeal and the Court of First Instance as the responsible journalism defence.

[50] *Flood*, above n 32.

[51] [2015] HKEC 61, HCA 1693/2011 (13 January 2015).

The court accepted that the defence was part of Hong Kong law, because the human rights considerations on which the introduction of the defence in UK law were based were, with reference to the Basic Law and Bill of Rights Ordinance, largely applicable here. However, on the facts of the case the defence was rejected by the court, rightly, it is submitted.

In the court's view, the defendant did not publish the article for the purpose of making known that a particular allegation had been made by a particular person. Rather, the defendant's purpose was to publish the article. The intention of the author was to make the allegations. In the words of Deputy Judge Lok, 'an article written in the name of an unknown person cannot possibly be described as a "report" that the anonymous author has written certain statements'. On this view, the case was not even one of repeat publication. The defendant magazine was, with the article's author, a primary publisher. In such circumstances the only defences available would have been the usual ones—justification and fair comment. On these facts, not surprisingly perhaps, neither was pleaded.

The court in its *obiter dicta* also confirmed that there is no such defence as 'neutral forum', according to which a defendant who publishes both sides of a dispute neutrally will not be liable for the publication of libelous material. If such a defence were to have been recognised, a blanket defence would be available to internet forum hosts for any libelous statements and counter-statements posted there, and as seen in the Court of Final Appeal decision in *Oriental Press Group Ltd v Fevaworks Solutions Ltd*,[52] that point has not been reached in the development of the common law.

Other Defences

Chau Hoi Shuen Solina Holly v SEEC Media Group Ltd[53] was concerned with the innocent dissemination defence, this time in the more conventional context of the print media. An issue of the monthly periodical *Caijing Magazine*, published in the Mainland and distributed in Hong Kong by the defendant, was found to contain material defamatory of the plaintiff, accusing her of corruption in relation to business activities in the Mainland. At issue was whether the defendant, as the distributor of the magazine, was liable for the defamation, or whether it could rely on the defence of innocent dissemination. The trial judge found that the defendant should have known of the defamatory material, on the basis that the magazine's heading on the cover[54] and its inclusion of the name of the well-known Hong Kong tycoon Mr Li Ka Shing, should have alerted the defendant to inspect the magazine for possible libel. The trial judge found the defendant negligent not only in failing to detect the defamatory material but also because it did not inspect the magazine on its delivery from China. Indeed, its distribution system was such that there was not even any opportunity for inspection.

[52] Above n 15.

[53] *Chau Hoi Shuen Solina Holly*, above n 20.

[54] 'Alliance of the newly appointed officials (or VIP). How did a group of young technocrats who stretched across business, commercial-industrial and forex sectors set up the two-way tollbooth on foreign investment approval, involving the richest Chinese man Mr Li Ka Shing, the richest man in China Huang Guang Yu, and also famous enterprises such as Siemens, Philips and Capital Group.'

In the Court of Appeal and the Court of Final Appeal the issue under consideration was whether the trial judge had applied the correct formulation of the innocent dissemination defence. The trial judge had applied the traditional formulation, for instance as applied by the Court of Final Appeal in *Oriental Press Group Ltd v Fevaworks Solutions Ltd.*[55] The appellant argued for an alternative formulation, based on the dissenting judgment of Lord Denning in *Goldsmith v Sperrings Ltd.*[56] Under that formulation, a distributor entitled to rely on the innocent dissemination defence would lose the defence only if he was or should have been aware that the publication contained an actionable libel (one for which there are no defences). This was not a trivial or academic distinction, and calls for the correct balance to be struck. A heavy duty could have a chilling effect. The traditional formulation puts distributors on guard and leaves them vulnerable to suit, as demonstrated by the instant case. Equally, the interpretation advanced by the defendant—that the defence would be lost only if the distributor knew or should have known that the material contained actionable libel—introduces problems of its own. In particular, how much legal knowledge about available libel defences can realistically be expected of a subordinate publisher such as a news agent? The Court of Final Appeal confirmed the traditional formulation. As such, subordinate publishers such as news agents and the like will be well advised to have some sort of monitoring system in place—one that can be shown to have been implemented—in order to have a reasonable case that it was not negligent in failing to detect libelous material in a publication it is distributing. How much will be required of a subordinate publisher is, as observed by Fok PJ, fact and context sensitive and will vary with circumstances. According to Fok PJ, this will generally mean that more may be required of a small-scale print distributor than, for instance, a busy internet host receiving thousands of posts. This raises the same problem identified in the discussion of *Fevaworks*: a more relaxed standard for the busy distributor and a more exacting one for the less busy (ie less commercially successful). Ironically, on this view, a distributor on the scale of Amazon.com might be under a lesser duty than a *South China Morning Post* delivery agent.

Damages

The issue of damages is often overlooked in the free speech/reputation debate. Unduly substantial awards can produce a chilling effect on free speech in the same way as unfavourably formulated libel rules. In two recent decisions, *Blakeney-Williams v Cathay Pacific Airways Ltd*[57] and *Oriental Daily Publisher Ltd v Ming Pao Holdings Ltd*[58] the Court of Final Appeal took the opportunity to set down a number of guidelines to be followed in the assessment of defamation damages, in order to ensure consistency, as well as moderation. In both cases, the Court confirmed the decisions of the Court of Appeal to significantly cut back the awards made at trial. In general, an appeal court will be slow to set aside an award of general damages made at trial, and will do so only where it regards the award as manifestly wrong,

[55] See discussion at above n 19.

[56] *Goldsmith v Sperrings Ltd* [1977] 1 WLR 478.

[57] *Campbell Richard Blakeney-Williams v Cathay Pacific Airways Ltd* (2012) 15 HKCFAR 261.

[58] *Oriental Daily Publisher Ltd*, above n 48.

or where the award is vitiated by some error made by the judge in assessing damages. An example of such an error is where in assessing general damages, the court has regard to awards made in cases that are not relevant or comparable to the one under consideration.[59]

The circumstances of the publication will be an important factor in the assessment of damages, including the means and extent of publication. According to the Court of Final Appeal, postings on the Internet made anonymously are likely to be taken less seriously than those made by known individuals whose pronouncements carry some weight, even more so where the posting is on a website forum with a constant and huge volume of turnover and thus less likely to attract attention.[60] Moreover, the fact that the publication is a repeat publication is also a relevant circumstance, normally but not always pointing to a lower award. The repeat publication could aggravate or lessen the sting of the original publication depending on the circumstances.[61]

The burden is on the plaintiff to prove, by inference as well as by direct evidence (if any), the fact of publication and its extent. Regarding Internet publications, it has been held in a Court of First Instance decision that there is no presumption that material placed on a generally accessible website has been published to a substantial albeit unquantifiable number of persons (whether within the jurisdiction or elsewhere).[62] On the other hand, it has been held that the 'viral' nature of social media and its potential to 'percolate' by way of the Internet can be taken into account in the assessment of damages.[63]

A corporate plaintiff can generally expect a lower level of damages as compared to an individual plaintiff because 'a commercial company has no soul and its reputation is no more than a commercial asset, something attached to its trading name which brings in customers'.[64]

The court is not duty-bound to award substantial damages. In *Christian Anthony Bullen v Oliva Fernandez Ibarra*,[65] where the evidence and the circumstances of the trivial slander made by the plaintiff English tutor's ex-wife to the plaintiff's tutorial client suggested no harm caused to the plaintiff, nominal damages of $1 (HKD) were awarded. So too in *Chan Kwing Chiu v Chan Chi Kau*,[66] concerning a dispute between members of a residential owners' subcommittee, where $5,000 (HKD) was awarded against each defendant.

In an individual case, there may be factors which aggravate or increase the injury to the plaintiff's feelings: a failure to apologise, or malice on the part of the defendant (in the sense

[59] As in *Blakeney-Williams*, above n 57, and *Oriental Daily Publisher Ltd*, *ibid*.

[60] *Fevaworks*, above n 15, [92].

[61] Per Ribeiro PJ in *Oriental Daily Publisher Ltd*, above n 48, [66], citing Simon Brown LJ in *Mark v Associated Newspapers Ltd* [2002] EMLR 38.

[62] *Oriental Press Group Ltd v Inmediahk.net Ltd* [2012] 2 HKLRD 1004 (CFI), citing *Al Amoudi v Brisard* [2007] 1 WLR 113, *Trumm v Norman* [2008] EWHC 116 (QB), and *Brady v Norman* [2008] EWHC 2481 (QB).

[63] *Cairns v Modi* [2012] EWCA Civ 1382 (CA); *John Raymond Luciw v Wolfgang Derler* (unreported, HCA 2148/2011, 29 July 2013, CFI). The court in *Luciw* found it 'reasonable to infer that the dissemination of the defamation by the use of Facebook meant that the publication of the defamatory statements were both inside and outside Hong Kong' ([35]). See also *Yeung v Google*, above n 25, [164]: 'In internet cases, there is no presumption of substantial publication.'

[64] Reyes J in *Yaqoob v Asia Times Online Ltd*, above n 38, [159], quoting Lord Hoffmann in *Jameel v Wall Street Journal Europe*, above n 30.

[65] *Christian Anthony Bullen v Oliva Fernandez Ibarra* (unreported, DCCJ 3008/2007, 10 February 2009, DC).

[66] *Chan Kwing Chiu v Chan Chi Kau* (unreported, HCA 505/2007, 23 July 2012, DC), plaintiffs' appeal dismissed (unreported, CACV 209/2012, 3 October 2013, CA).

of spite or an intention to hurt), or a plea of justification when it is not viable on the facts might be examples. In such cases the court may award aggravated damages.

To qualify for an award of aggravated damages, it is important that the plaintiff adduce some evidence as to injury to feelings. There is no basis for presuming aggravated pain and suffering in a given case: 'that must be a matter of evidence, depending on the circumstances, such as the robustness or vulnerabilities of the plaintiffs in question'.[67]

Moreover, the mere fact that a defendant sticks to its defence of justification and does not offer an apology does not mean that an award of aggravated damages is indicated. The decision, in good faith, to rely on justification and therefore to not offer an apology may be entirely reasonable in the facts of the case.[68] Given their function, it is evident that aggravated damages are not really a separate category of damages but are part of compensatory damages. Unfortunately, judges very often treat them as two categories.[69] This has the tendency to inflate the damages awarded, and also comes close to reintroducing exemplary (punitive) damages. This makes a good case for the adoption of a global award for aggravated and general damages, as has been adopted by the English courts.[70]

Conclusion

Some change is taking place, but needless to say, change is slow and incremental, and perhaps unavoidably, has produced inconsistent results in some of the decisions of the lower courts. The challenges being thrown up by the changing technology and the changing political environment do not lend themselves to obvious or simple solutions, certainly not to solutions with which everyone or even a majority would agree. An examination of the recent case law suggests that the courts are feeling their way slowly, understandably reluctant to commit to any political agenda, whether in support of a free Internet, or freedom of political speech. Development of defamation law in Hong Kong will be a step-by-step process and will be led by the courts. A picture is emerging of a legal environment that will not be particularly liberal in favouring freedom of speech and the press over protection of reputation, and that no significant breaks with Hong Kong's traditionally conservative approach can be expected.

[67] per Ribeiro PJ in *Oriental Daily Publisher Ltd*, above n 46, [128].

[68] As in *Blakeney-Williams*, above n 57, where the CFA agreed with the Court of Appeal's decision to set aside the trial judge's award of aggravated damages.

[69] See, eg, *Sin Cho Chiu v Tin Tin Publication Development Ltd* (unreported, HCA 6662/1997, 11 January 2002, CFI) and *Lee Ching v Lau May Ming* [2007] 3 HKLRD 623 (CFI).

[70] 'All the three heads of damages are "at large". In England, the practice in defamation cases has been to make a global award for general damages and aggravated damages instead of making separate awards for each head. In *Broome v Cassell & Co Ltd*, the House of Lords expressed preference for a single sum award even where there is an element of exemplary damages. A single sum award is convenient and reduces the risk of double-counting. It is particularly preferable for trial by jury. A split award has the advantage of underlining the factors considered for the different heads of damages and if the court has taken an unfavourable view of the defendant and the reasons. In this judgment, I shall make split awards in view of its obvious advantages'—see *Lo Sam Shing v Li Fong* (unreported, HCA 1803/2011, 14 March 2014, CFI) [135].

8

China's Defamation Law: The Contest Between Criminal and Civil Defamation Law

XU XUN*

Academic discussions of China's defamation laws have only a short history of around 30 years and have been divided into two phases. The start of the second phase in 2001 was when the development of defamation laws began to tread in deep waters—how to deal with the regulation of media and public expression on public issues became a typical dilemma. To this day, there remains no clear solution to the problem. Between academic debate and legislative inaction, the development of civil law has become weak, in turn giving criminal and administrative law the necessary space to grow and take force. The Joint Interpretation on Internet Speech Crimes and its application will become the new focal point of research and observation of China's defamation law.

The concept of 'Chinese defamation law' referred to in this chapter is an academic one, and refers to the relevant provisions and judicial interpretations of Chinese constitutional law, criminal law, civil law (especially tort law) and administrative law (especially public security administration and punishment law), which make up the framework of defamation law in China. A special set of practices exists in the area of defamation relating to media and media professionals and has always been an important point of study in Chinese defamation, garnering concerns of both the legal field and society alike.

Unlike Anglo-American defamation laws that have several hundred years of history, China's defamation laws have only been around for about 30 years. It was first introduced in 1979 as criminal law. If we look back at the timeline of China's defamation laws in the media, I believe the developments can be divided into two phases.

The First Phase: 1979 to 2001

The period starts in 1979, when defamation became a criminal offence, and ends with the Supreme People's Court's adoption of the Interpretation of the Supreme People's Court

* First presentation of this chapter was given in October 2013, at the University of Hong Kong's Media Law and Policy in the Internet Age Conference. The first edit of the chapter was made on 30 June 2014, while the second edit and final draft was made on 24 January 2016.

on Problems regarding the Ascertainment of Compensation Liability for Emotional Damages in Civil Tort in 2001. The distinguishing feature of this phase is the birth of Chinese defamation, the establishment of an initial framework, and plenty of judicial practice.

This phase enjoyed a rather long time span—a total of 22 years, with civil and criminal defamation law each developing in a timely manner and bringing preliminary systematic regulations to some of the more basic and fundamental issues. In fact, the extreme speed at which the country developed surpassed the hundred, or even few hundred years that more developed countries had taken to walk down the same path. (See Appendix 1 below for a detailed chronology of this phase.) A lot of academic research was done during this phase, but there were few academic debates. There are two points worth noting: firstly, that with the introduction of civil defamation, it was no longer appropriate to apply the criminal offence to reporters carrying out their job duties. Secondly, there was also a gradual increase in the number of claims brought by state agencies and officials against the media. This showed that the development of China's media defamation litigation was beginning to face much more deep-seated problems.

The Second Phase: 2001 to 2013

This period spans between the adoption of the Interpretation of the Supreme People's Court on Problems regarding the Ascertainment of Compensation Liability for Emotional Damages in Civil Tort in 2001 by the Supreme People's Court and the adoption of the Interpretation of the Supreme People's Court on Handling Criminal Defamation on the Internet by the Supreme People's Court and the Supreme People's Procuratorate in 2013. (See Appendix 2 below for a detailed chronology of this phase.) The main feature of this phase is the weak development of civil defamation law, resulting in the law's lessened impact on social relations, while criminal defamation and administrative law made great strides from legislation to implementation. The development of China's defamation laws began to tread in deep waters and establishing rules on expressing public issues became a prevalent problem.

The following features appeared in this particular period. Firstly, development of civil legislation was slow. From the timeline provided in Appendix 2 below, from 2001, it seemed that legislation for civil defamation in China entered a stagnant state. Although there were two National People's Congress decisions made in this period,[1] neither of them directly dealt with the problem of defamation. Since the entry into force of the Tort Law of the People's Republic of China in 2010, there has yet to be a judicial interpretation on civil defamation. In other words, there have not been much new developments in the area of civil defamation in the past decade.

I believe there are two reasons for this. The first explanation is that in the 1990s, when China underwent rapid economic development, there was a great need to solve problems

[1] See Tort Law of the People's Republic of China, which came into effect 1 July 2010 and The Decision of the Standing Committee of the National People's Congress on Strengthening Information Protection on Networks, introduced at the end of 2012.

using civil law. In debating how to draft up the civil codes, the preferred model was to introduce legislation in stages. Thus, contract law, property law, intellectual property law and marital law were not only promulgated in quick succession, but some have even been modified a few times. Personal rights law, on the other hand, was barely developed at all. The second explanation is that after the Supreme People's Court's two judicial interpretations on the right of reputation,[2] it could be said that the foundation of civil defamation laws had begun to take shape. But in terms of priorities, the need to develop defamation laws was not as urgent compared to the need for legislation to aid the development of the economy.

In fact, efforts from Chinese academics and the press circle to perfect civil defamation law never ceased. In 2002, a civil law scholar was commissioned to begin drafting the Draft Proposal of the Personal Rights Act of the People's Republic of China.[3] Since then, Professor Yang Lixin from the Law Faculty of the Renmin University of China directed at least two important research projects on similar topics.[4] The Chinese media were aware that development in civil defamation law was lacking, and in 2006, the All-China Journalists Association completed the Proposed Draft on a New Judicial Interpretation on Press Infringement on Reputation and Privacy. The document was formally submitted to the Supreme People's Court in April 2007, but no official reply was received.[5] During the consultation period on the drafting of tort liability laws, media law scholars and members of the All-China Journalists Association convened a special meeting to express their views and advocate for a special article or provision for 'media infringement' under tort law, but their suggestions were not adopted.[6] The results of these suggestions, comments and research show that although members of the academia may have yet to settle on the concept of 'media infringement',[7] from the start, they and professionals in the industry have all been concerned with the sluggish development of civil defamation. They have aspired and put in a great deal of effort to improve and perfect this area of law. However, until now, the legislative and administrative organs have not responded. Furthermore, the different opinions of academics and media professionals have given the indecisive legislative body a further excuse to postpone, or even shelve any legislative discussion on civil defamation.

[2] See the 1993 Reply of the Supreme People's Court to the Questions in the Trial of Cases Concerning the Right of Reputation and the 1998 Interpretation of the Supreme People's Court on the Trial of the Case Concerning Right of Reputation.

[3] See Wang Liming (ed), 'Foreword', *Zhongguo minfa dian cao'an jianyi gao ji shuoming* (Chinese Civil Law Draft Proposal and Instructions) (Law Press China 2004).

[4] See comments in the 2006 *Zhonghua renmin gonghe guo qinquan zeren fa cao'an zunjia jianyi gao* (People's Republic of China Tort Law Draft and Instructions) and the already published *Zhongguo meiti qinquan zeren anjian falu shiyong zhiyin* (Judicial Handbook on Media Infringement Cases) (People's Court Press 2013).

[5] See Xu Xun (ed), *New Research on the Tort of News Media* (China Law Press 2009) 337–340 for full text of the 2007 Proposed Draft.

[6] See Li Guomin and Wang Lili, '*Xinwen qinquan bu ke deng xian shi zhi*' (Media infringement should not be underestimated), *Procuratorial Daily* (23 February 2009); Song Shijing, '*Qinquan zeren fa cao'an: Si Da Xuannian dai Jiekai*' (Draft Media Tort Law: Four questions to be answered), *Procuratorial Daily* (2 November 2009); Wang Shouli, '*Zhongguo ji xie: meiti ying xiangyou si xiang huomian quan*' (ACJA: Media should be granted four immunities), *Southern Weekly* (29 October 2009).

[7] A heated debate arose during the consultation period on the drafting of tort liability law on the question of whether 'news infringement' or 'media infringement' should be regulated separately. Two renowned professors from the Law Faculty of the Renmin University of China headed the arguments with one affirming the view and the other opposing the view.

On 10 October 2014, the long-awaited Provisions of the Supreme People's Court on Several Issues concerning the Application of Law in the Trial of Cases Involving Civil Disputes over Infringements upon Personal Rights and Interests through Information Networks finally came into effect. In the space of 19 provisions and approximately 3,600 words, the legislation set out the litigation system to deal with infringement of personal rights through the Internet (including the right to reputation), a major advancement in Chinese civil defamation laws. However, to what extent this will slow the application of criminal defamation laws remains to be seen.

Secondly, in the wake of new media developments, a typical dilemma that arose was how to regulate the dissemination of information and the discussion of public issues. The public authorities tried several different methods to regulate expression.

Statistics showed that since the civil code (General Principles of the Civil Law of the People's Republic of China) came into force in 1987, state agencies and officials began to bring claims against the media for infringement of reputation, although this was not brought to light in the beginning. However, in 1995, these types of litigation became popular; the number of cases peaked in 1999 before gradually decreasing, until there were no more cases in 2007.[8] In other words, the phenomenon of state agencies and officials suing the media and other defendants took about ten years to adjust itself: rising from zero to a peak, and then falling back to zero. Since 2007, there were no more significant civil litigation in defamation anymore—in the areas concerning the expression of public issues, plaintiffs (that is, state agencies and officials who claim they were victims of libel) have all but abandoned reliance on the system of civil defamation.

At the same time, public prosecution of defamation began to appear more frequently. Statistics show that from 2006 to 2010, there were more than 20 cases of public prosecution of defamation or administrative detentions relating to suspected defamation. Persons facing allegations of defamation included normal citizens and media professionals, while alleged victims of defamation were almost always local party leaders. Most of these cases were later revoked or corrected.[9] The Ministry of Public Security issued a notice in 2009 pointing out that 'there were some local public security organs who were not able to correctly handle libel claims';[10] and the Supreme People's Procuratorate also issued a notice in 2010, requiring procurators to obtain approval from a higher-level procuratorate before issuing arrest warrants,[11] but it was still difficult to eliminate the widespread abuse of power

[8] See Zhu Li and Yang Huizhen, '*Zhongguo meiti qinquan anjian tongji baogao*' (General Report of News Media Infringement in China) in Xu Xun (ed), *An Inquiry into News Media Torts* (Law Press China 2009) 64.

[9] Lei Lili, '*Feibang de chu zui huayan*' (Research on the Decriminalisation of Libel) (Master thesis, Central University for Nationalities 2009).

[10] On 3 April 2009, the Ministry of Public Security issued a directive—'2009 Ministry of Public Security Directive on how public security organs nationwide should treat criminal defamation cases in strict accordance with the law'—stating that 'some local public security organs were not able to properly handle criminal defamation cases. On the surface it was caused by an inaccurate understanding of the law; on a deeper level, it was caused by internal contradictions and lack of clear understanding of the people's rights.' See *Fabao.cn* www.fabao.cn accessed July 2016.

[11] The Supreme People's Procuratorate increased the level of authority required for the approval of issuing arrest warrants for defamation charges in 2010, requiring that 'in the coming period, when public security organs request for an arrest warrant relating to defamation offences, and the Procuratorate after reviewing the case considers it necessary to make an arrest, higher level authority must be obtained.' (See *Procuratorate Daily*, 7 August 2010).

used to suppress public expression. Not only did Wang Lijun, the former head of the Public Security Bureau of Chongqing, use shuangqi lun (double effect theory)[12] to threaten media in flagrant violation of the law, he also used the re-education through labour system to sanction critics of the system. This resulted in a number of cases[13] that ultimately led to the abolition of re-education through labour from the Chinese legal system.

The examples above show that to control and shape public expression involves allowing citizens the right to make criticisms, suggestions, and complaints and to litigate against state agencies and government officials. But the development of civil defamation in China has remained sluggish, and after ten years of inaction, it was now insufficient and outdated. As a result, this gave way for criminal defamation and administrative sanctions to develop. At the rapid rate new media technology is impacting society, it is foreseeable that criminal litigation and administrative sanctions will only gain momentum going forward.

Thirdly, in an attempt to forcibly regulate defamation, the Supreme People's Court and the Supreme People's Procuratorate made defamation offences indictable on public prosecution in the Interpretation on the Criteria for Convicting and Sentencing Offenders who Spread Rumours Online that Defame Individuals or Organisations.

Chinese criminal law expressly provides that defamation is an offence only if complaints are made; that is to say, defamation is treated as private litigation. However, there is an exception: 'except where it causes serious harm to public order and national interests.' On 10 September 2013, the Supreme People's Court and the Supreme People's Procuratorate issued an interpretation to refine the exceptions to the general offence, which could either imply the possibility of greater use of public prosecution in the future, or be understood as a more stringent reading of the terms that make up the libel offence. The judicial interpretation also refined the scope of the offence by re-defining the meaning of 'fabricating facts to defame others' and 'in serious cases', greatly enriching the law regarding criminal defamation.

It is worthy to observe the judiciary's practice following the interpretation by the Supreme People's Court and the Supreme People's Procuratorate. The first case in which the interpretation was applied came from Gansu, where the detainee was a 17-year-old teenager. The police's misinterpretation of the law and its arbitrary use of the law not only led to widespread criticism of the incident,[14] this particular case also became a reminder to the public to stay vigilant of the authorities' gross interference with the freedom of expression.

[12] Former Chongqing Head of Security Bureau Wang Lijun said, 'From today on, whenever newspapers twist the truth to attack our security bureau and local police, we will prosecute the media company and its writer as one unit. If he mentions a particular member of the force and it leads to consequences, the local police will take the evidence to court and sue the writer, and the security bureau will sue the media company. This is called the "Double Effect Theory"' See Jiang Tao, '*Jingcha zhengdang weiquan yu Wang Lijun shangqi lun*' (Legitimate police powers and Wang Lijun's double effect theory), *Chongqing Evening News* (19 November 2010).

[13] '*Chongqing jiu cuo di yi an shengsu yinfa bei laojiao renyuan shensu langchao*' (Success of the first corrected case in Chongqing sparked wave of labour camp prisoners seeking redress), *Urban Times* (26 October 2012).

[14] Seventeen-year-old Yang Mou posted online his suspicions that the local police had mishandled a murder case. The police claimed that he had 'used the Internet to fabricate facts, caused a public disturbance and caused the online post to be forwarded 500 times' and detained him on the charge of 'creating a public disturbance'. See *Jinghua Daily* (19 September 2013). When the news got out, the police's opinion was widely questioned: the act of 'forwarding more than 500 times' was only applicable to a defamation charge, but not on a charge of creating a public disturbance. The police later stated that 'Yang Mou was still a minor, had actively cooperated with the

The Supreme People's Court and the Supreme People's Procuratorate issued the Joint Interpretation on Several Issues Regarding the Applicable Law in Cases of Using Information Networks to Commit Defamation and Other Such Crimes in September 2013, but there have been extremely few criminal defamation cases since its promulgation.

Some of the more well-known cases of public prosecution of defamation include: Qin Zhihui, also known as Qin Huohuo online, who was sentenced to three years in prison by the court of first instance for creating a public disturbance;[15] Fu Xuesheng, who was imprisoned for a period of two years and nine months for defamation.[16] Of course, there are also a number of cases where prosecution failed, such as the case of Liu Hu, a reporter from Guangzhou's *Xin Kuaibao* who was accused of defamation, although the case ended when prosecutors issued an official letter not to prosecute.[17] A point worth noting is that in all three cases of defamation, the defamed victims are either officials or influential people in society,[18] These events further illustrate what I meant by typical dilemmas above.

On 29 August 2015, the Chinese People's Congress issued the Ninth Amendment to the Criminal Law of the People's Republic of China, which added a third paragraph: 'If the defamed victim reports a case on information networks to the People's Court but has insufficient proof, the People's Court may request for police aid.' I believe the legal system has realised the difficulty of having natural persons search for defamation instances online, and thus, the new amendment is an effort to bring criminal defamation back to civil defamation. As for how effective this new law is would require further observation.

The threat of defamation litigation is the first enemy to the freedom of expression. Since the rule of law should hold minimal control over the right to free expression, we advocate that in regards to the regulation of expression, if we can self-discipline, then we do not need third-party controls; if things can be handled under civil law, then criminal law is not necessary; if private litigation is sufficient, then we do not need public prosecution. If it is appropriate to use alternative punishments (such as depriving a person's political rights, or imposing a fine), then one should not be deprived of their personal freedom. With

investigation and had shown sincere repentance. The provincial public security authorities therefore decided after investigation that they would withdraw the criminal charge accordingly, and give Yang a light sentence.' He was placed under administrative detention for just seven days. See Chinese National Radio (23 September 2013) http://cnr.cn accessed July 2016. The so-called 'dramatic ending' was due to citizens' heightened interest in the incident, which uncovered a number of old cases whose judgments were never executed. Under heavy criticism, the local police chief involved in the case was suspended. See '*Zhang jia chuan guanwang shenye fa xiaoxi xuanbu gong'an juzhang Bai Yongqiang bei tingzhi*' (Zhang province official website announces late night that police chief Bai Yongqiang has been suspended), *Jinghua Daily* (24 September 2013).

[15] See '*Qin Huohuo an panjue yaodian*' (The main points on Qin Huohuo's verdict), *Xinhuanet.com* (17 April 2014).

[16] See '*zhongshihua feizhou niu lang men deng yaoyan zhizao zhe fu xuesheng yin feibang zui huo xing*' (Fu Xuesheng found guilty of fabricating rumours about Sinopec official), *Xinhuanet.com* (13 November 2014).

[17] See '*yuan xin kuaibao jizhe liu hu bei mian yu qisu ceng shiming jubao huárun dongshi zhang song lin*' (Xin Kuaibao reporter Liu Hu, who reported on China Resources CEO Song Lin, exempted from prosecution), *Beijing Times* (12 September 2015); '*duihua "feibang an" bei ju jizhe Liu Hu: Zui hao de ziwo baohu jiushi bu jubao*' (A conversation with reporter Liu Hu, accused of defamation: The best protection you can give yourself is to not report), *ifeng.com special report episode 385* (11 September 2015).

[18] According to media reports, the three 'defamed victims' include government officials on the deputy ministerial level, judges, police chiefs, CPPCC members, leaders of large state-owned enterprises and generals.

defamation laws (including defamation of goodwill), public prosecution should only be a nation's last resort, and it should be held to the highest standard of judicial review. From the standpoint of the principles advocated above, it is difficult not to conclude that in the area of Chinese defamation law, civil law, criminal law and administrative law maintain an objective and correlative relationship, such that where one falls the other one rises. Freedom and regulation are a contrasting pair—where civil law is substandard, inadequate, disused, particularly where the government believes that it is incapable of maintaining order, criminal law and administrative law will be given reason and space to develop.

I believe, even though the international trend is to decriminalise defamation laws, that is, to remove the offence of defamation from criminal laws,[19] and even though a Chinese scholar has also suggested a four-step solution for speech crimes,[20] due to many factors at this point of time, China does not have the prerequisites to abolish public prosecution of defamation. The laws have very clearly set out the prohibitions regarding defamation, but under the shadow of the Cultural Revolution's legacy, and also limited by the country's media literacy, there is a serious lack of consensus amongst the ordinary people's standards of expression. Even intellectuals are prone to be held liable under the law for insult and slander.[21] For media professionals too, their regulatory bodies and professional norms are still a far cry from objective standards. In this Internet age where 'everyone has a microphone', there will indeed be individuals who will defame and disrupt social order with malicious intentions.[22] Of course, public society must always remain aware of the potential abuse of the criminal defamation system.

In order to truly decriminalise defamation, a series of significant adjustments to the existing system must be made, the very first being to improve the civil law system. The first thing to do would be to get civil defamation law out of its current state of inaction, which it has been in for the past ten years. Although the Provisions of the Supreme People's Court on Several Issues concerning the Application of Law in the Trial of Cases Involving Civil

[19] Zheng Wenming, '*Xifang guojia feibang fa zhong ruogan zhongyao wenti*' (Important issues surrounded defamation law in western countries) in *An Inquiry into News Media Torts*, above n 8, 299.

[20] Zhan Jiang and Qiao Zhenqi, '*Jiejue "yin yan huo zui" de si bu zou zhanlue*' (A four-step solution to "speech crimes") in *An Inquiry into News Media Torts*, ibid 135.

[21] Typical cases in this respect are 'the rant of Kong Qingdong' and 'the libel of Zhang Xian'. The defendant in the first case was Chinese professor Kong Qingdong from the Peking University. He was found guilty of defamation by the Court of First Instance in the Beijing Haiding district court, after he called Internet users 'dog traitors' on his blog. See '*Kong Qingdong Weibo maren'an yuangao zishu wo gao Kong Qingdong zhe yi nian*' (The case of Kong Qingdong: the plaintiff shares his year of suing Kong Qingdong), *Beijing Evening News* (13 May 2013). The defendant in the second case was Zhang Xian, an associate professor in inorganic non-metallic materials at the Wuhan University of Science and Technology, who spread false rumours about Yao Jiaxin (a convict on death penalty) and his father Yao Qingwei. Using his blog and Weibo account, he accused them of being a 'second generation army kid', 'second generation rich kid', 'army worms', and claiming that the 'Yao family has four estates'. He was found guilty of damaging the reputation of others in 2012 in the Xi'an Intermediate People's Court. See '*Yao Qingwei su Zhang Xian mingyu qinquan'an sheng su*' (Yao Qingwei successfully sues Zhang Xian for damage to reputation), *The Beijing News* (11 August 2012).

[22] See, eg, the 2009 case of the AIDS girl Yan Deli. After a failed relationship, her former boyfriend Yang Yongmeng deliberately retaliated by opening a Weibo account as Yan, claiming that 'she' has contracted AIDS and having lost hope in life, desired to get her 15 minutes of fame. At the same time, Yang also published a 'list of sexual contacts', building it from more than 200 contacts Yan had on her phone. The action caused widespread concern and the online posts went viral, causing panic in some areas. The case was publicly prosecuted and Yang received a three-year prison sentence for the insult. See '*Hebei aizi nu Yan Deli shijian zhizaozhe bei pan san nian*' (The accused in the Hebei AIDs girl Yan Deli case receives a three-year sentence), *Jinhua Daily* (10 April 2010).

Disputes over Infringements upon Personal Rights and Interests through Information Networks has come into effect, providing parts of a framework for online defamation in civil law, we are still a long way from having a civil defamation law that is sufficient and efficient. A long-term solution would be to bring the People's Republic of China Personal Rights Law to the legislation table as soon as possible, in order to enrich and improve the area of civil defamation law. Apart from legislation, we also need to see judges with the courage to explore options, and in their judicial practice, come up with solutions and breakthroughs in terms of the 'typical dilemmas' mentioned above. Only when public prosecution of defamation becomes a mere suspended sword, to have but not to use, can China truly begin to decriminalise defamation laws. And only when freedom of expression in China's constitution can find its footing, alongside building up effective self-regulatory bodies for media professionals and media agencies, will China have found the ideal form of freedom of speech.

Appendix 1: First Phase of the Development of China's Media Defamation Laws (1979–2001)

Legislation	Year	Judicial Practice
Defamation is established as an offence under criminal law, signifying the emergence of the concept of 'defamation' under new Chinese laws.	1979	
The 1982 Constitution is promulgated, announcing 38 new offences against libel and slander.	1982	
	1985	The first media lawsuit in China was a private defamation claim in Shanghai, brought by Du Rong against two reporters who reported on the French publication *Democracy and Law.*[23]
General Principles of the Civil Law of the People's Republic of China takes effect. Article 101 provides that all citizens enjoy the right to reputation.	1987	Shanghai sees a rise in defamation litigation against reporters, with most plaintiffs being normal citizens.
	1990	Beijing sees a rise in defamation litigation against reporters, with most plaintiffs being cultural and sports stars.

(continued)

[23] For details of the action and appeal, see Wang Song Miao, '*Xin Zhongguo xinwen guansi di yi an, rang ren yisheng tanxi*' (People sigh over New China's first media lawsuit), *Chinese News (Media) Fifty Selected Cases of Infringement and Analysis* (Law Press China 2009), 397.

Appendix 1: (Continued)

Legislation	Year	Judicial Practice
The Interpretation of the Supreme People's Court on Several Issues about the Trial of Cases Concerning the Right of Reputation was adopted, with 11 new provisions on registration, jurisdiction, reputation of the deceased, news criticism, the standard for truth and responsibility in civil defamation law.	1993	Rise in defamation litigation brought by commercial and legal entities; litigation occurring all over the country.
	1996	A court in Sichuan awarded RMB5,000,000 in damages, the highest in a media infringement case.
Criminal Law amended, with Article 221 providing two new defamation offences against reputation of businesses. Criminal defamation begins to distinguish between natural and legal persons.	1997	The Court of Appeal of Shenzhen Futian District successfully sued the *Workers' Daily* for damage to reputation, marking the first time a Chinese court brought an action against the media.[24]
The adoption of the Interpretation of the Supreme People's Court on Several Issues about the Trial of Cases Concerning the Right of Reputation further refined civil defamation law. The 11 provisions include internal control, reprint, internal mechanism to decide if civil litigation is appropriate, libel prosecution, state news sources, general news sources, and product and services supervision.	1998	
	1999	Actions brought by state agencies and officials against the media for damage to reputation reach a peak, with 16 cases per year.[25]
The Interpretation of the Supreme People's Court on Problems regarding the Ascertainment of Compensation Liability for Emotional Damages in Civil Torts was adopted; civil litigation of defamation sees gradual improvement.	2001	Defamation cases against the media entered a three to five years period of relative stability.

[24] See decision from the Intermediate People's Court in Shenzhen Guangdong province: 1995 见广东省深圳市中级人民法院民事判决书 (1995) 深圳特区中法民初字第 021号。

[25] See Zhu Li and Yang Huizhen, above n 8, 64.

Appendix 2: Second Phase of the Development of China's Media Defamation Laws (2001–2013)

Research and Legislative Proposals	Legislative Process	Year	Judicial Practice
Xu Xun noted that the trend of state agencies and officials bringing actions against the media posed a challenge to the legal system.[26]		2002	Fan Zhiyi's action against *The Oriental Sports Daily* failed. It is the first case where the Chinese court applied the public interest test.[27]
		2005	Dan Zhidong, a citizen from Shanghai, believed that removal of websites constituted an invasion of the right to freedom of expression, but the court dismissed his civil case. Dan Zhidong is hailed as the nation's first netizen to fight for his right to free speech on the Internet.[28]
Yang Lixin completed the 'Expert Proposal for Tort Liability Laws', creating nine special categories of' media infringement', including internet infringement.[29] The Legislative Affairs Commission consulted the media industry but opinions were split, with the All-China Journalists Association in the opposition.		2006	Cases of abusing unlawful defamation offences to sanction expression began to appear, including the Wuhe SMS case (Dong Guoping case),[30] and the Pengshui poem scandal (Qin Zhongfei case).[31] Most of the judgments in these cases were eventually corrected.

(continued)

[26] See Xu Xun, '*Zhongguo xinwen qinquan goufen de di si ci langchao*' (The Fourth Wave of Dispute on Media Infringement in China) *China Youth Daily* (11 February 2002).

[27] See Qingan (Shanghai) People's Court decision: (2002) 見上海市静安区人民法院民事判决書 (2002) 静民一民初字第 1776号。

[28] See *China Youth Daily* (7 April 2005); *Shanxi Evening News* (8 April 2005); *Oriental Daily* (14 June 2005).

[29] See Yang Lixin, *Zhonghua renmin gonghe guo qinquan zeren fa cao'an jianyi gao ji shuoming* (People's Republic of China Tort Law Draft and Instructions) (Law Press China 2007).

[30] See Li Shen, '*Wuhe Jiaoshi Duanxin an Yinchu Tanguan Shuji*' (Wuhe teacher's text message draws out corrupt party secretary) *Beijing Youth Daily* (*YNET.com*, 11 June 2010).

[31] See '*Pengshui si an*' (Pengshui Poem Scandal), *Baidu* http://baike.baidu.com/view/813180.htm accessed July 2016.

Appendix 2: (Continued)

Research and Legislative Proposals	Legislative Process	Year	Judicial Practice
The All-China Journalists Association officially submitted the 'Proposed Draft on a New Judicial Interpretation on Press Infringement on Reputation and Privacy', totaling 10 provisions.[32] No response was received.		2007	Cases brought against the media by state agencies and officials fall to zero.[33] Beijing Television reporter Zi Beijia, who created the cardboard-bun hoax, became the first reporter to be jailed for fabricating news and damaging others' business reputation.[34]
The issue of whether specific adjustments should be made in the tort laws relating to media infringement led to widespread open debates amongst academics.[35]		2008	Police in Liaoning, Xifeng County arrested reporter Zhu Wenna on the offence of attempt to libel, but case was dismissed.[36] This case became the first in which a journalist was prosecuted on defamation charges.
The Research Centre of Media Law at the Chinese University of Political Science and Law and the All-China Journalists Association jointly researched and submitted a draft on adjustments to be made in tort law regarding 'media infringements',[37] but the draft has not been adopted.	The Ministry of Public Security issued a notice, stressing that 'libel cases generally belong in private prosecution.'[38]	2009	From the end of October 2009 to August 2010, of the 16 more typical cases concerning the internet, 10 of them involved county officials.[39]

(continued)

[32] See *New Research on the Tort of News Media*, above n 5.

[33] See Zhu Li and Yang Huizhen, above n 8, 64.

[34] See Beijing No 2 Intermediate People's Court decision: 見北京市第二中級人民法院刑事判决書 (2007) 二中刑初字第 1763号.

[35] The arguments for both sides of the debate are encapsulated in Zhang Xinbao, '*Xinwen (Meiti) Qinquan Foudingshuo*' (News Media Infringement Negation Theory), *China Legal Science* (Issue 6, 2008); Yang Lixin, '*Wo guo de Meiti Qinquan Zeren yu Meiti Quanli Baohu—jian yu Zhang Xinbao Jiaoshou "Xinwen (Meiti) Qinquan Foudingshuo" Shangque*' (My Country's Media Tort Liability and Protection of Media Rights—Discussion with Professor Zhang Xinbao's 'News Media Infringement Negation Theory'), *China Legal Science* (Issue 6, 2011).

[36] See Yang Chengjun and Fan Chunsheng, '*Xifeng xian Gong'an ju Chexiao dui Zhu Wenna de Li'an, Juchuan*' (Public Security Bureau of Xifeng county to withdraw probe and arrest warrant on Zhu Wenna), (*Xinhua Net*, 9 January 2008) http://news.xinhuanet.com/legal/2008-01/09/content_7389210.htm accessed July 2016.

[37] See Li Guomin and Wang Lili, '*Xinwen Qinquan buke dengxian shi zhi*' (Media infringement should not be underestimated), *Procuratorial Daily* (23 February 2009); Song Shijing, '*Qinquan Zerenfa Cao'an: Si Da Xuannian dai Jiekai*' (Draft Media Tort Law: Four questions to be answered), *Procuratorial Daily* (2 November 2009).

[38] Above n 10.

[39] '*Wangluo dazi bao rang xianguan yaomo hua*' (County official 'demonized' online), *Banyuetan (China Comment)*, (*people.cn*, 12 January 2011).

Appendix 2: (Continued)

Research and Legislative Proposals	Legislative Process	Year	Judicial Practice
Yang Lixin started a project to create the *Judicial Handbook on Media Infringement Cases* that studies the trial principles of civil defamation.[40]	Tort Law of the People's Republic of China came into force, including 36 provisions that involve media and expression. The Supreme People's Procuratorate issued a notice to raise the level of authority required for approving arrest warrants for public prosecution of defamation offences.[41]	2010	Former head of Public Security Bureau, Wang Lijun, pitched *Shangqi Lun* (Double Effect Theory).[42] The nation saw a rise in police detention in defamation cases.[43]
		2011	Netizen Zhang Sha was detained by the police on a charge of defamation following comments she posted on the microblogging service, Weibo. The allegedly 'defamed' Ren Zhiqiang claims he was unaware of the events.[44]
Following the Fang Hong case, three lawyers suggested to the National People's Congress to hold a review on the constitutionality of the re-education through labour system.[45]	The Decision of the Standing Committee of the National People's Congress on Strengthening Information Protection on Networks was announced, requiring real names to be used on the Internet.	2012	In Chongqing, critics on the Internet were sanctioned through the re-education through labour system, following the Fang Hong case.[46] These cases are gradually being corrected.

(continued)

[40] See Yang Lixin (ed), 'Author's Note', *Zhongguo meiti qinquan zeren anjian falu shiyong zhiyin* (Judicial Handbook on Media Infringement Cases) (People's Court Press 2013).

[41] Above n 11.

[42] Above n 12.

[43] Above n 9.

[44] See '*Wangmin paishe qiangchai bei yi feibang juliu, Ren Zhiqiang cheng mei bao'an*' (Netizens filming demolitions were arrested on defamation charges, Ren Zhiqiang yet to make a police report), *Yangcheng Evening News* (8 December 2010) www.focus.cn accessed July 2016.

[45] See lawyer Yuan Yulai's blog post on JCRB.com: '*Yi ta shi laojiao an di san an: gei quanguo renda changweihui de weixian shencha jianyi*' (The third labour camp case: judicial review by the National People's Congress Standing Committee is suggested) (*JCRB.com*, 26 June 2012) http://yuanyulai.fyfz.cn/b/221372 accessed July 2016.

[46] Xie Yinzong, '*Chongqing jiu cuo di yi an shengsu yinfa bei laojiao renyuan shensu langchao*' (Success in the 'Chongqing corrected case' leads to rise in appeals from people under the reeducation through labour system) (ifeng.com, 26 October 2012) http://news.ifeng.com/mainland/detail_2012_10/26/18573280_0.shtml?_from_ralated accessed July 2016.

Appendix 2: (Continued)

Research and Legislative Proposals	Legislative Process	Year	Judicial Practice
	The Supreme People's Court and the Supreme People's Procuratorate issued an Interpretation on the Criteria for Convicting and Sentencing Offenders who Spread Rumours Online that Defame Individuals or Organisations, significantly narrowing the scope of criminal defamation.	2013	Several reporters were arrested on various charges.[47] The first case to be tried after the judicial interpretation came into effect involved a teen from Gansu suspected of a cyber crime. His case was dismissed.[48]

[47] Including *New Express Daily* reporter Liu Huyin, who reported on the Head of State Administration for Industry and Commerce and was detained by Beijing police on suspicion of defamation (*The Beijing News*, 11 October 2013); *Caixin Media* legal reporter Chen Baocheng, hailed as the 'anti-demolition reporter' by the media, was detained by Shandong police on suspicion of false imprisonment offences (See *China Youth Daily*, 23 August 2013).

[48] Above n 14.

9

The Philippine Supreme Court on Cyber Libel: Lost in Overbreadth

H HARRY L ROQUE, JR *

In 2014, the Philippine Supreme Court, voting 10–5, ruled in the consolidated cases of *Disini v The Secretary of Justice*,[1] that the provision in the Cybercrimes Prevention Act on cyber libel is constitutional.[2] In so doing, the Court caused the Philippines to infringe on its treaty obligation to protect and promote freedom of expression. The Court also defied a view of the United Nations Human Rights Committee (UNHRC) that asked the Philippines to ensure that imprisonment of journalists for conviction for criminal libel should not be repeated in the future. The Committee had previously asked the country, a State Party to the International Covenant on Civil and Political Rights (ICCPR) and its Optional Protocol, to review its criminal libel legislation.

In upholding the constitutionality of libel as provided in the Cybercrimes Prevention Act, the Court reasoned that Philippine jurisprudence was already in line with international standards of freedom of expression since its jurisprudence has adopted the meaning of 'actual malice' as laid down in the seminal case of *New York Times v Sullivan*.[3] It also ruled that the view expressed by the UNHRC did not expressly ask the country to repeal its criminal libel legislation. Moreover, it ruled that the application of libel on the Internet does not result in a chilling effect on the exercise of freedom of expression because the legislation purportedly will penalise only the original authors of libelous articles on the Internet.

This chapter seeks to dispute the grounds relied upon by the Court in its ruling. It will argue that while the Philippines has adopted 'actual malice' as defined in *New York Times v Sullivan*, it has done so together with the broad definition of actual malice under civil law. It includes false statements made out of hatred, ill-will, malevolence or contempt, which in practice will have a chilling effect, particularly on statements leveled against public figures on matters of public concern. Consequently, the inconsistencies under Philippine law

* The author was party petitioner to the constitutional challenge against the Cybercrimes Prevention Act of 2012 and argued that the law's provisions against libel and cybersex were unconstitutional.

[1] *Disini v The Secretary of Justice*, GR No 203335, 11 February 2014, accessible at www.lawphil.net/judjuris/juri2014/feb2014/gr_203335_2014.html accessed July 2016.

[2] Cybercrimes Prevention Act, Republic Act No 10175 (2012). It is reported that Senator Vicente Sotto III proposed the addition of the offence of libel to Senate Bill No 2796 in January 2012 because as he later stated, 'there are numerous abuses in technology, particularly the video and photo uploading and unnecessary write-ups and comments in social networking systems', see Norman Bordadora, 'Sotto admits he proposed online libel provision', *Inquier.net*, 2 October 2012.

[3] *New York Times v Sullivan*, 376 US 254 (1964).

on the definition of actual malice would still have the effect of hampering robust and public debate on public issues.

Moreover, this chapter will argue that by dismissing the constitutional challenge on libel itself on the basis of overbreadth without addressing the issue squarely, the Court has shown itself to be lost in the doctrine's meaning for failing to appreciate how the doctrine operates. Finally, this chapter will critically evaluate the Court's conclusion that the Philippines' obligations under the ICCPR do not require it to repeal its criminal libel legislation.

The Philippine Law on Libel

The Revised Penal Code provisions on libel define it as a 'public and malicious imputation of a crime, or of a vice or defect, real or imaginary, or any act, omission, condition, status, or circumstance tending to cause dishonor, discredit or contempt of a natural or judicial person.'[4]

The Philippine Supreme Court explained why defamation is punished:

> The enjoyment of a private reputation is as much a constitutional right as the possession of life, liberty or property. It is one of those rights necessary to human society that underlie the whole scheme of civilization ... 'The law recognises the value of such a reputation, and constantly strives to give redress for its injury. It imposes upon him who attacks it by slanderous words, or libelous publication, a liability to make *full compensation* for the damage to the reputation, for the shame and obloquy, and for the injury to the feelings of the owner, which are caused by the publication of the slander or the libel ...'[5]

Philippine criminal law is of Spanish origin. Its text is derived from the Spanish Penal Code's felony of *defamacion*. It was a felony prior to the advent of freedom of expression as recognised in the Universal Declaration of Human Rights (UDHR) and the ICCPR.

Consistent with the Spanish colonial crime of *defamacion*, Philippine criminal libel law proceeds on the basis that 'every defamatory imputation is presumed to be malicious, even if it be true, if no good intention and justifiable motive for making it is shown.'[6] Philippine jurisprudence grants this legal presumption of malice to statements made against private persons. A statement made against a public figure, is defined as one:

> who, by his accomplishments, fame, or mode of living, or by adopting a profession or calling which gives the public a legitimate interest in his doings, his affairs, and his character, has become a 'public personage'[7] is not entitled to this presumption and to convict for libel one must prove 'malice in fact.'

'Malice in fact' has been ruled by the Supreme Court[8] to include the definition of actual malice in *New York Times v Sullivan*:[9] the publication of falsity knowing that it is 'false

[4] Rev Pen Code, Art 353.
[5] *Worcester v Ocampo*, 22 Phil 42 (1912), citing from *Times Publishing Company v Carlisle*, 94 FR 761 (1899).
[6] Rev Pen Code 1930, Art 354, in force from 1 January 1932.
[7] *Ayer v Capulong*, GR No 82380, 29 April 1988.
[8] *Guingging v CA*, GR No 128959, 30 September 2005 and *Borjal v CA*, GR No 126466, 14 January 1999.
[9] *Sullivan*, above n 3.

or in utter disregard thereof.' It, however, also includes the civil law definition of actual malice, that is, ill-will, hatred, malevolence and contempt.[10]

Under Article 360 of the Revised Penal Code, persons who may be liable for libel include 'the author or editor of a book or pamphlet, or the editor or business manager of a daily newspaper, magazine or serial publication ... to the same extent as if he were the author thereof. The felony is punishable with up to 6 years of imprisonment.'[11]

The Cybercrimes Prevention Act defined libel as a 'content related' offence. Section 4(c)(4) of the law conceived of libel as a cybercrime offence: 'the unlawful or prohibited acts of libel as defined in Article 355 of the Revised Penal Code, as amended, committed through a computer system or any other similar means which may be devised in the future.'[12] Three other provisions of the new law are relevant to libel as a cybercrime:

> SEC. 5. Other Offenses.—The following acts shall also constitute an offense:
>
> (a) Aiding or Abetting in the Commission of Cybercrime.—Any person who willfully abets or aids in the commission of any of the offenses enumerated in this Act shall be held liable.
>
> (b) Attempt in the Commission of Cybercrime.—Any person who willfully attempts to commit any of the offenses enumerated in this Act shall be held liable.
>
> SEC. 6. All crimes defined and penalized by the Revised Penal Code, as amended, and special laws, if committed by, through and with the use of information and communications technologies shall be covered by the relevant provisions of this Act: Provided, That the penalty to be imposed shall be one (1) degree higher than that provided for by the Revised Penal Code, as amended, and special laws, as the case may be.
>
> SEC. 7. Liability under Other Laws.—A prosecution under this Act shall be without prejudice to any liability for violation of any provision of the Revised Penal Code, as amended, or special laws.[13]

Under the foregoing, more individuals other than those mentioned in Article 360 of the Revised Penal Code may be held liable for a cybercrime. This would include what the law describes as 'aiders and abettors.' Moreover, the higher penalty for libel as a cybercrime would mean incarceration for the person found guilty of violating the act, since the maximum penalty under the Cybercrimes Prevention Act exceeds the maximum allowable penalty for felonies subject to probation and parole. Worse, conviction for libel under this law can be by way of double jeopardy, since a person can be convicted for publishing the same article under the Revised Penal Code.

The Adonis Challenge to the Cybercrimes Prevention Act

Alexander Adonis is a radio broadcaster in Davao City, Mindanao. In 2007, he was convicted for libel for a story which he broadcasted involving a former Speaker of the House

[10] *Diaz v People of the Philippines*, GR No 159787, 25 May 2007 and *Fermin v People of the Philippines*, GR No 157643, 28 March 2008.

[11] Rev Pen Code, Art 355.

[12] Rep Act No 10175 (2012), s 4(c) 4.

[13] Rep Act No 10175 (2012), ss 5, 6, 7.

of Representatives representing the city where he was broadcasting from. The former Speaker was purportedly seen running around the hallway of a hotel in Manila after he was discovered 'in the act' by the husband of the woman with whom he spent the night. The incident has since been referred to in Davao city as the 'Burlesque King' incident.

As is usual in a country which has been described as 'semi-feudal', the then speaker of the House of Representatives, the fourth highest official of the land, sued Adonis for libel in his home district. Predictably, he was found guilty allegedly because he had actual malice in his broadcast of the false narration of the 'Burlesque King' incident. What was the basis for this actual malice? He was a political supporter of the City Mayor of Davao, the political nemesis of the House Speaker.

Adonis was meted the penalty of three years of imprisonment. He served two years of imprisonment, ironically in the same jail where drug pushers and other criminals whom Adonis helped send to prison in the practice of his profession as a journalist served their sentences.

Since the Philippines is a party to the First Optional Protocol to the ICCPR, and hence recognises the jurisdiction of the UNHRC,[14] Adonis filed a communication to the UNHRC complaining that the Philippines' criminal libel law violates freedom of expression as enshrined in Article 19 of the ICCPR.

Adonis prevailed in the UNHRC and for the first time, the Committee issued a view[15] that criminal libel law violates freedom of expression. This, according to the Committee, is because imprisonment is not proportional to the interest which the legislation seeks to promote, ie the protection of the right to privacy of private individuals. It also noted that there is an alternative—civil libel. It also reiterated its General Comment No 34 which provides that truth should be a defense and that public figures should have the onus of proving actual malice. It stated:

> The Committee recalls its General Comment No. 34, according to which defamation laws must be crafted with care to ensure that they comply with [Article 19], and that they do not serve, in practice, to stifle freedom of expression. All such laws, in particular penal defamation laws, should include such defences as the defence of truth and they should not be applied with regard to those forms of expressions that are not, of their nature, subject to verification. At least with regard to comments about public figures, consideration should be given to avoiding penalising or otherwise rendering unlawful untrue statements that have been published in error but without malice. In any event, a public interest in the subject matter of the criticism should be recognized as a defence. Care should be taken by States parties to avoid excessively punitive measures and penalties. States parties should consider the decriminalisation of defamation and, in any case, the application of the criminal law should only be countenanced in the most serious of cases and imprisonment is never an appropriate penalty.[16]

The Committee also mentioned in its view that the Philippines should take steps to avoid a repetition of the incident in the future, including the review of its criminal libel law.

Instead of complying with the foregoing, the Congress of the Philippines instead enacted the Cybercrimes Prevention Act, which recognised that all publications on the Internet

[14] The First Optional Protocol to the ICCPR establishes a complaint mechanism for individuals to file directly to the UNHRC.

[15] *Adonis v Republic of the Philippines*, UNHRC Communication No 1818/2008 (2011).

[16] ibid [8.9].

are also vulnerable to prosecution for libel as a cybercrime. This is an offence not subject to probation and parole and may render an accused liable for double jeopardy because again, libel is already punished under the Revised Penal Code. Hence Adonis brought his own petition to challenge the Cybercrimes Preventions Act.

The Legal Challenge

The Adonis Petition challenged libel as a cybercrime on two grounds: first, it is overbroad and should be struck down on its face; and second, it constitutes a violation of the principle of *pacta sunt servanda*, or that treaty obligations must be complied with in good faith.

On Overbreadth

The challenge on overbreadth was on the basis that the language used by both the Revised Penal Code and the Cybercrimes Prevention Act in their provisions on libel was so broad that it could encompass legally protected speech. A challenge on a statute based on overbreadth may be done when its very existence may cause a 'chilling effect' on the exercise of the right to free speech. The Adonis challenge on the basis of overbreadth was two-pronged.

First, since the Internet is a new technology, the language of the law as to who is responsible for libel is so broad that it is bound to include those in the exercise of the right of free speech. For instance, Adonis inquired that given the language of the Revised Penal Code on who may be held responsible for libel, who [should] would be held liable for it when the crime is projected onto the Internet? Certainly, the internet service provider (ISP), the telephone company, the service provider and the networking sites themselves may be deemed to be publishers of an allegedly libelous article on the Internet. Also, given that the language of the libel statute was drafted prior to the advent of the Internet, it is not clear as to who should be held liable for the various posts on different social networking sites. For instance, it is uncertain if 'retweeting' an allegedly libelous statement would make the person retweeting liable. In the same light, there is uncertainty as to the author when an allegedly libelous remark is reposted on Facebook. It is all the more uncertain if a 'like' on Facebook would make the person pressing the like button criminally liable either as a principal or for aiding and abetting.

Second, the role of intermediaries was not considered by the statute. Although the nascent norm is that intermediaries should not incur criminal liability, many states in Southeast Asia have in fact made them liable. In Thailand for instance, intermediaries have been meted long imprisonments for failure to immediately remove comments which violate the country's *lest majeste* law. Similar controversies are likely to arise as a consequence of the Cybercrimes Prevention Act, since it is unclear if an intermediary, because it can be argued that he is the publisher of a libelous remark appearing as a comment in a blog, could be held liable for libel.

Certainly, the development of international jurisprudence in this regard has not been well settled. Other than liability of intermediaries, American courts appear to be only in the process of determining if the 'like' button on Facebook is protected speech. If it is not, then it is conceivable that like buttons may be actionable for libel but subject to defences related to public figures and issues affecting the public interest.[17]

How the American courts will resolve the matter is of import to the Philippines because Philippine courts have often had the tendency to follow the American lead. The Philippines has not only adopted fully the doctrine of *Sullivan*, but also the concept of overbreadth in statutes affecting freedom of expression. In the Philippine case of *Estrada v Sandiganbayan*,[18] the Philippine Supreme Court adopted the concept of a facial challenge to statutes on the basis of overbreadth. This means that the governmental purpose may not be achieved by means which sweep unnecessarily broadly and thereby invade the area of protected freedoms. As the Court through Mr Justice Bellosillo said:

> [W]hen statutes regulate or proscribe speech and no readily apparent construction suggests itself as a vehicle for rehabilitating the statutes in a single prosecution, the transcendent value to all society of constitutionally protected expression is deemed to justify allowing attacks on overly broad statutes with no requirement that the person making the attack demonstrate that his own conduct could not be regulated by a statute drawn with narrow specificity. The possible harm to society in permitting some unprotected speech to go unpunished is outweighed by the possibility that the protected speech of others may be deterred and perceived grievances left to fester because of possible inhibitory effects of overly broad statutes.[19]

Based on the foregoing, Adonis then argued that, given conflicting jurisprudence on what constitutes 'actual malice' where the latest pronouncement is that it includes 'ill-will, hatred, contempt and malevolence,' the criminal libel statute should be declared void on its face because it can penalise two instances that would limit the debate on public issues.

The first would be the false statements regarding public figures made without knowledge or recklessness outside of fair and true report of any act performed by public officials in the exercise of their functions. The second would be true statements regarding public figures not covered by qualified privilege. Fear of criminal liability under these circumstances would serve as a prior restraint on their freedom of expression and their duty to inform the public as news reporters.

The Cybercrimes Prevention Act also poses a difficult questions on the issues of double jeopardy, equal protection, and the right to privacy. By providing that a conviction for libel under the Revised Penal Code is not a bar to another prosecution under the Act, a person is liable for punishment twice for the exact same libelous statement. Likewise, the fact that the Act's penal clause provides for a heavier penalty that precludes possibility of probation and parole provokes the query as to whether the difference in penalty is based on substantial distinctions. A primary author of the law, Senator Juan Ponce Enrile, justified the heavier penalty on the basis that a libelous remark on the Internet may be viewed in all parts of the world and by anyone with access to the Internet. But the question is whether Internet publication differs substantially from newspaper publications given their audience.

Theoretically, the Internet may be seen and accessed by more, but the reality is that not all posts on the Internet will receive heavy traffic and attract the same number of readers.

[17] See *Bland v Roberts*, No 12-1671, 2013 WL 5228033 (4th Cir, 18 September 2013) which held that 'liking' a political candidate's Facebook page was protected by the First Amendment of the US Constitution.

[18] *Estrada v Sandiganbayan*, GR No 148560, 19 November 2001.

[19] ibid.

Certainly, an obscure webpage with an allegedly libelous remark but only 30 visits should not warrant a heavier penalty for libel given that newspapers may have more readership than the overwhelming number of blogs and other publications on the net.

Even the enforcement of the statute is liable to violate the right to privacy. Under Section 19 of the statute, the Secretary of Justice is empowered, upon 'good reasons', to take down any website violating the law. This makes the Justice Secretary the investigator, prosecutor, judge and executioner in the same case.

On *Pacta Sunt Servanda*

Adonis argued that as a party to the Optional Protocol to the ICCPR, the Philippines was once more in breach of its obligation to protect and promote freedom of expression. He raised before the Court the UNHRC view which was issued in his favour, where the UNHRC determined that the sanction of imprisonment on Adonis was incompatible with Article 19 of the ICCPR and that the Philippines was under an obligation to take steps to prevent similar violations from occurring in the future, including by reviewing the relevant libel legislation.[20]

Although the UNHRC's views are themselves non-binding, Adonis argued that as taken from a body of experts, the views are authoritative declarations on whether a state complies with its treaty obligations. He invoked the decisions of the International Court of Justice to support the authority of UNHRC views: 'The Court ascribes great weight to the interpretation adopted by [the Committee] that was established specifically to supervise the application of that treaty.'[21] Despite the non-binding nature of the UNHRC's views, the Philippine Supreme Court has nonetheless chosen to apply them in previous cases. If the Supreme Court has applied non-binding views issued against other countries in the resolution of cases before it, why does it not apply a view that is against the Philippines itself in the resolution of a Philippine case?

Decision of the Court

The Philippine Supreme Court partially granted the petition of Adonis. Regrettably, what it denied was precisely the prayer that both cyber libel and libel be declared unconstitutional. The Court through Mr Justice Abad said:[22]

> Parenthetically, the Court cannot accept the proposition that its ruling in *Fermin* disregarded the higher standard of actual malice or malice in fact when it found Cristinelli Fermin guilty of committing libel against complainants who were public figures. Actually, the Court found the presence of malice in fact in that case. Thus:

[20] *Adonis*, above n 14, [10].

[21] *Ahmadou Sadio Diallo* (*Republic of Guinea v Democratic Republic of the Congo*), Merits, Judgment, ICJ Reports 2010, 639 (30 November 2010) [66].

[22] *Disini v The Secretary of Justice*, above n 1.

> It can be gleaned from her testimony that petitioner had the motive to make defamatory imputations against complainants. Thus, petitioner cannot, by simply making a general denial, convince us that there was no malice on her part. Verily, not only was there malice in law, the article being malicious in itself, but there was also malice in fact, as there was motive to talk ill against complainants during the electoral campaign.
>
> (citations omitted)

From the foregoing, it was clear that the Court did not appreciate that the definition of 'actual malice' other than that provided in *Sullivan* would render criminal libel unconstitutional under the overbreadth doctrine. The US Supreme Court has ruled that hatred and ill-will should not form part of the definition of 'actual malice':

> Even where the utterance is false, the ... Constitution ... precludes attaching adverse consequences to any except the knowing or reckless falsehood. Debate on public issues will not be uninhibited if the speaker must run the risk that it will be proved in court that he spoke out of hatred; even if he did speak out of hatred, utterances honestly believed to contribute to the free interchange of ideas and the ascertainment of truth [are not covered by libel].[23]

Concerning the View expressed by the UNHRC, the Court declared:[24]

> General Comment 34 does not say that the truth of the defamatory statement should constitute an all-encompassing defense. As it happens, Article 361 recognizes truth as a defense but under the condition that the accused has been prompted in making the statement by good motives and for justifiable ends. Thus:
>
> 'Art. 361. Proof of the truth.—In every criminal prosecution for libel, the truth may be given in evidence to the court and if it appears that the matter charged as libelous is true, and, moreover, that it was published with good motives and for justifiable ends, the defendants shall be acquitted.
>
> Proof of the truth of an imputation of an act or omission not constituting a crime shall not be admitted, unless the imputation shall have been made against Government employees with respect to facts related to the discharge of their official duties.
>
> In such cases if the defendant proves the truth of the imputation made by him, he shall be acquitted.'
>
> Besides, the UNHRC did not actually enjoin the Philippines, as petitioners urge, to decriminalize libel. It simply suggested that defamation laws be crafted with care to ensure that they do not stifle freedom of expression. Indeed, the ICCPR states that although everyone should enjoy freedom of expression, its exercise carries with it special duties and responsibilities. Free speech is not absolute. It is subject to certain restrictions, as may be necessary and as may be provided by law.

As to the attack on criminal libel on the ground of overbreadth, the Court did not address the issue squarely but only reiterated that defamation is not protected speech:[25]

> The Court agrees with the Solicitor General that libel is not a constitutionally protected speech and that the government has an obligation to protect private individuals from defamation. Indeed, cyber libel is actually not a new crime since Article 353, in relation to Article 355 of the penal code, already punishes it. In effect, Section 4(c)(4) above merely affirms that online defamation constitutes 'similar means' for committing libel.
>
> (citations omitted)

[23] *Garrison v Louisiana*, 379 US 64, 73 (1964).
[24] *Disini v The Secretary of Justice*, above n 1.
[25] ibid.

The Court attempted to temper its declaration upholding the constitutionality of libel on the Internet by ruling that only the author of the libelous statement may be held liable for violation of the law. It held that the provisions of the cybercrime law on aiding and abetting, insofar as it may consider those who repost, retweet, like or comment on blogs as guilty of the crime of libel as aiders and abettors, as being unconstitutional:[26]

> But the Court's acquiescence goes only insofar as the cybercrime law penalises the author of the libelous statement or article … Section 5 with respect to Section 4(c)(4) is unconstitutional. Its vagueness raises apprehension on the part of Internet users because of its obvious chilling effect on the freedom of expression, especially since the crime of aiding or abetting ensnares all the actors in the cyberspace front in a fuzzy way. What is more, as the petitioners point out, formal crimes such as libel are not punishable unless consummated. In the absence of legislation tracing the interaction of netizens and their level of responsibility such as in other countries, Section 5, in relation to Section 4(c)(4) on Libel, Section 4(c)(3) on Unsolicited Commercial Communications, and Section 4(c)(2) on Child Pornography, cannot stand scrutiny.
>
> (citations omitted)

It is strange that the Court considered aiding and abetting to cyber libel as unconstitutional on the basis of overbreadth and yet upheld the constitutionality of the crime itself. If the uncertainty on who could be held liable for a lesser penalty for aiding and abetting cyber libel could be a basis for there to be a 'chilling effect' on freedom of expression, why should not the penalty itself on defamation, where it could punish protected speech critical of public figures, not similarly result in the same chilling effect?

The reasoning of the Court is that since Internet communication is not exactly the same as paper publication, it is uncertain whether liking a Facebook entry, retweeting, favouriting a tweet, or reblogging could be punished as aiding and abetting to the crime of libel. What the Court failed to consider is that a facial challenge could be applied to cyber libel as a whole because these uncertainties on the Internet that the Court itself noted are precisely what makes it difficult to determine what should and should not be punished. The US and regional human rights bodies have already pronounced that criminal libel itself, because it could penalise protected speech, is overbroad.[27] Indeed, some tribunals have gone a step further and touched on the possibility of civil liability infringing upon freedom of speech:

> The effective exercise of freedom of expression implies the existence of conditions and social practices that favor it. It is possible for freedom of expression to be unlawfully curtailed by de facto conditions that directly or indirectly place those who exercise it in a situation of risk or increased vulnerability. The State must abstain from acting in such a way that favors, promotes, fosters, or deepens that vulnerability.[28]

[26] ibid.

[27] *Parmelee v O'Neel*, 145 Wash App 223, 186 P3d 1094 (Wash App Div 2); *Garrison v Louisiana*, 379 US 64, 73 (1964); *Cumpana and Mazare v Romania*, ECHR, Application No 33348/96, Judgment of 17 December 2004; *Sener v Turkey*, ECHR, Application No 26680/95, Judgment of 18 July 2000.

[28] Inter-American Court of Human Rights: *Uzcategui et al v Venezuela* Judgment of 3 September 2012 Series C no 249, [189]–[190]; *Vargas v Colombia* Judgment of 26 May 2010 Series C no 213, [172]; *Rios et al v Venezuela* Judgment of 28 January 2009 Series C no 194, [107]; *Perozo et al v Venezuela* Judgment of 28 January 2009 Series C no 195, [118].

As a further concession to the petitioners, the Court declared that the Cybercrimes Prevention Act, insofar as it authorises prosecution under the same law and under the Revised Penal Code, is unconstitutional for constituting double jeopardy:[29]

> Online libel is different. There should be no question that if the published material on print, said to be libelous, is again posted online or vice versa, that identical material cannot be the subject of two separate libels. The two offenses, one a violation of Article 353 of the Revised Penal Code and the other a violation of Section 4(c)(4) of R.A. 10175 involve essentially the same elements and are in fact one and the same offense. Indeed, the OSG itself claims that online libel under Section 4(c)(4) is not a new crime but is one already punished under Article 353. Section 4(c)(4) merely establishes the computer system as another means of publication. Charging the offender under both laws would be a blatant violation of the proscription against double jeopardy.
>
> (citations omitted)

Likewise, it declared that the provisions authorising real time data collection of data as unconstitutional for being violative of the right to privacy:[30]

> The authority that Section 12 gives law enforcement agencies is too sweeping and lacks restraint. While it says that traffic data collection should not disclose identities or content data, such restraint is but an illusion. Admittedly, nothing can prevent law enforcement agencies holding these data in their hands from looking into the identity of their sender or receiver and what the data contains. This will unnecessarily expose the citizenry to leaked information or, worse, to extortion from certain bad elements in these agencies.
>
> (citations omitted)

Finally, it also declared as unconstitutional the power granted to the Secretary of Justice to take down data or block websites:[31]

> Section 19 empowers the Department of Justice to restrict or block access to computer data:
>
> 'Sec. 19. Restricting or Blocking Access to Computer Data.— When a computer data is prima facie found to be in violation of the provisions of this Act, the DOJ shall issue an order to restrict or block access to such computer data.
>
> ...
>
> Without having to go into a lengthy discussion of property rights in the digital space, it is indisputable that computer data, produced or created by their writers or authors may constitute personal property. Consequently, they are protected from unreasonable searches and seizures, whether while stored in their personal computers or in the service provider's systems ... [T]he Government, in effect, seizes and places the computer data under its control and disposition without a warrant. The Department of Justice order cannot substitute for judicial search warrant.
>
> The content of the computer data can also constitute speech. In such a case, Section 19 operates as a restriction on the freedom of expression over cyberspace ... Section 19 merely requires that the data to be blocked be found prima facie in violation of any provision of the Cybercrime Law.
>
> ...

29 *Disini v The Secretary of Justice*, above n 1.
30 ibid.
31 ibid.

The Court is therefore compelled to strike down Section 19 for being violative of the constitutional guarantees to freedom of expression and against unreasonable searches and seizures.'

(citations omitted)

Concluding Observations

So criminal libel remains in the statute books of the Philippines. This, despite the UN Human Rights Committee's view that criminal libel is contrary to freedom of expression. When the Supreme Court had the opportunity to keep Philippine jurisprudence in line with international jurisprudence on freedom of expression, the Philippine Supreme Court has in effect decided that it will deviate from the former insofar as the definition of actual damage and the application of overbreadth to criminal libel statutes is concerned.

It must be said that there was a serious lapse in the Court's application of the overbreadth doctrine when it struck down only the crime of aiding and abetting the crime of libel. For while the Court in fact admitted the many ambiguities involved in retweeting, reposting, sharing, and liking on the Internet made it difficult to punish as aiding and abetting without infringing on freedom of expression, it failed to rule whether these acts can by themselves constitute libel, which imposes a heavier penalty including incarceration. In applying the principle of overbreadth, the Court mused:[32]

> When a person replies to a Tweet containing child pornography, he effectively republishes it whether wittingly or unwittingly. Does this make him a willing accomplice to the distribution of child pornography? When a user downloads the Facebook mobile application, the user may give consent to Facebook to access his contact details. In this way, certain information is forwarded to third parties and unsolicited commercial communication could be disseminated on the basis of this information. As the source of this information, is the user aiding the distribution of this communication? The legislature needs to address this clearly to relieve users of annoying fear of possible criminal prosecution.
>
> When a penal statute encroaches upon the freedom of speech, a facial challenge grounded on the void-for-vagueness doctrine is acceptable. The inapplicability of the doctrine must be carefully delineated. As Justice Antonio T. Carpio explained in his dissent in *Romualdez v Commission on Elections*, 'we must view these statements of the Court on the inapplicability of the overbreadth and vagueness doctrines to penal statutes as appropriate only insofar as these doctrines are used to mount 'facial' challenges to penal statutes not involving free speech.'
>
> But this rule admits of exceptions. A petitioner may for instance mount a 'facial' challenge to the constitutionality of a statute even if he claims no violation of his own rights under the assailed statute where it involves free speech on grounds of overbreadth or vagueness of the statute.
>
> The rationale for this exception is to counter the 'chilling effect' on protected speech that comes from statutes violating free speech. A person who does not know whether his speech constitutes a crime under an overbroad or vague law may simply restrain himself from speaking in order to avoid being charged of a crime. The overbroad or vague law thus chills him into silence.

[32] ibid.

> As already stated, the cyberspace is an incomparable, pervasive medium of communication. It is inevitable that any government threat of punishment regarding certain uses of the medium creates a chilling effect on the constitutionally-protected freedom of expression of the great masses that use it. In this case, the particularly complex web of interaction on social media websites would give law enforcers such latitude that they could arbitrarily or selectively enforce the law.
>
> Who is to decide when to prosecute persons who boost the visibility of a posting on the Internet by liking it? Netizens are not given 'fair notice' or warning as to what is criminal conduct and what is lawful conduct. When a case is filed, how will the court ascertain whether or not one netizen's comment aided and abetted a cybercrime while another comment did not?
>
> Of course, if the 'Comment' does not merely react to the original posting but creates an altogether new defamatory story against Armand like 'He beats his wife and children' then that should be considered an original posting published on the Internet. Both the Penal Code and the Cybercrime Law clearly punish authors of defamatory publications. Make no mistake, libel destroys reputations that society values. Allowed to cascade in the Internet, it will destroy relationships and, under certain circumstances, will generate enmity and tension between social or economic groups, races, or religions, exacerbating existing tension in their relationships.
>
> (citations omitted)

But what the Court seemed to have been confused about is the fact that despite the peculiar nature of the Internet, all criminal libel is still overbroad insofar as it may punish speech involving (1) false statements regarding public figures made without knowledge or recklessness outside of fair and true report of any act performed by public officials in the exercise of their functions; and (2) true statements regarding public figures not covered by qualified privilege. Hence, it is not just the peculiar nature of the Internet that makes the statute overbroad insofar as aiding and abetting libel is concerned. The very statute of libel itself should be declared unconstitutional on its face.

This much was said in the three dissenting opinions. Citing well-established American jurisprudence as incorporated in Philippine cases, Justice Leonen reiterated:[33]

> Taking all of these into consideration, as mentioned earlier, a facial attack of a provision can only succeed when the basis is freedom of expression, when there is a clear showing that there is an imminent possibility that its broad language will allow ordinary law enforcement to cause prior restraints of speech, and when the value of that speech is such that its absence will be socially irreparable.
>
> Among all the provisions challenged in these consolidated petitions, there are only four instances when the 'chilling effect' on speech can be palpable: (a) the 'take down' provision; (b) the provision on cyber libel; (c) the provision on cybersex; and (d) the clause relating to unbridled surveillance of traffic data. The provisions that provide for higher penalties for these as well as for dual prosecutions should likewise be declared unconstitutional because they magnify the 'chilling effect' that stifles protected expression.
>
> For this reason alone, these provisions and clauses are unconstitutional.
>
> …
>
> The ponencia claims that 'libel is not a constitutionally protected speech' and 'that government has an obligation to protect private individuals from defamation.'

[33] ibid. accessible at www.lawphil.net/judjuris/juri2014/feb2014/203335_leonen.pdf accessed July 2016.

I strongly dissent from the first statement. Libel is a label that is often used to stifle protected speech. I agree with the second statement but only to the extent that defamation can be protected with civil rather than criminal liabilities.

(citations omitted)

Chief Justice Sereno took particular note of how the Cybercrimes Prevention Act created an 'additional *in terrorem* effect' by introducing a qualifying aggravating circumstance for libel, ie the use of the Internet. By making the use of the Internet—something that is inextricably intertwined with modern life—a qualifying aggravating circumstance of a crime, the law cut deeply into the robust exercise of freedom of expression. The Chief Justice wrote:[34]

> One begins to see at this point how the exercise of freedom of speech is clearly burdened. The Court can take judicial notice of the fact that ICTs are fast becoming the most widely used and accessible means of communication and of expression. Educational institutions encourage the study of ICT and the acquisition of the corresponding skills. Businesses, government institutions and civil society organizations rely so heavily on ICT that it is no exaggeration to say that, without it, their operations may grind to a halt. News organizations are increasingly shifting to online publications, too. The introduction of social networking sites has increased public participation in socially and politically relevant issues. In a way, the Internet has been transformed into 'freedom parks.' Because of the inextricability of ICT from modern life and the exercise of free speech and expression, I am of the opinion that the increase in penalty per se effectively chills a significant amount of the exercise of this preferred constitutional right.
>
> The chill does not stop there. This increase in penalty has a domino effect on other provisions in the Revised Penal Code thereby further affecting the public's calculation of whether or not to exercise freedom of speech. It is certainly disconcerting that these effects, in combination with the increase in penalty per se, clearly operate to tilt the scale heavily against the exercise of freedom of speech.

Justice Carpio's dissent is closest to the message that this chapter is trying to convey. He took the majority to task for failing to see that while the presumption of 'actual malice' in Article 354 of the Revised Penal Code has been untouched since the Revised Penal Code was enacted in the 1930s, constitutional rights—particularly with regard to freedom of expression—have expanded rapidly since then. When the Cybercrimes Prevention Act adopted Article 354 wholesale, and the Act was challenged before the Court, it was precisely the opportunity for the Court to strike down a statute that has long been repugnant to freedom of expression as envisioned today. Moreover, by striking down the provision in the Cybercrimes Prevention Act (and by extension Article 354), the Court would have managed to reconcile Philippine statute with Philippine case law, which has long adopted *Sullivan*. To employ Justice Carpio's own words:[35]

> The actual malice rule and Article 354 of the Code impose contradictory rules on (1) the necessity of proof of malice in defamatory imputations involving public proceedings or conduct of a public officer or public figure; and (2) the availability of truth as a defense in defamatory imputations against public officials or public figures. The former requires proof of malice and allows truth as a

[34] ibid. Accessible at www.lawphil.net/judjuris/juri2014/feb2014/gr_203335_so_2014.html accessed July 2016.
[35] ibid. Accessible at www.lawphil.net/judjuris/juri2014/feb2014/gr_203335_so_2014.html#carpio accessed July 2016.

> defense unqualifiedly, while the latter presumes malice and allows truth as a defense selectively. The repugnancy between the actual malice rule and Article 354 is clear, direct and absolute.
>
> Nonetheless, the Office of the Solicitor General (OSG) argues for the retention of Article 354 in the Code, suggesting that the Court can employ a 'limiting construction' of the provision to reconcile it with the actual malice rule. The ponencia appears to agree, holding that the actual malice rule 'impl[ies] a stricter standard of "malice" … where the offended party is a [public officer or] public figure,' the 'penal code and, implicitly, the cybercrime law mainly target libel against private persons.'
>
> Allowing a criminal statutory provision clearly repugnant to the Constitution, and directly attacked for such repugnancy, to nevertheless remain in the statute books is a gross constitutional anomaly which, if tolerated, weakens the foundation of constitutionalism in this country. 'The Constitution is either a superior, paramount law … or it is on a level with ordinary legislative acts,' and if it is superior, as we have professed ever since the Philippines operated under a Constitution, then 'a law repugnant to the Constitution is void.' (citations omitted)

In summary, the Court had the golden opportunity to disentangle Philippine jurisprudence on 'actual malice' in libel, steer the Philippines in line with its international obligations, uphold the Constitution, and defend freedom of expression all in one day. Instead, it dropped the ball on the overbreadth doctrine. All this means is that for advocates of freedom of expression, the fight will continue: either Congress passes a new law and repeals the statute, or the Court rules anew on a case involving a person convicted for libel who will again argue that the criminal statute is void on its face.

10

Confidentiality of Journalists' Sources in Singapore: Silence is Not Golden

GEORGE HWANG*

Introduction

The *Norwich Pharmacal* order and interlocutory injunctions are two procedural tools often used by the Singapore courts in the areas of intellectual property and media law. However, in cases involving the media, the possible effects of such orders on freedom of expression must be considered. With interlocutory injunctions, the issue is prior restraint. With *Norwich Pharmacal* orders, it is the chilling effect on the flow of information. When such an application is granted, the newspapers and/or journalists are being ordered by the court to reveal their source of information.

The cornerstone of the newspaper rule is ensuring that potential sources do not shy away from providing information to the press. This flow of information ensures that the press is able to obtain and publish information which is in the interest of the public. An independent press which publishes and reveals information from unofficial sources is a necessity for democracy to thrive. A press which publishes only press releases is only a propaganda machine. The premise is that the public has a right to know. For democracy to truly function, the public must always be informed about the going-ons of society, government, public institutions or even establishments with many stakeholders so that they can make an informed choice. Total transparency remains a challenge. The press has an important role to investigate and expose the opaque but important parts to the public: this constantly makes governments and other large institutions accountable to our society which is why the press has been called *the fourth estate*.

A society with not only free press, but also an environment where whistleblowers and sources of information can feel safe to expose information is a necessity if we want to promote accountability, good governance, and democracy.

In the case of *James Michael Dorsey v World Sports Group Pte Ltd*,[1] Singapore's apex court, the Court of Appeal, heard two firsts: the issue of *Norwich Pharmacal* orders or their equivalent and the issue of journalist's confidentiality. Unfortunately, it based its decision purely on the

* The author was counsel for the appellant, Mr James Michael Dorsey.

[1] *James Michael Dorsey v World Sports Group Pte Ltd* [2014] 2 SLR 208 (CA), rev'g [2013] 3 SLR 180 (HC).

considerations for granting a *Norwich Pharmacal* equivalent. It only mentioned the newspaper rule when summarising the decision of the lower court judge. It neither discussed this rule nor brought up the free flow of information as a factor to be considered in granting such an order.

This silence is lamentable. Investigative journalism *is* important in Singapore. In 2005, one of Singapore's biggest and most respected non-profit organisations, the National Kidney Foundation (NKF), was hit by a corruption scandal. Alleged misuse of funds and corruption had been the subject of a handful of whistleblowers' complaints, but the matter exploded into the public realm when NKF's then CEO, TT Durai, sued Singapore Press Holdings (SPH) in 2004 for an editorial in the *Straits Times* written by its senior correspondent Susan Leong. The article raised incidents whistleblowers were discussing that Durai claimed were defamatory. In the midst of trial, when things such as a gold-plated tap in a private washroom were revealed, the case was settled. However, this led to the prosecution and conviction of TT Durai for corruption. Not only was there a shake-up in the management of NKF, legislation and regulations were amended to prevent future similar incidents with other non-profit organisations.[2]

This chapter will not discuss the defects of the newspaper rule. It laments the failure of the Court of Appeal to discuss the newspaper rule and the applicability of the policy reasoning for the rule within the context of Singapore. By keeping silent, it has missed the boat to give not only the mainstream press but also online 'newspapers' needed guidance on their relationship with the law.

Facts of the Case

The World Sports Group (WSG) is an international company that specialises in selling and exploiting commercial rights of sporting events, especially those across Asia and the Middle East. In 2009, associate company World Sports Football entered into a relationship with the Kuala Lumpur-based Asian Football Confederation (AFC), culminating in the Master Rights Agreement (MRA). This MRA was novated to WSG.[3] The novation took effect on 1 January 2010.

At the material time James Dorsey, the Defendant, was a senior fellow at the S Rajaratnam School of International Studies at Nanyang Technological University (RSIS). He ran a blog called 'The Turbulent World of Middle East Soccer' where he discussed how soccer intersects with Middle Eastern culture, politics and economics.[4] Part of the terms of his agreement with RSIS was to maintain and publish articles on this blog. He had been a journalist for such news organisations as the *Wall Street Journal*, the *Christian Science Monitor* and United Press International. He considered himself a journalist and worked to uphold the ethos of journalism.

[2] Charities (Amendment) Act (No 10 of 2007) introduced more checks and mechanisms for the government to oversee and control the board of trustees and overall 'to put in place a more robust and transparent regulatory framework' (Commissioner of Charities *Commissioner of Charities Annual Report For The Year Ending 31 December 2007* (2007) [3]).

[3] Novation is a process where a third party is brought into an existing contractual relationship to replace one of the contracting parties.

[4] The blog can be accessed at http://mideastsoccer.blogspot.sg accessed July 2016.

In the first half of 2011, the then AFC President, Mohammed bin Hammad, was embroiled in a corruption scandal for allegedly illegally offering bribes for votes in support of him being the president of Fédération Internationale de Football Association (FIFA). This led to him being banned by FIFA in July 2011. Although he successfully appealed against this ban in the Court of Arbitration for Sport in 2012, in December 2012, FIFA slapped him with a second ban, this time for life, for acting in 'conflict of interest' whilst he was the president of the AFC.

AFC hired PricewaterhouseCoopers Advisory Sdn Bhd (PWC) in July 2012 to investigate the financial state and activities of AFC during the time Mohammed was president. PWC's report (Report) was submitted to AFC, who in turn, submitted it to FIFA.

What PWC found with respect to the MRA and Mohammed was damning: no-bid contracts were severely undervalued, including the MRA, and Mohammed had allegedly received substantial sums of money from various people linked to the agreements AFC made during his presidency.

The Report generated a lot of interest in international media, and Dorsey blogged about it between 23 July 2012 and 22 September 2012. The case centred around an article published on 28 August 2012, entitled 'FIFA investigates: World Cup host Qatar in the hot seat'. He quoted from the Report and the MRA extensively in some of the posts, citing 'sources close to AFC' or 'sources', which he had never identified.

Meanwhile, on 30 July 2012, other mass media channels such as the Wide World of Sports, News.com.au, The Republic and Al Jazeera had reported that all the contracts between AFC and WSG were no-bid and considerably undervalued.

On 5 September 2012, WSG sought leave to serve pre-action third party interrogatories on Dorsey to find out the identity of the 'sources' he referred to, as well as to produce the MRA and Report.

WSG argued that the Report was defamatory and the source who provided Dorsey with the Report had published the same to Dorsey. The Report alleged or implied that WSG was complicit in AFC's corrupt activities. The ingredients for commencing a defamation action against the source were fulfilled. By the same action of communicating with Dorsey, it was claimed the source who provided the MRA or related information acted in breach of confidence. It follows, so it was argued, that Dorsey's comments were both defamatory and in breach of confidence. WSG did not specify what actions they would take, except that they wanted to know all the facts before deciding who to sue.

Journalists' Ethics

Singapore's National Union of Journalists expressly states that a journalist should protect the identity of his source. Section 8 of its Code of Professional Conduct reads: 'Every member shall respect all necessary confidence regarding sources of information and private documents.'[5]

[5] Section 8 of Singapore National Union of Journalists' Code of Professional Conduct as listed on EyeonEthics, accessible at www.eyeonethics.org accessed July 2016.

There is still no official international code of ethics that journalists subscribe to, but a journalist's obligation to confidentiality is written in most democratic countries' journalists' association code of ethics or the like. The International Federation of Journalists is the biggest union of journalist trade unions in the world, and it regularly speaks out in support of or against a government's laws or a court decision that would encourage or harm the protection of journalist sources. It only accepts as members journalist trade unions 'devoted to media freedom',[6] and it currently represents more than 600,000 journalists in 134 countries.

At the legal level, protection of confidential sources has been recognised internationally as a right that must be honoured by governments. It is within the scope of freedom 'to seek, receive and impart information' in Article 19(2), International Covenant on Civil Political Rights.[7] In 2005, the UN Commission on Human Rights spotlighted the need to 'ensure greater protection for all media professionals and for journalistic sources'.[8] The European Court of Human Rights has famously held in *Goodwin v UK* that '[p]rotection of journalistic sources is one of the basic conditions for press freedom'.[9] The African Union[10] and the Organization for American States[11] have also released declarations elaborating the right to protection of journalist sources.

Hearing History

It was a long winding road for the defendant Dorsey before the final victory. This was a David-and-Goliath story of an individual putting himself and his journalistic integrity before a multi-million-dollar enterprise. The case was first heard before the Registrar and the High Court before the Court of Appeal delivered the final decision.

Procedure Used

The applications were originally for pre-action third party discovery[12] and interrogatories for the purpose of identifying the source of the information which Dorsey possessed.[13] Discovery is a process by which documents are produced and interrogatories refer to

[6] Section 3(b) of the International Federation of Journalists Constitution 2013-2016.

[7] Singapore is not a signatory to this treaty.

[8] UN Commission on Human Rights, Res 2005/38 (19 April 2005).

[9] *Goodwin v the United Kingdom* [1996] ECHR 16.

[10] See Art XV of Resolution on the Adoption of the Declaration of Principles on Freedom of Expression in Africa, ACHPR /Res 62(XXXII)02: 'Media practitioners shall not be required to reveal confidential sources of information or to disclose other material held for journalistic purposes except in accordance with the following principles: the identity of the source is necessary for the investigation or prosecution of a serious crime, or the defence of a person accused of a criminal offence; the information or similar information leading to the same result cannot be obtained elsewhere; the public interest in disclosure outweighs the harm to freedom of expression; and disclosure has been ordered by a court, after a full hearing.'

[11] See Declaration of Principles on Freedom of Expression as approved by the Inter-American Commission of Human Rights in October 2000.

[12] O 24 r 6(1) for an order to be given pursuant to O 24 r 6(5) and r 7 for discovery.

[13] O 26A r 1(1) for an order to be given pursuant to O 26A r 1(5) and r 2 for the interrogatories.

questions posed to another party or non-party for the disclosure of information. The rules for pre-action third party discovery and interrogatories are worded similarly. Given that they have the same origins, the cases for one are considered to be relevant to the other.

At the Registrar

The Assistant Registrar (AR) hearing the application allowed all the interrogatories ascertaining the identity of the sources to be served on Dorsey.[14] However, she did not allow the discovery of the documents, the Report and MRA.

No report of the decision has been published. The authors' learned guess is that these documents do not reveal the identity of the source(s). They are also—at least in the case of the MRA—documents which WSG should possess. Hence, they were irrelevant to WSG's objective of finding out the identity of the source(s). Dorsey appealed to the High Court against the AR's decision regarding the interrogatories. WSG did not cross-appeal the disallowance of the discovery.

At the High Court

Judith Prakash J struck out some of the interrogatories but still ordered Dorsey to answer those relating to the source's identity and relationship to AFC and also the questions about whether Dorsey had been given a copy of the MRA and by whom.[15]

In coming to her judgment, Her Honour examined two main areas: (1) the law on pre-action third party proceedings for interrogatories with regards to defamation and confidential information; and (2) the newspaper rule in the context of Singapore.

Her Honour examined the law relating to pre-action interrogatories under O 26A r 1, citing *Norwich Pharmacal Co v Customs and Excise Commissioners*[16] and the rationale of ensuring access to justice for the plaintiff, which in this case meant identifying the tortfeasor in order to bring the suit. The judge also examined *British Steel Corp v Granada Television Ltd*[17] to stress that a balancing of interests test must be carried out in deciding to grant the order. On one side is the interest of the applicant in being able to exercise their legal right to bring action against a wrongdoer, and hence the right to the identity of that wrongdoer; on the other side is the public interest in the free flow of information. The Singapore courts had developed a substantial body of case law in interpreting O 26A, which emphasises that the courts will not allow interrogatories if they are not necessary or relevant either for disposing fairly of the case or to save costs.

Her Honour found a prima facie case of defamation in the blog post dated 28 August and a likelihood that either AFC or the sources had been in breach of confidential information. When balancing between the public interest in the free flow of information and protection of confidential information, the judge emphasised the importance of protecting the

[14] *Dorsey* (CA), above n 1, [11].
[15] *Dorsey* (HC), above n 1.
[16] *Norwich Pharmacal Co v Customs and Excise Commissioners* [1974] AC 133 (HL).
[17] *British Steel Corp v Granada Television Ltd* [1981] 1 AC 1096 (HL).

confidence breached by the source. Her Honour was satisfied that the public interest in free flow of information would not be harmed 'in the light of the prima facie probability that [the] sources were in breach of their legal obligations of confidentiality ...'[18]

The judge stated that the newspaper rule could not be used as a defence as there is no such rule in Singapore.[19] Further, she found it to be inapplicable as Dorsey was not a journalist as he was employed by Nanyang Technological University, an academic institute.

The Law at the Time of Appeal

The rules on procedure in Singapore for commencing a civil action in the High Court and Court of Appeal are not encapsulated in an Act of Parliament, unlike the criminal procedure.[20] The procedures are mainly in the Rules of Court. These rules are made by a rules committee formed pursuant to section 80 of the Supreme Court Judicature Act (SCJA).[21] No rules can be made without the consent of the Chief Justice and presentation to Parliament.

Origins of the Power

The Court's power to order pre-action discovery and interrogatories is derived from paragraph 12 of the First Schedule of the SCJA. This power was made express in 1993 with the amendment of the SCJA (Supreme Court Judicature (Amendment) Act 1993.[22] Prior to this, there were doubts as to whether the courts could grant a *Norwich Pharmacal* order in Singapore. However, since the amendment, even with the existence of O 24 r 6 and O 26A, Singapore's court has indicated that it retains the residual right to grant a *Norwich Pharmacal* order where necessary.[23]

Norwich Pharmacal v Customs & Excise Commissioner was an intellectual property case where the House of Lords based its decision on the inherent jurisdiction of the court. A *Norwich Pharmacal* order, unlike other pre-action discovery, is for the purpose of identifying persons only.[24] In this case, the plaintiff was a patent owner who was aware that someone had imported infringing products into the UK. However, it did not know the identity of the wrongdoer. The UK Customs & Excise Office was innocent; it did not have anything to do with the importing of the infringing goods except to store the infringing goods in its warehouse. It refused to reveal the identity of the importer, leaving the plaintiff with no one to sue, and hence with no legal remedies.

[18] *Dorsey* (HC), above n 1, [33].

[19] Citing *KLW Holdings Ltd v Singapore Press Holdings Ltd* [2002] 2 SLR(R) 477 and *Tullett Prebon (Singapore) Ltd v Spring Mark Geoffrey* [2007] 3 SLR(R) 187.

[20] Criminal Procedure Code (Cap 68, 1985 Rev Ed).

[21] Supreme Court Judicature Act (Cap 322, 2007 Rev Ed).

[22] Supreme Court Judicature (Amendment) Act 1993 (Act 16 of 1993).

[23] See *Wellmix Organics (International) Pte Ltd v Lau Yu Man* [2006] 2 SLR 117; *UMCI Ltd v Tokio Marine & Fire Insurance Co (Singapore) Pte Ltd* [2006] 4 SLR(R) 95.

[24] The main conditions and scope of the modern *Norwich Pharmacal* order are detailed in George Wei Sze Shun, 'Pre-Commencement Discovery and the *Odex* Litigation: Copyright versus Confidentiality or is it Privacy?' (2008) 20 *Singapore Academy of Law Journal* 591, 617.

The House of Lords decided that a third party who facilitated an infringement or a tort has a duty to assist the victim by producing the document revealing the identity of the tort-feasor. This is the case even if the third party's contribution is innocent. The rationale for this rule is that access to justice would otherwise be denied. The principle is summed up in the words of Lord Reid:

> [I]f through no fault of his own a person gets mixed up in the tortious acts of others so as to facilitate their wrongdoing he may incur no personal liability but he comes under a duty to assist the person who has been wronged by giving him full information and disclosing the identity of the wrongdoers.[25]

The Court balanced the plaintiff's access to justice and the privacy of the person from whom the information is sought. Should this person be an innocent bystander, no duty will be imposed upon him to reveal the information. He needs to have been embroiled, unwittingly or innocently, in the wrong committed by the unknown third party. In such a case, the public interest of access to justice overrides the freedom from interference of a private individual. The Court should also consider all the circumstances of the case before making the order. These include:

> such matters as the strength of the applicant's case against the unknown alleged wrongdoer, the relation subsisting between alleged wrongdoer and the respondent, whether the information could be obtained from another source, and whether the giving of the information would put the respondent to trouble which could not be compensated by the payment of all expenses by the applicant.[26]

Since then, the English cases have broadened the scope of the *Norwich Pharmacal* order such that the wrongdoing by the unknown third party need not be confined to tort, but also criminal acts. Also, the purpose for seeking the identity of the source is not confined to initiating civil proceedings. It could be to initiate criminal proceedings or to take self-help disciplinary proceedings including termination of employment.

The wordings of O 24 and O 26A themselves do not contain limitations as to the scope of these orders, except that they must be done against a third-party and hence preclude self-help remedies.

Burden of Proof

Whilst the applicant has to prove that the conditions in *Norwich Pharmacal* are met, the party resisting the order has to prove that the order is not necessary in order to dispose of the case fairly or to save costs. This is provided for in the black letter law itself: O 24 r 7 and O 26A r 2 put the onus on the defendant.[27]

[25] *Norwich Pharmacal*, above n 16, 195.

[26] ibid 199 (per Lord Cross).

[27] O 26A r 2 read: 'On the hearing of an application for an order under Rule 1, the Court, if satisfied that interrogatories are not necessary, or not necessary at that stage of the cause or matter, may dismiss or, as the case may be, adjourn the application and shall in any case refuse to make such an order if and so far as it is of opinion that interrogatories are not necessary either for disposing fairly of the cause or matter or for saving costs.'

The respondent can resist the application by arguing that the communication is absolutely privileged. However, this does not cover purely confidential communication or information. The newspaper rule, unlike solicitor-client privilege, does not fall within this category.

The conditions the plaintiff must prove are the following: (1) that the defendant had facilitated the wrongdoing of the third party; (2) that without the identity of the wrongdoer, the plaintiff would have no legal redress; (3) that the plaintiff has established that a wrongdoing has been committed; (4) that the identity of the source and/or the documents is relevant to the action contemplated; (5) that no question on confidentiality or privacy would arise; and (6) other relevant factors such as where the tort was committed, the relationship between the various parties, the nature of the wrongdoing and harm suffered and if the source could cause further damage.[28]

The cases so far have been silent on the degree of proof that a wrong has been committed required. *Norwich Pharmacal* orders are in a way similar to *Anton Piller* orders as both are based on the process of discovery. In an *Anton Piller* order, the plaintiff has to prove that there is an extremely strong *prima facie* case that a wrong has been committed as it is the civil equivalent of a search warrant. A *Norwich Pharmacal* order merely compels the production of documents revealing the wrongdoer's identity, and in an O 26A r 1(5) application, the defendant to the application merely has to answer the questions he is asked.[29] As such, a lesser burden may be expected. Lord Reid has said that the Court should only grant such an order when it is satisfied that there is no substantial chance that an injustice will be done.[30]

Newspaper Rule

The newspaper rule is an old common law rule that tries to recognise one of journalism's primary code of ethics: the confidentiality of sources. It is usually pitted against the general rule that one has the right to discover other participants in a tort, or the rule that one should identify a source when giving evidence. This gives rise to a tension between a journalist's ethical obligations and their legal obligations. Failure to comply with the latter would put them in contempt of court.

The newspaper rule is vague and imprecise, and even in jurisdictions where it is recognised it has been steadily eroded. It has never been an 'absolute privilege'. It is a 'rule of practice' that requires the Court to balance considerations relevant to the 'interests of justice',

[28] Professor Pinsler submits the following factors to be considered instead (see Jeffrey Pinsler, *Principles of Civil Procedure* (Academy Publishing, 2013) 653): 1. the applicant has a strong case against the potential defendant; 2. the information or identity is very likely to be accurate but cannot be obtained from any source other than the respondent; 3. it is absolutely necessary for the applicant to have access to the information in order to pursue his claim; 4. the respondent would be able to provide the information with ease; 5. no issue of confidentiality would arise; and 6. the respondent's costs (if any) in providing the information would be indemnified.

[29] O 26A r 1(5) reads: 'An order to administer interrogatories before the commencement of proceedings or to administer interrogatories to a person who is not a party to the proceedings may be made by the Court for the purpose of or with a view to identifying possible parties to any proceedings in such circumstances where the Court thinks it just to make such an order, and on such terms as it thinks just.'

[30] Lord Reid in *Norwich Pharmacal*, above n 16, [18]: 'The Court will then only order discovery if satisfied that there is no substantial chance of injustice being done.'

which is made up of the interests of the plaintiff seeking the identity of the sources, and the public interest in protecting the sources of journalist information.[31]

This nuance was recognised by the Singapore High Court in *KLW Holdings Ltd v Singapore Press Holdings*,[32] where it was held that instead of recognising the newspaper rule as a *rule*, the Court would instead conduct a balancing of interests approach, and in the pre-trial stage, it would lean in favour of the interests recognised in protecting the confidentiality of sources. The subsequent case of *Tullet Prebon (Singapore) Ltd v Spring Mark Geoffrey*,[33] however, cited *KLW Holdings* as being authority for not recognising a newspaper rule in Singapore. These two cases are discussed in detail in the next section.

Legislation in other jurisdictions have enacted 'shield laws' to codify and make certain the protection of the confidentiality of journalists' sources and confer a legal privilege from being asked to reveal their sources. The best examples of these shield laws can be found in 49 states (and the District of Columbia) in the US, although they differ in their scope and extent. The failure of the newspaper rule in bequeathing legal protection to journalists has been the major factor in proposing the introduction of shield laws. This is what happened in the US (the US Supreme Court case of *Branzburg v Hayes*[34] recognised no constitutional protection for confidentiality of sources) and recently, in Queensland, Australia (*R v Mcmanus and Harvey*,[35] 2007, where two journalists were convicted for contempt of court for refusing to comply with a court order to reveal their sources).

In England, the home of the newspaper rule, the rule itself has been codified in section 10 of the Contempt of Court Act 1981 in the aftermath of the House of Lords' decision in *British Steel*. The provision reads:

> No court may require a person to disclose, nor is any person guilty of contempt of court for refusing to disclose, the source of information contained in a publication for which he is responsible, *unless it be established* to the satisfaction of the court *that disclosure is necessary* in the interests of justice or national security or for the prevention of disorder or crime. (emphasis added)

Since its introduction, English case law has been focused on the definition or extent of 'the interests of justice', 'national security', 'prevention of disorder or crime' that override the protection against the need for disclosure. There is still no 'shield law' legislated by the English Parliament, but as stated previously, the European Court of Human Rights has ruled that ordering the revelation of a journalist's confidential sources without 'an overriding requirement in the public interest' is a breach of Article 10 (the right to free expression) of the European Convention on Human Rights.[36]

The newspaper rule' unlike a *Norwich Pharmacal* order or its codified progenies in Singapore ie O 24 r 6(5) and O 26A r 1(1), is a 'defence'. Further, it can be used not only in a *Norwich Pharmacal* application (pre-action third party proceeding), but in an interlocutory application or at trial: in *Goodwin*, the plaintiff had already obtained an interlocutory injunction against the journalist in the local court.[37] However, it has been observed that

[31] *British Steel*, above n 17, 1128 (per Lord Denning MR).
[32] *KLW Holdings*, above n 19.
[33] *Tullet Prebon*, above n 19.
[34] *Branzburg v Hayes*, 408 U.S. 665 (1972).
[35] *R v Mcmanus and Harvey* [2007] VCC 619.
[36] *Goodwin*, above n 9.
[37] ibid.

attempts to apply it outside of a *Norwich Pharmacal* situation have not been met with much success.

Precedents on Point

The only reported cases in Singapore involving the newspaper rule are *KLW Holdings* and *Tullet Prebon*.

In *KLW Holdings*, the applicant had in 2000 acquired a company, Barang Barang Pte Ltd, from Sonny Boey and Alvin Chua. Part of the acquisition deal was that the sellers, Sonny Boey and Alvin Chua, would remain working with Barang Barang Pte Ltd. The applicant stopped paying the two individuals on grounds that they had breached the anti-competition clause in the acquisition agreement by setting up a competing business.

The respondent published a story which, according to the applicant, was defamatory. It gave the impression that it had defaulted in its payment and was insolvent. There was no breach of confidential information belonging to the applicant. The applicant took out a pre-trial discovery application for the following documents: notes of the interview; and working drafts of the article.

The application was dismissed. The High Court judge who heard and dismissed (yes, the appeal was dismissed) the appeal decided that the newspaper rule did not apply to Singapore. He refused to examine whether issues such as free flow of information and investigative journalism were in the public's interest as it has to be considered in light of whether there is a responsible press. In his view, there was no necessity to decide the case based on the newspaper rule. (I hope it is now clearer. The sentence is a synopsis of what can be found in page 283 of the judgment) He refused to apply the rule, which has stood for over a hundred years in England, but had no history in Singapore.

The judge stressed that 'No argument was advanced to persuade [him] that if the rule is not recognised, the newspaper's sources of information would cease to come forward.' He was concerned with recognising a rule with ill-defined boundaries. With regards to the facts before him, he took into account that it was an application for pre-action discovery. As such:

> slightly different considerations (from an interlocutory proceeding) apply. Prima facie … the courts are entitled to lean in favour of confidentiality … Confidentiality must, therefore, be observed unless the greater interests of justice demand otherwise. The burden of proof lies with the applicant.[38]

The judge endorsed the Australian High Court's decision in *John Fairfax & Sons v Cojuangco*,[39] where the public interest in having a free flow of information was balanced with that of the plaintiff's access to justice. He considered that disclosure was not necessary in a defamation case as the plaintiff would have recourse against the journalist or newspaper. Whether or not there was libel was a question for the trial and disclosure of source was irrelevant here. There was also no danger that the plaintiff would continue to suffer any harm unless positive steps were taken.

[38] *KLW Holdings*, above n 19, [10].

[39] ibid [11] endorsing *John Fairfax & Sons v Cojuangco* (1988) 165 CLR 346 (HC).

In *Tullet Prebon*, there was a prior dispute between the plaintiffs and the defendant which was settled. The settlement was that BGC pay the plaintiff an undiscloseable sum. This was crystallised with a confidentiality clause. It was claimed that the sum was what BGC initially offered to settle the case before trial started. Reuters (respondent's employer), Straits Times and Business Times reported the quantum. The contemplated action against the source was breach of confidential information.

The plaintiffs sued BGC for non-payment. BGC's defence was that the plaintiffs breached the confidentiality clause in the settlement agreement. It was thus discharged from performing its obligations. Both the plaintiffs and defendants sought leave of court to serve interrogatories on non-parties to discover the source of the leak. The plaintiffs served on Shanley of Reuters and the defendants, Straits Times and Business Times. The application against Straits Times and Business Times were granted and the journalists disclosed their source.

On appeal, the High Court decided that the journalist, Shanley, had to disclose his source on grounds of fairness. Both Straits Times and Business Times were ordered to do the same on the basis that like cases should be decided alike.

The Court remarked that it would be unrealistic to expect the plaintiffs to find out the answer from another source when the information had been passed to the journalist by an unnamed source on a confidential basis. It would be akin to searching for a needle in a haystack.

The Court held that there is 'no newspaper' in Singapore and endorsed Justice Choo's decision in *KLW Holdings* that the Court could have regard to the desirability of preserving confidentiality: 'What is spoken in confidence ought to be kept in confidence. Confidentiality must, therefore, be observed unless the greater interests of justice demand otherwise.'[40]

Court of Appeal's Decision

The Court of Appeal, comprised of Sundaresh Menon CJ, Chao Hick Tin JA and VK Rajah JA, allowed the appeal and dismissed WSG's application for pre-action interrogatories. The written judgment was delivered by Justice Rajah with which the other members of the bench concurred. In his introductory paragraph, he wrote: 'The grant of a pre-action interrogatories, while not exceptional, is not usual. It requires the court to take a multi-factorial approach that necessitates the answering of a number of questions.'[41]

The Court summarised the case law underpinning O 24 (pre-action discovery) and O 26A (pre-action interrogatories), the 'juridical undergirding' of the *Norwich Pharmacal* order, and the UK Civil Procedure Rules to come up with 'essential principles'. These principles are as follows: there is a threshold of relevance that must first be satisfied, and then there is a test of *necessity*. This necessity has several facets, the most important of which is the claimant's 'real interest' in obtaining the information, as the Court shall not allow the 'sniff[ing] around' of potential actions.[42] Other facets include 'notions of proportionality,

[40] ibid [10].
[41] *Dorsey* (CA), above n 1, [1].
[42] ibid [47].

the availability of alternative avenues to obtain the information and how intrusive those interrogatories are'.[43] The Court will also take into heavy account whether the applicant has immediately commenced proceedings against an identified party at the time of the application.

The applicant would have to finally convince the Court that it is just to allow them to get information even before the commencement of the proceedings and their circumstances are extraordinary enough to warrant the intrusive procedure. The Court will take all these factors into account to arrive at its decision.[44] (too many use of phrase, 'multi-factorial approach')

The Court noted that WSG's claims were not very clearly defined, ie: who they wanted to take action against, and what for. However, the Court accepted that WSG wanted to go after the 'sources' more than Dorsey himself. The Court also helpfully summarised the potential causes of action in this case as shown in the following table:[45]

Potential claims as against/ cause of action	Defamation	Breach of confidentiality
Dorsey	— Dorsey made comments defamatory of WSG on his blog posts	— Unclear what breach of confidentiality Dorsey could have committed; possibly breach of *equitable* duty of confidence by knowingly disclosing information which he knew to be confidential.
Sources	— The sources facilitated Dorsey's defamation by supplying him with material to make those statements/ defamatory statements. — The sources published defamatory material contained in the PWC Report to Dorsey and possibly third parties. — Unclear where this might have taken place as no assertions were made.	— Breached duty of confidentiality by providing the two confidential documents, the PWC Report and/or the MRA, to third parties, including Dorsey. — Unclear where this might have taken place as no assertions were made.

It rejected the High Court's finding that WSG would be left without an effective legal remedy because Dorsey would rely on a fair comment defence if WSG was to sue him. They noted that the High Court's reliance on *Fairfax* was ill-suited because the newspaper in that case could rely on section 22 of the Defamation Act which conferred upon them a privilege, which is different from Dorsey's possible defence of fair comment. It was too premature for the judge to decide how the defamation case would go. Besides, the statutory limitation

[43] ibid [48].
[44] ibid [50].
[45] ibid [51].

period of six years was not close to running out. Even if Dorsey had a defence and won at trial, there was enough time for WSG to commence an action against the source. Therefore, the Court was not satisfied that WSG would be left without an effective remedy if they only had Dorsey to sue for defamation.

Another factor the Court considered was the information on Dorsey's blog. This information, the catalyst of WSG's complaint, was already reported by international media. Hence, it was already in the public domain. The Court noted that WSG was not singled out in these reports. It seemed like there was no malicious intent behind the 'sources' or Dorsey against WSG in leaking and writing about the information.

The Court also looked disfavourably upon WSG's failure to sue Dorsey, immediately, for defamation—if they were so concerned about the damage to their reputation, they would have acted with more alacrity. The Court was also not content as to WSG's singling out of Dorsey in this action when other journalists and international media also covered the news. There was no evidence that WSG had taken any other steps to find the identity of the 'sources' apart from serving the interrogatories on Dorsey.

The Court also disagreed with the High Court judge that there was sufficient nexus in this case to Singapore simply because the information might have been passed through the Internet, and that Dorsey resided in and blogged from Singapore. It emphasised that the burden was on WSG to persuade the Court that the discretion should be granted in their favour, and in this case, there was no evidence to suggest that Dorsey had received the information in Singapore. The Court does not have jurisdiction to order interrogatories to aid proceedings *outside* Singapore. Therefore, even if there were *prima facie* causes of action against Dorsey, these factors for the Court weighed against granting the application.

Finally, the Court discussed the wider public interest in exposing corruption. It discussed the iniquity rule, in which the Court will not enforce an obligation of confidentiality if the confidential information is related to serious misconduct. Singapore's stance on corruption can be seen from its ratification of the United Nations Convention Against Corruption, and the enactment of the Prevention of Corruption Act.[46] There is only more reason for exercising the discretion against the interrogatories.

This was the only public interest factor that the Court of Appeal discussed extensively. It mentioned the newspaper rule once in discussing the High Court's judgment and repeated that it was not applicable in Singapore, and that a 'balancing of interest' approach would be applied instead.[47] It did not mention the rule when summarising the law or in its decision.

In short, the Court of Appeal's reason for allowing the appeal was because it considered the High Court judge to not have taken all the relevant factors into account, hence giving wrong weightage to those in WSG's favour. There is also an issue of proof. It considered WSG not to have proven all the factors which it should have for a pre-action third party interrogatory order to be made.

[46] Prevention of Corruption Act (Cap 241, 1993 Rev Ed).

[47] *Dorsey* (CA), above n 1, [18], referring to *Dorsey* (HC), above n 1, [19].

Comment on the Court of Appeal's Decision

The Court of Appeal's decision is interesting in light of the new trend of in taking a more active role in its decision-making. However, where freedom of expression issues are concerned, we are getting silence. This silence is undesirable because of its traditional tendency to reject foreign authorities or arguments in this area.[48] The silence does not allow us to build up a body of cases, decisions and arguments which can be refined into principles. Even worse, it could lead the press and the legal profession to interpret the silence as an implied rejection of the 'newspaper rule' or its underlying policies.[49]

A More Active Court of Appeal?

The new Chief Justice indicated in his speech at the Opening of the Legal Year 2013[50] a greater willingness for the Court to appoint *amicus curiae* for complex issues. In its hearing to challenge the constitutionality of section 377A, Penal Code, the presiding judge, Justice Andrew Phang, in an unprecedented move, handed to counsels for both parties documents found in the British Library.[51] Even though no *amicus curiae* was involved in Dorsey's appeal, we still can detect the Court's proactivity in the number of cases the Court cited in its decision. There were at least 12 not submitted by counsels on both sides.[52] However, none of these 'extra' cases cited, apart from *Ashworth, British Steel* and *John Fairfax*, were on the newspaper rule or freedom of expression. What was disappointing was that these three cases were not used for these purposes.

When looking at this trend, could the silence on the newspaper rule be on purpose? Whilst Dorsey did not expressly make any submissions on the newspaper rule, there were submissions that the High Court judge was wrong in holding he was not a journalist and giving undue weightage to the public interest of free flow of information. If the Court was

[48] The Singapore courts have not adopted a more pro-freedom of speech stance in defamation cases, rejecting other common law approaches such as *Reynolds v Times Newspapers Ltd* [2001] 2 AC 127 and *Lange v Atkinson* [2000] 3 NZLR 385: see *Review Publishing Co Ltd and another v Lee Hsien Loong* [2010] 1 SLR 52 and *Lee Hsien Loong v Singapore Democratic Party* and others [2007] 1 SLR(R) 675.

[49] This spectre could happen if the dicta are forgotten by later cases or legal writings.

[50] Sundaresh Menon CJ, *Response by Chief Justice Sundaresh Menon at the Opening of the Legal Year 2013 and Welcome Reference for the Chief Justice*, 4 January 2013.

[51] The documents, consisting of correspondence between the governor of the day and London, indicated a legislative purpose of the male sodomy offence.

[52] See, eg, *Anglo Irish Bank Corp plc v West LB AG* [2009] EWHC 207 (Comm); *Ashworth Hospital Authority v MGN Ltd* [2002] 1 WLR 2033; *Asta Rickmers Schiffahrtsgesellschaft mbH & Cie KG v Hub Marine Pte Ltd* [2006] 1 SLR(R) 283; *Clift v Clarke* [2011] EWHC 1164 (QB); *Kneale v Barclays Bank plc* [2010] EWHC 1900 (Comm); *Long Beach Ltd v Global Witness Ltd* [2007] EWHC 1980 (QB); *Navigator Investment Services Ltd v Acclaim Insurance Brokers Pte Ltd* [2010] 1 SLR 25; P v T Ltd [1997] 1 WLR 1309; *President of the State of Equatorial Guinea v Royal Bank of Scotland International* [2006] UKPC 7; *R (Mohamed) v Secretary of State for Foreign and Commonwealth Affairs (No 1)* [2009] 1 WLR 2579; *Rugby Football Union, The v Consolidated Information Systems Ltd* [2012] 1 WLR 3333; *Tan Seow Cheng v Oversea-Chinese Banking Corp Ltd* [2003] SGHC 30; *United Company Rusal plc v HSBC Bank plc* [2011] EWHC 404 (QB); *XL London Market Ltd v Zenith Syndicate Management Ltd* [2004] EWHC 1182 (Comm).

of the opinion that the judge did not take into account a full spectrum of factors, to omit comment on the most salient factor, ie: freedom of expression, is unsatisfactory.

Silence Is Not Golden

The Court of Appeal's silence on the newspaper rule is a missed chance to illuminate us on what it thinks about the newspaper rule. This case marks not just the first time a *Norwich Pharmacal* case appeared before the Court of Appeal, but also the first time for the Court to consider the issue of confidentiality of journalists' sources.

Though the High Court discussed the newspaper rule in the previous case *KLW Holdings*, there are flaws in Justice Choo's reasoning that need to be brought out. All the points in Choo J's decision on the newspaper rule are unsound. Those points were (1) that it is an old English rule; (2) that the applicability of the rule needs to be examined within the context of whether Singapore has a responsible press; and (3) the lack of argument to show that the rule if not recognised will lead to the drying up of sources.

Being an old English rule does not make it inapplicable, even if there have yet to be cases recognising the rule in Singapore. *KLW Holdings* is the first reported case on confidentiality of journalists' sources before the High Court of Singapore since independence. This is a common law rule. Singapore has a common law tradition. The lack of precedence does not make it irrelevant.

As for having to examine the press culture in Singapore, we believe that there is no need for it. There is no guarantee that today's responsible press will not be irresponsible tomorrow. It is impractical to examine the press culture each time such a case comes before the court. Also, a different type of press or journalist will appear before the Court each time. We cannot presume an immutable and homogenous mindset amongst all journalists.

The issue of responsible journalism ought to be handled on a case-by-case basis. Any fear of irresponsible journalism can easily be overcome by examining the conduct of the journalist for the case itself. A list of criteria such as that in the English *Reynolds* case can be developed.[53]

Finally, the judge's comment on lack of argument proffered in support is effectively asking for evidence on a point which is impossible to prove. Few sources will come forward to state that without the rule, he would not be providing the information.[54] Balanced by the media's belief and defence of this rule, including going to jail for contempt, the chilling effect for the lack of such a rule can be said to be presumed. Further, we submit that this is an assumption about human behaviour which is self-evident. It is like asking for proof that absolute power corrupts absolutely, to support Montesquieu's separation of power theory. We submit that the universality of the rule's application would be the most persuasive.

There is an important difference between applying the *Norwich Pharmacal* type of balance of interests approach and recognising and applying the newspaper rule. The newspaper rule

[53] *Reynolds*, above n 48.

[54] JM Brabyn, 'Protection Against Judicially Compelled Disclosure of the Identity of News Gatherers' Confidential Sources in Common Law Jurisdictions' (2006) 69 *Modern Law Review* 895, 926.

does *not* confer an absolute privilege or immunity to journalists;[55] it sets up how the balance is to be applied. It shifts (or to be more exact, adds to) the applicant's burden to persuade the court that it is necessary to order the disclosure of the source.

This is why it might sound odd for *KLW Holdings, Tullet Prebon* and the High Court in *Dorsey's* case to state that the newspaper rule does not apply because 'the balance of interests' approach is the correct one. *Recognising the newspaper rule does not forego a balancing approach. Apart from shifting the burden of proof as aforementioned, the newspaper rule serves as an express reminder to the court as to what public policies should be kept in mind when applying the balancing of interest approach.* The High Court in *Dorsey* did not do a very good job of recognising just what the public interest in 'free flow of information' entails, and the Court of Appeal, unfortunately, did not address the question at all.

One might argue that this is a very fine, if not pedantic, difference in the ultimate application of the two approaches. But the recognition of the newspaper rule is more than just academic posturing: how the court treats it and its underlying policies is a reflection of how the court views the press in society. In the Singaporean context, this becomes even more important.

It can be said that the newspaper rule presumes that freedom of expression is integral to a democracy. This is based on the theory that it promotes the free flow of information, without which sources may dry up. The important role the press plays as a watchdog in a democracy necessitates this rule and the values behind it.

When we discuss the newspaper rule, it can be said that we weigh the public interest underpinning the free flow of information with the applicant's interest in access to justice. Whilst access to justice can be looked at from the point of view of individual private interest as well as that of the public interest, the free flow of information is necessarily only a matter of public interest. There is no private interest involved in the press' need for free flow of information.

In cases such as *British Steel* and *John Fairfax* the free flow of information is one of the many factors to be considered in the granting of a *Norwich Pharmacal* order. In Singapore, the free flow of information in itself has never been considered in the granting of *Norwich Pharmacal* or O 24 and O 26A orders. The closest a Singapore court came to this was in *KLW Holdings*, which expressly endorsed *John Fairfax* for the proposition that the state will not compel the revelation of sources unless the necessity for justice between the parties demands it.[56]

In many other common law jurisdictions, *John Fairfax* has come to stand as one of the most 'liberal' cases on the newspaper rule.[57] It is therefore interesting to see it cited in the first Singapore case on the newspaper rule which rejected the existence of the rule.

The newspaper rule itself has been a slippery, baffling creature that the English and common law courts cannot seem to define satisfactorily. The most the judges in newspaper

[55] *John Fairfax*, above n 39, [13]: 'It is a fundamental principle of our law, repeatedly affirmed by Australian and English courts, that the media and journalists have no public interest immunity from being required to disclose their sources of information when such disclosure is necessary in the interests of justice.'

[56] KLW Holdings, above n 19, [11].

[57] Even though *Fairfax*, the media company, lost against the order for the disclosure of the sources in this case, the High Court of Australia suggested that there is no reason why the newspaper rule as a rule of practice is to be confined to a pre-trial or interlocutory stage of a defamation action (above n 39, [14]).

rule cases can agree on is that it is a *rule of practice*, but what it was, and is now, based on, is still fiercely debated. We can see the range of views in this debate in *John Fairfax* and *British Steel:* the unanimous judgment of the High Court of Australia in *John Fairfax* surveyed and summarised the landscape of the newspaper rule cases and found that the reasoning behind the rule had changed from a more procedural reasoning of relevancy[58] to a public interest value in the free flow of information. In *British Steel*, the speeches of the Law Lords and justices show a diversity of understanding of the newspaper rule, the extreme being Lord Denning and Lord Salmon,[59] whose view of the rule as being grounded on the public policy interest of free flow of information was rejected by the majority (as well as by the High Court of Australia in *John Fairfax*).[60]

Another issue lies in the extent of the rule itself: is it limited to interlocutory defamatory actions, or can it be applied to trials, or actions not based on defamation? There is also the debate as to whom the newspaper rule covers: limiting it to people working on 'newspapers' sounds too outdated in an age of technology and blogging.[61] Whilst in 2002 we had a few well known bloggers who commented on issues of public interest, today we have online 'newspapers', such as The Online Citizen and TR Emeritus. This issue was raised by Dorsey's counsel when submitting that the High Court judge erred in finding him not to be a journalist.

We do not wish to plunge into these lively debates in this chapter. They are only mentioned to emphasise the fact that the Singapore courts missed their chance to engage with them in the *Dorsey* case.

Despite many courts trying to ground it to procedural reasons, the recognition of the newspaper rule itself is a recognition of the public policy interest in the protection of journalist sources, and/or the free flow of information. In effect, the newspaper rule shifts the balancing of interests in *Norwich Pharmacal* orders and the like in favour of the journalists from the start. This exercise *is* a reflection of a society and the values which it places

[58] Relevancy has always been an important ingredient for pre-action discovery or interrogatory cases; the court is highly suspicious of the applicant party abusing the process for 'fishing expeditions'. See *Ching Mun Fong v Standard Chartered Bank* [2012] 4 SLR 185 where the Court of Appeal affirmed the rejection of the application for pre-trial discovery because the applicants were 'raid[ing] the cupboards of the respondent for the purposes of finding fault' and that O 24 r 6 and r 7 codified the public policy grounds against this kind of behaviour ([42]).

[59] Lord Denning's statement in the Court of Appeal case of *British Steel*, above n 16, 1129: 'The public has a right of access to information which is of public concern and of which the public ought to know. The newspapers are the agents, so to speak, of the public to collect that information and to tell the public of it'. This was approved in Lord Salmon's dissent in the House of Lords (ibid 1189).

[60] *John Fairfax*, above n 39, [13].

[61] *Cornec v Morrice* [2012] IEHC 376. The facts of the case are highly complicated. It involves a cult figure suing for defamation in Colorado. Applications for letters rogatory were made in the court of Ireland against two persons—one a journalist, Ms Talland; and the other, a blogger, Mr Garde which could lead to the revelations of their sources. The blogger, a former theologian was considered a specialist in the area which he was blogging—cults. Hogan J declined to give effect to the letters rogatory for both and applied the same test to the blogger, even though he was not a 'journalist in the strict sense of the term'. He opines that the traditional distinction between journalists and laypeople have 'broken down' in the recent decades, 'not least with the rise of social media'. He further emphasises that this blogger's activities fall within the scope of educating the public. Such a person can readily constitute an 'organ of public opinion' in the Irish Constitution. Further, there is high 'constitutional value' in ensuring his right to voicing these opinions should not be compromised. He is of the view that 'critical information in relation to the actions' of cults would dry up if the blogger could be compelled to reveal the information sought. See [65] to [70].

much importance on; it is also a reflection of pragmatism that can change from case to case depending on—as the judges always remind us—'the necessity of justice'.

So far the common law cases on newspaper rule reveal two things: firstly, for a 'rule', it is hardly set in stone, and its boundaries flow and ebb from case to case; secondly, most judges are, rightly or not, suspicious of placing too much power in an institution, especially in favour of the amorphous concept of the 'press' whose members may not always be noble self-sacrificing paragons of journalism.[62] No judge has talked of the newspaper rule without talking about how it should be limited; even Lord Denning in *British Steel* added an important caveat that the journalists should prove themselves to be responsible and worthy of the privilege under the rule.[63]

Recognising the newspaper rule will not be introducing a foreign idea that lacks precedent and is also grossly out-of-place in a twenty-first century Singapore society. The policy objectives of free flow of information is in sync with the government's goals of ensuring accountability and good governance. At the very most, it will only place a stick in the sand to guide not just the court, but also Singaporean journalists and the public, as to where free flow of information and the press, as an important institution of a democratic society, stand in the eye of the law.

There are many layers to Justice Choo's brief, but important decisions, the two most important of which are (i) in substance recognising the newspaper rule as a rule of practice while holding it to be, in name, inapplicable in Singapore;[64] and (ii) in pre-action third party discovery, the court is entitled to lean in favour of confidentiality of the source's identity unless greater interests of justice demand otherwise.

KLW Holdings remains the only case in Singapore to substantively discuss and tackle the question of the newspaper rule and the issue of the protection of journalist confidential information. Despite its flawed reasoning, it is in danger of being reduced to merely standing for the proposition that the newspaper rule does not apply. Had the Court of Appeal looked more closely at the issue, it would have noticed that the legal landscape has changed since *KLW Holdings*. In 2012, 10 years after the *KLW Holdings* decision, the ASEAN Human Rights Declaration[65] was signed by all 10 member states of the regional political grouping. Article 23, the provision on freedom of expression is similar to Article 19 of the Universal Declaration on Human Rights, except for the notion sharing information through any medium regardless of frontiers. This would have been a good chance for the Court of Appeal to re-examine the law in view of Singapore's new international obligations.

[62] A case that deals with less-than-stellar journalists is *British Steel*, above n 17, where the journalists in Granada had not told BSC's Sir Charles Villiers in reasonable time beforehand that they had the papers with them so that he could prepare for his interview with them, and they had also mutilated the papers when they 'complied' to send them back to BSC. Even Lord Denning, who had said that there was a public interest in journalist protection of confidential sources subject to the rule that the journalist must act responsibly, found that in this case, the journalists had fallen under the standard.

[63] *British Steel*, ibid 1130: 'It seems to me that the rule—by which a newspaper should not be compelled to disclose its source of information—is granted to a newspaper on condition that it acts with a due sense of responsibility. In order to be deserving of freedom, the press must show itself worthy of it. A free press must be a responsible press. The power of the press is great. It must not abuse its power. If a newspaper should act irresponsibly, then it forfeits its claim to protect its sources of information.'

[64] *KLW Holdings*, above n 19, still recognises the 'default' position that the court will honour confidential obligations owed by the journalist to their sources, unless it is shown that the necessity of justice requires otherwise. Even though Choo JC refused to call it by its name, this is effectively the newspaper rule at work.

[65] ASEAN Human Rights Declaration, adopted by the Heads of State/Government of ASEAN Member States at 19 November 2012.

Finally, it is worth noting that in common law jurisdictions such as England and Australia, the newspaper rule has been largely supplanted by arguments based on codified journalist shield laws, or the constitutional freedom of speech.[66] Journalists in Singapore do not have such luxury. The Singapore Parliament shows no zeal in legislating or clarifying laws for the benefit of journalists.[67] While the freedom of speech is a constitutional right in Singapore, case law[68] suggests that we are still a long way away from relying on our constitutional right to freedom of speech for the purposes of protecting the free flow of information. Therefore, if the government is loath to offer legislative or other protection to the media, the Singapore courts should at least clarify the scope and applicability of the newspaper rule, or its substantive application by another name, so that journalists can have greater legal certainty as to when they may or may not need to reveal their confidential sources.

Is the Glass Half Full?

Despite the above criticisms of the Court of Appeal's judgment, we would like point out that it was indeed a very welcome judgment which clarified the law on O 24 and O 26A, in Singapore. What we found most heartening were the following two aspects of the judgment: (1) the focus on the intrusive nature of O 24 and O 26A orders; and (2) mentioning the public interest in bringing corruption to light as a factor to be considered.

It might seem that the Court of Appeal took extra precaution in not mentioning the role that journalists and free presses play in bringing corruption to light—this is in keeping with the theme of the judgment as a whole. However, we take the more optimistic view that recognising the public interest in whistleblowing and exposing iniquities such as corruption is only a step removed from recognising the public interest in having a legal environment that fosters protection of journalists' confidential sources and investigative journalism. The policy behind protecting whistle blowers is to encourage the free flow of information where corrupt practices are detected. This is to promote good governance. This is the same rationale for the newspaper rule.

[66] With the adoption of the European Convention of Human Rights and the *Goodwin* judgment, above n 9, journalists are not limited to only s 10 of the Contempt of Court Act 1981 when pleading against divulging confidential sources. See *Ashworth Hospital Authority v MGN Ltd* [2002] 1 WLR 2033, [38] (per Lord Woolf): 'there can be no doubt now that both section 10 [of the Contempt of Court Act] and article 10 [of ECHR] have a common purpose in seeking to enhance the freedom of the press by protecting journalistic sources.' Australia has journalist shield laws on a federal level since the passing of Evidence Amendment (Journalists' Privilege) Bill 2010. Currently, five Australian states (New South Wales, Victoria, Tasmania, Australian Capital Territory, Western Australia) have varying degrees of protection of journalist privilege under their relevant evidence legislation. New Zealand has a Protection of Journalist's Sources provision under s 68 of their Evidence Act 2006 (NZ), and this inspired the Australian journalist privilege provision in ss 126G and 126H of the Evidence Act 1995 (Commonwealth).

[67] Mark Cenite has argued that the Singapore government has over-legislated the freedom of speech area, but the laws are so vague as to cause uncertainty that results in a chilling effect over the media. Mark Cenite, 'Too Much Legislation, Too Little Expressions' in Kalinga Senevitratne and Suganthi Singarayar (eds), *Asia's March Towards Freedom of Expression and Development* (AMIC Singapore 2006).

[68] According to the Court of Appeal in 2009, 'the notion that "[t]he press discharges vital functions as … a watchdog" (per Lord Nicholls in *Reynolds* (HL) at 205) is not accepted. The media has no special role beyond reporting the news and giving its views on matters of public interest fairly and accurately … the media's role in Singapore has hitherto been and continues to be limited to what Lord Nicholls referred to in *Reynolds* (HL) as 'the traditional activities of reporting and commenting', see *Review Publishing Co Ltd v Lee Hsien Loong* [2010] 1 SLR 52, [277–278].

Conclusion: Why, When and Who?

The Court of Appeal, by not discussing the newspaper rule and its policy reasoning, has not provided much assurance to journalists and has left lawyers handling future cases with uncertainty. Should a similar fact situation such as Dorsey's arise in the future, what is clear is that someone in WSG's position should file a writ against the journalist, then apply to the court for information on the source. O 24 and O 26A, like *Norwich Pharmacal* orders, are pre-action third party applications. The possibility of being granted an order against a journalist to reveal his sources in interlocutory applications is untested. The defence lawyer will need to then go through all the technical requirements of an interlocutory application either for discovery or for interrogatories to defend the confidentiality of the source's identity despite the issue being one of free flow of information.

Like most issues, when deciding on the policy of protecting the identity of journalists' sources, we should ask ourselves, 'why, when and who'? Why should we protect the identities of journalists' sources? When should we protect these identities or the confidence? Who should be able to make use of this protection?

Why?

The courts in major common law jurisdictions have never questioned the wisdom of the free flow of information. They have merely tried to control the ability of the papers or journalists to use it indiscriminately by stating that it is not an absolute privilege. The objective of the free flow of information is to promote transparency, accountability and good governance. These are aims shared by Singapore's government. Hence, there is no reason for the newspaper rule or the free flow of information policy not to be adopted by the courts.

When?

This is the difficult question. We do not want the rule to lead to irresponsible journalism. The policy behind a *Norwich Pharmacal* order is to ensure access to justice. When the newspaper rule is used as a defence against a *Norwich Pharmacal* order, two major principles clashes. This is the reason why no judge is willing to state that the newspaper rule is one of 'absolute privilege'. It will place the responsibility of ensuring good governance at the total discretion of the press. This is why the courts have preferred a 'balancing approach'. It is submitted that the court should come up with a set of criteria to be applied on a case-by-case basis.

Who?

The court should decide or give a set of criteria on when a blogger or online-only newspaper reporter can avail himself of the protection of the newspaper rule. It is a pity as the facts in the case presented such a chance. Dorsey was an academic at the material time. His contract with the Nanyang Technology University included a clause that he had to maintain his blog, 'The Turbulent World of Middle East Soccer'. He considered his job when writing for his blog as one of a journalist. Should a blogger with specialised knowledge in an area be able to find solace in the newspaper rule[69] or should we look at his methodology when gathering information and writing?

It is unsatisfying to read cases with issues that seem to hover in the background. Everyone involved in the *Dorsey* case knew there was a freedom of expression issue. It has resulted in the Court of Appeal discussing the subject of corruption which shares the same policy reasoning for protecting sources and emphasising their privacy or the intrusive nature of O 26A r 1(5). It is unsatisfying when the 'why' is clear. As for the 'when' and 'who', they are the job of the court. We should always address matters for what they really are. Only then will our media be given proper guidance and syndromes such as the much disliked 'OB markers' and self-censorship disappear.

[69] *Cornec v Morrice*, above n 60.

Part C

Legal Regulation of the Media and Internet

11

Challenges for Communications in a Changing Legal Landscape

ROLF H WEBER*

Media play a central role in modern societies and have a direct interrelation with politics since governing political bodies regularly have a substantial interest in information-driven processes. During the last 20 years, however, communications were exposed to major technological changes which did and do not only have an impact on daily life but also on the legal landscape. An additional challenge comes from the globalisation of communications making it more and more difficult to safeguard a national media regime, ie a certain 'harmonisation' of cross-border rule-making appears inevitable. This chapter addresses the legal issues arising from different elements of the new media environment which need to be reconsidered in order to respect the technological conditions of the online world; furthermore, the general political perceptions of rule-making must also be taken into account. Thereafter, technology as a means of media control regulation is addressed. Finally, the pillars of a new media governance framework are outlined.

Based on the new technologies, the character of communications changed causing major challenges for media enterprises. In addition, control and surveillance mechanisms introduced by national legislatures and private enterprises (technology leading to media control) make it necessary to develop fresh participatory approaches having their foundations in multi-stakeholder concepts and power distribution models. Openness, interoperability and neutrality must become the major pillars of the media landscape and should be complemented by a newly designed media governance framework encompassing improved legitimacy and accountability elements imposed on the participants of the media landscape.

Elements of the New Media Landscape

From One-way Communication to Interactive Communication

Initially, communication took place one-way between a sender and one or more personally defined receivers. Later, this 'simple' communication was complemented by mass

* The author would like to thank his research assistant Ulrike I Heinrich, attorney-at-law, for her valuable support in the preparation of this chapter.

communication, founded on the idea of mass production and distribution,[1] namely newspapers, cinema, radio and television. This sort of communications takes place one-way between a source and a large number of receivers being classed as one-to-many-communication.[2] In so doing, messages are indirectly and unilaterally mediated to a disperse public.

In the middle of the nineteenth century, electronic communications and new forms of visual media complemented and partly transformed the existing print culture.[3] In addition, being defined as both the specific communications technology and the social, political, and economic structure within which these technologies are used,[4] the media landscape substantially changed in the course of the last three decades especially caused by the introduction and establishment of the Internet, an international online databank allowing the sharing of linked multimedia documents. The ongoing development of the World Wide Web resulted in additional challenges to the 'media environment'.

In this context, the terms 'offline communication' and 'online communication' are at stake. While forms of communication outside the Internet area like talking on the telephone, writing letters or even speaking face-to-face are referred to as 'offline communication', the term 'online communication' encompasses the communications via networked computers[5] and can be dated back to the late 1960s when United States (US) researchers first developed protocols that allowed the sending and receiving of messages by use of computers. In light of the spread of personal computers in the 1980s, online communication became available to the public at large.

Since the percentage of people having Internet access and using web-based systems for the search and purchase of products or the cultivation of contacts has grown vastly, civil society gradually started to replace traditional face-to-face communication by using e-services.[6] Accordingly, it comes as no surprise that by now working without Internet access is almost inconceivable, at least in developed countries.

From Contents Produced for Many to Individual Contents

Along with the World Wide Web's development, global communication as a new form of communication evolved, shifting communication from a local to a worldwide level.[7] In fact, the Internet became so important for societal communication that the participation of all

[1] Kalyani Suresh, 'Journalism and Mass Communication' (2003), ch 2 www.peoi.org/Courses/Coursesen/mass/fram2.html accessed July 2016.

[2] Despite its large reach, the traditional mass communication by print and electronic media faces a lack of scope for feedback by the audience.

[3] Andrea L Press and Bruce A Williams, *The New Media Environment: An Introduction* (Wiley-Blackwell, 2010) 12.

[4] ibid 8.

[5] Mark Warschauer, 'Online Communication' in Ronald Carter and David Nunan (eds), *The Cambridge Guide to Teaching English to Speakers of Other Languages* (Cambridge University Press, 2001) 207.

[6] Geke van Dijk and Shailey Minocha and Angus Laing, 'Consumers, channels and communication: online and offline communication in service consumption' (2007) 19 *Interacting with Computers* 7.

[7] Mohammad Shamsuddoha, 'Globalization to Glocalization: A Conceptual Analysis' (2008) University of Chittagong, Working paper, 4 http://papers.ssrn.com/sol3/papers.cfm?abstract_id=1321662 accessed July 2016.

was included in the agenda as a substantial political task.[8] Uniting all kinds of stakeholders, the Internet's range of services and information is continuously growing, granting all the possibility to participate, regardless of geographic or social barriers.[9] Since prices of communications' exchanges over online networks have become quite cheap (in view of the necessary hardware and software as well as the fees payable for the online services) economic barriers for users are hardly relevant (anymore).

Currently, social networks such as Facebook and Twitter are among the most discussed phenomena in the online world, technologies that connect a large part of the world's population. For becoming part of the social networks' community and getting the ability to react immediately to published information and therewith continuously change one's role from a receiver to a sender of information, Internet users only have to create a new account. Within this interactive communication, every participant has the ability to be a receiver and a sender; in both functions, the individual is able to read, view and contribute, the latter without any substantial financial effort. Accordingly, contents published on the Internet are no longer produced for many users only, but also for a definable group of interested receivers.

From Short Living Information to Always Traceable Information

Previously, the lifetime of information announced via television, radio or newspapers was quite limited since the repeated access to the information was not easily possible. Nowadays, by participating in social networks such as Facebook or Twitter, Internet users increasingly transfer their real life into the online world and thereby announce large amounts of private data to the public. Once published, these data (images, personal information) stay available virtually for an unlimited period of time.

Privacy interests do not correspond to the eternal life of data in the Internet. Therefore, more and more frequently the question is raised whether individuals have a so-called 'right to be forgotten'. Such a right would conceptually entitle an individual to request from a social network or another Internet provider to remove/delete a certain piece of information from the Internet. This right to be forgotten has recently been acknowledged by the European Court of Justice that requested Google to remove the information about a Spanish citizen having fallen bankrupt in the late 1990s from the search engine services.[10] The data protection perception on the two sides of the Atlantic is quite different in respect to the viability of a right to be forgotten.[11] However, irrespective of the technical problem that the deletion of the information by Google does not necessarily lead to a complete 'disappearance' of the information, the legal scope of the European Court's opinion is not so broad as partly assumed. The right to be forgotten can only be invoked if the information

[8] Bernd Holznagel and Pascal Schumacher, 'Die Freiheit der Internetdienste' in Wolfgang Kleinwächter (ed), *Grundrecht Internetfreiheit* (Eurocaribe Druck, 2011) 14.

[9] Hans Peter Dittler, 'Besonderheiten der Internetkommunikation' in Kleinwächter, ibid 40.

[10] Case C-131/12 *Google Spain SL, Google Inc v Agencia Espanola de Protección de Datos, Mario Costeja* González (ECJ, 13 May 2014).

[11] Daniel Fisher, 'Europe's "Right to be Forgotten" Clashes with US Right to Know' (Forbes, 16 May 2014) www.forbes.com/sites/danielfisher/2014/05/16/europes-right-to-be-forgotten-clashes-with-u-s-right-to-know/ accessed July 2016.

has a direct impact on the reputation of the concerned person and if the event dates back to a time which should no longer be relevant for the present.[12]

Visions of Political Power in the Digital Age

As mentioned, the new technologies influencing the media landscape particularly concern the practical importance of the Internet. Not surprisingly, political forces attempt to have a stake in the development of the Internet.

Need for a Redesign of the Sovereignty Concept due to Globalisation

Communications' exchanges can also constitute a means of power; consequently, politics are important in the media environment and need to be assessed in connection with the rising importance of the Internet. Traditionally two visions of political power exist, namely the dominance of state power, being founded on the sovereignty concept that goes back to the Westphalian Peace Treaty of 1648,[13] and the power distribution approach that relies on a variety of stakeholders.[14] For centuries, international treaty making was a domain of state power; however, the globalisation by way of the Internet has led to a loss of the nation states' sovereignty.

Legal doctrine has discredited the traditional sovereignty notion in several ways during the last few years with manifold reasons for the trend. On the one hand, private and professional activities became more and more of a cross-border nature. With regard to the fact that sovereign borders are blurring in the light of global communications' possibilities that lower barriers to social and commercial intercourse geographically, legal rules and systems, based on the principle of territoriality, lose importance.[15] In this context, already at the end of the twentieth century, the then UN Secretary General Kofi Annan expressed the opinion that a global era would require global engagement and that necessary actions in favour of humanity could not embark on the basis of the traditional approach looking at sovereignty.[16] Consequently, the competence of states to regulate cross-border activities must be redefined.

On the other hand, the concept of sovereignty is deeply interwoven with international law and abandoning sovereignty requires very serious thoughts about the substitute that could efficiently fill the gaps left by its absence.[17] New players in the rule-making processes

[12] Case C-131/12, above n 10, [94].

[13] Rolf H Weber, 'New Sovereignty Concepts in the Age of the Internet?' (2010) 8 *Journal of Internet Law* 12, 13.

[14] Alexander Klimburg, 'The Internet Yalta' (Center for a New American, 5 February 2013) 1 www.cnas.org/sites/default/files/publications-pdf/CNAS_WCIT_commentary%20corrected%20%2803.27.13%29.pdf accessed July 2016.

[15] Weber, above n 13, 12; Warren B Chik, 'Customary internet-ional law: Creating a body of customary law for cyberspace. Part 1: Developing rules for transitioning custom into law' (2010) 26 *Computer Law and Security Review* 1, 7, 10.

[16] John H Jackson, 'Sovereignty—Modern: A New Approach to an Outdated Concept' (2003) 97 American Journal of International Law 782, 787.

[17] Weber, above n 13, 12; Jackson, ibid 790.

need to assume and execute certain tasks. In particular, intermediaries (for example, service providers) in the Internet have gained a strong power in shaping norms, even legal norms, giving such kind of customary norms an (potentially) acceptable legitimacy.[18]

Bearing in mind that internationalisation is a political concept but globalisation is a sociological approach which should have an impact on the efforts to achieve socio-economic equity,[19] a shift towards a 'post-Westphalian mode of frame-setting' is being discussed, namely one that emanates from the emergence of 'other structures, both extra- and non-territorial'.[20]

Emergence of the Multi-stakeholder Concept and Power Distribution as Alternative

Throughout the past decade experience has shown that governance, in particular Internet governance, urgently needs to involve more players, traditionally not granted with sovereign power[21] since the joint involvement of all stakeholders having the necessary know-how is desirable[22] to strengthen the public's confidence in decision-making processes.[23] Besides that, public participation contributes to increasing the governing bodies' transparency and accountability.[24]

Accordingly, the inclusion of all stakeholders in governance and rule-making processes (multi-stakeholder concept) has become a hotly debated topic. A first most remarkable approach has been developed by the Working Group of Internet Governance (WGIG) preparing the second World Summit on the Information Society (WSIS) in 2005 (Tunis); the WGIG Report has identified, a number of roles and responsibilities of the various stakeholders, such as governments, the commercial world, civil society and the academic/technical community.[25] Thereby, the interests of the parties involved should not be defined by any specific group, but through (procedural) participatory mechanisms that reflect the views of the whole society.[26] The respective design of the multi-stakeholder concept depends on the given factual situation.

[18] Timothy S Wu, 'Cyberspace Sovereignty?—The Internet and the International System' (1997) 10 *Harvard Journal of Law and Technology* 647, 666.

[19] Marianne I Franklin, *Digital Dilemmas. Power, Resistance, and the Internet* (Oxford University Press, 2013) 45.

[20] Nancy Fraser, 'Reframing Justice in a Globalizing World' (2005) 36 *New Left Review* 69, 82/83.

[21] Timothy William Waters, 'The Momentous Gravity of the State of Things Now Obtaining: Annoying Westphalian Objections to the Idea of Global Governance' (2009) 16 *Indiana Journal of Global Studies* 25, 33.

[22] Rolf H Weber, 'International Governance in a new media environment' in Monroe E Price and Stefaan Verhulst and Libby Morgan (eds), *Routledge Handbook of Media Law* (Routledge, 2013) 367.

[23] Rolf H Weber, 'Visions of Political Power: Treaty Making and Multistakeholder Understanding' in Roxana Radu and Jean-Marie Chenou and Rolf H Weber (eds), *The Evolution of Global Internet Governance: Principles and Policies in the Making* (Schulthess, 2013) 96.

[24] Rolf H Weber, 'Internet Corporation for Assigned Names and Numbers' in Christian Tietje and Alan Brouder (eds), *Handbook of Transnational Economic Governance Regimes* (Martinus Nijhoff, 2009) 326.

[25] Working Group on Internet (WGIG), 'Report of the Working Group on Internet Governance' (Château de Bossey June 2005) 4 www.wgig.org/docs/WGIGREPORT.pdf accessed July 2016.

[26] Rolf H Weber, 'Future Design of Cybespace Law' (2012) 5 *Journal of Politics and Law* 1, 8.

Notwithstanding the details of this concept, it is clear that multi-stakeholder participation calls for the inclusion of civil society and a bottom-up process. Even if the various actors of civil society are independently organised, common strategies must be developed; the multi-stakeholder model has the potential to rely on an ever increasing participation by those with interests, capacities, and needs in respect of communications' exchanges.[27] In view of the legitimacy aspect of contributions from civil society the following factors should be taken into account: openness, transparency, accessibility, accountability, credibility, consensus-driven approach.[28] The links between the different elements must be developed through the multi-disciplinary examination of the relevant question incorporating social-legal, economic, policy-oriented and game theory studies.[29]

Re-establishment of State Intervention through Fragmentation of Global Networks

As mentioned, political forces have always been interested in playing a role in the media environment. This assessment is also true for modern media; governments have recently worked towards getting involved in the online world's organisation and administration. During the last few years, especially with regard to the Internet's triumph, many countries more and more intensified this interest by claiming that the current, mainly private order of the Internet would impair their national security.

For quite some time now, particularly shown prior to and in the course of the World Conference on International Telecommunications (WCIT) in Dubai (December 2012), advocates of a so-called 'cyber-sovereignty' approach have raised their voices louder, being of the opinion that, for public interest and security reasons, control over the Internet including the right to regulate the activities occurring in the Internet as far as accessible by the domestic population should remain in the competence of national governments.[30] For renewing the existing regulations[31] of the International Telecommunication Union (ITU), the independent United Nations specialised agency for information and communication technologies, its member states assembled at the WCIT and were caught in contradictory debates.

Prior to the WCIT, the Non-Commercial Users Constituency (NCUC) published several motions discussing the promotion of cyber-security, human rights on the Internet, the participation of all stakeholders involved (multi-stakeholderism) as well as the role of governments in the Internet. Besides, advocates of a liberal approach to Internet regulation identified freedom of expression and privacy as key policy issues, apart from the discussions surrounding the new top-level domains. These debates became only possible, since, for the

[27] Rolf H Weber and Romana Weber, 'Social Contract for the Internet Community? Historical and Philosophical Theories as Basis for the Inclusion of Civil Society in Internet Governance?' (2009) 6 *script-ed* 90, 94; Avri Doria, 'Use [and Abuse] of Multistakeholderism in the Internet' in Radu and Chenou and Weber, above n 23, 135.

[28] Joe Waz and Philip J Weiser, 'Internet Governance: The Role of Multistakeholder Organizations' (2012) 10 *Journal of Telecommunications & High Technological Law* 331, 342/43.

[29] Ian Brown and Christopher T Marsden, *Regulating Code: Good Governance and better Regulation in the Information Age* (The MIT Press, 2013) 200.

[30] Weber, above n 23, 98.

[31] The existing International Telecommunication Regulations (ITR) were developed in 1988.

first time in the ITU's history, the entity also invited some civil society representatives to attend the conference and made a huge part of the negotiation documents transparent. During the second half of 2012 many voices raised concerns that the free environment of the Internet could be endangered by the WCIT; thousands of delegates went to Dubai to participate in the WCIT-discussions.

The interests and expectations of the conference participants regarding the new regulations' content diverged to a great extent. With regard to the fact that most important motions (such as the initiative of the United Arab Emirates and some other countries at the end of the first week)[32] were discussed in closed rooms and that civil society representatives were hardly heard in the plenary sessions, the potential of the multi-stakeholder concept has been partly perverted during the WCIT's negotiations. In a nutshell, the negotiations have shown three different visions of political power: while 'cyber-sovereignty'-oriented governments such as Russia, China or Saudi Arabia advocated for an extension of the mandate of the ITU to include Internet governance topics, proponents of a liberal approach such as the US and some allied countries envisaged only implementing minor modifications of the existing regulations since in their opinion the multi-stakeholder approach represented the best way to regulate the Internet.[33] Apart from the two 'extreme' positions, a good number of ITU member states such as India, Brazil, South Africa or Egypt followed neither of the two visions completely but represented a moderate approach[34] by rejecting Internet censorship and closed networks on the one hand but by also fearing that the US could use Internet governance as a diplomatic tactic on the other hand.

In the meantime the tensions of the WCIT have been (at least partly) dissolved. Particularly at the NetMundial[35] in Sao Paolo in April 2014 the final Declaration[36] was negotiated by manifold stakeholders and participation at the conference was open to everybody (with equal speaking time). However, care must be taken that the NetMundial does not remain a single event and that the multi-stakeholder spirit is taken over by other institutions, particularly the ITU.

Technology as Media Control Regulation

Technology as Regulation

For quite some time social scientists define the organisation of communication through the function of a system-specific 'code'; such kind of code is seen as a binary opposition

[32] After two weeks of fruitless discussions, the Iranian representative called for a vote on the inclusion of the 'right of access of Member States to international telecommunications services' into the ITR Preamble, Weber, above n 23, 99.

[33] Weber, above n 23, 99.

[34] Klimburg, above n 14, 2.

[35] Global Multistakeholder Meeting on the Future of Internet Governance: the first conference bringing together thousands of participants from governments, private sector, civil society, technical community, and academia from all around the world.

[36] The non-binding statement contains a set of common principles and important values contributing for an inclusive, multistakeholder, effective, legitimate, and evolving Internet Governance framework by recognising that the Internet is a global resource which should be managed in the public interest, www.netmundial.org/principles.

between a positive and a negative value.[37] The legal system is co-extensive with its coded communicative operations; therefore, Luhmann[38] introduced a system-internal distinction between coding and programming (leading to an allocation of the code values in particular situations).[39]

In the Internet context, the concept of code-based regulation was introduced by Lessig[40] (without specific reference to Luhmann) who outlined and discussed a complex interrelation between four forces, namely law, markets, social norms, and architecture.[41] Lessig's approach relates 'information' to 'code solutions' that are linked to the economic model of property and liability rules as entitlements.[42] By adding 'architecture' to the well-known concepts of 'law', 'markets', and 'social norms' Lessig attempted to take into account the constraints of nature, physics, and technology as determinants of the cyberspace's foundation.[43] Architecture is based on the code being described as the design of the hardware and the software elements for the network (ie the Internet) and of the communication elements allowing these elements to interact with each other; the constraints of the code are self-executing and apply without specific intervention from the participants.[44]

In a nutshell, Lessig argued that code is overtaking the functions of law. Designing cyberspace through software code is thus becoming a powerful regulatory activity.[45] Lessig distinguished between the 'East Coast Code' encompassing laws as a product of the conventional legislative processes (in Washington DC) and the (modern) 'West Coast Code' being based on technology (as developed in Silicon Valley).[46] Conventional law-making is a product of deliberative democratic processes and reflects the system of checks and balances.[47] By contrast, the technological code is simply built into the hardware or software; however, even if the code creation is cheaper and faster, the consequence occurs that code is opaque for civil society.[48]

Obviously, the question of who is in control of and responsible for the code is of utmost societal importance. According to Lessig, the states should prevent the Internet from turning into a place perfectly controlled by commercial entities; furthermore, states should take steps to alter or supplement the architecture in order to reflect public policy.[49] Thereby, the analytical and theoretical approach turns to a political assessment and is losing its technical (neutral) character. The issue of the control structure has a political impact causing questions such as[50] (i) How much state regulation is necessary to secure collective values in the given technical architecture? (ii) Can society accept the aggregation of individual

[37] For further details see Niklas Luhmann, *Legitimation durch Verfahren* 3rd edn (Suhrkamp, 1993) 165–213.
[38] Prof Niklas Luhman was a well known German legal sociologist of the 20th century.
[39] Luhmann, above n 37, 93, 189.
[40] Prof. Lawrence Lessig is a US Law Professor (Harvard, before Stanford and Chicago) and a political activist.
[41] Lawrence Lessig, *Code and Other Laws of Cyberspace* (Basic Books, 1999) 88.
[42] Lessig, ibid 25ff.
[43] ibid 87.
[44] ibid 236/37.
[45] Lawrence Lessig, *CODE version 2.0* (Basic Books, 2006) 32.
[46] Lessig, ibid 72.
[47] Mira Burri, 'Controlling new media (without the law)' in Price and Verhulst and Morgan, above n 22, 335.
[48] Burri, ibid 2013, 336.
[49] Lessig, above n 41, 98 and 109.
[50] Rolf H Weber, *Regulatory Models for the Online World* (Schulthess, 2002) 99.

preferences? (iii) Are choices among architectures necessarily political making collective decision-making imperative? (iv) Can code or architecture be established as a semi-autonomous, semi-distinct social domain?

Furthermore, Lessig's concept relying very much on a technological determinism does not appear to adequately distinguish between the actual status and the desired outcome of code solutions and is underestimating the power of social developments.[51] In addition, perfection of control may be unachievable since at least in theory any code control may be circumvented by another code and often a code fails to realise perfect control over user behavior since it does not operate in a regulatory vacuum.[52]

Nevertheless, technology influences both the interactions within the media environment that are to be regulated (ie the subject of regulation) and its regulability (ie the possibilities and conditions of regulation).[53] Looking from this technological angle, an assessment of the media framework's developments since the publications of Lessig does at least not allow an optimistic outlook.[54] Code is increasingly used as a mechanism of control in cyberspace as shown by the hereinafter discussed examples of Internet filtering and digital rights management. But attempts to overcome code restrictions can also be identified, not only through the legal establishment of openness and access rules but also by way of technical possibilities that allow limits on the application scope of certain codes.

Technology as Enforcement Tool

Technology can be used as an enforcement tool. As creators of technological codes, states as well as private enterprises are relevant.

Internet Filtering

From the side of states the most commonly applied technologically enabled form of control is Internet filtering. Censorship is (allegedly) justified by (often autocratic) regimes with reference to national security, social/cultural reasons, public order or need of restricting the use of Internet tools for what might be deemed inappropriate or improper.[55] Despite all hopes that the Internet would enable individuals to 'route around' censorship, many governments have proven adept at extending state control into cyberspace.[56] In fact, states can apply different measures, apart from the traditional blocking and filtering, to take down information from the Internet or to build a pervasive culture of self-censorship preventing 'unsuitable' content from being created and published online.[57] In addition, the Edward

[51] Victor Mayer-Schönberger, 'Demystifying Lessig' (2008) *Wisconsin Law Review* 713, 736–739.

[52] Chris Reed, *Making Laws for Cyberspace* (Oxford University Press, 2012) 213.

[53] Burri, above n 47, 338.

[54] But the assessment of Burri, ibid 336/37 appears to be too pessimistic.

[55] Rolf H Weber, 'ICT Policies Favouring Human Rights' in John Lannon and Edward Halpin (eds), *Human Rights and Information Communication Technologies: Trends and Consequences of Use* (Hershey, 2013) 27.

[56] Burri, above n 47, 332; Ronald Deibert and John Palfrey and Rafal Rohozinski and Jonathan Zittrain (eds), *Access Denied: The Practice and Policy of Global Internet Filtering* (University Press Group Ltd, 2008).

[57] Weber, above n 55, 27.

Snowden revelations have made it transparent that the US and many other states apply extensive surveillance mechanisms.[58]

From a technical perspective, a range of filtering mechanisms and processes for blocking an Internet user from visiting certain website are available, such as DNS tempering, URL filtering, IP address filtering, deep packet inspection, HTTP proxy filtering, geolocation filtering, and denial of service attacks.[59] Furthermore, there are numerous ways in which businesses can be complicit in censorship.[60] For example, mandatory licensing proceedings can be used to make the business conditional upon adherence to specific requirements such as blocking access to certain information.[61]

Notwithstanding more sophisticated applications, Internet filtering remains a relatively old technology, particularly if compared to code and architecture. From a technological perspective, Internet filtering is less a modality of control than a tool of identification and selection.[62] A major problem consists in the fact that such governmental intervention is not transparent, ie civil society cannot assess its legitimacy and accountability. Furthermore, due to the cross-border nature of the problem, judicial control is only in place to a very restrictive extent, and the 'outsourcing' of certain activities to private entities executing enforcement measures is additionally worsening the legal framework.[63]

Digital Rights Management

Private control mechanisms using technology in order to regulate access to the Internet are available in the case of installation of so-called digital rights management systems (DRM). Originally DRM systems were a measure to strengthen copyright protection; the entertainment industry attempted to avoid 'illegal' downloading of music and films by 'wrapping' digital content into a technologically protected 'package'. As a result, persons not knowing the decryption devices were not able to have access to the protected digital contents.[64] In the meantime, however, DRM systems have lost importance as a means of enforcing copyright claims since most systems can be hacked quite easily and the entertainment industry is looking for other measures of protection.

DRM systems regulating access to information are even more problematic than those attempting to protect copyright. At least in Western countries, the freedom of information

[58] In summer 2013 the computer analyst Edward Snowden revealed top-secret NSA documents leading to revelations about US surveillance on phone and internet communications; subsequently it turned out that many other states apply surveillance mechanisms, too.

[59] William H Dutton, Anna Dopatka, Michael Hills, Ginette Law and Victoria Nash, 'Freedom of connection—freedom of expression: The changing legal and regulatory ecology shaping the Internet' (19 August 2010) Report prepared for UNESCO's Division for Freedom of Expression, Democracy and Peace www.unesco.org/new/fileadmin/MULTIMEDIA/HQ/CI/CI/pdf/wsis_igf5_executive_summary_freedom_expression.pdf accessed July 2016.

[60] European Parliament, *Information and Communications Technologies and Human Rights. Directorate-General for External Policies of the Union* (EXPO/B/DROI/2009/24, PE 410.207, June 2010) www.europarl.europa.eu/meetdocs/2009_2014/documents/droi/dv/2_4_puddephattstudyv2_/2_4_puddephattstudyv2_en.pdf accessed July 2016.

[61] Weber, above n 55, 27.

[62] Burri, above n 47, 333.

[63] ibid.

[64] See in general Joan Van Tassel, *Digital rights management* (Focal, 2006).

is usually guaranteed by a nation's constitution (apart from international instruments such as the UN International Covenant on Civil and Political Rights).[65] Furthermore, access to information fosters innovation[66] since a broader part of civil society can participate in the development of new inventions. Therefore, the informational rights of civil society should not be conditional on a payment, since privileged access to knowledge and scientific data, news and archives can create a deep divide with unknown implications. Dominant stakeholders must also be restricted in blocking rival content threatening their own commercial interests, for example by transforming open platforms into 'walled gardens'. Consequently, openness must remain a key objective of Internet regulation; typical examples of such freely accessible 'systems' are open software and Wikipedia for contents.

In addition, it should not be overlooked that the application of Internet filtering measures as well as the application of DRM systems is not transparent, ie the user can hardly know who has installed technical measures. The lack of transparency is a further problem in the media landscape since the importance of clear information sources and free information distribution are key pillars of an open society.

Elements of a New Media Governance Framework

Necessity of a New Media Governance Framework

As a result of extensive developments in the information and communication technologies—media such as newspapers, books, films, and broadcast were complemented by the ubiquitous Internet—communication practices and the traditional media environment changed to a great extent. Developing into a global network for sharing information and ideas the Internet became a valuable tool in everyday life and a phenomenon encompassing social, cultural, economic, and legal facets. In so doing, this new medium helped to open new horizons for connections between people.

Accordingly, a new media governance framework is needed. With regard to the absence of harmonised rules related to potential regulatory areas, and in light of corresponding risks to freedom of expression, a universal media governance framework comprising appropriate regulations and having their own special characteristics and particularities is needed to create legal certainty. Similar to international private law, the focus needs to be on societal interests. In this context, it is of the utmost importance to remove the existing democratic deficits that accrue from media ownership, filtering and censorship. Besides, an increased co-operation between international bodies and the inclusion of private actors, like media enterprises and recipients of information, is needed.

[65] United Nations, *International Covenant on Civil and Political Rights* (16 December 1966) www.ohchr.org/en/professionalinterest/pages/ccpr.aspx accessed July 2016.

[66] Burri, above n 47, 335.

Recognition of the Openness Principle

Freedom of information/communication and freedom of access to the infrastructure to receive information/communication are of utmost importance in the new media landscape. In line with the well-known slogan 'information wants to be free'[67] Lessig proclaimed in his book *The Future of Ideas*[68] that free resources are essential for creativity and innovation. The 'bridges' between sender and receiver of communications are the networks; freedom and power are affected by the degree of their openness, ie by the extent 'to which individuals can bob and weave between networks to achieve their designed behavior, perceptions, or outcomes'.[69]

Recently, the inventor of the World Wide Web, Tim Barners-Lee, proposed to agree on a 'Magna Carta' in order to protect and enshrine the independence of cyberspace as means for communications' exchanges since the web he created 15 years ago has become under increasing attack from governments and corporate influence. According to Barners-Lee, it is important to ensure an 'open, neutral system'[70] and to generate a digital bill of rights and an open Internet.

The freedom of communications' exchanges in the online world corresponds to the principle that the world must be seen as a public sphere in a universality concept that enshrines multiple publics with manifold interests.[71] The European Commission's vision for the cyberspace landscape consists in a single un-fragmented resource that is endangered if each national legislator develops its own network with the objective to intervene into the cross-border flow of information.[72] The openness of communications' exchanges in cyberspace also is a key element of the 'Internet Universality' concept of UNESCO as outlined in a working paper of September 2013; this 'Internet Universality' is constituted by the R-O-A-M concept of Rights, Openness, Acceptability, and Multi-stakeholder.[73]

Importance of Technological Interoperability and Neutrality

Technological interoperability and neutrality are notions that relate to infrastructure, not to media services in a substantive understanding. However, if the infrastructure is not freely accessible for all members of civil society, the respective restrictions will have a negative impact on the viability of the media landscape.

[67] This slogan was coined by Stuart Brand at the first Hackers' Conference in fall 1984; see Andrew D Murray, *The Regulation of Cyberspace: Control in the Online Environment* (Routledge-Cavendish 2007) 76, 77 fn 7.

[68] Lawrence Lessig, *The Future of Ideas: the fate of the commons in a connected world* (Random House, 2001) 167.

[69] Yochai Benkler, 'Network Theory: Networks of power, degrees of freedom' (2011) 5 *International Journal of Communication* 721.

[70] Jemima Kiss, 'An online Magna Carta: Berners-Lee calls for bill of rights for web', *Guardian*, 12 March 2014, accessible at www.theguardian.com/technology/2014/mar/12/online-magna-carta-berners-lee-web accessed July 2016.

[71] Rikke Frank Jørgensen, *Framing the Net. The Internet and Human Rights* (Edward Elgar Publishing Ltd, 2013) 83–89; Robert Uerpmann-Wittzack, 'Principles of International Internet Law' (2011) 11 *German Law Journal* 1245, 1248.

[72] See Joanna Kulesza, *International Internet Law* (Routledge, 2012) 141 with further references.

[73] See UNESCO Discussion Paper, 'Internet Universality: A Means Towards Building Knowledge Societies and the Post-2015 Sustainable Development Agenda', 2 September 2013, accessible at www.unesco.org/new/fileadmin/MULTIMEDIA/HQ/CI/CI/pdf/news/internet_universality_en.pdf accessed July 2016.

'Interoperability' means the interconnection of networks; interoperability functions can exist on four broad layers of complex systems, namely the technology layer, the data layer, the human layer, and the institutional layer.[74] For the media landscape, the human layer is of utmost importance since it provides the ability to communicate, such as through a common language. Interoperable systems usually make life easier and increase efficiency.[75] The wider the choice available to media users, the higher is their ability to take advantage of their communications' freedoms.[76]

'Technology neutrality' means that normative rules should abstain from favouring or discriminating against any particular technology.[77] For example, if a rule favours digital radio communications, the providers of analogue radio will have difficulties to survive. Even if direct discrimination is not introduced, indirect influences of norms can force some providers to modify their services, potentially at some expense. Rules promoting technology neutrality should attempt to achieve a functional equivalence between different modes of activities and the non-discrimination between technologies with equivalent effects. Furthermore, a rule-maker can achieve a basic level of neutrality between different technological implementations by providing the possibility to modify a non-compliant service in a way that it becomes compliant. However, neutrality is not always desirable (if policy reasons play a role, for example);[78] in a particular media landscape, public service obligations might be a justification for favouring a specific television provider.

Key Functions of Information Intermediaries

Service providers of any kind have gained an important gatekeeper function in the communications markets (search engine providers, social networks etc.). The availability of information and the different ways communications can be exchanged depend on these service providers. Their functions are very important so that antitrust rules must be enforced if a gatekeeper role is exercised by way of market misuse.[79] In addition, media law should be re-conceptualised with respect to liability issues in respect of the own illegal activities of information intermediaries as well as of illegal information exchanges initiated by their customers. A fair balancing is required in view of the need to encourage innovation in the provision of media online services and the need to protect individual rights, such as the right to protect one's reputation.[80] In other words, the legal rights and responsibilities of Internet intermediaries related to information exchanges facilitated by their customers are to be delineated afresh.[81]

[74] John Palfrey and Urs Gasser, *Interop: The Promise and Perils of Highly Interconnected Systems* (Basic Books, 2012) 5, 6.

[75] Palfrey and Gasser, ibid 11.

[76] Brown and Marsden, above n 29, 23.

[77] Reed, above n 52, 192.

[78] ibid 193–199.

[79] The gatekeeper Google is constantly criticised of misusing its market power.

[80] Jacqueline D Lipton, 'Cyberlaw 2.0' in Sam Muller, Stavros Zouridis, Morly Frishman and Laura Kistemaker (eds), *The Law of the Future and the Future of Law: Volume II* (TOAEP, 2012) 145.

[81] Lipton, above n 80, 144.

This task has a close connection to jurisdictional challenges and the impact of conflict of law principles on the substantive assessment of the rights and obligations of intermediaries. The main reason for the importance of jurisdiction and conflict rules consists in the fact that the hereinafter discussed legal interoperability in respect of substantive legal rules has not advanced very far. Indeed, a more harmonised approach to substantive rules governing rights and obligations of intermediaries, particularly for issues such as privacy, intellectual property, and defamation might lessen the pressure on jurisdictional and conflict questions.[82]

Specific Challenges with Content Requirements

For the time being, a global media governance framework does not exist, although media policy occurs not only at the national level but also at the regional and international level.[83] This lack of harmonised media rules is mainly due to the different cultural and social perceptions of media content.

From a theoretical perspective, the question of legal interoperability is arising: the more similarities between national media regulations are given, the more likely media services can be offered by cross-border distribution. The most well-known case showing disparities in legal rules is the case of *LICRA v Yahoo!* The *Tribunal de grande instance* in Paris confirmed the illegal nature of the sale of memorabilia of the Nazi period under French law by a US enterprise in 2000 (thereby approving the competence of the French courts for this case).[84] The principle of legal interoperability which does not necessarily require a total harmonisation of media rules should attempt to lay the foundations for the recognition of some basic substantive principles (such as freedom of expression and privacy) in different circumstances.[85] Using such understanding of legal interoperability facilitates the cross-border rendering of media services.

Furthermore, the discussions around the keyword 'media governance' deal with the question of how developed governance principles can be used for the regulation of media, especially with regard to the fact that media regulation ranges between state control and self-regulation. Additionally, a differentiation is made between the traditional, hierarchically oriented 'governments' and the 'governance' describing the general process of overcoming problems among the different actors involved.[86] Encompassing co-regulation[87] and self-regulation, media governance refers to both private actors and the state that align their media policy on the one hand and the media organisations' own internal regulations on the

[82] ibid 148.

[83] Werner A Meier, 'Demokratie und Media Governance in Europa' in Hans-Jürgen Kleinsteuber and Sabine Nehls (eds), *Media Governance in Europa: Regulierung—Partizipation—Mitbestimmung* (VS Verlag, 2011) 37.

[84] RG:00/0538 of 22 May and 22 November 2000.

[85] Palfrey and Gasser, above n 74, 180–183.

[86] Werner A Meier/Joseph Trappel, 'Medienkonzentration und Media Governance' in Patrick Donges (ed), *Von der Medienpolitk zur Media Governance* (Herbert von Halem Verlag, 2007) 253.

[87] The Interinstitutional Agreement on Better Lawmaking of 16 December 2003 (2003/C 321/01) defines co-regulation as 'the mechanism whereby a Community legislative act entrusts the attainment of the objectives defined by the legislative authority to parties which are recognised in the field (such as economic operators, the social partners, non-governmental organisations, or associations)'.

other hand.[88] The fact that the media environment is characterised by various aspects such as journalistic, political, social, economic, and legal elements speaks against the existence of only one media market.

Outlook

Media governance must be classified as a work in progress tackling central questions such as: who rules the communication channels, in whose interest, by which mechanisms, and for which purposes?[89] With regard to the fact that the existing enormous number of inconsistent domestic media regulations fails to cover the wide range of new problems arising from the constantly developing media environment, changes are reasonably required to establish a new governance framework making uniform arrangements regarding many relevant regulatory areas. Taking into account the substantial changes of the forms of communication and ongoing globalisation, the emerging problems require an international media governance framework.

Particularly with the growing influence of some international bodies, questions of their legitimacy and accountability have arisen.[90] Hence, for being most widely accepted, a sustainable media governance framework should first of all concentrate on legitimacy and accountability aspects.

Traditionally, legitimacy describes a concept primarily relevant to sovereign states as subjects of international law. With regard to the fact that the Internet's development has generally led to an increase in influence of the organisations and entities engaged with the 'World Wide Web', multidisciplinary research should analyse to what extent the same criteria for assessing states' legitimacy can be applied to international entities in the media field.

With regard to the enhancement of the governing bodies' accountability, standards need to be introduced that hold them accountable, at least on an organisational level; in this context, information should be made more readily available to the concerned recipients and consultation procedures as well as some sort of sanctions need to be established.[91]

In addition, there needs to be a focus on the participation of civil society by following a multi-stakeholder approach. Regulations are required for including private actors to help them to raise their voices. Within recent political events like the 'Jasmine Revolution'[92] during which governments tried to shut down Internet and mobile communications for hindering their opponents to organise and telling the world the truth about the current proceedings. In order to avoid such events, a new media governance framework needs to determine internationally-binding regulations encompassing areas like Internet filtering and censorship.

[88] Meier and Trappel, above n 86, 43, 44.

[89] Rolf H Weber and Mirina Grosz, 'Legitimate governing of the Internet' (2009) 3 *International Journal of Private Law* 316.

[90] As in the case with the Internet Corporation for Assigned Names and Numbers (ICANN).

[91] Weber, above n 22, 370.

[92] Starting in Tunis in 2010/2011 the 'Jasmine Revolution' led to far-reaching political changes in several North African states.

12

Self-regulation of the Press in the United Kingdom

LORD HUNT OF WIRRAL

History

The press in the UK has been subject to self-regulation for 60 years, beginning with the creation of a voluntary Press Council in 1953 and the Press Complaints Commission in 1991.

In the 1980s, a small number of publications failed, in the view of many, to observe the basic ethics of journalism. This in turn reinforced a belief among politicians that the Press Council, which had also lost the confidence of some in the press, was not sufficiently effective.

The Government asked David Calcutt QC to consider the matter and he published his report in June 1990. Rather than suggesting new statutory controls, he recommended the setting up of a new Press Complaints Commission (PCC) in place of the Press Council. The press set up the independent PCC at the beginning of 1991.

A committee of national and regional editors produced for the very first time a formal Code of Practice (Code) to administer. All publishers and editors committed themselves to abiding by the Code and to ensuring secure and adequate funding of the PCC.

What the PCC Did

The PCC's primary function was to deal with complaints—relating to the editorial content of newspapers and magazines and the conduct of journalists.[1] The PCC sought to negotiate remedial action and agreed settlements for complainants, issued rulings on complaints and publicly censured editors for breaches of the Code.

On the issue of privacy, there was another core function of the PCC, which, perhaps because it was so confidential in nature, received relatively little mention in public—our anti-harassment service. The PCC regularly passed on requests to editors that their journalists cease contacting individuals and so prevent media harassment. This took the form of a private advisory notice, or in more serious and urgent cases, we issued what was known

[1] The website of the Press Complaints Commission is still accessible at www.pcc.org.uk accessed July 2016.

as a 'desist notice', requesting that journalists or photographers cease their approaches immediately. This service had a markedly high success rate, with journalists and editors appreciating that, if an individual had made it clear that he or she did not wish to speak to the media, then persistent questioning or pursuit would be in breach of the Editors' Code of Practice. Time and time again, we heard from members of the public who used this service and expressed their gratitude to the PCC for the sudden end to media harassment. This demonstrated the relationship the PCC had with the press—one marked by mutual understanding and respect.

The PCC in Transition

As the full extent of the phone-hacking scandal emerged, it became apparent that the public and politicians had lost confidence in the existing system. When I applied in late 2011 for the position of Chairman, I had already concluded that the PCC must be replaced by a new and credible regulator, armed with the powers that the PCC had lacked. I did so on the basis that in my view the PCC had never been a regulator: it had never had any powers of investigation or enforcement, and it had never been able to bind participants into long-term membership. By a cruel twist of fate, I was not the only 'new kid on the block'—just a few months earlier, there had been a fresh infusion of independent Commissioners, all of whom were individuals of the highest calibre. Quite justifiably, when they almost immediately found themselves in the middle of a political firestorm, which was the direct consequence of earlier decisions for which they personally bore no responsibility, nerves frayed somewhat. They all stuck with it, however, for which I remain very grateful.

For most of the time I was there, the PCC was in a transitional phase, as we negotiated the basis of a new, tougher, regulatory system. The governance I inherited was far from ideal: members of the Commission were all both members of the company (with duties to themselves) and also directors of the company (bound by law to act in the best interests of the company). In more placid times, the conflict between those two functions was more potential than actual, but in these straitened times, I needed, as chairman, to be able to speak with authority to politicians, campaigners and the press. We therefore moved towards a much leaner governance structure. Meanwhile the Commission continued with its primary job: commenting on the weekly papers produced by the office team and, at our regular meetings, taking collective decisions on the tough cases that had not been resolved informally. I wish our critics could have seen and heard for themselves the exceptional quality of those discussions.

The primary responsibility of the board and executive director was to give our full support to our staff at all times and to maintain the important, fast, free and fair service we continued to provide to the public. When the time came, the directors of the PCC only took a decision about how best we could contribute to the creation of a new system of effective and independent self-regulation of the press. I personally thought the Leveson Report was a balanced and very fair document and, on the day of release in December 2012, I gave my personal view, which was that it should be accepted *in toto*. Unfortunately, there were aspects of the Leveson model that proved unacceptable to significant elements within the press, so an amended version was eventually adopted.

Implementing Leveson

In his report, Sir Brian Leveson was very clear that it should be the job of the industry to address the failures of the past by creating a new regulator: 'by far the best solution to press standards would be a body, established and organised by the industry, which would provide genuinely independent regulation of its members ...'[2]

The publication of the Leveson Report was followed by an intense period of negotiation, in only some which I and/or the PCC played any part. Plans were finalised in the industry for the introduction of a new independent regulator that would replace the PCC—the Independent Press Standards Organisation (IPSO). The establishment of IPSO did not depend on approval of a Royal Charter, as the Prime Minister made clear to Parliament on 18 March 2013: The Royal Charter does not set up a self-regulator; that is for the press to do.[3]

IPSO, which was launched on 8 September 2014, is a complete break with the past, and delivers all the main Leveson recommendations:

- A majority of independent members at every level, and no industry veto on appointments.
- The power to impose £1m fines for serious or systemic wrong-doing.
- Upfront corrections and adjudications—whether editors like it or not.
- A standards and compliance arm with investigative powers to call editors to account.
- An Arbitration Service to offer a speedy and inexpensive alternative to the libel courts, subject to the successful conclusion of a pilot scheme (dealing with the new 2013 Defamation Law).
- A whistleblowers' hotline.
- A warning service to alert the press, and other media such as broadcasters, when members of the public make it clear that they do not wish to be the subject of media attention.

The implementation of these changes represented arguably the most stringent media regulatory body in the Free World. The greatest tribute I can pay to IPSO (at the time of writing—early 2016) is that the organisation itself has never made the headlines, in any of the main news media. Journalists and newspapers still get things wrong, but in a quietly efficient manner, IPSO has been doing its job.

The Political Impasse

Until the 2015 general election at least, the big debate in Britain related not so much to the regulator itself, but more to the body that has the power to 'recognise' regulators. In his

[2] Lord Justice Leveson, *Report on An Inquiry into the Culture, Practices and Ethics of the Press*, Vol IV (London, The Stationery Office, 2012) 1758, accessible at http://webarchive.nationalarchives.gov.uk/20140122145147/http://www.official-documents.gov.uk/document/hc1213/hc07/0780/0780_iv.asp accessed July 2016.

[3] House of Commons Hansard Debates, 18 March 2013, cols 630–637, accessible at www.publications.parliament.uk/pa/cm201213/cmhansrd/cm130318/debtext/130318-0001.htm#13031811000708 accessed July 2016.

report, Lord Justice Leveson recommended that there should be a body made responsible for formally 'recognising' the new press regulator to ensure that it conforms to the requirements of the Leveson Report. Crucially, and controversially, he said the mechanism for formal recognition should be enshrined in legislation.

During the course of cross-party talks, there emerged the alternative proposal of establishing a recognition body by Royal Charter instead of having it enshrined in (or 'underpinned by') legislation enacted by Parliament.

The Conservative Party—then in coalition with the Liberal Democrats—produced a draft charter, which was rejected by its coalition parties, the opposition Labour party and campaigners for tougher press regulation. Under pressure from campaigners, the three main political parties then produced a draft Royal Charter, which, they maintained, satisfied the substance of the Leveson principles without the need for any new 'press law'. The press responded with their own Royal Charter, accepting many of the provisions of the politicians' draft, but differing in certain material respects.

One area of dispute is on how (or, in practice, if) the Royal Charter could be amended in the future. The press did not want Parliament to be able to initiate, block or approve any future changes to regulation. Instead they proposed a system of independent self-regulation in which the regulator, the trade bodies and the regulator's panel would all have to agree to any changes, in a 'triple-lock' system. The political parties, on the other hand, proposed that a two-thirds majority in Parliament should be enough to amend the Charter. This is how the matter now stands: the Charter is circumscribed by two acts of Parliament, the Crime and Courts Act 2013 and the Enterprise and Regulatory Reform Act 2013.

It was this aspect that the press really opposed. It was not the threat of £1 million fines, nor the proactive investigative arm, nor the 'upfront' corrections and adjudications: it was the prospect of politicians being able to set and adjust the rules for the print and online media. In a sense, therefore, the stumbling block was not one of practicalities, but one of principle. The press felt they simply could not accept this 'crossing of the Rubicon.'

In due course, the Privy Council formally endorsed the government's Royal Charter in autumn 2013. So far, however, no newspaper has said it will sign up to any regulator that applies for recognition under the Charter and the impasse continues. The Press Recognition Panel is up and running, chaired (at the time of writing) by Dr David Wolfe, but it has not, so far, recognised any regulator, although the Impress regulator (responsible for regulating a number of local or 'micro' news publishers) has applied for recognition. If Impress is recognised, that will potentially trigger adverse consequences for newspapers that have not signed up to a recognised regulator.

The Virtues of Self-regulation

It is my strongly held belief that only effective self-regulation can preserve freedom of expression, whilst also inculcating a sense of responsibility into our print journalism. I have not yet seen a convincing argument for statutory regulation of the press. Indeed I have genuine and profound misgivings about directly involving the state in anything that might chill freedom of expression arbitrarily and unnecessarily.

There is good reason why we have shied away from statutory regulation of the press ever since the Licensing Act was repealed in 1695. Winston Churchill stated:

> A free press is the unsleeping guardian of every other right that free men prize; it is the most dangerous foe of tyranny … Under dictatorship the press is bound to languish, and the loudspeaker and the film to become more important. But where free institutions are indigenous to the soil and men have the habit of liberty, the press will continue to be the Fourth Estate, the vigilant guardian of the rights of the ordinary citizen.[4]

Even Karl Marx—not a visionary I often find myself quoting with approval—recognised in 1842 that:

> The free press is the ubiquitous vigilant eye of a people's soul, the embodiment of a people's faith in itself… It is the spiritual mirror in which a people can see itself, and self-examination is the first condition of wisdom.[5]

We all agreed from the outset that the print media must take positive action in order to regain the trust and confidence of the British people. We must ensure that the decline in ethical standards and internal controls at some newspapers, which led to unacceptable, outrageous and illegal behaviour, must never be allowed to happen again. Above all, it is essential that IPSO continues to demonstrate that the result of all these once interminable-seeming discussions and debates is indeed a new regulator with effective sanctions and teeth, truly independent both of the industry—and also of politicians.

[4] Speech by Winston Churchill, 1949, cited in the Leveson Report, vol I, above n 2, 56.

[5] See generally Padmaja Shaw, 'Marx as Journalist: Revisiting the Free Speech Debate' (2012) 10 *tripleC* 618 accessible at www.triple-c.at/index.php/tripleC/article/view/389 accessed July 2016.

13

Regulatory Responses from a Southern Archipelago

URSULA CHEER

Introduction

New Zealanders are enthusiastic adopters of new technology and our use of the Internet has been described as at near saturation point.[1] In a 2013 survey, 81 per cent of respondents rated the Internet[2] as important or very important. Importance ratings of offline media were very different—the proportion who rated offline (or mainstream) media as important were: television (47 per cent), radio (37 per cent) and newspapers (37 per cent). Although watching television is an important leisure activity for people of all ages, 80 per cent of respondents aged 16 to 29 said the Internet is important or very important for entertainment purposes.

In this technological landscape, New Zealand, like other legal systems, is facing challenges arising from harms caused by the publication of online speech. Existing forms of speech regulation are being tested and some adaption has occurred. In addition, the government recently commissioned an investigation into whether gaps exist in the law but ultimately rejected suggestions for a new grand regulator.

This chapter examines the contextual background of current media regulation in New Zealand and the challenges presented by the proliferation of online speech. It considers proposals from the New Zealand Law Commission for a new grand-regulator covering mainstream and new media, and the rejection by the government of those proposals. The chapter then examines the current patchwork of regulation applying to online speech and the introduction by the government of a Harmful Digital Communications Bill, a controversial response to cyber-bullying. Although there are many positive elements to this current patchwork of regulation, overall the system of regulation is too complex, inaccessible and lacks cohesion. The lesson from the New Zealand experience suggests a grand regulator dealing with both offline and online speech is the most desirable solution to take account

[1] Andy Gibson, Melissa Miller, Philippa Smith, Allan Bell and Charles Crothers, 'The Internet in New Zealand', World Internet Project New Zealand 2013, 4, www.aut.ac.nz/__data/assets/pdf_file/0007/424816/wipnz2013final.pdf accessed July 2016. Ninety-two per cent of respondents said they currently used the Internet.

[2] Including online media such as streamed radio.

of the rapid changes brought about by convergence and to preserve and balance free speech and the rights of those harmed by published speech.

Background

New Zealand is a remote archipelago in the South Pacific. Geographically it is 1.1 times the size of the UK, and 244 times the size of Hong Kong, but it has a tiny population of only 4.2 million people. Still a constitutional monarchy, politically the country is a stable democracy utilising a mixed member proportional representation voting system every three years. Economically it is one of the most open markets in the world. Population ethnicity is made up of nearly 74 per cent European descendants of mid nineteenth-century colonists, with the next largest group being nearly 15 per cent indigenous Maori. The Asian population at close to 12 per cent is the next largest and the fastest growing ethnic group in New Zealand.[3]

Media Ownership

Population growth aside, it remains true that New Zealand media audiences are small—among the smallest in the world. There is not much of a market to fight over, but what market exists is governed only by basic competition legislation and mostly owned by off-shore interests. There are only four major commercial players, three of which are foreign-owned; these are APN News & Media (Australian but with a large stake held by Irish company, INM), Fairfax Media (trans Tasman), MediaWorks (Canadian, then Australian, recently in receivership) and Sky TV (Australian, previously controlled by Rupert Murdoch). Cross-media ownership and promotion is common: APN News & Media and Fairfax Media dominate the print media in New Zealand, while MediaWorks and Sky TV dominate commercial television, and MediaWorks and APN dominate radio networks. Change in ownership by these off-shore media proprietors is constant. For example, in 2013, the German Bauer Media Group bought APN's magazine stable. Additionally, financial institutions have been replacing media companies as media proprietors since 2010. By 2012, financial institutions such as equity funds owned over 50 per cent of APN and Fairfax Media, and in 2013 Rupert Murdoch's News Corporation sold all 44 per cent of its shares in SKY TV, now dispersed among various financial institutions.[4]

Alongside this ever-changing commercial market sits a small public broadcasting sector which is nonetheless constantly shrinking as government withdraws funding and increasingly applies commercial imperatives. This is made up of the state broadcasters TV1, TV2, TV1 and TV2 Plus (which simply repeat programming from both channels an hour later),

[3] *2013 Census*, New Zealand Government www.stats.govt.nz/Census/2013-census/profile-and-summary-reports/quickstats-about-national-highlights/cultural-diversity.aspx accessed July 2016.

[4] Merja Myllylahti, *New Zealand Media Ownership Report 2013* (AUT Centre for Journalism, JMAD, 28 November 2013) www.aut.ac.nz/__data/assets/pdf_file/0010/427681/JMAD-2013-Report.pdf accessed July 2016.

Maori Television, and Radio New Zealand and the Concert Programme. Only the latter two broadcasters carry no advertising.

Character of New Zealand Media

What then is the character of the New Zealand media, apart from being mainly foreign-owned? It is often said that the New Zealand media is well behaved. Even our highest court has said so, and though this was 13 years ago now, it remains largely true. In *Lange v Atkinson*, the leading defamation case, the Court of Appeal endorsed the following view of the New Zealand print media, contrasting it with that in the United Kingdom:[5]

> The combination of the smallness of the population with the fact that the dailies are not national papers produces low circulation figures ... Another consequence of the regional character of the dailies is that there is not the same competition that can arise, and has arisen, in the United Kingdom between national papers ... Another difference is that some of the British dailies have close associations with particular political parties; competing political positions are by contrast often expressed in the opinion pages of individual New Zealand dailies and weeklies.

The court additionally endorsed the view that 'New Zealand has not encountered the worst excesses and irresponsibilities of the English national daily tabloids'.[6] But it also noted that the responsibility and vulnerability of the press are critically dependent on its ethics and practices, ownership structures and the independence of editors.

In contrast to this assessment of the New Zealand print media, there is a more recent view that broadcast media is becoming more tabloid in New Zealand, both in style and in the use of intrusive news-gathering methods, and that the print media is aping this development to some degree.[7]

In fact, a 2012 controversy called 'Cuppagate' ignited concerns that some New Zealand media might be involved in illegally breaching privacy. Prior to the November 2012 election, the Prime Minister, John Key, referred the matter of an audio recording he said was illegally obtained to the police. Mr Key and a political ally, Mr Banks, had held a meeting to which media were invited in the week running up to election day. The two men enjoyed a cup of tea in a café, but prior to having discussions, media were asked to remove themselves to a position outside where they could film but not record the conversation. After the meeting, Mr Key discovered a recording device had been left on the table. A cameraman, Bradley Ambrose, who owned the device, obtained a recording remotely from it, which he later

[5] *Lange v Atkinson* [2000] 3 NZLR 385, [34].

[6] ibid. The court referred to a view put forward by journalist Karl Du Fresne, in a publication: *Free Press Free Society* (Newspaper Publishers Association of New Zealand, 1994), 26, 34, that: 'some British tabloids have thrown away the rule book in their pursuit of sensational exclusives. Invasion of personal privacy, fabrication of interviews and the obtaining of information by dishonest means have become the norm in the down-market tabloid press.' Sir Douglas Graham, at the time the Minister of Justice, was also quoted by the court and Du Fresne as saying at the New Zealand Press Council's 20th anniversary that 'Compared to our British counterparts, media intrusion into our daily lives is rather tame, but I do not believe the standard of journalism is by any means inferior. If anything, quite the contrary.'

[7] See Judy McGregor and Margie Comrie eds, *What's News? Reclaiming journalism in New Zealand* (Dunmore Press, 2002).

released to a newspaper when Mr Key accused him of deliberately recording the conversation using '*News of the World* tactics'.[8] The question was whether Mr Bradley had intentionally intercepted a private communication using an interception device.[9] The newspaper refused to release the recording on the basis that it could be breaching a further provision prohibiting disclosure of such communications.[10]

A media storm erupted, focussed on the content of the tape. No mainstream media released it, although hints about its content were reported once another political candidate, Winston Peters, suggested in a campaign speech that the Prime Minister had made derogatory comments about the elderly on the tape. Although the Prime Minister's popularity did not diminish, Mr Peters, whose political future was in doubt, was returned to Parliament after obtaining a sufficient share of the list vote. The cameraman, Mr Bradley, meanwhile sought a declaration that the discussion between Mr Banks and Mr Key was not a private one. The judge refused to adjudicate on the grounds that insufficient facts were before her and the police had not completed their investigation.[11]

Following the election, Mr Key continued to refuse to consent to the release of the tape or to stop the police investigation, even though the tape became available on the Internet. The police eventually announced they would not prosecute Mr Ambrose who had written a letter of regret, but delivered a warning to him and to media that his actions were probably illegal and any publication of the tape would be also. However, the tape had been leaked long since by prominent media law bloggers linking to it. They argued the meeting which was essentially a publicity stunt in a public cafe could never have been private, and any media publishing the tape would not be in breach of the criminal law either.

In a postscript to the story, a newspaper sought the police file on the matter under the Official Information Act 1982 and discovered that the logs of Mr Ambrose's text messages and phone calls were disclosed by a telephone company after police served a search warrant on the company when investigating the incident. The text messages appeared to confirm that the recording was inadvertent, not a deliberate *News of the World*-style conspiracy as the Prime Minister had claimed.[12] It appears that in terms of disclosing media misbehaviour, the incident was no more than a 'storm in a teacup'. There was no real criminal conduct that constituted a breach of the Prime Minister's privacy. Undoubtedly the police pursued the inquiry zealously, but probably not overly so. They were in fact entitled to pursue a warrant and uplift relevant communications from Mr Bradley to investigate his possible commission of an offence, and if this looks heavy-handed, then that is possibly because referring the matter to the police in the first place was so.

If 'Cuppagate' is indicative of the sort of controversy that exposes the state of media behaviour and freedom in New Zealand, then, compared to some of our Pacific neighbours and indeed, to the UK, we are doing quite well. One problem, then, is not that our press lacks freedom but that freedom may be taken for granted. An examination of the current state of media law in the jurisdiction does reveal that although there have been many developments which have opened up the law, vigilance, and possibly change, are still required.

[8] 'Teapot Tape saga costly for cameraman' (*TV One News*, 26 March 2012).

[9] Crimes Act 1961, ss 216A-B.

[10] ibid, s 216C.

[11] *Ambrose v Attorney-General* [2012] NZAR 23.

[12] Bevan Hurley, 'Police seize Cuppagate Texts' (*New Zealand Herald*, 4 August 2013) www.nzherald.co.nz/nz/news/article.cfm?c_id=1&objectid=10907972 accessed July 2016.

Legal Restrictions on Media Freedom

How free is the New Zealand media? In 2014 it was ranked ninth in the world in the Press Freedom Index. Meanwhile, the UK was at 33. No Asian countries were in the top 25 per cent of the table, while many of those countries are among the bottom 45 places. New Zealand is always quite high on the list, where rankings are based on an assessment of pluralism, media independence, environment and self-censorship, legislative framework, transparency and infrastructure in each country. The factors I have noted above, our civic stability and our distance from other markets and conflicts undoubtedly contribute to this result.[13] A steady relaxation of media law restrictions has also played a part, though, as noted above, this cannot be taken for granted. Relevant aspects of the law are examined below.

Criminal Libel

Until 1 February 1993 defamation was punishable as a specific criminal offence. However, this was repealed by the Defamation Act 1992.[14] The government attempted to revive a form of criminal libel in 2001 but was successfully resisted by the media. A clause in the Electoral Amendment Bill (No 2) 2001, making it an offence to expose between writ day and polling day any untrue statement that defamed a candidate and was calculated to influence votes, was inserted into the Bill as part of a last minute proposed amendment. Following a meeting with media representatives concerned about their ability to report on the election, the provision was dropped from the Bill.[15] Any new forms of criminal libel would probably now be inconsistent with the rights and freedoms in the New Zealand Bill of Rights Act 1990, and therefore require a report to Parliament, thus hopefully also prompting a public outcry.[16]

Sedition

Though still on the statute book, sedition offences appeared obsolete by 1989 when there was a failed attempt to repeal them.[17] Then in 2004, a surprisingly successful prosecution was brought against a Mr Selwyn, a man who took part in an axe-attack on the Prime Minister's Auckland electorate office and who was linked to flyers found at the scene of the attack and elsewhere. The use of sedition laws against Mr Selwyn was inappropriate because the main concern of the police in this case appeared to be preventing incitement to violent behaviour. However, this conviction was unfortunately followed by a charge

[13] Press Freedom Index 2013, *Reporters Without Borders* http://en.rsf.org/press-freedom-index-2013,1054.html accessed July 2016.

[14] Crimes Act 1961, ss 211–16; repealed by s 56(2), Defamation Act 1992. See *Single v Church* (unreported, CP 22/93, District Court, Napier, 10 May 1994) one of the last prosecutions for criminal defamation. It was unsuccessful.

[15] The government drafted a limited corrupt practice provision instead: Electoral Act 1993, s 199A.

[16] See New Zealand Bill of Rights Act 1990, ss 4, 5, 6, 7, 14.

[17] Crimes Bill 1989, which was not enacted into law.

in March 2007 of a Dunedin bar tavern owner for publishing a seditious document, which was an offer to students of a chance to win a petrol-soaked couch and to swap petrol for beer. While the innkeeper accepted diversion in the case, the inappropriate nature of the charge at least added weight to a recommendation of the New Zealand Law Commission that our sedition laws should be repealed and not replaced, following a brisk consultation.[18] The Commission concluded that the offences were too wide, were in breach of the New Zealand Bill of Rights Act 1990, were unclear, and had been used to muzzle vehement and unpopular political speech. The Commission also concluded that criminal behaviour covered by the sedition provisions could be punished under other existing criminal provisions. The recommendations were accepted by the government, which accordingly consigned the sedition laws to the 'dustbin of history'.[19]

Blasphemy

Unfortunately, we have retained the offence of blasphemous libel, although prosecutions are rare—in fact there is only one reported example.[20] However, the offence carries a penalty of up to a year's imprisonment.[21] Fortunately, the leave of the Attorney-General is necessary before a prosecution may be brought.[22] The constituents of blasphemy are nowhere defined in our statute; all the legislature has done is to define what it is not:[23] 'It is not an offence … to express in good faith and in decent language, or to attempt to establish by arguments used in good faith and conveyed in decent language, any opinion whatever on any religious subject.'

Publications, including films, continue to provoke some persons to threaten proceedings for blasphemy, but no prosecutions have been commenced. In February 2006, the New Zealand media became involved in an international controversy over what many Muslims considered were blasphemous caricatures of the Prophet Mohammad that had been published previously by a Danish newspaper. Wellington's *Dominion Post* and the Christchurch *Press* joined a number of European newspapers in re-printing the Danish cartoons. Amidst threats of blasphemy action, the Human Rights Commission hosted a meeting between interest groups, which resulted in the release of a statement.[24] In this statement, the parties affirmed without dissent the importance of freedom of the media, but also noted that such freedom is not absolute, and comes with responsibilities. Those responsibilities included sensitivity to diverse cultures and beliefs and recognition of the diversity within cultures and beliefs, responsibility to inform the community about diverse cultures and beliefs and the provision of dialogue and channels of communication between the media and faith

[18] See Law Commission, *Reforming the Law of Sedition* (LC R 96, 15 March 2007) www.lawcom.govt.nz/our-projects/sedition accessed July 2016.

[19] 'Govt agrees to put sedition laws "in dustbin of history"' *New Zealand Herald* (New Zealand, 8 May 2007). See also Crimes (Repeal of Seditious Offences) Amendment Act 2007, 07/96, introduced 8 June 2007.

[20] *R v Glover* [1922] GLR 185.

[21] Crimes Act 1961, s 123.

[22] ibid s 123(4).

[23] ibid s 123(3).

[24] Human Rights Commission, *Press release: Statement from media and religious representatives* (9 February 2006).

communities. Nonetheless, the meeting acknowledged that the media has to make difficult calls on such issues on a daily basis and these need to be considered in an international context of conflict, and accepted that the media which published the cartoons did not set out to insult or offend, only to inform. Those media apologised for the offence caused but did not resile from the decision to publish, based on the context at that time. The two newspapers also gave an undertaking not to publish the cartoons again.[25]

In spite of the view that blasphemy is a dead letter, some time ago our Court of Appeal examined and indirectly endorsed a role for the offence to continue to play. In *Mendelssohn v Attorney-General*,[26] the Court examined the rights protecting religious freedom in the New Zealand Bill of Rights Act 1990[27] and held the Bill did not impose positive duties on the state in any relevant sense to protect religious freedom. The Court also examined New Zealand's international obligations, and noted that Article 18 of the International Covenant on Civil and Political Rights 1966 protects freedom of religion, but primarily affirms a freedom from state interference. In the Court's view, Article 20 unambiguously requires protective action in favour of religion, but only in limited extreme situations. New Zealand entered a reservation to this article which stated that it had legislated in various relevant areas. In *Mendelssohn*, the Court of Appeal identified the relevant legislation referred to in the reservation as including the crime of blasphemous libel.

In spite of *Mendelssohn*, it is apparent the crime of blasphemy serves little practical purpose any longer in the law. The intervention of the Human Rights Commission in the Prophet Mohammad cartoon controversy prevented a further testing of blasphemy laws in New Zealand, and in particular, whether they survive the Bill of Rights and whether they apply to non-Christian religions. Blasphemy is anomalous in a secular society, and represents a threat to freedom of expression.

Hate Speech

New Zealand also retains limited hate speech regulation which is now rarely engaged. Section 131 of the Human Rights Act 1993 makes it a criminal offence to publish or broadcast threatening, abusive, or insulting statements, these statements being intended and likely to excite hostility or ill will against, or bring into contempt or ridicule, any group of persons in New Zealand on the ground of the colour, race, or ethnic or national origins of that group of persons.[28] The offence is a summary one and is punishable by imprisonment for a term not exceeding three months or to a fine not exceeding $7,000 (NZD). It goes by the name of 'inciting racial disharmony'. The Attorney-General must consent to any prosecution.[29]

Section 61 of the Human Rights Act provides civil sanctions for published racist remarks. Complaints based on this racial disharmony provision may be made to the Race Relations Conciliator, whose office is part of the Human Rights Commission. The remedies are not

[25] The cartoons were published again worldwide in 2008, although not by the *Press* or the *Dom Post*.
[26] *Mendelssohn v Attorney-General* [1999] 2 NZLR 268, [16]–[18].
[27] New Zealand Bill of Rights Act 1990, ss 13, 14, 15, 17, 20.
[28] See *Brooker v Police* [2007] 3 NZLR 91, [61].
[29] Human Rights Act 1993, s 132 (HRA 1993).

punitive, but if the matter is not settled through conciliation, it can be referred to the Human Rights Review Tribunal, which may among other remedies uphold the complaint, issue a declaration that the Human Rights Act has been breached, award damages, or make a restraining order. Damages may be significant, covering pecuniary loss, loss of benefit, and humiliation, loss of dignity, and injury to feelings. The threshold for invoking the civil sanction is lower than for section 131.[30]

The media are exempt from liability for accurately reporting the remarks of others under section 61(2), which provides:

> It shall not be a breach of subsection (1) of this section to publish in a newspaper, magazine, or periodical or broadcast by means of radio or television a report relating to the publication or distribution of matter by any person or the broadcast or use of words by any person, if the report of the matter or words accurately conveys the intention of the person who published or distributed the matter or broadcast or used the words.

The exception for the media seems to apply only to their reporting functions and to accurate reports. This means publication of items such as letters to the editor is not covered. Furthermore, in determining accuracy, the Office of the Race Relations Conciliator may investigate and pronounce on media ethics and standards.[31] 'Newspaper' means a paper containing public news or observations on public news, or consisting wholly or mainly of advertisements, being a newspaper that is published periodically at intervals not exceeding three months.[32]

How section 61 affects the media will vary, depending on the facts of the case. Although one or two early complaints against media were upheld,[33] more recent decisions indicate that the New Zealand Bill of Rights freedom of expression now ensures a high threshold for complainants before section 61 will be invoked. The Race Relations Conciliator issued a *Statement on Race Relations* in 2008[34] which sets out the principle of freedom of expression and the limitations on it, being sections 131 and 61 of the Human Rights Act. This emphasises that the right to freedom of expression in the Bill of Rights Act prevails if the words are simply offensive. It also notes that section 131 requires not only a likelihood that the words will excite hostility, contempt or ridicule, but also an intent to do so.

In 2013, the Human Rights Commission noted that complaints received under section 61 comprised a relatively high area of complaint. A large number of these complaints were generated from comments made by high profile public figures and reported in the media. However, in the course of making submissions on the recent Bill dealing with harmful digital publications, the Commission stated that the threshold for an offence under section 61 is now so high as to render it inoperable, and called for a review of the hate speech offence.[35]

[30] For a fuller discussion of the provisions, see *Burrows and Cheer: Media Law in New Zealand*, 7th edn (LexisNexis 2015) 634.

[31] See Grant Huscroft, 'Defamation, racial disharmony, and freedom of expression' in Grant Huscroft and P Risworth (eds), *Rights and Freedoms: The New Zealand Bill of Rights Act 1990 and the Human Rights Act 1993* (Wellington NZ, Brooker's, 1995), 198.

[32] HRA 1993, s 61(3).

[33] *Proceedings Commissioner v Archer*, HR Law and Practice 2(2) September 1996, 117–18.

[34] Race Relations Commissioner, *Race Relations in Aotearoa New Zealand: Whanaungatanga ā Iwi: Statement on Race Relations* (New Zealand Diversity Forum 2008) www.hrc.co.nz/files/7314/2405/1388/25-Aug-2008_11-45-29_Race_Relations_final_Aug_08.pdf accessed July 2016.

[35] Human Rights Commission, *Annual Report 2013* (New Zealand, October 2013) 20–21.

It would indeed be timely for a review of these incitement provisions in the Human Rights Act, carried out in conjunction with a review of the law of blasphemy, as suggested above.

Name Suppression

After considerable lobbying and commentary by media, passage of the Criminal Procedure Act 2011 established a new legislative regime for the granting of name suppression in criminal cases and took effect in March 2012. The provisions were intended to make obtaining interim suppression at first appearance easier, but imposed more onerous requirements at a later stage. Open justice is the presumption. However, this will be displaced where publication of the name would be likely to cause extreme hardship to the defendant. The specification of extreme hardship is new, as is a provision stating that the fact that a defendant is well known does not, of itself, mean that publication of his or her name will result in extreme hardship. Judges are now required to give reasons for their decisions and it has been clarified that media have standing to be heard on the matter. To obtain an interim injunction, only an arguable case has to be shown.[36] The cases involving decisions made under the new legislation are now being eagerly monitored, although there is little indication of a different approach to that taken under the previous law being applied and the old leading cases continue to be referred to.[37]

General Civil Laws

The general laws impacting freedom of expression and media in particular are also developing in ways that admit greater freedom of expression. In defamation, the most significant development has been the recognition of a political discussion qualified privilege defence that appears to be maturing into a public interest defence.[38] And although New Zealand has recognised a robust tort of breach of privacy and the beginnings of a tort of breach of seclusion, this has been in conjunction with provision of strong public interest defences,[39] or the potential for them.[40] Furthermore, injunctive relief in defamation and privacy should be restrained. The High Court recently declined an application for an interim injunction in a privacy case involving anticipated publication in mainstream media, even though it had considerable sympathy for the plaintiff's position. The judge referred to the defendant as a responsible news media organisation which could reasonably be expected to give a balanced report on the matter. This meant the high threshold for injunctive relief based on anticipated publication had not been crossed.[41]

[36] Criminal Procedure Act 2011, pt 5, sub-pt 3: Public access and restrictions on reporting, ss 197–211.

[37] See, eg, *R v R* [2015] NZCA 287.

[38] *Lange v Atkinson* [1998] 3 NZLR 424, *Lange v Atkinson*, above n 5; *Osmose New Zealand v Wakeling* [2007] 1 NZLR 841 (HC); *Dooley v Smith* [2012] NZHC 529; *Smith v Dooley* [2013] NZCA 42; *Cabral v Beacon Printing* [2013] NZHC 2684; *Karam v Parker* [2014] NZHC 737.

[39] See *Hosking v Runting* [2005] 1 NZLR 1; *Andrews v TVNZ* [2009] 1 NZLR 220.

[40] *C v Holland* [2012] 3 NZLR 672, [96].

[41] *Clague v APN News and Media Ltd* [2013] NZAR 99. See also *TV3 Network Services Ltd v Fahey* [1999] 2 NZLR 129.

Regulation of Online Media—New Zealand Models

It will be apparent that, somewhat like Canada,[42] New Zealand has a comparatively well-behaved press that enjoys freedoms considered a luxury in some countries in the Asia-Pacific region. We do, however, have multiple forms of media regulation, some industry-based, some government-imposed. Like all of our neighbours in the region, we are moving to adapt our laws to the online era. What follows is a discussion and analysis of the various forms of media regulation currently maintained or developing in New Zealand which impact on online speech.

A Grand Regulator?

Like the UK and Australia, New Zealand recently examined how its media is specifically regulated. Although the review was not prompted by unethical and illegal behaviour such as that displayed by media in the UK, in developing its recommendations, the New Zealand Law Commission was clearly very conscious of the battle played out on the other side of the world over what form media regulation might take. Similar to the experience in the UK, however, the Commission had to beat a narrow path between media strongly advocating for as much freedom and as little state interference as possible, and the public and media commentators and other parties seeking to ensure responsible and ethical media.

The specific task for our Law Commission was different, however. Its role was to investigate whether the growth of new media has led to gaps in the regulatory regime which require addressing. In a report released in March 2013 after two years investigating the current state of regulation and consulting closely with mainstream media, new media and other stakeholders, the Commission recommended that the current complex system of media regulation involving a statutory authority for broadcasters, the Broadcasting Standards Authority (BSA) and a self-regulatory Press Council for the print media, be replaced with one over-arching regulator known as the News Media Standards Authority (NMSA).[43]

NMSA would enforce one set of standards across all publishers of news irrespective of format or method of distribution. It would accept and resolve complaints relating to news, current affairs, news commentary and content like documentaries and factual programming.

As recommended by the Commission, membership of NMSA would be voluntary, but both mainstream and new media would be incentivised to join by being promised in return the privileges in laws such as those which currently give mainstream media presumptive access to courts, and exemptions from the operation of the likes of the Privacy Act (a data protection act which could impede the ability of media to engage in newsgathering) and the Fair Trading Act (which criminalises false commercial speech) Members of NMSA would

[42] See Jared A Mackey, 'Privacy and the Canadian Media: Developing the New Tort of "Intrusion Upon Seclusion" with Charter Values' (2012) 2(1) *Western Journal of Legal Studies* 3, at 8.

[43] See Law Commission, *The News Media Meets 'New Media'* (2013), NZLC Report 128, http://r128.publications.lawcom.govt.nz/ accessed July 2016 (New Media Report).

also get access to certain defences in the Defamation Act so long as their reports are fair and accurate. NMSA would be independent of both media and government. An independent panel would be appointed to work on its membership.

Members of NMSA would fund the body, although the government would provide some funding for its recommended research function. The Authority would be a 'one-stop shop' covering three previously separate media platforms—print media, broadcasters, and online and anything between. It would also develop a mediation service, and appeals would be heard by an independent body. NMSA would have power to make take down orders, correction orders, apologies, rights of reply and censure. The members of NMSA would not be compelled to comply with orders made, but would agree to be bound by its rulings by signing a contract beforehand.

The Commission also recommended that all statutes which give privileges or exemptions specifically to the news media should be amended to include a new and consistent definition of 'news media', which would include new media. Under this definition, news media would have to meet specified statutory criteria:

- a significant element of their publishing activities involves the generation and/or aggregation of news, information and opinion of current value;
- they disseminate this information to a public audience;
- publication is regular and not occasional; and
- the publisher must be accountable to a code of ethics and to the NMSA.

Bloggers could therefore meet this definition and take advantage of journalistic privileges and exemptions if they are prepared to develop a code of ethics.

Voluntary membership of the Authority was recommended to make the body as attractive to media as possible. What about media who opted not to join? The Commission observed that non-members would still be covered by other laws such as those relating to defamation and privacy, and statutes like the Privacy Act. They would also be subject to new laws recommended by the Commission in a Briefing Paper on cyberbullying—a criminal offence and special jurisdiction in the District Court which would deal with speech that causes serious harm online.[44]

The recommendations about NMSA and cyberbullying were co-dependent for the full symmetry of the review reforms to be realised However, the government cherry-picked the cyberbullying recommendations and agreed to implement those but not the more significant recommendations on media regulation generally. Justice Minister Judith Collins noted that the regulatory review was not driven by a crisis of confidence in the mainstream media, and thought the media in New Zealand had already made good progress in dealing with the challenges posed by the impact of technological convergence on the news media. She concluded there is no pressing need for statutory or institutional change of the regulatory bodies.[45] This outcome is regrettable, for reasons which will now be examined.

[44] The Harmful Digital Communications Bill which implements the Law Commission Briefing Paper on Cyberbullying is discussed further below. See Law Commission, *Harmful Digital Communications: The adequacy of the current sanctions and remedies* (Ministerial Briefing, 15 August 2012) (Harmful Digital Briefing).

[45] New Zealand Ministry of Justice, *Government Response to Law Commission Report 'News Media meets New Media'* (October 2013) www.justice.govt.nz/publications/global-publications/n/news-media-meets-new-media-government-response-to-law-commission-report accessed August 2015.

Mind the Gap

The Minister's conclusion ignored the fact that gaps in the law still exist in New Zealand. Most of these revolve around the question of what and who comprise new media, and the connected question of whether new media can or should take on the privileges and responsibilities of mainstream media. For example, in October 2013, a controversial New Zealand blogger revealed that a recently re-elected Mayor of New Zealand's largest city had had an adulterous affair in a blog entry containing private and salacious detail.[46] Although there appeared to be public interest in the disclosure, many commentators argued the detail constituted an invasion of privacy.[47] Mainstream media picked up the story but did not republish the salacious detail. Had the Mayor wanted to complain, he had nowhere to go as the blogger did not operate a complaints system nor was he subject to any other regulatory system.

Additionally, this same blogger has claimed journalistic source privilege in separate defamation proceedings brought against him by a businessman for comments on his blog.[48] This case raised for the first time the issue whether a member of new media could claim a privilege only available in the past to mainstream media. The question at issue arose from the Evidence Act 2006 which captures in statute a presumption in favour of protection of journalists' sources that can only be displaced if a court finds it is in the public interest to order disclosure.[49] The Evidence Act defines a journalist as a person who in the normal course of their work may be given information by an informant in the expectation it will be published in a news medium. Further, a news medium is a medium for the dissemination of news and observations on news to the public or a section of the public.[50]

The blogger publishes a mixture of information, much of it gossip, private detail and opinion, but has also broken important news stories from time to time. In this case, the blogger used the Evidence Act 2006 to resist a discovery order obtained by the plaintiff who was suing him for publication of various blog posts. The plaintiff wished to test the blogger's defence of honest opinion, and therefore sought discovery of emails held by the blogger that he had acknowledged belonged to the plaintiff. The blogger claimed journalist source protection in relation to the emails, arguing that at the time of the relevant blog posts, he was a journalist in terms of the Evidence Act.[51] After noting that the legislation provides an exemption from compellability rather than an entitlement to a particular type of privilege,[52] Asher J found that at the time of the posts, the blogger and his blog *did* fit the definition of a journalist and a news medium in the Evidence Act. Although the style of journalism might be criticised and could be dramatic and abusive, the expression was

[46] See Scott Morgan and Kirsty Johnston, 'Len Brown affair a "new low" in NZ politics', *Stuff.co.nz* (Auckland, 22 October 2013) www.stuff.co.nz/national/politics/9309297/Len-Brown-affair-a-new-low-in-NZ-politics accessed July 2016.

[47] See the compelling arguments made by media lawyer and blogger, Steven Price, 'Can Len Brown sue for invasion of privacy?', *Media Law Journal*, 17 October 2013 www.medialawjournal.co.nz/?p=620 accessed July 2016.

[48] *Slater v Blomfield* [2014] 3 NZLR 835.

[49] Evidence Act 2006, s 68.

[50] ibid s 68(5).

[51] Evidence Act 2006, s 68(5).

[52] *Slater v Blomfield* [2014] 3 NZLR 835, [32].

vigorous and coherent and the Judge had before him no evidence of consistent inaccuracy or deceit.[53] The blog was published regularly and the blogger derived revenue from it. Overall, the blog was not of such low quality that it was not reporting news.

This case demonstrated that the journalist source privilege can apply to new media such as blogs. However, the blogger was ultimately ordered to comply with the discovery order because the blog posts related to a private dispute and it seemed likely the emails were obtained illegally by the blogger's sources. This diminished the importance of protecting the sources in terms of public interest and there would be no real chilling effect from ordering disclosure which might affect media sources generally. Additionally, the extreme nature of the attack on the plaintiff and an allegation of a planned attack involving the sources meant there was public interest in disclosure of the sources. Ultimately, after a specific fact-weighing exercise, the Judge found that the protection in the Act was not available to the blogger.[54]

If bloggers can be treated as media under some parts of the law, entitling them to freedom from compellability in court in some circumstances, such freedoms should be accompanied by an obligation to take on media responsibilities, such as the basic requirements of fair, truthful and balanced reporting that are reinforced through regulatory complaints systems. However, currently bloggers and other new media in New Zealand are not obliged to subject themselves to any form of regulatory system. The recommendations of the Law Commission would have plugged this gap, making all media subject to one grand regulator.

Having rejected any major regulatory change for the time being, the government expected the existing regulatory schemes, the BSA and the Press Council, to continue to improve their systems of oversight. This put considerable pressure on these two bodies but does appear to be happening to a degree. These regulators, which have previously only dealt with print and broadcasting media, are changing to deal with some of the challenges presented by new media. Their tentative expansion may offer insights for other jurisdictions.

Expanding Powers of Existing Regulatory Bodies

The Press Council

Like its UK counterpart (pre-Leveson), the Press Council[55] deals with the print media and is a self-regulatory body which depends on the voluntary co-operation and compliance of those who agree to belong to it. It has no statutory power to enforce decisions or impose sanctions but creates an expectation that each member of the Press Council will publish an adjudication upheld against it.

The Press Council extended its coverage and expanded its powers in March 2014. The Council now offers a new form of membership to non-newspaper digital media which

[53] This finding was seen as controversial in the light of allegations made in the book, *Dirty Politics*, published during the defamation proceedings by investigative journalist, Nicky Hager. See *Slater v Blomfield* [2014] 3 NZLR 835, [3]–[4].

[54] Evidence Act 2006, s 68(2). See also *Police v Campbell* [2010] 1 NZLR 483.

[55] The New Zealand Press Council www.presscouncil.org.nz accessed July 2016.

agree to membership conditions, with membership fees determined by size and commercial and non-commercial status. Currently three digital media have joined the regulatory scheme.

The Council's decisions still lack the penalties which a court of law or the BSA can impose, in that, apart from the Council website database, decisions against a print publication only receive publicity in the relevant publication itself. However, the Council has attempted to strengthen its sanctions process by taking to itself powers to direct where an adjudication should appear in a publication, based on a requirement for fair prominence. For example, where an article has been published on one or more of the first three pages of a newspaper, the council is now able to direct an adjudication to be published on page three. Similar placement requirements cover magazines and websites. All electronic copy that persists and is deemed to be conveying inaccuracy must be noted as having been found incorrect and why. Where the potential harm outweighs the need to keep the public record intact, the Council may go so far as to require the removal of story elements or the taking down of a story in its entirety.[56]

The Council has also been developing forms of mediation. However, in 2012 it mediated or resolved only six per cent of complaints, and in 2013, even less, at four per cent. This may be because there is a concern not to displace the development of a clear body of precedent in the form of actual decisions.

The Council received 142 complaints in 2013 compared to 157 for the previous year. It issued decisions on 61 complaints in the 2013 year, five less than the 66 decisions in the 2012 year.[57] The uphold rate for 2012 was 28 per cent, which is high for the Press Council but similar to the year before. In recent years, the uphold rates of the Council and the BSA appeared to reverse, with the Council upholding more complaints than the BSA. This may have been because the Council carried out the extensive review of its procedures described above following criticism that as a self-regulator, it tended to take a light-handed approach.[58] However, in 2013, the uphold rate dropped rather dramatically back to 18 per cent. The reasons for this are as yet, unclear and the result may only be a temporary one.

The Broadcasting Standards Authority

The Law Commission has described the BSA[59] as a Crown entity established by statute which operates within a co-regulatory content regulation environment. Complaints are only referred to the BSA if the complainant is first dissatisfied with the handling of their complaint by the broadcaster (except for privacy, where complaints can be made directly). All broadcasters are covered by its jurisdiction and it is able to apply a range of sanctions including compensatory damages in privacy cases, and other commercial penalties such as forcing a broadcaster to forego advertising revenue by broadcasting commercial-free for up to 24 hours. The BSA can also order publication of an approved statement where it finds

[56] Press Statement 23 March 2014—NZ Press Council to extend coverage, gain new powers, www.presscouncil.org.nz/articles/Press_Council_-_Press%20statement_230314.pdf, accessed 4 May 2015.

[57] *Annual Report of the New Zealand Press Council* (2013), 7.

[58] The BSA also changed its complete membership.

[59] Broadcasting Standards Authority http://bsa.govt.nz/ accessed July 2016.

a complaint is justified (unlike the Press Council), and it can make costs awards. Failure to comply with a BSA order is an offence carrying a fine of up to $100,000 (NZD).

Until recently, the BSA usually upheld about 25 per cent of complaints. However, the Annual Reports for 2013 and 2012 record significant decreases in the number of complaints received (136 in 2013 and 195 in 2012, compared to 250 in 2011) and in those upheld (16 per cent in 2013 and 10 per cent in 2012. It issued 99 decisions in the 2013/14 period and upheld only 12 per cent of complaints. These reductions are significant. The BSA has changed membership during this time and has suggested the changes may flow from a more robust and integrated analysis of freedom of expression. This iteration of the Authority also prefers to uphold complaints but make no order. In 2013, it dealt with 85 per cent of uphold decisions in this way and in 2012, 65 per cent. The standards breached in the decisions where an order accompanied the uphold were accuracy, fairness and privacy.

The BSA has begun consulting with broadcasters about the broadcasting codes with a view to developing a modernised, user-friendly, single code in the form of a handbook. The idea is to develop a single set of standards, the application of which would be dependent on context and medium. Consultion closed at the end of August 2015.

However, the BSA is not taking on any special jurisdiction in relation to online content of New Zealand broadcasters. This is probably because the main broadcasters have collaborated to address the issue on a voluntary basis, by setting up a new self-regulatory body dealing specifically with online content. This new body is examined below.

A New Self-regulatory Body

Online Media Standards Authority (OMSA) for Broadcasters

While the government was considering the Law Commission recommendations for regulatory reform discussed above, the main television broadcasters Television New Zealand (TVNZ), SKY/Prime, MediaWorks TV, and Maori Television, Radio New Zealand, The Radio Network and MediaWorks Radio developed an industry-led body to regulate the identified unregulated area of online news and current affairs content, which came into being on 1 July 2013. OMSA now provides a free complaints process overseen by a Complaints Committee with a separate Appeals Committee. The Complaints Committee is chaired by a retired Court of Appeal Judge and has four public members and three broadcasting industry representatives. The Appeals Committee is chaired by a retired High Court Judge and has two other members.[60]

The new body is modeled on the self-regulatory Advertising Standards Authority (ASA)[61] and the NZ Press Council. OMSA has published a code of standards, which include balance, accuracy, fairness and privacy among others. There is no special reference to freedom of expression in the code but it is stated that freedom of speech and social responsibility underpin the code and that application of the code observes the principles of natural justice.

[60] See Online Media Standards Authority www.omsa.co.nz/ accessed July 2016.

[61] See Advertising Standards Authority www.asa.co.nz/ accessed July 2016.

OMSA's jurisdiction extends solely to complaints about news and current affairs content published online by any of its members that is not subject to a complaint to any other regulator, ie the BSA and the Press Council.

Where a complaint has been upheld, publishers have to publish OMSA's decision, or a fair summary of it, on their website with similar prominence to the original publication. All OMSA decisions are published on its own website. OMSA will also entertain other remedies based on remedy principles which include the acknowledgment of errors, publishing of corrections and replies with appropriate prominence, and the offering of apologies where justified.

OMSA seems accessible in that it is possible to complain directly online. However, the procedure differs from the BSA or the Press Council in that there is an extra step called Initial Consideration of Complaints which is intended to weed out complaints that should not proceed. The Chair can summarily dismiss complaints that fall outside OMSA's jurisdiction, are trivial or vexatious, or do not disclose an arguable breach of the Code of Standards. This is modeled on the ASA model and is useful in weeding out claims with no foundation but does leave considerable power in the Chair. If complaints get through this step, OMSA will investigate and mediate if possible.

An examination of the first OMSA decisions reveals the system is operating in a practical fashion with an emphasis on robust decisions by the Chair at the Initial Consideration stage. None of the first eight complaints were upheld. Five have been found by the Chair to have no grounds for proceeding further, one decision was treated as settled, one was rejected by the Chair as being out of time, and the remaining decision was the only one to proceed to consideration by the Committee, but was ultimately found to have no grounds to support a breach of the code.

The decisions are easily accessible online and not excessively long. The Chair checks that the story is a unique entry on a website of a signed-up member, and then refers the complaint for a preliminary response from the broadcaster involved. Once that is received, the Chair uses the questioned story content, the complaint, the preliminary response and the standards to determine whether the complaint contains an arguable breach of the code that should go to the Committee for decision.

Only those who are a party involved in the relevant news or current affairs story can complain about lack of fairness.[62] OMSA has also noted that it is important story headlines as well as content comply with the code requirements, especially in the online environment where audiences are most likely to browse using headlines.[63] It appears content on Facebook pages is unlikely to be seen as news and current affairs, and that comments posted in response to such content are seen as providing balance in any event.[64]

The complaint OMSA treated as settled involved an old image used by Television New Zealand in a story that wrongly suggested a church had been burned to the ground in Malaysia.[65] TVNZ removed the photograph, attached a note explaining the removal, and

[62] *Wood v Radio New Zealand*, OMSA 13/002.
[63] *Cumming v Radio New Zealand*, OMSA 13/003.
[64] *Ngaro v Radio Network*, OMSA 14/003; *McCallum v MediaWorks Ltd*, OMSA 14/001.
[65] *Mitchell v TVNZ Ltd*, OMSA 14/002.

apologised to the complainant. As the material complained about had been removed, there appeared to be no point in referring the matter to the Committee.

The complaints procedures require a complaint to be lodged within 14 days of the content first being posted on the publisher's website. In one decision, the complaint was rejected because it came four days too late.[66] The 14-day requirement does not really meet the stated objective of reflecting a balance between the immediacy and ongoing nature of online publications, the need to provide a reasonable opportunity to complain and the time needed for proper consideration of complaints. Requiring a complaint to be made within 14 days from first posting gives priority to immediacy rather than to the fact that information can remain online indefinitely, and, when compared to the BSA, which requires a complaint to be made within 20 working days of the broadcast concerned, appears miserly. If more apparently weighty complaints are rejected in future because of this requirement, or the Chair is regularly asked to grant exceptions to the time limits,[67] the 14-day period may be unfair and require revisiting. Furthermore, if the uphold rate of complaints is below that of the other regulatory bodies, OMSA's credibility as an online industry regulator may be called into question, as was the case with the Press Council. These reservations aside, currently OMSA appears to provide a serious and efficient complaints process, though the small number of complaints received have not placed it under any real pressure as yet, and uphold rates are yet to be established. If the uphold rate of complaints turns out to be below that of the other regulatory bodies, OMSA's credibility as an online industry regulator may be called into question, as was the case in the past with the Press Council.

As noted above, the government rejected the Law Commission's comprehensive and thoughtful recommendations for one grand regulator, and instead, accepted connected recommendations intended to deal with online cyber-bullying.[68] These may also have impact on media and are accordingly discussed below.

New Statutory Regulation of Seriously Harmful Online Speech

While the Law Commission was investigating the need for reform of New Zealand's laws to take account of the advent of digital media,[69] the government became most concerned about the high profile issue of cyberbullying and other online harmful publications which were seen to negatively impact on children and young people in particular. This could be described as responding to a moral panic of the kind that tends to follow changes in technology—classic examples include the development of the printing press, the camera, and videotape technology, all means by which more and more people have obtained mass-access to new forms of information and entertainment. In any event, the New Zealand government, like other governments worldwide, wished to be seen to be responding to this societal concern and therefore asked the Law Commission to fast-track part of its general review and provide it with a briefing paper on the issue of cyberbullying.[70]

66 *Maurice v TVNZ Ltd*, OMSA 13/005.
67 See www.omsa.co.nz/how-we-work/time-limits/ accessed July 2016.
68 Law Commission, Harmful Digital Briefing, above n 44.
69 Law Commission, New Media Report, above n 43.
70 Law Commission, Harmful Digital Briefing, above n 44, 5.

The Commission investigated the prevalence of such harms, carried out empirical research and received submissions from interested parties. It concluded that reform of the law was necessary and possible based on a series of recommendations in a special briefing paper.[71] The government enthusiastically embraced the briefing paper and in November 2013, it introduced the Harmful Digital Communications Bill,[72] which passed into law two years later.[73]

The Act provides a civil regime based on a set of communication principles and an approved Agency with the power to receive and assess complaints about harm caused by digital communications. The Agency will focus on mediating the complaint and seeking voluntary take-down if appropriate, but has no powers to make orders. If the complaint cannot be resolved at this level, the complainant may take the matter to the District Court.

The Act also contains a criminal offence of posting a harmful digital communication with intent to cause serious emotional distress punishable by up to 2 years imprisonment, or a fine.[74] Online content hosts have protection from criminal or civil liability if they follow a complaint and take-down procedure in the Act.[75] Only these provisions are currently in effect. The civil regime will not commence until the government appoints an appropriate Agency by 2017.

The regime is based on a set of Digital Communication Principles, which are:

Principal 1

A digital communication should not disclose sensitive personal facts about an individual.

Principal 2

A digital communication should not be threatening, intimidating, or menacing.

Principal 3

A digital communication should not be grossly offensive to a reasonable person in the position of the affected individual.

Principal 4

A digital communication should not be indecent or obscene.

Principal 5

A digital communication should not be used to harass an individual.

Principal 6

A digital communication should not make a false allegation.

Principal 7

A digital communication should not contain a matter that is published in breach of confidence.

[71] ibid.

[72] Harmful Digital Communications Bill 2013, 168-1: www.legislation.govt.nz/bill/government/2013/0168/latest/DLM5711810.html accessed July 2016.

[73] Harmful Digital Communications Act 2015.

[74] ibid, s 22.

[75] ibid, ss 23–25.

Principal 8

A digital communication should not incite or encourage anyone to send a message to an individual for the purpose of causing harm to the individual.

Principal 9

A digital communication should not incite or encourage an individual to commit suicide.

Principal 10

A digital communication should not denigrate an individual by reason of his or her colour, race, ethnic or national origins, religion, gender, sexual orientation, or disability.

Both the approved Agency and courts must take account of the communication principles and act consistently with the rights and freedoms contained in the New Zealand Bill of Rights Act 1990 when operating under the Act.[76]

The principles cover most of the forms of harmful speech recognised in New Zealand law. It is possible, then, that they would regulate more speech and have more serious effects than regulation of offline speech. The Act contains a number of safeguards against this. First, only an individual who has suffered harm can make a complaint. Harm is defined as serious emotional distress.[77] Thus the threshold is high. Second, a Court can only consider a complaint if the Agency has already attempted to deal with it, and then only if there has been a serious, repeated or threatened breach of one or more of the Principles, and this has caused or is likely to have caused harm.[78]

The remedial powers in the Act are practical and extensive. The Court may make interim orders pending determination of an application for a final order.[79] Both interim or final orders can take the following forms:

— an order to take down or disable material;
— an order that the defendant cease the conduct concerned;
— an order that the defendant not encourage any other persons to engage in similar communications towards the affected individual;
— an order that a correction be published;
— an order that a right of reply be given to the affected individual;
— an order that an apology be published.[80]

The following orders can be made against content hosts:

— an order to take down or disable public access to material;
— an order that the identity of the author of an anonymous or pseudonymous communication be released to the court;
— an order that a correction be published;
— an order that a right of reply be given to the affected individual.[81]

[76] ibid, s 6(2).
[77] ibid, s 4.
[78] ibid, s 11
[79] ibid, s 18.
[80] ibid, s 19(1).
[81] ibid, s 19(2).

There is also power to direct orders to apply to third parties, to order a declaration that a Principle has been breached, and to order suppression of names.[82] Such declarations would not bind a host of offshore websites, but are intended to have symbolic effect.

A court is required to consider a number of factors before making an order, including the purpose of the communicator, and whether the communication was intended to harm. This does not mean lack of fault will result in no order being made. In some cases, even if there is no fault at all, it may still be a good idea to order removal of material from the Internet, or publication of a correction in a relevant form. However, the inclusion of this factor means that the issue of fault must be addressed and weighed in some way before any order is made. The Act also requires the question whether the communication is in the public interest to be addressed, as well as the truth or falsity of the statement. Additionally, a court must consider the occasion, context and subject matter of the communication, the content of the communication and the level of harm caused, the extent to which the communication has spread beyond the original parties, the age and vulnerability of the affected individual, the conduct of the defendant, including any attempt to minimise the harm, the conduct of the affected individual or complainant, the technical and operational practicalities and the costs of an order, and the appropriate individual or other person who should be subject to the order.[83]

The Harmful Digital Communications Act 2015 establishes an unknown, new and quite complex legal regime that will impact on online speech differently to the same speech in another medium. A number of serious issues arise. First, it is currently unknown what body will become the 'approved agency' responsible for the bottom 'mediating tier' of the civil regime. The government has put the appointment out to tender and this part of the regime must take effect by 2017. Netsafe was suggested as an appropriate body by the Law Commission in its Briefing Paper that resulted in the Act.[84] Netsafe is an independent, non-profit organisation set up to promote safe, confident and responsible use of online technologies. As such, it is an interest group established to advance the cause of victims of cyberbullying and other harmful online speech.[85] It is not clear that Netsafe would approach complaints in a balanced and nuanced way, especially when freedom of expression issues arise.

Second, whatever agency is appointed, it is crucial that it is properly resourced to deal with valid complaints and weed out the frivolous ones, and simply deal with what are likely to be numerous complaints, given the extent of online communication now. It would be highly undesirable to create an attractive complaints regime like the Office of the Privacy Commissioner, and then set it up to have a backlog of cases, as has happened there.

Third, it is questionable how accessible the low-level civil complaints process implemented by the Agency will be. This is because there is doubt about how much real interest there will be in mediation[86] Most victims will seek take-down as soon as possible. The Agency will not be able to make take down orders and before a Court can make an interim order, or an order of any kind, the Agency must have tried to mediate or otherwise

[82] ibid, s 19(4).

[83] ibid, s 19(5).

[84] Law Commission, *Harmful Digital Communications: The adequacy of the current sanctions and remedies*, (Ministerial Briefing, 15 August 2012), 18, 130.

[85] www.netsafe.org.nz accessed July 2016.

[86] Harmful Digital Communications Act 2015, s 8.

negotiate the complaint. If the Agency cannot prevent publication through its processes, an order may come too late. Therefore it is questionable how useful will it be to go to the Agency rather than directly to the ISP and ask them to take the material down, as most reputable ISPs do currently in any event.

Further, the Act provides safe harbour protection for ISPs[87] which, once notified of offending material, must use the special processes in the legislation to notify the poster of the material as soon as possible but within 48 hours of the complaint. The poster then has 48 hours to respond. If the poster cannot be identified, the material can be taken down in the meantime. Following the process immunises the ISP against any possible legal claim by the complainant. Take-down regimes are being used world-wide now but their effectiveness is not yet established. NewZealand ISPs, especially if they are small businesses, will be inclined to take-down as soon as possible to avoid trouble. That in itself has a chilling effect on freedom of expression. However, if they do prefer to take down immediately instead of following the 48 hour plus 48 hour period requirement in the Act to get in touch with the poster first, they cannot claim the safe harbour protection in the Act. It is therefore uncertain how useful the safe harbour provisions will be in practice.

Fifth, the criminal offence does set the liability threshold requirements high, as they should be, but there is a risk that children may be unnecessarily criminalised, and indeed, so will adults who have just been stupid and thoughtless. Whether or not prosecution follows is a matter of police discretion, and there is no transparency as to how that discretion will be used. Police will require adequate training and resourcing to ensure the offence is not over-used and prosecuted.

Sixth, many of the communication principles may encourage frivolous or vexatious complaints. The Act contains provisions to allow the Agency[88] or a District court to weed these out and the publication has to have caused harm which is serious enough (there has to have been a threatened serious breach, a serious breach or a repeated breach of one or more of the communications principles, and the breach has to have caused or be likely to cause harm to an individual).[89] However, some principles are problematic because they require very difficult judgments to be made before the Agency can decide if a principle has even been breached. For example, principle 3 which states that a digital communication should not be grossly offensive to a reasonable person in the position of the affected individual. This might easily prompt a Muslim to complain about cartoons of the Prophet, which, as described above, have been published by newspapers in New Zealand. It is unknown whether the Agency will be required to put itself in the shoes of a reasonable Muslim, or a reasonable but culturally aware non-Muslim. In any event, it is clear that the principles could capture publication by media with the consequent effect of involving media in the time-consuming mediation process which is likely to be pointless in any event if the publisher regards the publication as being in the public interest. The result may be forced engagement for media in the further processes in the District Court, which may involve a significant cost and time commitment. Although the Act requires the public interest to be taken into account, this is only one factor to be weighed in the process and is not set apart

[87] ibid, ss 23 and 24.
[88] ibid, s 8(3).
[89] ibid, s 12(2).

as a media defence. That is indeed what the Law Commission recommended, but it also suggested that media be exempt from the Act if they belonged to NMSA, the grand regulator recommended as part of the larger media regulation review.[90] However, since the government rejected that report, the Harmful Digital Publications Act was passed without any real consideration of the need for a media defence. The impact of this will be costly for media.

Finally, under the Harmful Digital Communications Act, media will still be able to maintain their own varied regulatory complaints processes and complainants can choose to use those rather than the Act provisions.[91] And therein lies a further problem. Such legislation does not exist in a vacuum. It is important to consider regulatory reforms in the context of the existing law and regulatory environment. The New Zealand government, in concentrating on plugging one gap, has missed a valuable opportunity to create coherent law reform. The final section of this chapter analyses the online regulatory road map that is in the process of being created in New Zealand.

Conclusion—a Mess or a Map?

The Harmful Digital Communications Act renders seriously harmful online speech unlawful. It provides a range of remedies for serious emotional harm, including a take-down procedure. Its processes enhance accessibility and affordability of the law within the special jurisdiction of civil complaint established under the Act. A low-level complaints process allowing for prompt removal or correction of damaging speech where appropriate is highly desirable.[92] However, a weakness of this model may be that harm does not currently cover pecuniary loss, and complaints processes based on forms of mediation, and then appeal-like resolution in a lower court, may not be appropriate in very acute cases where significant financial loss has occurred as well as serious emotional harm.

Far more problematic is that the Act increases the proliferation of regulatory schemes dealing with online speech in New Zealand to the point of incoherence. An individual wishing to complain about published online speech is faced with a series of confusing choices. For example, if a person currently wishes to complain that something seriously untrue was broadcast on a broadcaster's website, she or he must first establish the story is not exactly the same as any which was actually broadcast. If it **is** the same, then the complaint should go to the broadcaster concerned and perhaps ultimately to the BSA. If it is a unique online story, then a complaint can be made to OMSA, provided the broadcaster is a signed-up member. Alternatively, complaint will eventually be able to be made to the approved Harmful Digital Communications Agency so long as the individual can show he or she suffered serious emotional harm and is interested in the complaint being mediated between the parties by the agency. If the complaint cannot be resolved, the matter will go to the District Court so long as there is serious, repeated or threatened emotional harm, but not if there

[90] Law Commission, Harmful Digital Briefing, above n 44, 126.

[91] See *Media Law in New Zealand*, above n 30, 753.

[92] It could be a more radical means to remedy most forms of published speech harms, as I argue in 'Divining the Dignity Torts—A Possible Future for Defamation and Privacy', (in A Kenyon (ed), *Defamation and Privacy*, (forthcoming, CUP)).

is only pecuniary loss. The individual may prefer to bring a civil action using the tort of defamation to pursue pecuniary loss and would need to be advised about this.

Each of these options is based on different codes, standards, principles or elements of liability. While each regulatory body may maintain an excellent website, such as that of the BSA (which outlines how to complain), and makes the process as easy as possible (as the OMSA website attempts to do), it is inevitable that potential complainants will need some sort of legal advice to negotiate a path through this remedial minefield. Regrettably, the simplicity of the schemes themselves is outweighed by the complexity of the overall remedial landscape. In this context, it was a mistake for the government to reject the idea of a grand regulator in the form of a New Media Standards Authority put forward by the Law Commission in 2013.[93] Although the recommendations of the Commission needed fine-tuning, such an Authority would have had jurisdiction to deal with complaints about speech published by both old and new media, and could have done so in a scheme which took the emphasis off the platform of delivery and placed it, rightly, on the words involved and any resulting harms.

One comprehensive regulatory body covering all platforms of delivery is easy for the public to locate, and one standard complaints process based on a single code of practice is far more accessible than the remedial patchwork we currently use in New Zealand to deal with online speech harms. This deficient system is largely the result of populist parliaments with a short three-year term which have had no compelling reason to take on the might of a reasonably well-behaved media, and instead have focused any reforming zeal on single issue aspects of media regulation that have high public acceptance. In the meantime, the patchwork quilt of regulation that is largely a product of history continues to prove itself unfit for purpose in the digital age. Such a mélange means the government is doomed to revisit the issue of coherent regulation that takes account of the need to preserve freedom of speech while balancing the interests of those who may be harmed by speech in a rapidly changing digital world. And indeed, the process has already begun over again. The New Zealand government is now investigating content regulation in the context of a converged world, and is seeking submissions on the idea of a new Media Content Standards Act, among other suggestions.[94] However, the consultation period is ludicrously short[95] and the project cannot take account of print media voluntary regulation.

While it is certainly true that it is much more difficult to get agreement and buy-in to grand regulatory schemes from the stakeholders involved, in the long run, they give greater coherence, fairness and efficiency to the law. If any lesson can be learnt from the New Zealand experience, that should be it.

[93] See the discussion above of 'The News Media meets "New Media"', above n 43.

[94] Content Regulation in a Converged World, Discussion Document, Ministry for Culture and Heritage, 25 August 2015. The paper is part of a large cross-government response to the issue of convergence on legislation: see p 5.

[95] Submissions were due by 16 October 2015.

14

Privacy Down Under

PETER BARTLETT*

Introduction

The year 2014 was an important one for Australian privacy law. As medium and large private sector organisations and Commonwealth government agencies conformed to new data protection laws, the Australian Law Reform Commission's inquiry into *Serious Invasions of Privacy in the Digital Era* came to a close. The growing prominence of privacy reform stems in part from the belief that threats to personal privacy are increasing. Rapid advances in technology, changes in the way information is recorded and stored, big data, and the rise and use of social media and the sharing of personal information in all kinds of forms through the Internet, all contribute to the perception that privacy is under siege. A recent survey conducted by the Office of the Australian Information Commissioner shows that Australians are more concerned about their privacy than ever before.[1] According to Mark Zuckerberg, each year people will continue to share twice as much information as they did the previous year.[2]

Lawmakers in Australia, just like their counterparts in the United States (US), the United Kingdom (UK), Europe, and many other jurisdictions are grappling with the challenge of formulating laws to protect personal privacy. The task is complicated because to some extent, an individual's right to an appropriate level of personal privacy must be balanced with the fundamental right to freedom of the press, freedom of speech and the public's right to know. There are also issues of defining precisely what personal privacy is and developing the technical instruments to realistically protect it. The way the Internet works (which is where so much information is shared and gathered for free) relies on an exchange between the individual and the Internet service they are using—a trade-off between giving up some of their privacy rights in exchange for free access to services or information. Different jurisdictions are approaching the issues in totally different ways, with contrasting emphasis and results. This chapter covers developments in Australia and examines how these issues have been approached.

* Prepared with the assistance of Tarryn Wood and Veronica Scott.

[1] Office of the Australian Information Commissioner, *Community Attitudes to Privacy Survey*, Research Report (2013). The OAIC is the data protection regulator.

[2] Mark Zuckerberg, *Zuckerberg's Law* (Facebook Developers Conference, 6 November 2008).

History of the Common Law

One important matter that has affected the way the Australian common law has developed in relation to privacy, is that unlike the US and European Union, there is no constitutionally protected right to privacy in Australia. Consideration of the impact of developments in these jurisdictions on Australian law needs to be undertaken with caution.

In 1937, Australia's highest court decided that no general right of privacy existed at common law. The case, *Victoria Park Racing and Recreation Grounds Co Limited v Taylor*,[3] concerned the question of whether an operator of race meetings could prevent someone from broadcasting race descriptions from outside the track. Despite the case concerning the rights of an organisation, rather than an individual, the High Court's ruling was, for many years, interpreted as foreclosing the development of any common law right to privacy in Australia.[4]

The leading case on personal privacy in Australia is the 2001 High Court decision of *Australian Broadcasting Corporation v Lenah Game Meats Pty Limited*.[5] In this case, the High Court left open the possibility for the Australian common law to develop to protect personal privacy, either under a freestanding tort or through an extension of the law of breach of confidence. In doing so, the High Court fundamentally challenged existing interpretations of *Victoria Park Racing*.

The case concerned graphic video footage of possums being stunned, then having their throats cut. Trespassers had installed hidden video cameras on the property of a licensed possum killing and processing factory operated by Lenah Game Meats (LGM). They recorded the activities of the abattoir, then later retrieved the footage and cameras. The video was supplied to an animal liberation organisation which, in turn, supplied it to the Australian Broadcasting Corporation (ABC) for television broadcasting. LGM applied to the Supreme Court of Tasmania for an interlocutory injunction to restrain the ABC from distributing, publishing, copying or broadcasting the video. The application was dismissed at first instance, but this decision was reversed by the Full Court of the Supreme Court of Tasmania on appeal. The High Court allowed the ABC's appeal and refused to grant the injunction sought by LGM.

Although the ultimate decision was not revolutionary, comments made by the Court have had significant implications for privacy law in Australia. The case addressed two principle issues: (1) whether an interlocutory injunction could be granted in the absence of an established cause of action; and (2) whether there was a right to privacy upon which LGM could rely.

In relation to the issue of a right to privacy, four judges departed from the decided view, holding that *Victoria Park Racing* did not stand as an obstacle to the development of a tort of invasion of privacy.[6] Despite this, all members of the Court stopped short of finding that such a tort existed. Gaudron, Gummow and Hayne JJ all concluded that whatever development may take place in the field of privacy, it would be to the benefit of natural, not

[3] *Victoria Park Racing and Recreation Grounds Co Limited v Taylor* (1937) 58 CLR 479 (*Victoria Park Racing*).
[4] Australian Law Reform Commission, *Unfair Publication: Defamation and Privacy,* Report No 11 (1979),113.
[5] *Australian Broadcasting Corporation v Lenah Game Meats Pty Limited* [2001] 208 CLR 199 (*Lenah*).
[6] ibid 248 (Gummow J and Hayne J), 277 (Kirby J), 321 (Callinan J).

artificial, persons.[7] This stance on corporations allowed the Court to postpone the question of whether a tort for invasion of privacy should be developed. Of all the justices, Chief Justice Gleeson was most resistant to the idea of a freestanding tort of privacy, taking the view that 'the lack of precision of the concept of privacy is a reason for caution in declaring a new tort of the kind of which the respondent contends.'[8] He appears to have been proved right.

Although the High Court did not determine whether a tort of invasion of privacy existed in Australia (the judgment highlighted several major challenges facing the development of any such a cause of action), the decision in *Lenah* unequivocally opened the door for significant changes to the way the common law of Australia could protect personal privacy. Even the Chief Justice acknowledged that 'the law should be more astute than in the past to identify and protect interests of a kind which fall within the concept of privacy.'[9] The case marked a turning point.

There have been three cases in lower state courts and one appellate decision of particular relevance to the development of Australian laws on privacy since the decision in *Lenah*. The first, and most controversial, was a decision of Skoien DCJ in the Brisbane District Court in *Gross v Purvis*.[10] Conceding that it was a 'bold step', His Honour held that an individual has a civil cause of action for damages based upon the right to privacy.[11] In his view, the High Court's decision in *Lenah* indicated that the time had arrived to consider how and to what extent privacy should be protected at common law. His Honour identified what he considered to be the essential elements of a new cause of action for invasion of privacy. These were:[12]

(a) a willed act by the defendant;
(b) which intrudes upon the privacy or seclusion of the plaintiff;
(c) in a manner which would be considered highly offensive to a reasonable person of ordinary sensibilities; and
(d) which causes the plaintiff detriment in the form of mental, psychological or emotional harm or distress which prevents or hinders the plaintiff from doing an act which he is lawfully entitled to do.

His Honour found that a defence of public interest could be raised to a tortious claim for invasion of privacy, but that it was not available on the facts of the case.[13] The plaintiff, Alison Grosse, had engaged in a sexual relationship with the defendant, Robert Purvis, for a period of six months. After that time, relations between the parties deteriorated. The plaintiff complained that the defendant had stalked her and cited over 70 specific incidents of threatening conduct.

The plaintiff claimed damages for invasion of privacy, harassment, intentional infliction of physical harm, nuisance, trespass, assault, battery and negligence. The trial judge found that the plaintiff had developed a post-traumatic stress disorder as a result of the defendant's

[7] ibid 257 (Gummow J and Hayne J), 232 (Gaudron J).
[8] ibid 225–6.
[9] ibid 225.
[10] *Grosse v Purvis* [2003] QDC 151 (*Grosse v Purvis*).
[11] ibid [442].
[12] ibid [444].
[13] ibid [447].

conduct and awarded $178,000 (AUD) in damages, which included an award for invasion of privacy.

Although *Grosse v Purvis* is noteworthy, its significance should not be overstated. Skoien DCJ emphasised that he was not attempting to formulate a general cause of action and that the decision was strictly confined to its facts. Further, as a decision of the District Court, it has limited value as a precedent and is not binding on other courts.

Giller v Procopets,[14] a case originally heard by a single judge of the Victorian Supreme Court, was the next, and more important decision in relation to the development of a tort of privacy. The plaintiff, Ms Alla Giller, claimed for damages for distress and hurt caused by the defendant showing and threatening to distribute a video of her and the defendant, Mr Boris Procopets, engaged in sexual activities while they were in a relationship. The video surveillance had been conducted covertly on several occasions, and later with the plaintiff's consent. Gillard J found that the defendant had shown the video to a third party, left a copy of the video with the plaintiff's father, and threatened to show it to others including the plaintiff's employer.

The plaintiff alleged that distribution of the videos by the defendant gave rise to three causes of action in breach of confidence, intentional infliction of emotional distress, and invasion of privacy.

In relation to the plaintiff's claim for breach of confidence, Gillard J found that:[15]

— during their sexual activities a confidential relationship existed between the parties;
— what appeared on the video tape was a portrayal of information of a confidential nature; and
— showing of the video would constitute unauthorised use of the information by the defendant.

However, Gillard J held that the plaintiff failed to prove that she was entitled to damages, although His Honour acknowledged the opinions of commentators who argued that damages for injury to feelings should be available in breach of confidence cases, where the action is being adapted to protect privacy and personal reputation.

In relation to the plaintiff's claim for breach of privacy, Gillard J held that neither UK nor Australia law recognised a cause of action based on breach of privacy.[16] The plaintiff appealed to the Court of Appeal of the Victorian Supreme Court. In its decision handed down in December 2008, the Court held that Giller was entitled to recover $40,000 (AUD), including $10,000 (AUD) for aggravated damages for breach of confidence relating to the use and threatened use of the videotapes.[17] The Court of Appeal also held that damages could be awarded for mere distress caused by breach of confidence. Neave J, who gave the leading judgment, found that no Australian decision indicated whether damages for breach of confidence could be awarded for mere distress, but that there was significant English authority supporting the proposition.[18] Again drawing on the UK decisions, the Court of

[14] *Giller v Procopets* [2004] VSC 113 (*Giller v Procopets).*
[15] ibid [149].
[16] ibid [187].
[17] *Giller v Procopets* [2008] VSCA 236.
[18] Her Honour considered in particular *Campbell v MGN* [2004] 2 AC 457; *Douglas v Hello! Ltd* [2001] QB 967; *Cornelius v De Taranto* [2001] EMLR 12.

Appeal held that aggravated damages were available for breach of confidence, although exemplary damages were not.[19] The Court of Appeal made no reference to the lower court decisions of *Grosse v Purvis* and the third case of *Jane Doe v ABC* (discussed below).

Prior to the Court of Appeal's decision, the conflicting stances taken in *Grosse v Purvis* and *Giller v Procopets* created incoherence in the law (although the decision of the Victorian Supreme Court in *Giller v Procopets* carried more weight than the District Court judgment).

The final relevant lower court decision concerning the development of a common law tort for invasion of privacy in Australia is the decision of Judge Hampel of the County Court of Victoria in *Jane Doe v Australian Broadcasting Corporation*.[20] This judgment pre-dated the appeal decision in *Giller v Procopets*. The plaintiff, Jane Doe, had been attacked and raped by her estranged husband, YZ (their names were suppressed). He was tried, convicted and sentenced on two counts of rape and one count of common law assault. On the day of sentencing, the ABC broadcast three radio news bulletins concerning the case which identified Jane Doe by reporting YZ's name, that he had been sentenced for rapes within marriage, the offences had occurred in Jane Doe's home and the suburb which she lived. One of the bulletins also named Jane Doe as the victim.

Jane Doe brought proceedings against the ABC, the reporter and the news producer for negligence, breach of statutory duty under section 4(1A) of the Judicial Proceedings Reports Act 1958 (Vic), which prohibits publication of information identifying the victim of a rape or sexual offence, breach of confidence and breach of privacy. The ABC argued that the plaintiff should be limited to a claim for damages for defamation—any injury suffered was a result of publication and was compensable in defamation proceedings; defamation was the appropriate forum for the action because this would preserve the coherence of the law and defamation law had well established checks and balances between freedom of speech and rights of individuals.[21] Hampel J rejected these arguments, stating that the plaintiff sought damages for the loss of protection of her identity, not for the vindication of her reputation.[22] The ABC would probably have had a complete defence under defamation law.

At trial, in relation to the claim for breach of confidence the ABC argued that the plaintiff could not succeed in an action for breach of confidence because it did not owe her a duty of confidence, and in any event, the information had lost its quality of confidentiality before the broadcasts. Drawing on the approach of the UK courts in *Douglas v Hello! Ltd* and *Campbell v MGM Ltd*, Hampel J held that the obligation of confidence now extends to a wider range of people than had previously been the case and that 'it is no longer necessary for there to be a relationship of trust and confidence in order to protect confidential information.'[23] Her Honour acknowledged that care had to be taken in considering UK decisions concerning privacy because the Human Rights Act 1998 requires courts to take into account the rights enshrined in the European Convention for the Protection of Human Rights and Fundamental Freedoms, including a right to privacy and freedom of expression

[19] ibid [437] and [439].

[20] *Jane Doe v Australian Broadcasting Corporation & Ors* [2007] VCC (Unreported, Hampel J, 3 April 2007) (*Jane Doe v ABC*).

[21] ibid [55].

[22] ibid [62]–[63]. An application for leave to appeal this decision to the Court of Appeal was also refused, the court finding that a trial of the facts was required (no findings of this decision are formally recorded.)

[23] ibid [110], citing *Douglas v Hello! Ltd*, above n 18, and *Campbell v MGM Ltd*, above n 18.

(as this chapter noted at the outset). Despite this, Her Honour's decision was clearly guided by UK jurisprudence.

Hampel J was satisfied that identifying a person as a victim of a sexual assault is confidential information because the person to whom this information relates would have a reasonable expectation that it would remain private, particularly in light of the prohibition on publication in section 4(1A). Her Honour considered that the confidential nature of the information was not lost simply because the plaintiff's identity was disclosed in open court, she had reported the rape to the police or she had informed 14 people of the assault before the broadcast. However, Her Honour also justified her decision on the basis of *Campbell*, which demonstrated that information does not have to be secret to satisfy the test of private or confidential. Hampel J concluded that the ABC had breached its obligation of confidence to Jane Doe.

In relation to breach of privacy Hampel J held that 'invasion, or breach of privacy is an actionable wrong which gives rise to a right to recover damages.'[24] Her Honour distinguished the Supreme Court decision in *Giller v Procopets*, noting that since that decision, there had been a rapidly growing trend, particularly in the UK, towards protection of an individual's right to personal privacy. Her Honour considered that a breach of privacy would be made out where there was 'an unjustified publication of personal information.'[25] The test is slightly different from the *Grosse v Purvis* formulation. However, Hampel J specifically stated that she was not attempting to articulate a general cause of action and was merely identifying the principle applicable to the facts before her. In this case, the wrong was the publication of personal information, in circumstances where there was no public interest in publishing it and where there was a prohibition on its publication.[26]

Hampel J awarded the plaintiff $234,190 (AUD) damages including $85,000 (AUD) general damages for the tortious causes of action (negligence and breach of privacy) and $85,000 (AUD) for breach of confidence. The ABC appealed the decision but settled the claim before it reached hearing.

Grosse v Purvis and *Jane Doe v ABC* constitute important developments in Australian privacy law. However, their significance must not be overstated. Both were decisions at first instance and do not create a binding precedent. As noted above, it is revealing that neither case received significant attention in the Court of Appeal's decision in *Giller v Procopets*. Further, the factual scenarios in both cases were relatively unusual and were not examples of the types of behaviour that a tort for breach of privacy would generally be aimed at preventing. In *Jane Doe v ABC* the breach of the plaintiff's privacy occurred through human error at the ABC and the action for invasion of privacy was not strictly necessary, given that the plaintiff could already establish its case on the basis of the breach of Judicial Proceedings Reports Act 1958 (Vic). Finally, the inconsistencies between *Grosse v Purvis* and *ABC v Jane Doe*, and the fact that the Court of Appeal was unwilling to conclusively determine whether Australian law recognises a tort of privacy in *Giller v Procopets*, clearly indicate that this area of law remains unsettled in Australia.

[24] *Jane Doe v ABC*, above n 20, [157].
[25] ibid [164].
[26] ibid [163].

The uncertainty was highlighted in a recent decision the Queensland District Court.[27] The Court refused to strike out a claim for breach of confidence and invasion of privacy against Yahoo!7 in relation to the misuse of photos. A fake account was set up on Yahoo!7 by one of the defendants using the photos (which had been published elsewhere) and offensive and abusive posts were published on the account. The District Court Judge said that he would be 'hesitant to strike out a cause of action where the law is developing and is unclear'.[28] However it remains to be seen whether the plaintiffs will have any success at trial.[29]

The enduring lack of a definitive statement on the issue from the higher courts of record in this country suggests that the courts would prefer to leave the formulation of any tort to Parliament.

Legislative Protections

As noted above, in contrast to the position in the UK, Europe generally and the US, Australian law does not give any general protection to an individual's right to privacy. Legislation protects privacy to a limited extent by protecting the identity of victims of sexual assault, regulating the use of listening devices and the ability to carry out telecommunications interception and restricting direct marketing. Privacy is also incidentally protected through the common law of trespass, nuisance and confidentiality. There is also federal, state and territory based legislation which protects personal information (or data).

Privacy Act 1988 (Cth)

In 1988, the Commonwealth Government enacted the Privacy Act 1988 (Cth), designed to regulate the collection, storage and use of personal information by Commonwealth government agencies. In 2000, changes to the Act also brought the private sector under its regulation. Further amendments to this Act came into force in March 2014, creating one set of 13 unified privacy principles which apply to both the private sector and government, called the Australian Privacy Principles (APPs).[30] The Act requires compliance with these principles, a breach of which will be an interference with privacy and a breach of the Act. These principles regulate the type of personal information that can be collected, the method of collection and the information to be provided to individuals about collection of their personal information and use of the information. They also establish requirements for storage of personal information to ensure it is protected against loss, unauthorised access, use, modification, disclosure or other misuse. The Act also establishes the office of the Commonwealth Privacy Commissioner. Significantly, the Act only protects personal information, as opposed to an individual's physical privacy. There are also a range of substantial

[27] *Doe v Yahoo!7 Pty Ltd & Anor* [2013] QDC 181
[28] ibid [311].
[29] There have been no reported decisions in this matter since 2013.
[30] Privacy Amendment (Enhancing Privacy Protection) Act 2012 (Cth).

exceptions, including for small businesses with an annual turnover of less than $3 million (AUD), for media organisations in the course of journalism, and for employers in respect of employee records.[31]

Uniform Defamation Laws

Prior to the introduction of national defamation laws in 2006, Queensland, Tasmania and the Australian Capital Territory required defendants to prove not only that the publication was true, but that it was published for the public benefit. In New South Wales, the publisher had to prove truth and that the publication was published in the public interest. This public benefit or public interest criterion provided some degree of protection to plaintiffs' privacy interests. For example, in *Mutch v Sleeman* a statement that a member of parliament was a 'brutal wife basher', derived from an allegation made by the plaintiff's ex-wife during divorce proceedings, was not protected by the defence of truth because even if the allegation was true, it was not in the public interest to publish such information.[32] The public interest element of the truth defence served to protect plaintiffs' interests.

However, as a result of the new uniform defamation laws introduced throughout Australia in 2006, truth alone became a complete defence to publication of defamatory material (this was despite many lobbying for an additional public interest requirement).[33] In developing the new laws, the Standing Council on Law and Justice (comprised of the Attorneys-General of the Commonwealth and states and territories and the Minister of Justice of New Zealand) acknowledged that privacy was a legitimate interest in need of protection and expressly referred to Article 17 of the International Covenant on Civil and Political Rights (to which Australia is a party) which states that 'no one shall be subjected to arbitrary and unlawful interference with his privacy.'[34] It ultimately concluded however, that a defence of truth alone was appropriate.[35] The Western Australian delegation in particular, argued that it was inappropriate to include a public interest element in the defence to protect privacy interests because instead of protecting privacy indirectly through defamation laws, a law specifically aimed at privacy interests could be developed.[36] This change in the law of defamation removed any suggestion that defamation laws protect personal privacy.

[31] Privacy Act 1988 (Cth), ss 6C(1), 7B(4) and 7B(3) respectively.

[32] *Mutch v Sleeman* (1928) 29 SR (NSW) 125; New South Wales Law Reform Commission, *Invasion of Privacy*, Consultation Paper 1 (May 2007) www.lawreform.justice.nsw.gov.au/Documents/cp01.pdf accessed July 2016.

[33] Defamation Act 2005 (Vic), s 25.

[34] International Covenant on Civil and Political Rights (adopted 16 December 1966, entered into force 23 March 1976) 999 UNTS 171, Article 17. Victoria and the Australian Capital Territory also have state-based human rights charters which each include a right not to have one's privacy unlawfully or arbitrarily interfered with, see Charter of Human Rights and Responsibilities Act 2006 (Vic), s 13(a); Human Rights Act 2004 (ACT), s 12(a). However these acts only apply to public authorities.

[35] Model Defamation Provisions 2005, prepared by the Parliamentary Counsel's Committee and approved by the Standing Committee of Attorneys-General on 21 March 2005, accessible at: http://webarchive.nla.gov.au/gov/20141215115204, www.lccsc.gov.au/sclj/archive/former_sclj/standing_council_publications/2005_publications.html accessed July 2016.

[36] SCAG Working Group of State and Territory Officers, *Proposal for Uniform Defamation Laws* (July 2004) 22–23 www.justice.qld.gov.au/_data/assets/pdf_file/0018/21636/uniform-defamation.pdf accessed July 2016.

Codes of Conduct

In addition to these indirect privacy protections, the radio and television codes of conduct, which must be developed under the Broadcasting Services Act 1992 (Cth) and are regulated by the Australian Communications and Media Authority (ACMA), also contain privacy obligations. ACMA has privacy guidelines for broadcasters which supplement these codes of conduct and provide guidance on how ACMA will respond to complaints about breaches of the privacy provisions of the codes.[37]

The Commercial Television Industry Code of Practice, for example, states that 'in broadcasting news and current affairs, licensees must not use material relating to a person's personal or private affairs, or which invades an individual's privacy, otherwise than where there is an identifiable public interest reason for the material to be broadcast.'[38] The advisory note to practitioners states that particular care should be taken in respect of people in vulnerable positions, for example, bereaved relatives or survivors of traumatic accidents.[39] It also states that stations should not identify an individual when commenting on the conduct of a group of people and that journalists observe standards (such as those developed by the Australian Press Council, discussed below) for the handling of personal information required by their stations.[40] The Code of Conduct and Guidelines developed by Commercial Radio Australia include similar privacy requirements, in particular, the requirement not to broadcast a person's personal or private affairs unless there is a public interest in doing so.[41]

In June 2008, a new Internet Code of Conduct made under the Broadcasting Services Act 1992 (Cth) was released. The Code includes provisions for online safety and enables Hosting Services Providers to become Family Friendly Content Services Providers. It requires Family Friendly Content Services Providers to have a link on their website to a safety page, which in turn includes links to web pages containing appropriate information about user rights to privacy.[42]

The Australian Press Council has also developed privacy standards to which member organisations can subscribe. It requires adherence to the following: 'in gathering news, journalists should seek personal information only in the public interest'[43] and 'personal information gathered by journalists and photographers should only be used for the purpose for which it was intended.'[44]

The Australian Press Council has also developed a specific set of standards that apply to the type of contact that the print and online media make with patients in hospitals, nursing homes and similar institutions. These cover amongst other things, identification of the

[37] Australian Media and Communications Authority, *Privacy guidelines for broadcasters* (December 2011).

[38] ibid 32.

[39] ibid 59.

[40] ibid 60.

[41] Commercial Radio Australia, *Code of Conduct and Practice* (23 September 2004), 6 www.acma.gov.au/webwr/aba/contentreg/codes/radio/documents/cra-codeofpractice.pdf accessed July 2016.

[42] Internet Industry Association, *Internet Industry Code of Conduct* (24 June 2008), 22 www.acma.gov.au/webwr/aba/contentreg/codes/internet/documents/content_services_code_2008.pdf accessed July 2016.

[43] Australian Press Council, *Statement of Privacy Principles* (Standards of Practice, 1 December 2001) www.presscouncil.org.au/privacy-principles/ accessed July 2016.

[44] ibid.

media and informed consent.[45] This was prompted by the prank telephone call made by Australian DJs at one of Southern Cross Austereo's radio stations to the King Edward VII hospital in London, where the Duchess of Cambridge was being treated for morning sickness. The nurse who put the call through took her own life following the incident. ACMA also investigated the incident and as a result (among other actions) imposed an additional condition on the station's commercial radio licence for a period of three years, that it will not broadcast the words of an identifiable person unless that person has been informed in advance that the words may be broadcast or, if recorded without the person's knowledge, they have consented to the broadcast of the words.[46] Although these industry codes provide some protection for privacy interests, it has long been argued that their enforcers are paper tigers with no power to impose penalties. Therefore, the strength of privacy protections, particularly in the context of the Internet, is questionable.

Steps by the Australian Law Reform Commission (ALRC)

In 1979 the ALRC published Report No 11, *Unfair Publication: Defamation and Privacy*,[47] in which it recommended the introduction of some privacy protection in Australia. The ALRC was however, conscious to strike a balance between privacy and other competing interests. It noted that 'the price, in terms of freedom of speech, must not be excessive.'[48]

The ALRC examined the general tort of privacy available in the US, Europe and Canada, where a plaintiff had 'an action for damages whenever there is a substantial, unreasonable infringement of his [or her] privacy.'[49] It found that there were strong arguments in favour of creating a general right along American lines. This approach would overcome the stultifying effect of previous decisions like *Victoria Park Racing* which denied a right to privacy, and would enable the courts in Australia to formulate specific principles over time, as had occurred in the US and Europe.[50] The ALRC was concerned, however, that until the courts had developed a comprehensive jurisprudence, there would be considerable uncertainty as to the scope of the general right. The ALRC concluded that 'at least in the short and medium term, the price of a general right of privacy might exceed the benefits gained.'[51]

The ALRC went on to assess the merits of introducing a specific and closely circumscribed tort and considered that 'if the courts would in time distil a general right down to specific principles, why not do so immediately?'[52] The ALRC recommended 'legislative protection against serious, deliberate exposures of a person's home life, personal and family relationships, health and private behaviour.'[53]

[45] Australian Press Council, *Specific Standards on Contacting Patients* (July 2014) www.presscouncil.org.au/specific-standards/ accessed July 2016.

[46] ACMA, 2DayFM 'Royal Prank' broadcast, Media Release (17 July 2015) www.acma.gov.au/theACMA/Newsroom/Newsroom/Media-releases/2dayfm-royal-prank-broadcast accessed July 2016.

[47] Australian Law Reform Commission, *Unfair Publication: Defamation and Privacy*, Report No 11 (1979).

[48] ibid 121.

[49] ibid.

[50] ibid.

[51] ibid 122.

[52] ibid.

[53] ibid.

The specific tort advocated by the ALRC was intended to prevent a wide range of conduct, but was also directed at some specific incidents that have occurred in Australia and overseas. These included the identification of a victim of sexual assault, publication of the name and address of the witness to a murder, photographing by the media of two 15-year-olds who had gone on a 'five day Romeo and Juliet elopement', filming someone in the street without consent, media investigations into the personal life of a television journalist separated from her husband and the taking of paparazzi photographs of a woman who gave birth to quadruplets.[54] In order to achieve these aims, the ALRC proposed the introduction of legislation prohibiting publication of sensitive private facts:

> A person publishes sensitive private facts concerning an individual where the person publishes matter relating or purporting to relate to the health, private behaviour, home life or personal or family relationships, of the individual in circumstances in which the publication is likely to cause distress, annoyance or embarrassment to a person in the position of that individual.[55]

The ALRC recognised that in order to balance competing interests, a claim for invasion of privacy 'must yield to any legitimate public interest in exposure.'[56] It considered the availability of a public interest defence to be critical. Other suggested defences included consent, privilege and publication under legal authority.[57]

The ALRC's recommendations in its 1979 report were not implemented. This was perhaps because the Federal Government at the time was awaiting the outcome of another ALRC investigation exclusively on privacy law. This further report, released in 1983, noted the negative effects that intrusive modern technology, enhanced official powers and new business activities were having on people's privacy. Despite this, the ALRC recommended that a general tort of invasion of privacy should not be introduced in Australia because 'such a tort would be too vague and nebulous.'[58]

After a significant interlude, in January 2006, the then Australian Attorney-General asked the ALRC to 'conduct an enquiry into the extent to which the Privacy Act 1988 (Cth) and related laws continue to provide an effective framework for the protection of privacy in Australia.'[59]

Although not mentioned in the terms of reference, it is perhaps not a coincidence that the inquiry was announced in the same month that the new uniform defamation laws came into force in most Australian states and territories, deleting the indirect privacy protection afforded by the truth/justification defence to defamation.

The ALRC published its final report, *For Your Information: Australian Privacy Law and Practice*, in August 2008. It recommended 295 changes to existing privacy laws, the majority of which related to data privacy in the Commonwealth Privacy Act 1988. Most significantly, however, the report recommended the introduction of a statutory cause of action for serious invasion of privacy.[60]

[54] ibid 118–119.
[55] ibid 124.
[56] ibid 121.
[57] ibid 132.
[58] Australian Law Reform Commission, *Privacy*, Report No 22 (1983) 24.
[59] Australian Law Reform Commission, *For Your Information: Australian Privacy Law and Practice*, Report No 108 (2008).
[60] ibid 2585.

In arriving at this recommendation, the ALRC appears to have been heavily influenced by a fear that the development of a common law tort of invasion of privacy would lead to 'piecemeal and fragmented privacy protection.'[61] The ALRC ultimately proposed a surprisingly wide cause of action for 'serious invasion of privacy', available where a plaintiff can show that in the circumstances:[62]

(a) there is a reasonable expectation of privacy; and
(b) the act or conduct complained of is highly offensive to a reasonable person of ordinary sensibilities.

It recommended that the new legislation contain a non-exhaustive list of the types of acts or conduct that could constitute an invasion of privacy, including where:

— there has been a serious interference with an individual's home or family life;
— an individual has been subjected to unauthorised surveillance;
— an individual's correspondence or private written, oral or electronic communication has been interfered with, misused or disclosed; and
— where sensitive facts relating to an individual's private life have been disclosed.[63]

The ALRC expressly declined to follow the American model, which includes unauthorised use of a person's identity or likeness and placing a person in a false light, within the general tort for invasion of privacy.[64] It found that these types of conduct are more closely aligned with other areas of the law, such as defamation.

The ALRC did not recommend a public interest or fair comment defence, which it had originally proposed when it called for submissions. It argued that its formulation of the elements of the proposed cause of action (namely the 'highly offensive' threshold in the second limb) removed the need for a public interest type defence.[65] However, this is not necessarily the case. Designating the public interest as something for courts to consider when determining whether an act is highly offensive puts defendants in a significantly weaker position than having a specific public interest defence designed to protect freedom of speech.

The ALRC did recommend three defences to invasion of privacy. These were that the act or conduct was incidental to the exercise of a lawful right of defence of person or property, was required or authorised by law, or that publication was, under the law of defamation, privileged.[66] These would not however, compensate for the absence of a public interest defence, particularly in light of the extensive remedies proposed, including damages, an injunction restraining publication, an apology, an account of profits and a corrections order.[67]

It is worth noting that while the ALRC recommended the statutory tort be included in the Privacy Act, it did not also recommend the removal of the exemption in the Act which exempts acts done by media organisations in the course of journalism where the

[61] ibid 2536.
[62] ibid 2584.
[63] ibid.
[64] ibid 2565.
[65] ibid 2578.
[66] ibid 2585.
[67] ibid 2582.

organisation observes published standards about how it deals with privacy—these include the Australian Press Council Standards referred to above.

June 2014 ALRC Inquiry

The Australian Law Reform Commission was yet again tasked with reviewing privacy protections in Australia in June 2013. Issued by the former Labor government, the ALRC inquired and reported on 'the issue of prevention of and remedies for serious invasions of privacy in the digital era'. The Inquiry was issued on the back of growing concern regarding the ability of existing privacy statutes to address:

— the rapid growth in capabilities and use of information, surveillance and communication technologies;
— community perceptions of privacy; and
— relevant international standards and the desirability of consistency in laws affecting national and transnational dataflows.[68]

March 2014 saw the release of the ALRC Discussion Paper.[69] The Final Report issued in June 2014 recommended the introduction of a statutory tort for 'serious invasions of privacy' in a new Commonwealth Act.[70] The Report recommends a number of elements for the proposed tort, including:

— confining the tort to intrusion upon a person's seclusion, or misuse and/or disclosure of their private information;[71]
— requiring invasions of privacy to be intentional or reckless in order to be actionable;[72]
— confining the tort to situations where a person in the position of the plaintiff would have a reasonable expectation of privacy, in all the circumstances;[73]
— allowing only 'serious' invasions of privacy to invoke the new Act;[74]
— allowing the new Act to be actionable *per se* and allowing damages for emotional distress to be awarded;[75] and
— requiring that the court be satisfied that the plaintiff's interest in privacy outweigh the defendant's interest in freedom of expression and any broader public interest, providing a non-exhaustive list of public interest matters.[76]

[68] Australian Law Reform Commission, *Serious Invasions of Privacy in the Digital Era*, Issues Paper No 43 (2013) (*ALRC Issues Paper No 43*).
[69] Australian Law Reform Commission, *Serious Invasions of Privacy in the Digital Era*, Discussion Paper No 80 (2014) (*ALRC Discussion Paper No 80*).
[70] Australian Law Reform Commission, *Serious Invasions of Privacy in the Digital Era*, Final Report No 123 (2014) (*ALRC Final Report No 123*).
[71] ibid ch 5.
[72] ibid ch 7.
[73] ibid ch 6.
[74] ibid ch 8.
[75] ibid.
[76] ibid ch 9.

This last point sets out the 'balancing exercise', in which courts weigh privacy against other important public interests, such as freedom of speech. Interestingly, this balancing act forms an element of the tort rather than a defence, which shifts greater onus on plaintiffs to show that the balancing act falls in their favour. The Report concluded that a cause of action for serious invasion of privacy would be better developed by an Act of Parliament than being left to develop in the courts.[77]

Interestingly, the ALRC also turned its head to 'innovative ways in which the law may reduce serious invasions of privacy in the context of an increasingly pervasive digital environment.'[78] The discussion paper considered a number of reforms including:

— unifying the range of surveillance device laws currently operating throughout the States and Territories;[79]
— strengthening the equitable cause of action for breach of confidence by legislation enabling courts to award compensation for emotional distress;[80]
— enacting a new Commonwealth harassment Act to consolidate existing protections;[81]
— providing the Australian Information Commissioner with additional functions that allow them to intervene in court proceedings or assist the court as *amicus curiae*.[82]

Future Directions?

The report on serious invasions of privacy is the most impressive to come out of the ALRC, but as with previous reports it will be of interest to see whether the Government will act on any of its recommendations. At the time of writing the Attorney-General George Brandis had not made a formal comment on the Report's findings, though he has voiced his opposition to a tort of privacy in the past.[83] A spokesperson for the Attorney General did however say after the ALRC Report was released 'the Government has made it clear on numerous occasions that it does not support a tort of privacy'.[84] Given that legislative reform in this area is likely to be a lengthy process, it is possible that the courts will in the meantime have another opportunity to consider whether a cause of action for breach of privacy exists at common law. Since *Lenah*, the tide has gradually turned towards greater protection of privacy in Australia and in the recent years we have seen the first two decisions where courts (albeit lower courts) have awarded damages for breach of privacy. The developments in this area are still clearly going to take some time. The cases of *Jane Doe v ABC* and *Grosse v Purvis*,

[77] ibid 24.
[78] *ALRC Discussion Paper No 80*, above n 66.
[79] *ALRC Final Report No 123*, above n 67, ch 14.
[80] ibid ch 13.
[81] ibid ch 15.
[82] ibid p 317.
[83] Chris Merritt, 'Brandis rejects privacy tort call', *The Australian* (Sydney, 4 April 2014) accessible at www.theaustralian.com.au/business/legal-affairs/brandis-rejects-privacy-tort-call/story-e6frg97x-1226873913819 accessed July 2016.
[84] Paul Farrell, 'Law Reform Commission seeks right to sue for victims of privacy violations', *The Guardian* (3 September 2014) accessible at www.theguardian.com/world/2014/sep/03/law-reform-commission-seeks-right-to-sue-for-victims-of-privacy-violations accessed July 2016.

while notable, arise from unusual facts and are not binding on other courts. Significantly, the only appellate court decision to consider the tort of privacy, *Giller v Procopets*, did not clarify the position, instead preferring to look to protections under the equitable remedy for breach of confidence. This may reveal a reluctance by the courts to make any significant determinations on privacy law while the ALRC's work is yet to be fully considered by Parliament.

Beyond the legal uncertainties, there are practical challenges associated with privacy protection. In a world of constantly changing technology, regulators and law enforcers will always be one step behind and this will affect the level of protection offered by new privacy laws. Further, there is also some question as to whether generations X, Y and beyond, who more freely give out personal information and publicise private details on social networking sites, such as Facebook, Twitter and YouTube, will even want the law to develop privacy protections.

International developments suggest that ultimately, the Australian courts or legislature will have to provide greater protection of personal privacy. Previous ALRC reports, the NSWLRC report and the approach of the lower courts in *Grosse v Purvis* and *ABC v Jane Doe* suggest that this will probably be along the lines of a US style tort for invasion of privacy. While this would have many advantages for many people, it is not without consequences in terms of freedom of the press and free speech. Privacy is undeniably a significant human right, but it must not be forgotten that free speech and freedom of the press are fundamental to the success of any democratic society. Any tort or statute should adequately reflect the need to balance these competing rights, just as the laws of defamation do.

15

Two Faces of Freedom of the Press in Indonesia's Reformation Era

T MULYA LUBIS

Introduction

After the fall of the Suharto regime in 1998, political reformation towards democracy is evident in Indonesia today. The democratic aspirations following the fall of the authoritarian regime can be summarised as three major agendas. First, reformation in civilian and military relations through the establishment of civilian supremacy in politics, the removal of the dual-function doctrine of the military and the abolition of the military faction in the legislative body. Second, democratisation of political life by promoting a multi-party system. Third, the promotion of a wider range of civil liberties including press freedom. The rise of press freedom in Indonesia was signified by Law No 40 (1999). By this law, state control over the press industry by the Surat Ijin Usaha Penerbitan Pers (Permission Letter of Press Publishing) (SIUPP) mechanism was diminished. Under the Suharto regime, the life of the press really depended on the SIUPP. SIUPP was a powerful government instrument used to control the media. It could be used arbitrarily by the state to ban media groups that were not aligning with state policy. Since the end of the SIUPP era, press freedom has grown fast and has become an integral part of democratic politics in Indonesia. Press freedom today is not just a name or object of right, it is a privilege used by the actors in the political process.

The press has a vital function in the democratic process; it is a bridge between the rulers and the people. That is why the press is referred to as the fourth estate of power, which functions to control the legislative, judicial and executive layers of government. It is also a means by which the public can voice their aspirations. Some observers have even considered that of these four pillars, the press is the only one that still performs appropriately.[1]

After the reformation era began in 1998, the importance of press freedom to seek and convey information to the public became evident. This was marked by a Decree of the People's Consultative Assembly of the Republic of Indonesia No XVII/MPR/1998 on Human Rights. One of the provisions in the decree states that every person possesses the right to

[1] Eks Chief of Judges of Constitutional Court said that from the four pillars of democracy, only press alone keeps it healthy and in the correct position, see www.merdeka.com/politik/mahfud-md-dari-4-pilar-demokrasi-hanya-pers-yang-masih-sehat.html accessed July 2016.

communicate and obtain information in accordance with the United Nations' Universal Declaration of Human Rights, of which Article 19 stipulates: 'Everyone has the right to freedom of opinion and expression; this right includes freedom to hold opinions without interference and to seek, receive and impart information and ideas through any media and regardless of frontiers'.

The freedom of expression is guaranteed in the Indonesian Constitution, namely in Article 28 E clauses 2 and 3 and Article 28 F of the 1945 Constitution amendment. The first article provides that the freedoms of association and assembly, and expressing one's thoughts orally and in writing, will be stipulated by law. Further, Article 28 F has become a legal umbrella of the press, which states that everyone has the right to communicate and obtain information to develop one's personal and social environment, as well as the right to seek, acquire, possess, keep, process and convey information by using all available channels.

As the implementation of these constitutional provisions, Law No 40 from 1999, regarding the Press, was issued. This Press Law is different from the previous regulation;[2] it devolved control of the press away from the government to the community. As mentioned in Article 2, 'Freedom of the press is a manifestation of the people's sovereignty, which is based on the principles of democracy, justice and rule of law'; likewise Article 4 clause 1, which stipulates that freedom of the press is an essential right of the people in the context of upholding justice and truth, as well as promoting and educating the nation. This clearly shows that the Press Law positioned the press as a representative of the people, one that ensures that the processes of democracy, justice and the rule of law function properly through the disclosure of information to the public.

To support this, and also in accordance with Article 15 clause 1 of the Press Law, an independent Press Council was formed in an effort to develop freedom of the press and to improve the life of the national press. The active role of the community in developing the freedom of the press and guaranteeing the right to obtain the necessary information is contained in Article 17, which stipulates that the community can perform monitoring activities and report violations of the law and ethics, and technical errors made by the press, and submit proposals and suggestions to the Press Council.

This law also paved the way for the liberalisation of the press so that the press industry can thrive. The Press Law eliminated the requirement to submit the SIUPP (a press publication business licence) as a condition of publishing, eliminated censorship and banning of the press, and provided a protection mechanism to journalists with a minor criminal record, all of which previously inhibited press freedom.

The impact of the Press Law was that the press industry flourished. Based on data collected by the Association of Newspaper Publishers (SPS) regarding the number of media printers, in 1997 Indonesia had 289 publishers. By 1999 the number had jumped dramatically to 1,687.[3] Press Council data shows that in 2011 there were 671 electronic media companies, 1,081 electronic printing media companies and 631 print media companies without a chief editor.

The strengthening of the freedom of the press is also evident from the existence of the Memorandum of Understanding (MoU) Between the Indonesian National Police (Polri)

[2] Law No 11 of 1966 in conjunction with Law No 4 of 1967 in conjunction with Law No 21 of 1982.

[3] Satrio Saptohadi, 'Pasang Surut Kebebasan Pers di Indonesia' (2011) 11 *Jurnal Dinamika Hukum*, 135.

and the Press Council Regarding Coordination of Law Enforcement and Protection of Freedom of the Press (dated 9 February 2012). One provision of the MoU coordinates the law enforcement response to public complaints about news reporting; the Indonesian Police will not immediately act on such reports; they will direct the parties involved in a dispute to take gradual steps, from the right of reply, to the right to correct, and finally submission of a complaint to the Press Council, while the entire offence relating to the code of conduct will be referred to the Press Law.[4] However the legal force of this MoU is very weak as it is an agreement lasting for a period of only five years.

Public Perceptions Regarding Freedom of Expression

Also important is how freedom of the press has transformed the community; it has made a positive impact on society. A BBC World Service poll, which was conducted by GlobeScan, found that, amongst other countries, freedom of expression in Indonesia is quite good.[5]

The survey asked interviewees if they perceived the press in Indonesia to be free. A total of 73 per cent answered that it was free, 18 per cent that it was moderately free and only 3 per cent that it was not free. Similarly, there was a perception that it was free from government control, a total of 69 per cent answering that the press was free and only 27 per cent that it was not.

Results regarding perceptions about freedom of expression on the Internet and in public places were also good. A total of 57 per cent said that the Internet was a safe place to express their opinions and 38 per cent said that it was not. With regard to discussing an issue in public, 78 per cent felt free and 21 per cent did not.[6]

These findings of the BBC poll were reinforced by the 2012 BPS (Statistics Indonesia) sociocultural data, which indicated the increasing need of the community for information and entertainment facilities.[7] Television is the medium for information and entertainment that is of most interest to the public. From 2006 to 2012, the level of public participation in televisual media increased steadily, while radio and newspaper media experienced a significant decline. In 2006, the percentage of the population aged 10 and older watching television was 85.9 per cent, and this increased to 91.55 per cent by 2012. The percentage of people who listened to the radio, by contrast, decreased significantly, from 40.3 per cent in 2006 to 18.55 per cent in 2012. Further, the percentage of people who read newspapers or magazines in 2006 was 23.5 per cent, and this had decreased to 17.66 per cent by 2012.

[4] The MoU was signed by the Chief of National Police, General Timur Pradopo, and the Chief of the Press Council, Prof Bagir Manan. A part of the MoU says that where there is a law broken by the press news, legal action in such a case should be referred to the Law No 40, 1999. See www.tribunnews.com/nasional/2012/02/10/ini-isi-mou-dewan-pers-dengan-polri.

[5] Collection of field data was conducted in February 2014, with a margin of error of +/– 2.9–4.9 % using the face-face methodology. The total sample size was 1,000 adult residents in urban areas (Bandung, Jakarta, Makassar, Medan and Surabaya having 27 per cent of the national population of adult citizens).

[6] 'One-in-Two Say Internet Unsafe Place for Expressing Views: Global Poll', *BBC World Service* (March 2014) http://downloads.bbc.co.uk/mediacentre/bbc-freedom-poll-2014.pdf accessed July 2016.

[7] Statistics Indonesia, www.bps.go.id, accessed July 2016.

The percentage of the population aged 5 and older who accessed the Internet in 2012 was 15.36 per cent (measured over a period of three months).

Along with increased public access to the Internet, online media has grown rapidly. According to a survey conducted by the marketing research firm MarkPlus Insight and the *Marketeers* online magazine, from 2012 to 2013 there was an increase of 22 per cent in the number of Internet users in Indonesia. In 2013 there were 74.6 million Internet users in Indonesia, up from 61.1 million in 2012. The study also calculated the penetration of the Internet community—those persons spending at least three hours on line each day. There are at present 31.7 million people in the Indonesian Internet community, up from 24.2 million a year ago, a rise of 30 per cent. As to the most frequently searched-for information on the Internet, the Indonesian community, for the most part, searched for news (54.2 per cent) followed by entertainment (16.3 per cent), movies (10.2 per cent), sport (8.7 per cent) and music (8.5 per cent). More specifically, the data showed that users searched for political news (7.4 per cent), soap operas (6 per cent), celebrity news (5.5 per cent), gossip (5.2 per cent) and educational content (5 per cent). With regard to online news, according to this survey the top three news websites were Detik, Kompas and Yahoo.[8]

Similarly, there has been an increased use of social media by the public. The Ministry of Communications and Informatics (Kemenkominfo) revealed that Internet users in Indonesia reached 63 million in 2013. Of that number, 95 per cent used the Internet for social networking. The Director of Information Services of the Directorate General of Information and Public Communication (IKP), Selamatta Sembiring, said that the most accessible social networking sites are Facebook and Twitter. Indonesia ranks as the fourth largest Facebook user group and the fifth largest Twitter user group in the world. Meanwhile, according to data from Weber Shandwick, a public relations and corporate communications services provider for Indonesia, there are about 65 million active Facebook users. There are 33 million active users per day, 55 million active users using mobile equipment to access the Internet per month and 28 million active users who use mobile devices per day.[9]

Barriers to Freedom of the Press

While public enthusiasm for the Internet has surged, there is a law that potentially undermines the freedom of expression on line, namely Law No 11 of 2008 regarding Electronic Information and Transaction (ITE Law). This ITE Law is intended to protect personal data and citizens from fraud and defamation through the Internet. However, in practice, the ITE Law is considered as not having clearly defined defamation and thus has often been used as a means of silencing freedom of expression on line. The penalties provided are even more severe compared to those in the Criminal Code, with a maximum of six years in prison and fines of up to one billion Indonesian rupiahs (US$98,000).

The Institute for Policy Research and Advocacy (Elsam), a human rights NGO in Jakarta, stated that since the ITE Law came into force in 2008, 37 cases relating to the implementation

[8] See www.techinasia.com/facebook-asia-numbers-q3-2013/, accessed July 2016.

[9] http://kominfo.go.id/index.php/content/detail/3415/Kominfo+%3A+Pengguna+Internet+di+Indonesia+63+Juta+Orang/0/berita_satker#.Vh_bqkugH0E accessed July 2016.

of that law have been registered, consisting of 32 cases relating to Article 27 clause 3, concerning insult or defamation, and five cases relating to the article prohibiting the spreading of hatred. These last five cases involved Prita Mulyasari, Donny Iswandoro, Johan Yan, Anthon Wahyu and Pramono dan Benny Handoko. From these five cases, the Prita Mulyasari case received massive public attention. Prita was sued by Omni International Hospital for defamation after she complained about the hospital's service in an online mailing list.[10] The Benny Handoko case was also widely published in the Indonesian media. Benny, a Twitter Celebrity, was sued by the politician Misbhakun for defamation of character. A panel of judges at the South Jakarta District Court found Benny guilty of violating Article 27 of the 2008 Electronic Information and Transaction (ITE) Law on defamation.[11]

Although freedom of the press has been rated by many Indonesians as functioning well, there is a variety of legal cases that have entrapped the press. In 2004 alone, according to the Alliance of Independent Journalists (AJI) annual report, there were 32 cases against the media and journalists. First among these was the case of contempt against the President that ensnared the Editor, Supratman, of *Harian Rakyat*, a daily newspaper. He was declared guilty and sentenced to six months in prison with 12 months' probation. He was convicted of intentionally insulting the President under Article 134 in conjunction with Article 65 clause 1 of the Criminal Code, which was later found by the Constitutional Court to be unconstitutional.[12] The second group of cases involved lawsuits claimed against *Tempo* magazine by businessman Tomy Winata.[13] An online and print media journalist, Radar Nusantara, with the initials of DQ, was officially named as a suspect; he was arrested and detained by the Muba Police. This was related to news released the previous month stating that the architect of corruption in Muba was the District Head of Muba.[14]

As a result of those cases, a view evolved from various groups that it would be appropriate for the Press Law to be regarded as *lex specialis*, which is intended to protect the press from the bondage of the criminal law. However, the Press Law could not yet be implemented as a *lex specialis* since it caters only for three press offences, namely the violation of religious norms, moral norms and the presumption of innocence (Article 5 clause 1). There are still many press offences that have not been catered for, such as the offence of making a false report, the offence of defamation, the offence of disclosing classified government material, and so on. Since those offences are not yet regulated in Law No 40 of 1999, laws and regulations outside the Press Law will continue to be utilised.[15]

[10] See www.thejakartapost.com/news/2009/06/05/blame-game-starts-over-misuse-law-prita-mulyasari-case.html accessed July 2016.

[11] See www.thejakartapost.com/news/2014/02/06/twilebrity-gets-jail-term-defamation.html accessed July 2016.

[12] See Naomita Royan, 'Increasing Press Freedom in Indonesia: The Abolition of the Lese Majeste and "Hate-sowing" Provisions' (2008) 10 *Australian Journal of Asian Law* 290.

[13] Gunawan Mashar, 'Wartawan Makassar Gelar Aksi Keprihatinan Vonis Tempo', Detik News (17 May 2004) http://news.detik.com/read/2004/05/17/232940/157350/10/wartawan-makassar-gelar-aksi-keprihatinan-vonis-tempo accessed July 2016.

[14] Sierra Syailendra, 'Beritanya cemarkan bupati, wartawan media online ditahan', Sindo News (15 September 2013) http://daerah.sindonews.com/read/783208/24/beritanya-cemarkan-bupati-wartawan-media-online-ditahan accessed July 2016.

[15] Tjipta Lesmana, 'Kebebasan Pers Dilihat dari Perspektif Konflik, antara Kebebasan dan Tertib Sosial' (2005) 2(1) *Jurnal Ilmu Komunikasi Universitas Atma Jaya Yogyakarta* 1–14.

Other barriers include the not-finalised cases of violence against journalists and the ongoing intimidation of journalists. The AJI reported that there were 26 cases of violence against journalists between January and August 2013. In addition, according to AJI, there were at least 12 cases of journalists being murdered. Eight of the 12 murdered journalists' cases are still in limbo and their perpetrators have not been brought to justice.[16] In 2014, AJI declared the police as enemies of press freedom, with 11 reported attacks on journalists by police from May 2014 to May 2015. The attacks allegedly committed by the police topped the 37 recorded attacks against journalists from 2014 to 2015.[17]

Obstructions to freedom of the press also come from Law No 7 of 2012 regarding Social Conflict Management (PKS Law). In Articles 26, 27 and 28 of the PKS Law, the District Head/Governor/Minister, appointed by the President, has the absolute authority to restrict anyone entering the area of conflict or to leave the area. This restriction can be used to limit journalistic investigations into possible legal violations committed by the government within an area of conflict.

Freedom of the press is also threatened by a number of articles of Law No 17 of 2011 regarding State Intelligence (Intelligence Law). Intelligence Law is considered to be full of 'loophole articles'. Article 1 clause 6 defines intelligence secrets in a broad and disordered manner. It even exceeds the definition of exempt information as stipulated in Law No 14 of 2008 regarding Freedom of Public Information. The power of various public agencies, such as ministries and non-ministerial government agencies, to conduct intelligence activities (Article 9 paragraph (e) of the Intelligence Law) leads to the authority to divert information as 'secret intelligence' of ministries and non-ministerial government agencies. In this way, the efforts of the press to monitor, criticise and correct government agencies can be criminalised as a form of leaking of intelligence secrets. Journalists could be jailed for up to ten years for exposing documents containing allegations of suspected fraud and corruption by a government agency. Other articles deemed to be dangerous to the freedom of the press are Articles 32 (relating to the authority of wire-tapping of intelligence apparatus), 26 (relating to the prohibition on opening and/or divulging confidential information), and 44 and 45 (relating to criminal sanctions as stipulated, namely ten years in prison, or seven years and/or a fine of hundreds of millions of Indonesian rupiahs).[18]

On 5 January 2012, AJI, together with four non-governmental organisations and 13 individuals, filed a judicial review of laws passed by the Plenary Session of the House of Representatives on 11 October 2011 in the Constitutional Court (MK). However, the MK rejected the petition on 10 October 2012.

[16] Those cases still uncertain include the following: Fuad Muhammad Syarifudin aka Udin (journalist of Bernas Daily Yogyakarta, died on 16 August 1996); Naimullah (journalist of Sinar Pagi West Kalimantan Daily, found dead on 25 July 1997); Agus Mulyawan (journalist of Asia Press in East Timor, died on 25 September 1999); Muhammad Jamaluddin (TVRI cameraman in Aceh, found dead on 17 June 2003); Ersa Siregar (RCTI journalist in NAD, died on 29 December 2003); Herliyanto (freelance journalist of the Sidoarjo Delta Pos Tabloid in East Jave, found dead on 29 April 2006); Adriansyah Matra'is Wibisono (local TV journalist in Merauke, Papua, found dead on 29 July 2010); Alfred Mirulewan (journalist of the Pelangi Tabloid in Maluku, found dead on 18 December 2010) (Kabar3.com, 30 April 2014).

[17] See www.thejakartapost.com/news/2015/05/03/aji-declares-police-enemies-press-freedom.html accessed July 2016.

[18] See http://news.detik.com/kolom/2588071/koalisi-pemilik-media-dalam-pilpres-2014 accessed July 2016.

Televisual Media and Politics

It is no secret that present media ownership is closely related to political interests, whereas during the legislative elections in early 2014, and also in previous times, the link between media ownership and political affiliation was not so obvious. However, during the presidential elections in 2009 and 2014, the political affiliation of media ownership became more open and visible to the public.[19]

There were at least two camps that were clearly affiliated politically with the presidential candidates. First, there was Media Group (Media Indonesia, Metro TV and Tabloid Prioritas) owned by Surya Paloh (Chairman of the Central Executive Council of the National Democratic Party) affiliated with Jokowi-Kalla. Secondly, Viva Media Group (TV One and viva.co.id) and ANTV, owned by Bakrie (Chairman of the Golkar Party) and affiliated with Prabowo-Hatta.

A media group that was also clearly affiliated in the presidential elections was the MNC Group (Koran Sindo, RCTI, MNC TV and Global TV), which is owned by Hary Tanoesoedibjo, who supported Hanura in the legislative elections and Prabowo-Hatta in the presidential elections.

One group that was not so obviously affiliated, although it tends to support Jokowi-Kalla, was the Trans Corp owned by Chairul Tanjung.[20] Trans Corp had a close relationship with the Democratic Party and with Susilo Bambang Yudhoyono during the past political leadership. Finally, there was the Televisi Republik Indonesia (TVRI), which is not affiliated with any political group due to its status as a State Owned Enterprise.

Many have argued that the affiliation of the media to a political force is inevitable and reasonable, and as long as the supervision performed by the KPI (the independent anti-corruption body) is done effectively, relations between the media and political factions are acceptable. One issue is that beyond the macro relationship there are some things that should be seriously considered, namely the independence of the media and the principle that the media are always associated with public life; and therefore the media, regardless of who owns them, still have a responsibility to the public. In this regard, we became aware that at the beginning of the presidential election a number of media leaders imposed specific actions to 'suppress' their own journalists; consequently a number of cases arose where workers in the media were not free—not because of any government or political pressures but due to the leadership authority within the media itself.

In principle, this issue relating to media political camps is an alarming matter. These political media camps can eliminate the independence of the media and ultimately destroy the substance of journalistic work as defined in the Journalism Code of Ethics. Article 1 stipulates: 'Indonesian journalists have an independent attitude, produce accurate and balanced news, and are not bad intentioned'. The Journalism Code of Ethics also asserts

[19] The splitting position among the media became extreme during the last presidential election in 2014. Metro TV, owned by the media tycoon Surya Paloh, stood on the Jokowi Widodo side, while TV One, owned by Aburarizal Bakrie, stood for Prabowo Subiyanto. Booth television engaged in the 'pool war' until the end of the election process.

[20] See www.solopos.com/2014/03/17/kampanye-pemilu-2014-chairul-tanjung-dan-dahlan-iskan-gabung-demokrat-496573 accessed July 2016.

further that what is meant by independent is 'to report events or facts in accordance with conscience without any interference, coercion and intervention from any other party including the owner of the press company'.

Conclusion: Two Faces of Freedom of the Press in Indonesia Today

Power tends to corrupt. In a society where not everyone can read and write, literacy is a form of power. In a society where the workers are not able to voice their aspirations due to fear of losing their jobs, the work-system is an authoritarian form. In a society in which a handful of owners control systems of mass communication, the media is power. This dimension was expressly stated by Brian Martin as follows:

> Mass media are inherently corrupting. A small number of owners and editors exercise great power over what is communicated to large numbers of people. Mass media should be replaced by participatory media organized as networks, such as telephone and computer networks. Strategies to supersede mass media include changing one's own media consumption patterns, participating in alternative media and using nonviolent action against the mass media.[21]

After the era of reform, the acceptance of freedom of the press and the independence of the media is taken for granted. In the conventional view, freedom of the press is usually defined as a condition in which intervention in the press by the government is absent. Indonesia and various other democratic countries implement a guarantee of freedom of the press in their legal system and constitution. However, other factors, such as the influence of economic pressure, and historical, cultural and social conditions, often need to be viewed as issues that determine, or at least have an influence on, media independence and its ability to fulfil its function as public media.

Also recognised by many actors in the European press is that, in a democracy, after the mushrooming of the media industry, two of the most important barriers to the freedom of the press are investigative reporting and plurality of content. In this region, intervention in the media no longer comes from the government against the media leaders but from a few actors, mostly media owners, against media workers. These symptoms are caused in part by a merger between political power and media power. One of the most obvious examples of this issue is what happened in Italy when Silvio Berlusconi won the election in 2008. Berlusconi revived a monopoly in the world of television and public broadcasting as well as using the power of the media under his control to win over a variety of political and business rivals. With this kind of power system, media workers in those companies that were monopolised will be more controlled and shaped by the media owners. Another example comes from Germany where there were strong fears after it became known that journalists' e-mail communications were being monitored, not only by the government but also by the owners of the media companies. In response to this, the White Paper on European Communication Policy, which was published by the EU in 2006, put forward

[21] Brian Martin, *Information Liberation* (Freedom Press, 1998).

new demands for the creation of wider press freedom and diversity of citizen participation in public communication.[22]

In Indonesia today, concerns similar to those seen in Europe are also appearing. Research conducted by Yanuar Nugroho and others, with very detailed evidence and data, came to the conclusion that the condition of the Indonesian media was as follows:

> Centralising in media industry is happening as an inevitable consequence of capital interest that drive the development of the media industry in Indonesia. Media oligopoly currently happening is endangering citizens' rights to information because the media industry is profit oriented and media firms have represented lucrative business overviews that can be shaped by the interests of the owner and as such, the media business has become very beneficial to those who are seeking power.[23]

With the above developments, we are seeing two faces of the freedom of the press in Indonesia. The first is that of a free press in a democratic society still struggling with the intervention of various new forms of power—of the government and of corporations. This is the freedom of the press that grows as a power to resist outside intervention. Second, the freedom of the press is also determined by an internal dimension, namely the power that grows as a consequence of the press being an industry where the owners are involved in the pursuit of political power. Freedom of the press was previously threatened by state intervention or other external factors; the situation has evolved to one in which freedom of the press can also be killed by itself and its own powers.

Whilst it is true that through the enactment of the Law No 40 in 1999 the Indonesian press enjoys freedom, this kind of freedom, unfortunately, is bestowed only on the actors who hold the power in the media. The Law No 40 is limited in protecting the freedom of the press. In situations where the media industrialist is engaged in political contest, the press freedom could easily be misused to serve private interests and to violate wider public rights. Based on the experiences of how media were used during the last two general elections, it seems that Indonesians need more regulation to ensure political fairness and to limit not press freedom but the power behind the press.

[22] Andre Czepek, Melanie Hellowig and Eva Nowak (eds), *Press Freedom and Pluralism in Europe Concepts and Conditions* (The University of Chicago Press, 2009) 9–10.

[23] Yanuar Nugroho, Sita Laksmi and Dinita Putri, *Memetakan Lanskap Industri Media Kontemporer di Indonesia* (Series: 'Laporan Berseri: Engaging Media, Empowering Society: Assessing Media Policy and Governance in Indonesia through the Lens of Citizens' Rights') (Jakarta, Ford Foundation, March 2012).

INDEX

Page locators in **bold** indicate information in tables.